21/-

BACK NUMBERS

The Victorian family in an Edwardian marriage group

Back row—left to right: Arthur; Best Man; Aunt Maggie; Uncle John; Bridegroom; fiancée of Winnie; Aunt Bessie; Uncle James. *Middle row—left to right:* The Victorian Girl; Aunt Maria; Doris, a Gaiety Girl who married Jack; Daisy, the Bride; Winnie, her sister, both daughters of Uncle Charles; Aunt Mary. *Seated on ground:* The Victorian Boy—and Jack

BACK NUMBERS

A Disturbance of the Dust of Yesteryear
Written for Back Numbers
by a Back Number—

W. MACQUEEN-POPE

With 84 Illustrations

HUTCHINSON
Stratford Place London

Hutchinson & Co. (Publishers) Ltd.

London   Melbourne   Sydney   Auckland
Bombay   Cape Town   New York   Toronto

First published 1954

*Printed in Great Britain
by The Anchor Press, Ltd.,
Tiptree, Essex*

A TRIBUTE

FROM HER HUMBLE FRIEND AND ADMIRER

TO THAT GRACIOUS LADY

JULIA NEILSON

IN WHOM IS EMBODIED

THE BEAUTY, GRANDEUR AND DIGNITY

OF THE

VICTORIAN AND EDWARDIAN ERAS.

A QUEEN OF THE STAGE

AND QUEEN OF OUR HEARTS,

SHE HAS GIVEN US

MANY HAPPY MEMORIES

Contents

List of Illustrations

9

Explanation

SOME years ago I wrote a book called *Twenty Shillings in the Pound*, which earned me many friends. It has also brought me many delightful gifts which have been some compensation for the depredations made by the Inland Revenue officials on my little trickle of royalties. I have received, too, not only heartening letters but souvenirs of the times about which I wrote—the period between 1890 and 1914. I ended there because in that year the Golden Sovereign vanished to be replaced by paper notes, which never were, never have been, and never will be worth twenty shillings in the pound.

Old and treasured books have been sent to me, photographs, pictures and prints, newspapers of the 'nineties of immense interest and—to me —of great value; all sorts of Victorian and Edwardian Treasures. On the shelf of my office stands a half-pint milk-can, made of pewter, such as the milkman used to leave for us instead of the very hygienic glass bottles of today—there it is, with its little handle, by which it used to hang on the railings if nobody was at home to take it in (and nobody stole it in those distant but honest days). Lots of things like that. But perhaps most precious of all was a square cardboard-box filled with cotton wool in which nestled—a real golden sovereign—dated 1898 and bearing Queen Victoria's head. That has become an heirloom. I showed it to my grandchildren, whose immediate query was: "What did you get the medal for?" They had never seen a sovereign, of course, nor have so many of the young people whom I meet. Well, I got that medal for writing a book, and I hope I earned it fairly. But the donor of the sovereign had not done with me, bless her. She is a very charming lady indeed, who is (God help her!) a fan of mine. She and her husband and their three children have a wonderful farm in Huntingdon—an unspoilt bit of England lying off the beaten track. The name is Jordan. And for the Christmas of 1953 she sent me what was, in the days of the sovereign, its necessary companion—a sovereign purse. Something never seen today because its use has vanished, but very dear to me and to those of my generation. That, too, is an heirloom and now the sovereign lives in the engraved silver purse and goes everywhere with me. It has become one of my most potent mascots.

What apparently pleased my readers was the fact that I had awakened their memories and thereby given them back their youth. They recalled doing the things about which I wrote, wearing the clothes I described, going to the places I mentioned, playing with the toys recalled—doing all the things which the book set forth. They remembered these because it was a book about the Middle Classes, and we who were of it all did much the same sort of things. But my letters were not exclusively from middle-aged and elderly people, which pleased me as much as it surprised me. A large number of young people wrote to me, too, and said how interested they were to know how people lived in those days—that it enabled them the better to understand the points of view of their parents and grandparents. That gave me pride. Letters have come from all over the world—and from people of other races. A very popular visiting Royalty, here for the Coronation of our Queen, not only read that book but took a copy home for her son to read. . . .

For one of my objects was to show, to the best of my poor ability, what late Victorian and Edwardian life was really like and what manner of people were that sturdy Middle Class before the time came for their annihilation.

That mighty organization, the British Broadcasting Corporation, both on its Sound and Television services, seems quite convinced that Victorian and Edwardian atmosphere is complete by references to or the sight of a hansom cab, an aspidistra, a tall hat, a soldier in a 'pillbox', an antimacassar and a sentimental ditty. Well, there was a good deal more to it than that. Being tired of misrepresentation by people who really cannot be blamed because they don't know (except that they do not take the trouble to find out), I wrote that book, as one who was of it and did know, to put on record exactly what it was like. Apparently I succeeded. I appear to have given a great deal of pleasure by recalling so many memories and reawakening the spirit of youth, for all the letters (they still come in, by the way) were of the highest approval. There was, of course, the exception which came from a lady who was kind enough to correct my Latin and to upbraid me for a statement that the men of that period were nervous of 'clever' women and fought shy of what I had called 'Blue Stockings'. She was one of those erudite ladies, she informed me. But I noticed that she was still unmarried. . . .

To awaken memories has always been my aim, for my belief is that memories are the best things in the world. They are possessions which nobody can snatch away, which no taxation can deplete or disperse, they are personal belongings—even what my friend 'Wemmick' would have called 'Portable Property'—of the utmost value. They are that part of Youth which, despite Shakespeare's dictum, can and does endure.

But I could not get everything into that book. So here I am again. This is no sequel. I do not believe in them. It is a 'follow-up' or, shall we say, extension. I am trying to use a larger canvas, to do my best, unskilled as I am, to go further back in Time and picture events before my own period by means of men and women whom I knew and saw. For the rest I will endeavour to picture it as it really was—for, after all, I lived through those years and I can remember. I have a gift of memory. It is about the only thing for which I have any renown. So I shall use it to the uttermost, and if there is a slip now and again it will, I think, be a very minor one.

I shall, I know, be accused by some reviewers (if the book gets reviewed at all) of being rambling and discursive. I know all about that and I warn them that this will probably be a rambling and discursive book. But it will nevertheless keep within its frame. I make no pretence at elegant literary style. What I try to do is to write as I talk. For years past I have talked in public to many thousands of persons, for amongst the trades I ply is that of lecturing. The listeners seem to like it, for I am always asked to go again—several times, indeed. And those who send me the letters tell me they like the way I write. Well, no praise is due for that because it is the only way I know. I try to make the book talk to the reader instead of giving him—or her—the task of just reading it. And to do that I just have to be myself. I would much rather hear a man talk to me in his own natural way without weighing every word and carefully rounding each point, than I would listen to a conversationalist whose object was 'style'. Anyway, I have no literary style—and it is not one of the virtues, if virtue it can be, which I propose to assume.

I shall also be accused of dealing in superlatives.

Well, I do. But they are not really superlatives, they only seem so to the present generation. This wonderful thing called Progress has caused the world to shrink in every way and the inhabitants of this world to shrink with it. So the period about which I write will seem to moderns much larger than life—and it was indeed much larger than life as lived today. It was a gay, flamboyant, virile age, full blooded, well fed and very well clothed. It did not deal in understatement.

Also, of course, to me it was My Period and therefore the best. Everybody's own period is always the best. The young people will find that out soon enough. It is good that it should be so, otherwise life would be intolerable. Young people find no faults with the lives they lead. Why should they? It is the only life they know. As the years gather, they notice alterations and what they did when they were young seems so much better than what they do now. The more years you live, the larger the perspective. You are aware of change and you have a standard of comparison. You always come down in favour of the Past. I have lived a good many years and under six sovereigns. I was born under Queen Victoria. I belong, basically, to the age of the horse and steam. It has been my good —or bad—fortune to see more Progress and alteration in the space of my life than had happened during the two succeeding centuries. I have watched and observed this progress. I accept and marvel at the miracles which to young folk are just everyday events. To me and countless others an aeroplane is still a marvel, radio and television twin miracles. My grandson did not believe me when I told him that I remembered the days when a motor-car was so remarkable a sight that people stopped to watch it go by. And often jeered, too. That the vast majority of them had never seen an aeroplane and indeed that I well remembered when there were no such things. He could not understand that when I was young—in fact until I was well on in life—there was also no such thing as radio. All those to him were ordinary everyday affairs. He thinks already in terms of Space Ships and is quite sure that he will, one day, visit the Moon. He probably will, too, for he is a determined lad bent on doing what he wants. And he will, in turn, tell his grandchildren of the, to them, primitive things of his youth, when it was considered a bit surprising that a plane could travel at 750 miles an hour, that the breaking of the sound barrier was a big event and that there was amazement when a plane crossed the Atlantic and arrived in America at the same time, by the clock, that it had left London. All those children will wonder how the poor wretches of today got on at all. That is, if they are there to wonder and have not been atomized out of existence. But my grandson, I am sure, will hanker after his own days—which by comparison will be leisurely days when there was plenty of time and nobody really rushed about, just as we think of our youth. Therefore you cannot really make comparisons between one era and another in general terms. You can only set down what those eras were like and how people lived in them. You may have your own ideas as to which was best—and who shall say you are wrong? Likes and dislikes are personal things. But the great thing is to get the picture right. Not just an impression and a sketch with a background of deduction but a photographic likeness of things as they were —even a stereoscopic three-dimensional one, as far as print will allow.

So, in this book, I shall try to draw that picture or develop that photograph from the negative of my own memory, from pictures and printed pages brought into focus by knowledge—that delineation of an Age so near in time but so different in method, texture, and thought as to be almost unbelievable. As I try to show how people lived and what life was like, I shall maybe make some comments. But young readers, if any, are at liberty to disregard them. Others will form their own views according to their age.

People speak of the Good Old Days. But others speak of the Bad Old Days. Both are right. It is, again, a personal affair. What was good for some was bad for others. It all depends on who and what you are —and were. But if they were not so entirely good, as some hold, they were not so entirely bad, as others claim. It is best to strike an average —and to keep to the truth in the chosen line one takes. I am always being told how thankful I should be for the blessing of living in a Welfare State. So far as I can see, that Welfare State is a Debtor instead of a Creditor Nation, of high costs of living and wages which never catch up, of constant Strikes and upheavals, of the perpetual danger of and preparation for War. Also, that it is no longer a mighty power ruling a fifth of the globe but one which is pushed around and generally insulted. I am told that the Welfare State is a free State—but nobody explains why the youth of that State has to waste some of its golden years by military service, of a compulsory nature, whereas the youth of the wicked old world—that large portion of it which was British—had no such shackle. We are also told that by giving away what used to be our Empire we are presenting the precious gift of Freedom to countless millions of souls. They do not seem much better off and each such severance makes life more difficult for the inhabitants of the Welfare Islands—the Islands of the Blessed. Nor can I see that it is good to have money which can hardly buy anything, and to have quantities of good, decent hard-working citizens reduced to poverty in their old age—for most of them the Welfare State holds no promise of assistance at all and only harrows them by taxation. Nor do I understand how much better off I am—for all this Welfare—or many thousands like me who have worked hard all their lives and now find themselves denied any rest in the declining years because of the necessity of paying for these times of Social Security— although there seems little security of the great blessing of peace—and who realize that at sixty-six years of age they are far, far worse off than they were at twenty-six. That is selfish, of course, and anti-social, but it has to be considered when taking stock of former times. And in spite of all the Freedom in this wonderful welfare world of Freedom and Equality, it seems strange to old-timers that people should be actively persecuted for their political opinions. That used to happen several centuries ago, but never in those bad old days of Victoria and Edward.

But here I fear I digress. One must go forward, and as one progresses down the years one is apt to remember more of that which was pleasant than that which was unpleasant. The good takes on a brighter hue, the bad seems to fade. That is one of the compensations of age. But it is necessary to remember about both and to recall the discomforts, of which there were many (but they were not realized then), as well as the comforts, of which there were a lot (accepted then as being perfectly natural). I shall try to record both.

This book is by no means an autobiography—even a sketchy one. I do not believe in autobiographies. Very few people can write a good one because very few people know themselves. The task would be beyond me, even if I wanted to attempt it, which I do not. Many people of my profession—I am of the Theatre—write their own life stories. Few of them succeed. You cannot see yourself as others see you. And always to my mind it is the people you have met and the things you have seen which are so much more interesting than the things you have done—so why not write about them and not about yourself?

Also I dislike the personal pronoun. I use it here in this Explanation so as to get rid of it afterwards. I have never had a high opinion of myself. I do not like my own personal appearance. I am not 'my type' at all. I dislike looking in mirrors, and when engaged upon the necessary act of shaving—which of all things I dislike most—I never meet my own eyes but concentrate on that particle of the face over which the razor is passing. To me, a room full of mirrors is a horror. I was lured into a maze of mirrors once in a side-show at an exhibition and it nearly drove me mad. This is not affectation but the solemn serious truth. So, no autobiography.

Nobody is interested in a very ordinary person like me, who has done nothing of note, who cannot even make money, but apparently many people are interested in the people I have met, the things I have seen and the events in which I have had the good luck to be involved. So the background of this book will be personally impersonal, if that can be understood.

We are going back in time, if the reader is still sufficiently interested to accompany me further. We are going to visit a road in a London suburb as it was in late Victorian and early Edwardian days and we are going to explore a house in it. I shall endeavour to give full details of that house, its contents and its surroundings, because all of them have altered today. Not even the house stands, although those which were its neighbours and replicas of it still do so. We are going to meet the people who lived in that house, because they were typical Victorians and, later, Edwardians. I admit here and now that they are the members of the maternal side of my own family. But many people will also recognize them as their own relations too, I expect, and will start thinking about their own Aunts and Uncles and what 'characters' they were. It seems to me that there were more 'characters' in the world then than there are now, but then, of course, there was no Equality—which is something of a steamroller. But generally speaking all Victorians had much in common and lived much the same sort of lives. They had their own idiosyncrasies, of course—for those were the days of Individuality. Nobody then, despite that belief in the conventions, which was only another name for good manners, wanted to be just like the people next door. And in those days they knew the people next door and knew them well. Nowadays it is not impossible to live next door to a family for years and not know them at all. But these people were Victorians and many will discover amongst the characters their own Uncle Will or Auntie Flo. I assure them they are not—they are actually my own Aunts, Uncles and Cousins. Any similarity is entirely coincidental—as they say today to avert the law of libel.

There is also a Victorian Boy who creeps through the book. He grew up into an Edwardian youth and young man, a Georgian husband and father, and is now an Elizabethan grandfather. He is there simply as Chorus to this story—as Shakespeare employed that character—and also to record the world of that time as it appeared to a growing child, who found his horizon widening as his years increased but who never forgot anything he saw and very little of what he heard. He is also there to show how changeless childhood is—how the children of today, except for details of progress, have exactly the same outlook on life and like and dislike the same things as did the Victorian child—as had the children down the ages ever since civilization began. Children have the same minds, they are all born little savages, with the same mentality as their forbears of pre-history—and they have to learn in their little lives what it took the world thousands of years to accomplish. But they all start alike and would not feel strange at all if suddenly faced with a Saxon boy or Norman girl—their outlook in the main would be the same. For that Elizabethan grandfather watches his grandchildren doing things as he did, saying just what he said, thinking as he thought, and having the same likes and dislikes. It is not merely heredity—it is the same for all. He knows, because he is one of the lucky ones who remembers and has perhaps never quite grown up—which gets him into all sorts of troubles at times. And it may be that some who have not that gift of memory unless evoked will find that something in this book rekindles it—and will get back their youth again thereby.

But the main inspiration of this book comes from another and less personal source. It comes from a place which is nowadays almost unknown, save in old houses, and in few of them, for they are now mostly divided into flats—but which was one of the great strongholds of Yesteryear. That place is something which in older days every house above the status of a cottage had beneath its roof—and only just beneath its roof—a room which was known as the Box Room or the Lumber Room. The name did not matter, the object was the same.

Today has its problems, so had Yesterday. Today one of the acutest of the problems is that of Housing. Yesterday had its housing problem too, but in reverse. It was not the general public who worried then as to how they were to get a house. The boot was on the other leg. It was the landlord who had the headache—who worried as to how soon he could get rid of the house property he had created, either by sale or by the much more general method of letting on rental. There were the older houses and there were the ever-growing new 'estates' on the edges of the rapidly swelling bulk of London—those new estates which were, in the technical phrase, 'ripe for development'. Which really meant that what had been fields, woods and meadows, and pleasant countryside, became rows and rows of houses in rows and rows of Streets. Not that they were called 'streets' on those new estates. That was far too urban. They were Roads, Drives, Crescents, Walks, Avenues—and as the development went on they also became reinforced by 'Close' and even 'Way'. Shopping centres became Broadways, Pavements or Parades . . . and always London stretched outwards, setting its bounds like those of the Empire of which it was the Capital—wider still and wider. . . .

Nothing must be urban—for these were the Suburban districts. This period was indeed the apotheosis of Suburbia. Suburbs were nothing new even then—but people were still moving outwards, to get what they thought was fresher air in which to sleep—but the distance they could go was governed by the speed and means of transport. In the early period of this book, the motor was either non-existent or just a toy of the very rich. Not everyone could afford a carriage, only the small minority, and few of the suburbans possessed such things—so the distance they could live away from their work in the City or the West End (mostly the City) was governed by the railway trains, the trams and the buses. The better-class suburban travelled to work by train—the working classes used the horse transport. Those means of transport had done much to break down the old-fashioned idea of living over one's business or shop. And as means of transport improved, so people moved out further and further and enterprising builders bought land and covered that land with houses. They were always a bit ahead of the demand—they got the land cheaper that way—and when they bought, they built and hoped for the best. What it really meant was that there were houses for all and to spare.

There was another unseen force which drove the people of London outwards. However urbanized they had become, there was latent in them that desire for the countryside which had fostered their forefathers. Love of the country never dies in the inhabitants of these islands. They wanted fresh air, they wanted space and, above all, they wanted a garden. That was an essential. It is not so strongly marked today when people live in clusters in blocks of flats but it is still there—and will come on top again when things get easier—if ever they do. Flat life is not native to this race, it is forced upon it as a necessity. The Europeans, and the Americans, like it—prefer it—but the British (and perhaps more especially the English) really prefer a house. There are many reasons why they have to live in flats and the Welfare State is one of them. But that outward movement had gone on for years and by the time this book begins its chronicle, what had once been smart, prosperous suburbs in the early years of Victoria's reign, were going downhill fast and some had already decayed. What had once been mansions inhabited by well-to-do merchants had become private hotels, boarding houses, or taken to trade. The original owners had not given them up for lack of means but had simply moved further away from Town, which constantly chased them. Thus the heart of London was ringed, as it still is, by layers of slowly decaying habitations, districts descending the social scale, passing from residential areas into those of commerce and trade, and even into slums. But something remained of ancient grandeur as will be seen. . . .

It was the young people who were the pioneers of the outward movement. That was natural. As they decided to marry they would look towards the new world of new suburbs, where it was cheaper to live than nearer in, and they would invade the new districts where the new houses stood, row upon row, smart, spick and span, and with 'every modern convenience' as then understood.

You would see those new houses, especially on Saturday afternoons, being inspected by young couples, who were 'engaged', rather embarrassed, and slightly furtive or else self-consciously and uncomfortably defiant, whilst the emissaries of the landlord or builder, and sometimes the builders themselves, hovered about them, very polite, very courteous, knowing what difficult and shy prey this was to get on the hook or in the net, knowing that it was easy to startle and put to flight—playing them as an expert fisherman plays a hooked fish, pointing out the advantages, the up-to-date improvements, the cheapness, the low rates, the easy access to Town, drawing a picture of residential bliss which seemed only to be equalled in Elysium. Each had their own methods. But always in their eyes was an anxious expression. They wanted desperately to effect a sale or a rental—for all this was done by private enterprise, this building, not by local authorities with rates behind them, and there were banks and overdrafts to worry about. Well those builders knew that there were so many houses from which to choose all around London.

Those young couples did not have to pay immense sums for houses, they did not have to put down a crippling amount by way of deposit and then saddle themselves with a mortgage for years. If they wanted to buy—they could do so—£350 was the price of a very nice house. But the landlord was only too anxious to rent his property—from £26 up to £45 a year, according to size and locality.

Few of those inspecting couples made up their mind at once. The young lady, if the preliminary view had been satisfactory, would return on a week-day with her Mother, who would view the place with an experienced eye and point out its drawbacks and advantages. Or the couple might return with their respective parents, *en masse*, and get the full benefit of mature judgment. If it got that far, the landlord cheered up—for it usually meant business.

Very few young couples wanted a flat, although there were such things. They had all been born in houses and so had generations before them. They had not acquired the idea of communal life. To them, an Englishman's home was his castle. It was true, too, in those days.

For many years those people of that age were free agents. Until the First World War had run its course, they had not become the slaves of The Machine. None of those early houses, early so far as the period under review is concerned, had a garage, which is now a prime necessity. Today people will sacrifice anything to get a house with a garage because they own a car which is their master. But then, cars were either not there at all, or were the playthings of the rich. So the young couples did not want a garage. They wanted a nice house, with a couple of living rooms, not too many stairs, two, three or four bedrooms, a kitchen, a scullery, a bathroom and a nice bit of garden. All those things they could get at a most reasonable rate.

The houses changed style as the era ripened. The Victorian type was followed by the Edwardian, a much lighter and more cheerful building fashion. Red brick displaced the yellow brick of former years, and red-tiled roofs were preferred to slates—'cooler in the summer and warmer in the winter' was the idea of the tiles. They wanted a front door, and a side door for the tradesmen, and they got it. And just before the First World War the type of house changed again, growing even brighter and less laborious to work—not that the labour question mattered much, for there was plenty of domestic labour, both permanent (they hoped) and casual.

It was a spacious age. People disliked being cramped. They did not have to take what they could get, like the people of today who are faced with shortage of accommodation. They could take their pick—and they did. In all those houses there were not only rooms but room. It was necessary, it appeared, to have room 'to swing a cat'. What this really meant nobody ever knew. Most of the houses when occupied certainly contained a cat, but nobody ever saw it being swung. Why, indeed, should it be? No cat would have liked it and a cat being a most intelligent animal it would have left the house at once should such a thing have been attempted. But that was the phrase everybody used. Maybe it had an older and darker significance like so many 'sayings', maybe it meant room to swing a cat-o'-nine-tails. Who can say for certain? But room to swing a cat they must have. They were not forced, like the modern folk, to live in what they would have regarded as a couple of cupboards with a corner partitioned off and called by courtesy a kitchenette. Not they. They wanted rooms so that they could fill them with possessions. For it was a Possessive Age. They wanted as much furniture as possible, a maximum, not a minimum. They wanted as many ornaments and pictures as could be crammed in. They wanted bookcases and bookshelves filled with books, which they actually purchased if they liked them. There were lending libraries then but people bought books. Authors could live in some comfort then—literature had not become a part-time occupation. They wanted cabinets in which to keep their greatest treasures. Every house which had any pretence at culture and style had a piano and the majority of the owners could play that piano. Bedrooms were as full as the living rooms, and the kitchen was packed with domestic apparatus. It was not a question of having half a dozen cups, saucers and plates and hoping for the best—there were whole services of the same pattern. . . . Everything was in greater supply and far more solid than today.

It may cause surprise in the minds of modern young couples that a couple starting life sixty years or so ago should have wanted four bedrooms. It must be borne in mind that the Family was then the hub of civilization and the question of their raising a family was in their minds—not mentioned to landlords or house agents because that would be indelicate, but known and understood by all. Also, the maid must have a room, for they could not only afford a maid, they could get one. And apart from that, there was the Absolute Necessity—the thing which was as imperative to them as the garage to their descendants. And that was the Box Room or the Lumber Room. That they must have. . . .

For after one or two years of married life everybody found they had a lot of things which were no longer wanted or which had become redundant. Indeed, they had such things as soon as they were married, because quite a lot of wedding presents were of no use to them and often heavily over-subscribed and duplicated. There were always far too many cruets, and one young couple received no less than eight pairs of silver or plated entrée dishes. . . . But these things simply could not be thrown away. For one thing, they were possessions and therefore must be kept. For another, they might come in useful one day—and, also, in case of wedding presents, the donors might come on a visit and then their gifts simply must be on show. So they went into the Box Room. Or the Lumber Room. Both names were right—it was a matter of family custom which was used. Bags and trunks were kept there—hence the Box Room; discarded articles were kept there—hence the Lumber Room.

They were amazing places—for although they did not know it, their owners were not only writing their own autobiographies there but also a complete history of their times. For there was something of everything in a box room. They were the store houses of an epoch of social history. It is a pity so few of them endured, for they would have been of immense value to antiquarians of the future. Those remarkable people can build up a whole era from a fragment of tile—and conjure races of men from a splinter of bone. What rewards could they not have reaped from a Victorian or Edwardian box room—those Home Museums of near-antiquities? But the two world wars wiped out the box rooms as they wiped away so much from a world which was peaceful and pleasant. The Age of Possessions became the Age of Doing Without. Even those old Victorian Houses which survive—how many of them still retain those domestic museums? So few as to be negligible. The room once sacred to lumber must now support life. For most of them are sub-divided into flats and there is no room for lumber there. Or what the modern world calls lumber. For what was in the Box Room belonged to Yesterday—it was the Treasury of Yesterday—the treasure cave of Family Life. But now family life is at a discount. Yesterday does not matter any more. Today is all important—Tomorrow? Well, deal with that when it comes. So the Box Room has gone. It is really a pity, for they were magic places. Everything went into them and nothing ever came out—yet they were never full. A search through them was as thrilling a voyage as could be taken, a sentimental journey without equal today. For they contained things which represented everybody in the house, in the family and even connected with the family. Nobody was ever surprised at what turned up in the Box Room; Aladdin's lamp itself would have seemed quite normal and evoked no amazement. Away up there, under the tiles or slates, next to the sky, stood the store-house of memories—the kingdom of the discarded yet retained. Junk of all sorts and sizes, the family history in material form—relics of youth, things which recalled those who had passed on. You could come across anything from an old bone saltspoon to a grandfather's clock—a christening mug to the first drawing-room carpet. But in every box room you would always find two things. There was always a pile of old magazines which were always going to be bound—but never were—and a heap of old newspapers put there because there was something so important in them that it had to be kept for reference—but nobody referred. There they were—The Back Numbers, in the holy of holy of Back Numbers, the Box Room. Despite the implied contempt in the phrase, Back Numbers are things of great potency. They hold, they grip, they compel. So long as they are really Back Numbers nobody can resist them. Once begin to glance through them and you are lost. You must go on, you are absorbed. The Past has you, whether you believe in it or not. Young people are held by them as well as old folk. But the young find amusement and something at which to laugh. The old people find much more than that —they find their youth enshrined—in every page—in every advertisement. 'I remember that,' they say—and they realize that they are Back Numbers themselves. But what of that? Back Numbers are grand things, full of interest, capable of giving joy, and of bringing content. Back Numbers to a Back Number proves that Youth is not so far away after all—only just around the corner and that it is possible to look back . . . through those old pages. And a Back Number has another advantage over the current issues of humanity, too. For he or she still possesses a box room of their own—their Memories, stored with the lumber of the years—possessions which cannot be destroyed or thrown away. That is the purpose of this book—to lead people into the Box Rooms of their minds and let them search there—and to show the young what manner of folk and what sort of life those Back Numbers knew when they too were fresh from the Press of Creation. So, if you like Back Numbers, come along.

If not, there is still time to switch on the Television. . . .

CHAPTER ONE

This Desirable Residence

ALTHOUGH the heart and core of Victorian and Edwardian life could be found in the Box or Lumber Rooms of the house in which they lived, it is not possible to proceed there straight away, for the Box Room was part of the house and the house was part of the street in which it stood, and as all pictures must have a frame it is necessary to get a proper idea of what those things were like. So the exterior must be called to mind first, and the house itself. . . .

'This Desirable Residence' is the favourite description still affixed by agents and property owners who are themselves desirous of disposing of something obviously to be desired. That label was used in Victorian days and the house which concerns this chronicle certainly lived up to that description.

It stood in the Best Road in a select suburb in the North of London and, more than that, in the Best Section of that Best Road. All districts then had Best Roads, the houses in which were larger, more imposing, dearer and therefore more desirable than lesser habitations in lesser roads. Those Victorian days were times of sharp Class Distinctions, and there were sub-divisions in all the sections of the great Classes—and in none more marked than in the Middle Class. A 'good address' was most important—where a family lived mattered a lot, socially. To live in one of the best houses in the best road was a matter of satisfaction not unmixed with pride in those who did so, and a matter of regret in those who did not—but that regret was mixed with determination amongst the younger members to achieve ultimate residence in the best road.

It was an ambition they strove to realize. It may have been snobbish but it was a genuine incentive. Those young people, who did not live in a Welfare State, believed in 'getting on' and imagined that their success

depended on their own efforts. They were as old fashioned and unen-
lightened as that! But very often they realized their ambition.

This particular road was—and is—about six miles from Charing
Cross. The district was already quite built up, there were no derelict
fields or wasteland awaiting engulfment by the builders. London had
already flowed past it but it was then at the height of its glory and had
not started to lose its quality. It showed no sign of tarnish all through the
period. The road was very long and almost straight, running practically
north and south. Across its extremities ran busy main roads thronged
with traffic and life, but the road itself had calm and detachment, which
two things graced all such roads in the days of Queen Victoria. It was
wide and spacious. It was then quite modern with all the latest improvements.

It was by no means monotonous. It was not just a double row of
houses all alike. It had variety because it had been built in sections by
different builders, each of whom had contributed his own style of
architecture to the desirable residences. There were two bisecting roads
which divided the thoroughfare into three parts, all of which were
different to the others. The middle section was the largest, the longest
and the best. Here again two builders had been at work, one at a slightly
later period than the other—so there was even a best portion of the best
section of the best road—the top half of the aforesaid middle section,
which contained the largest and most ornate houses. For some time this
section had come to a dead end, before a different builder contributed
rather smaller but still desirable residences on the vacant ground. These
houses were only small by comparison with those they adjoined; today
they would seem immense and indeed most of them now hold three or
four families. But they were smaller than the very Best Houses, whose
residents told visitors who were coming to see them for the first time
that theirs was one of the Big Houses. The family concerned in this
chronicle, who were the first residents in their desirable residence, could
give their visitors an even more explicit direction and say that theirs
was 'the last of the big houses'—and so it was. These houses had been
built in the 1870s. The road had a royal name but is now a 'Drive'.

The northern half was quite different to the middle and lower section
and had been built a bit before. The houses there were double fronted
and detached. They had two floors and attics. They formed a little settlement of their own around a large granite-built church dedicated to St.
John. These houses were all of the same pattern and design and ended
at the first bisecting road. Then the large houses began. They were not
double fronted or detached; although they gave the appearance of being
semi-detached it was really an optical illusion. But they were big and

most imposing and were, by general consent, the aristocrats of the road. Then began the block of houses which were more squat and smaller than they, although mansions by modern reckoning, until the second bisecting road was reached. Here were other large houses, but not quite so good or so desirable as those in the upper and middle sections, either in appearance or convenience. They stretched to the very end of the road and even amongst that section there were different kinds of houses, some much more desirable than the others—those on the eastern side backed on to a bowling green, which gave them considerable light and air and which they said was almost countrified. But that second bisecting road was something of a social barrier, people below it seldom knew or were known by those residing in the upper section—and indeed they were a considerable way off. But that crossroad was something in the nature of the salt on the banqueting table. The people who lived below it were 'in' the road but not quite 'of' it. The houses were the oldest and, already, even when this tale begins, at the extreme end one showed a card in the window which had the legend 'Apartments'. . . .

It is, however, with the middle section of the road and with one particular house in it with which this book mainly deals. Its residents, although well aware they lived in the best part of the best road, showed no discrimination on that account to their neighbours. Perhaps they did adopt a slightly more august air with the neighbours in that bottom end of the road—as residents in Mayfair might have adopted to people of West Kensington. They felt they were the senior members of the village, settlement or kraal, what you will, but it was understood that all people living in this road were of equal social standing. That did not apply to those who were without the pale by even a few yards, who dwelt in adjoining roads which were not the best road. These people, although neighbours, were not admitted to the status of friends. They might, by long residence and impeccable behaviour, qualify to a 'bowing' acquaintanceship, or a few words exchanged in a shop, unless of course there existed a bond of friendship not based on residential qualifications. In a few special instances, for some reason, probably membership of a church or chapel, some individual or even family from one of the lesser roads might gain admission as guests to one of the Best Houses. But she—it would be a lady in most instances—would not be honoured by an invitation to the 'At Home Day', which might be the second Tuesday, the first Wednesday or the third Thursday of the month. Not that invitations were issued for such functions. Friends knew that was the day on which the lady of the house was officially at home and it was therefore good form to call. She would inform new acquaintances, whom she considered worthy, what her 'Day' was. It was also engraved on her visiting cards—and visiting cards were essential then. Knowing the day and being sure that you would be welcome, or at least expected, you called as in duty bound. The residents of the lesser roads knew all about these days, they had their own—but they never called then. They knew they were not of the inner circle. When they called it was on an 'off' day and by appointment. They would be given tea, it is true, but not out of the Silver Teapot and not in the Drawing Room, but out of an earthenware pot and downstairs. There would be plenty to eat but no ceremony. They would be proud, however, to be on such terms as that, for in those days people 'knew their place'. And they would wear their best things and newest clothes for the visit.

This 'Best Road' was about ten minutes' easy walking from its local station from whence steam trains took the male residents to their offices in the City or the West End. If the City was the goal, then the gentlemen took the train to Broad Street or Moorgate Street; if the West End was required, it was a question of going to King's Cross and thence by bus or cab—or District Railway. Later, one of the earliest tubes linked this suburb with the City and later still, with the West End. From that moment, the neighbourhood declined. There is something in the burrowing nature of tubes which undermines residential values. . . .

This suburb had many amenities. At each end of the desirable road of desirable residences there was a Park. The shopping centre was only five minutes away. And there were horse trams and buses for shorter distances than the journey to town—not lightly undertaken then, for these were the days of the Horse. The main roads along which these vehicles ran were considered very busy ones indeed, but it was possible to cross them at any point you wished with an absolute minimum of rush and no danger at all, unless you went out of your way to court disaster. It was a matter of considerable difficulty to get knocked down or run over in those slow, dull days of Victoria. It seldom happened, even to children. Progress has altered all that.

The desirable residences in the best part of the best road were four stories high. Actually there were more, as will be discovered when the interiors are dealt with. They were quite a law unto themselves for they had no actual ground floor. There was a semi-basement, a first floor, a second floor and a top floor—and landings in between.

The house to be visited stood aloof from the road—as they all did—by means of a front garden. This had a low brick wall to close it in, surmounted by iron railings and an iron gate. The railings were shaped like spears and not a few boys cast envious eyes on them. Railings and gates were painted according to the taste of the householder, mostly brown, green or maroon. But one house broke away from the others. The owner painted his railings and gate black and gold. Although it looked quite imposing it did not find favour with the rest of the inhabitants. It was regarded as ostentatious and in bad taste and consequently in bad form at a time when unconventionality was vulgar and failure to conform to rule a social sin. Despite the flutter caused, the gentleman with a taste for black and gold took no notice. He kept on having them repainted in the same way and finally this very regrettable eccentricity was accepted. But nobody imitated this bizarre touch. On entering the front garden, there was a lawn on the right flanked by two flower beds. One was filled with evergreens and that running along the road held lime trees. The lawns were sometimes replaced with gravel with a pedestalled urn in the middle, but grass was the most usual and a peculiarity of those lawns was the extremely luxuriant crop of daisies they all produced. They were quite snowy with the little flowers. The lawn did not reach to the house but the ground fell away into an area in a species of rock garden or fernery and ferns grew quite luxuriantly. Mixed with the ferns in the selected house were periwinkle and creeping jenny and the effect was pleasant. It was possible to go right down into the area and of course small boys did so, clambering down through the ferns and over the lumps of clinker which stood for rocks. It had many uses for them. It was a cave, a camping place on the banks of the Amazon (suggested by the luxuriance of the ferns) and on many occasions the Pass of Glencoe or, alternatively, Killiecrankie. It was also a very handy place of ambush for sudden sallies against hostile gangs.

From the gate ran a pathway, either of flags or tessellated pavement, which ended at the foot of the Front Steps. These Front Steps were important and imposing. They ascended to the Front Door in a stately manner and there were nine of them. They had bordering walls with broad balustrades which ascended from flat square sections on either side which bore an ornament of some kind. It might be stone eagles, their wings half opened as if meditating a flight they never undertook. It might be stone lions, *couchant regardant*, or it might be stone vases of generous proportions which either held a species of petrified pineapple or really lived up to their name by being filled with earth and in summer were radiant with geraniums.

These front steps were quite large and rather steep, but the first of them at the foot of the flight was long and flat. In the middle of it was— —the Coal Hole. There, right in front of the house, right in the fairway of the state entrance, the Front Door, was a round hole covered by a circular plate of iron which was either painted black or blackleaded. Coal was delivered at houses in those days with a minimum of delay by private enterprise—it was not Nationalized. You could have as much as you wanted and the coal merchant was always anxious for you to have more. The usual order for this particular type of house was two tons at a time. It was good coal, of first-rate quality, with a minimum of slack, and if any slate or stone was detected the coal merchant trembled in his boots. The cost of the very best coal was from 16s. to 20s. a ton —the latter considered very expensive indeed. Of course, the miners had no baths, a deprivation they shared with about half of the whole community—and did not get as high pay. But it did not cost them as much to live and they managed to own their whippets just the same— and indulge in sport.

The coal came to the houses in carts drawn by large horses—flat carts with rails round them, rising to an arc at the horses' end. The coal-man seemed blacker and grimier than his successor today. For one thing, he worked longer hours and handled far more coal. A great deal of coal was used. It was the main—almost the only—form of heating. Hardly anyone had gas-stoves and there was very little electricity in suburban houses, or anywhere else. So the consumption of coal was considerable, for summer and winter alike there had to be hot water and that meant coal. There was no central heating, no immersion heaters, just coal, good and plentiful. Everyone was aware that it was the basis of this country's wealth, and despite the vast amount consumed at home, millions of tons were exported and fortunes made. It had not then been discovered economic to make it in such short supply and so dear that it was as cheap to import it from abroad. There was so much that it was hawked about the streets by the chaldron and delivered without grumble anywhere at any time.

The coalman's clothes were nondescript, basically of corduroy, the trousers being fastened round the knees with a strap like a navvy's. He wore a kind of leather sleeveless waistcoat, with a tight-fitting cap of black leather, with a long tail like a beaver's, which covered his shoulders and most of his back, upon which the sacks rested as he carried them. His boots were immensely heavy with iron-shod soles. He walked up the centre path of the front garden and shot the coal down the hole. He did it with a dexterous twist at the last moment, the coal cascading over his shoulder—and most of it going down the hole. Naturally there was a good deal of mess, for to get the last lumps out he held the sack over the hole. There would be quite a lot left on the step and a little trail up the path. He swept up in a casual way which would have suited most males but not a single female. There was coal dust all over the step which had been so white. The coalman was cheerful, despite his dirt and grime, and although his voice was raucous, for he cried his wares as he came along, he had a bright and lively nature. His delivery made, he reported at the side door, where a mysterious piece of paper was signed—nobody ever read it—got his tip (threepence or sixpence, quite good money then) and departed. He seldom rode in his cart unless it was empty, and not often then. He walked beside his horse.

But there was that coal hole, all dirty, spoiling the front steps which should have shone so white and snowily, and smirching the whole appearance of the house, in days when appearance counted for much. It was a point of honour and pride to keep those steps spotless. This was made difficult by the non-utilitarian position of the coal hole. There was no disguising the fact that coal had been delivered and a mess made. The coal and the coalman made work for everybody, the only person benefiting from the absurd position of the coal hole was the coalman himself, for it made a short 'carry' for him. Not that he would have minded much—in some poorer houses he carried sacks right up the stairs.

Those front steps, intended by the architect to be a 'feature', were a real liability. They were swept down every day and were completely washed down once a week. Not only washed but whitened by hearthstone. This job was not done by the domestics, although in times of great stress it might fall upon them, but was performed by a strange race of outcasts—rather like the 'Untouchables' of India—who were called Step Girls. Sometimes they were, indeed, girls, sometimes young women and they could be middle-aged and elderly. But they were Step Girls just the same. It was a distinct calling, perhaps it ran in families. Every house had its own girl, who came to 'do the steps' always on a regular day and at the same time. She worked at many houses and kept a strict time-table. These women supplied their own rags and cloths, and often their own hearthstone, the householder supplying hot water in pails, scrubbing brushes and any other implements required. The house under observation always supplied hearthstone, but that was entirely optional. These women washed down those steps, scrubbed them and hearthstoned them, with immense labour, speed and skill, and with great energy, leaving them spotless, resembling a drift of newly fallen show. It seemed a shame to use those steps after the step girl had exercised her art upon them. They worked on their knees, wearing coarse aprons of sacking, and they worked hard and with a will. It was their pride to make those steps shine—and they did. Theirs was a backbreaking job, really heavy manual labour.

These women, apparently, had no names, and no contact with anyone in the house except in the way of business. Children were not allowed to go near them, let alone speak to them. This served the double purpose of keeping the children's feet off the clean steps and preserving their whiteness and the children's minds from contamination. For these step girls were social outcasts of the lowest station. The servants held no conversation with them, just giving them the water and things they knew they wanted. The front path was cleaned down as well and, also, in the case of this house, quite a long flight of steps leading to the side door. It took about an hour and used up several pails of water. They were paid the sum of sixpence. This was apparently satisfactory for no more was ever demanded. It was the standard rate for the job. They were most regular in their attendance. They were always on their job. Bad weather was their bugbear for it interfered with their earning capacity, but it had to be very bad weather indeed to prevent them from cleaning the steps. If they were ill, they sent a deputy, they never let down their customers. Nobody knew their names or where they lived. They wanted that money and sixpence had a real value then. If they had a good connection, they earned quite a lot of money, as money went then, during a week. A skilled step girl could make herself fifteen to eighteen shillings a week and that was comfortable. Newcomers to a neighbourhood never enquired as to where they could find a step girl. There was always one attached to the house. She would turn up, knock at the side door and announce that she had come to clean the steps. Change of tenancy meant nothing to her, the steps were still there. Some of the older Victorian houses must have had three generations of step girls at work on them. And in the case of new estates and fresh houses, well, those step girls turned up from nowhere and carried on. It would seem they allocated the houses according to some strange ballot of their own. There was no poaching on each other's preserves, each girl had her own houses and the occupants had no say or choice in the matter. It was a strange affair altogether.

These women paid little attention to their own personal appearance, but they were never dirty, despite their work. The younger ones wore their hair in steel curlers all the week, probably removing them for the festive Saturday nights and Sundays. They seldom wore coats, even in winter, but had shawls round their shoulders. Their boots were always disasters, it was a marvel how they kept on the feet. Their headgear varied from a man's cap to a black straw hat of the same pattern as a 'gent's boater' or, if elderly, a bonnet which always fell away from the head and stood straight out from the neck when they were not leaning forward. The caps, hats or bonnets were fixed with hatpins on to the heads of hair. Their hours of work were from early morning until about 2 p.m. in the best roads, never later than that because the afternoon in Victorian times was the period of leisure and visiting. They worked later in inferior thoroughfares but that would 'never do' in the best house-

Her Majesty Queen Victoria

Above: A second Best House in a second
Best Suburban road

Below: A second Best Suburban road during the hour when the ladies
dressed—in the afternoon

holds—a visitor might arrive and find the steps being cleaned! There was a fiction that this never happened and that the steps shone through natural causes. Having done their job, they would return the pails, brushes, etc., to the side door and draw their sixpence. The more kindly employers would, on occasions, present them with old clothing and boots, and parcels of 'pieces'—odds and ends of food, scraps off the joint, bones, stale cake and the like. These were accepted with a curt grunt of thanks, but not of a servile nature. These things were received not as charity but as a custom and part payment. Although they belonged to the very lowest stratum of society as then constituted, they had the independence of spirit which came of the knowledge of a job well done. They took pride in that. If anyone had told them they were slaves, the answer would have been such as the maker of the remark would not have forgotten. They died, of course, from time to time, but always a successor arrived on the right day and at the right time, announced briefly that she had succeeded to the job—and carried on. She may have been one of the same family as the deceased or she may have inherited it by verbal last will and testament. Nobody ever knew.

It was, however, one of the laws of nature that coal was always delivered just after the step girl had done her job and gone. Or, at latest, the day following. Then a servant, or the odd man, had to whiten the step which had been sullied because it bore the coal hole. But they never did it with the same art and efficiency as displayed by that now vanished race, the Step Girls.

The path leading from the gate to the steps was in two portions, as stated, one either paved or tessellated and the other of gravel—the latter leading to the side steps which led downwards to a long passage and the Tradesmen's Entrance or side door. No tradesmen ever went to the front door. If he did he lost the custom. No tradesman ever gave more than a single knock—that was the Law as of the Medes and Persians. The only persons other than a visitor who ever went to the front door were the telegraph boy and the postman. They had to, because that was where the letterbox was. The postman gave a double knock, a rat-tat. If he had a parcel, a package too large for the orifice of the letterbox, or a registered letter, he gave a double rat-tat, and waited for the door to open. A similar double rat-tat also meant a telegram. That opening took some time if the family were busy and would entail a good deal of shouting up and down the stairs as to who was to answer the door. It was, of course, the job of the parlour-maid, but she might be right at the top of the house. However, the postman did not mind waiting, he had plenty of time. There were six deliveries a day in some parts, the last being about nine o'clock at night. The postage for a letter was One

C

Penny. It reached a destination in the same district as that in which it was posted in about two hours. Today, a letter bearing a twopenny-halfpenny stamp may achieve a journey of five miles in seven and a half hours but is more likely to take twenty-four. Postmen then looked much the same as now, but the caps changed. Early in the period the caps had a flat brim, which stuck out. Later they curved down in front and also at the back and a postman wearing the new model was heard to say that he did not know if he was going or coming. Parcels came in horse-drawn vans, being protected by wire netting inside and often by a dog as well. Yet there were hardly any robberies.

These best houses, in this particular section of this best road, were of yellow brick, but time had toned it to grey. It was a point of honour to keep them well painted and 'pointed'. A shabby exterior was a sign of financial weakness and that must never be admitted. The long passage alluded to gave them the appearance of semi-detachment, whereas actually they were joined together. They were oddly built, in many respects, but they were very commodious and comfortable. They had large windows and large airy rooms. Pokiness was something to be despised. The semi-basement room which faced the front had a bay window composed of three large panes. And the bay carried on up to the first floor, where the roof of it formed the floor of a little balcony outside the windows, which were set flat, of the second floor front bedroom. This balcony had a balustrade of small stone pillars. The architect had intended this as a feature. In the house being visited, the feature was naturally never used as a balcony but it came into its own when Queen Victoria celebrated her Diamond Jubilee. The ladies of this Victorian house had a nephew who came up from the country to stay with them for this great historic event. To please the boy, always their chief consideration (and also to get a bit ahead of their neighbours), they decorated the front of the house. The entire road was gay with flags and bunting although miles away from the route of any procession. The Victorian house flew its flags, a Union Jack, a White Ensign, the Tressured Lion of Scotland, a St. Andrew's Cross (they were Scots) and a St. George's Cross as well. The family did it well. But they went further than that. Buying some quarter of a mile or so of red, white and blue material, probably cheap muslin, they draped the house therewith from the windows and intertwined the patriotically coloured material through the pillars of the miniature balcony. The effect was striking. The neighbours were envious and some copied the idea. That material was not thrown away after use; it was kept, as were most things of that age, and it came out again for other rejoicings, such as the Reliefs of Ladysmith, Kimberley and Mafeking in the Boer War. That was the last occasion—the family had moved by the time Edward VIIth came to the throne.

The bay windows in the semi-basement were protected by stout iron bars, which was true of all the windows on that floor, back and front. The windows of the first-floor front were of the same size as those below them but were not protected. On the next floor there were three large flat windows, one over the front door and, above that, the windows were of the attic variety, standing out from the roof.

At the top of the front step was a porch, flanked by pillars and rather like a small Greek temple. The front door itself was big, like everything else about that house, and had its two top panels of opaque glass. In some houses the glass was coloured, in others heavily frosted, the idea being that those outside should not see inside. Once in the porch a visitor was safe from observation. If he or she had managed to get up the front steps unobserved, nobody inside knew who they were nor could they find out. Not all callers were welcome, even in those days of security. But nobody dreamed that a day would come when in response to a knock on the door the lady of the house would be struck down with a cosh and lie unconscious and maybe dying whilst her house was rifled. The undesirability of a caller then was of a different nature. It might be a persistent salesman risking his luck at the front door against all convention or it might be an annoying person to whom one was always out. In that case it was a problem as to who was to open the door if the correct servant was not available. But as it was quite a walk from the gate to the front steps and up them and as somebody was usually keeping observation on the road, interlopers seldom got by. But, having secured the porch, they were faced by a bell and a knocker, both of brass. You did not press the bell, you pulled it. It was not electric, it worked by wires. Perhaps that is too optimistic a phrase—it is better to say that it had worked by wires although nobody in the house could remember its doing so, even though they were the first tenants. There was a legend to the effect that it had worked once but not for long. So anyone pulling the bell had a long wait coming. At one time this family had an electric bell installed, a great innovation. It had a round brass plate with a little ivory knob in the middle, which bore the legend 'Press' in black. It operated on wet batteries which soon ran out. As no one in the house understood the first thing about electricity, let alone batteries, and as the men who had installed it knew hardly any more, that bell joined its brother who had to be pulled, in a duet of silence. It was no good ringing the bell. Regular visitors knew this and applied themselves to the knocker. Successful knocking depended on two things: the whereabouts in the house of the servants or members of the family who happened to be at home and the loudness of the knock. Visitors knocked according to their temperaments. And knocking was a great exhibition of character. Knocks varied from a gentle rat-tat-tat to a good, hard thumping series of double knocks. Some indeed used a kind of crescendo—starting quietly and finishing fortissimo—and some the reverse. The gentle knockers had to smarten up their ideas before the knock was heard, and even then it took a long time to get to the door for the purpose of opening it. By the time the visitor got in they were either irritated or humble, according to their type. Of course, on days when visitors were expected, the parlour-maid took up a strategic position in the hall.

The architect of those houses was indeed a man of weird ideas. He ran that long passage down to the side door which was the tradesmen's entrance and which indeed most of the family used, if they did not want to climb the steps and get out their latchkeys. The side door was opposite the kitchen and got answered promptly. But the architect had several different levels in his houses and he tacked pieces on outside. It was such a section that joined these houses together, out of sight of the road and so the semi-detached illusion was created. Such an adhesive section went across this long passage from the first floor up to the third floor. It contained some important rooms, too. The side door was painted and had an iron knocker but no letterbox. The passage had a brick party wall along it, to divide it from next door, and it was a small boy's delight to walk along the top of that wall, which provided all the thrills of a tight-rope act. The house was roofed with slate and had pipes climbing all over it, not at the front but at the back and side.

The road was straight and ran slightly downhill, with just a suggestion of a curve at its southern end but not enough to interfere with the vista of well over half a mile. It was lit by gas lamps and it had an air of prosperity, security and peace all over it. It was almost a self-contained community, socially, but of course it held no shops, although it did contain a private school, but that was regarded as Culture.

It had two doctors, one at the top and one two-thirds of the way down. Both wore tall hats and frock coats and were never seen in any other attire. Had they been less formal, they would have lost the confidence of their patients. One (he at the top end) was English and he did his rounds on foot. The other was a Scot and he visited in a brougham; nobody knew if this was hired or his own property. No need to say which had the largest practice or which was regarded as the best doctor. It did so happen that the Scot was by far the best, but had he not been so the carriage would have convinced everyone coming into the neighbourhood that he was the foremost medico. The Englishman, a curious little fellow, had been there first and built up his connection which he held with the tenacity of his race.

Life went very pleasantly in that Best Road, as it did in so many just like it all over the Kingdom. It was a life governed by security, which was based upon the commercial supremacy of this nation and the value of its golden sovereign, on integrity and on leisure—and also on convention. For those very conventions, now so derided, gave people a sense of responsibility and they lived up to it. Those Victorians had a sense of quality, and they not only gave it but demanded it. Those Best Roads were places of tranquillity such as cannot be found today. The busy time was the morning. The men went off to business, the children went off to school, the servants were sweeping down the front, polishing the knockers and bells, cleaning the windows, and the ladies went out shopping. The result of that shopping led to more activity, for nobody then needed to carry their purchases home. So errand boys went up and down the road, carrying their baskets, butcher boys in their blue jackets with striped aprons called at the houses with a sort of elongated wooden tray on their shoulders, with handles at each end—like a stretcher with shortened arms and truncated—on which were the joints. Or the butchers' carts dashed round at a very swift pace—at least twelve miles an hour—made like 'dog carts' with a box in the body to carry the meat. These butchers' carts, which always had a good horse between the shafts, were regarded as dangerous—they came round corners so quickly and elderly people cursed them for their speed.

The milk float rattled up and down the road, like the Roman Chariot it resembled, laden with churns and cans; or the more leisurely milkman on foot pushed his vehicle—something like a large perambulator with four wheels, which also carried its churns, and lots of little pewter cans for delivering the milk. These had handles and could be hung on railings. The milk flowed into jugs direct from the churns or it was ladled out with a pewter dipper—there were no glass bottles and it was all gloriously unhygienic. The milkman sold butter, too, and little brown jars of cream, real rich cream, and would announce his presence by shouts of what sounded like 'Milk-aheaow'. All the goods were delivered in the morning, that was the pèak bustle time of those distant days. Greengrocers' carts, fully stocked, moored themselves to the kerb whilst the man in charge called at adjacent houses. He not only delivered what was known as 'the order' but would display attractive samples of fruits in season, punnets of strawberries, enticing baskets of greengages—and he did very well. To give colour there was an occasional hurdy-gurdy with a monkey, a series of regular visits by piano organs, also with monkeys, and sometimes with dancing dolls on top which waltzed stiffly to every tune, whether it was in waltz time or not. There might even be a German band—regarded by most people as a congregation of spies—who played their music round a lamp post, daytime or evening, with a rather larger ration of 'oom-pah' from the heavy brass than was really necessary. It might have even six performers, two of whom would be boys, and those boys would sing sentimental German songs (not too badly) and would go round to collect coppers in their peaked caps. Such children as were not at school, the younger ones, who had gone out to play, would find great joy in a one-man band, in which the solitary performer produced a far greater proportion of noise than music, and would sometimes be thrilled by a dancing bear—a rather subdued but solemn animal of dirty yellowy-browny-white, led by an Italian, which sat up, danced (or what passed for dancing in a bear) and caught the pole his leader threw to him. Children of a timid nature would take refuge in their gardens and peer through the gates, whilst the bolder gathered round but were ready for instant flight. But all the youngsters would ask their parents to contribute coppers—and the bear leaders did very well. Some of the piano organs had a woman attached, dressed in contadino costume, who had a couple of budgerigars which would, for the very reasonable sum of one penny, condescend to perch on a little stick held in the woman's hand and then select from a tray a tiny envelope which contained the fortune of the contributor of the penny. The birds were never called budgerigars then, but love birds, and the lady in charge had long dangling brass ear rings and a flashing smile. She did a roaring trade with the servants, who were seldom disappointed in the birds' choice of their future.

In season, vendors of lavender would slowly traverse the road, crying their wares in the manner of the older times, and men chanting 'Fine clothes props' bearing forked saplings over their shoulders found a ready sale, for much washing was done at home. Other men who were apparently wire workers also hawked their wares with cries of 'A fire guard, a lampshade, only six pence'. But all that happened as a rule between 8.30 a.m. and 1 p.m. There was very little noise, for all vehicles were horse-driven. Errand boys might give vent to piercing whistles and send out blood-curdling yells of 'Wait for us' to other boy friends similarly employed and seen in the distance. They would carry on conversations at over a quarter of a mile range—and always they whistled, but they whistled tunes, not that ear-piercing sibilance without any melody which one encounters today. But one motor-bike today can make more noise than a small army of such leathern-lunged lads. If there was serious illness in a house, the road immediately outside was covered with straw or tan, to deaden the noise of traffic.

In the afternoons these roads relapsed into a graceful peace, they seemed to take a siesta. Hardly a cart went along. There might be a Carter Paterson, London Parcel Delivery or Pickford's van driving slowly by, its two occupants scanning the windows to see if a card bearing the name of their firm summoned them to call and collect a parcel. If they saw one, they stopped, collected the parcel and it went on its way. Imagine it! They called at a house which wanted them, and saved the occupants much trouble. It was their business—it was a service they gave and the job was done with expedition and efficiency. Hardly anything ever went astray and the charge was very small. All you had to do was put the card in the window, and the card was supplied free.

On summer afternoons there would be the water cart, that tank on wheels drawn by a leisurely horse. By means of a pipe at the back, pierced with many holes, this cart sent its cool water spraying fountain-like over the dust of the macadamed roads, and caused such a fresh fragrance that the memory of its aroma lasts down the years. Roads were not tar-sprayed then and this fact gave an added charm, for every such road had its complement of house-martins, those gay, cheerful blue and white birds which flashed to and fro and made their nests under the eaves of those houses out of mud collected from those very roads. Tar-spraying has driven them from the suburban roads where they were once plentiful and which they graced with beauty.

There would be a few foot passengers—people out visiting or returning from shopping expeditions, but mostly the afternoons were quiet, serene and peaceful, almost cloistral. There was renewed activity when the children came home from school and, later, around half-past six and half-past seven when the Gentlemen returned from the City.

Evening settled in with renewed peace. The only vehicles would be cabs or broughams taking residents out to the Theatres, dinners or parties. A bicycle or two might pass up and down, but not many—and sometimes a piano organ played in the dusk. Occasionally the peace was broken by a shocking, frightening sound of men and boys rushing along, shouting, ' 'Orrible Murder—Latest News—Full Details—'Orrible Murder.' Murders were then comparatively rare events and servants were sent out to buy a paper. But there was seldom any news of the 'Orrible Murder in them, for these men and boys were known as catchpennies, although the papers they sold were priced at only one halfpenny each. If a penny was tendered they never had time to give change—they did not wait for obvious reasons. Lights twinkled in the lamp posts and in the windows of the houses. One could hear pianos and there might be a party in progress, and even the sound of singing might penetrate to the street. But it would be human music, no blaring loud-speakers, for the miracle of radio had not arrived. The jingle and hoof-beats of a hansom cab would go by—but mostly it was very quiet.

The moon, if there was one, would look down on a scene of peace —no motors, changing gears, being driven into garages with resulting noise. Just a long, peaceful road, quite motionless, save for one thing —the Policeman on the Beat. That quiet, unobtrusive figure, in the blue uniform and helmet. He seemed ubiquitous, he seemed to turn up everywhere, watching with apparent casualness, pausing here and there, standing still and almost invisible at corners as he surveyed a double vista, flashing a light from his lantern on windows, gates and doors. Always there, never far away, day or night, he was the reason for that tranquillity, that freedom from crime and violence, the reason for one's being able to sleep peacefully in bed without fear of loss or a crack on the skull. Also the reason why there was so very seldom any news of that ' 'Orrible Murder' in the catchpenny's paper. The policeman on the beat, known to everyone and knowing everything and everybody, made this country the safest and most law-abiding in the world—an unarmed guardian of the Peace, he certainly saw to it that Peace was kept. . . .

CHAPTER TWO

Desirable Residents

BEFORE dealing with the intimate life and inhabitants of the special Desirable Victorian residence selected, it is necessary to still further gild the frame of the picture and perhaps to glaze it, so that the people, events and things to be considered closely should have every focus brought to bear.

The inhabitants of this Best Road were people of the prosperous Middle Class which might—and indeed did—consider themselves of that nebulous section of it called 'Upper', although that was usually conceded to the landed gentry and professional walks of life. The predominant note here was Commerce, although there were a sprinkling of the Professions (as well as the two doctors who were general practitioners, of course, and not of the upper walks of Specialism). There was an architect or two, a couple of solicitors, and a good many who were 'retired'. There were also some spinsters of mature years and ample means. But the 'retired' gentlemen had been in commerce and nobody in the road was in 'trade' or 'retail business'. It was all very respectable and refined indeed. Most of the houses contained families—many grown up but still there—but there were exceptions. Next door to the selected house lived, for many years, an old lady and gentleman. They were elderly, he had a grizzled beard and hair which was white, she had silver hair. They both habitually wore black, the lady affecting bonnets in the winter and large floppy black hats in the summer, fastened perhaps for additional security by a kind of scarf under the chin. They had three servants and they lived all alone except for a little black-and-tan dog, a miserable little beast which was perpetually shivering, but to which they were quite devoted. They never seemed to go out alone. He was 'retired', though from what nobody ever discovered. Their next-door neighbours, the family to be met with, would bid them good day but were never invited to call, nor did they invite the old couple. But they were considered excellent neighbours for they were very quiet and eminently respectable. They never had any visitors, they had no family as far as could be found out, they never entertained. They would go out walking, always together, and every summer a cab came and they went for a month's holiday with innumerable trunks. They never appeared to do anything though from time to time the old gentleman might be observed in the large garden, watching the jobbing gardener at work. Sometimes they would sit there, in the midst of the trim flower beds and neat lawn, he in a soft felt hat (as a change from the invariable topper worn outdoors) and she in a black dress, black silk apron and little lace cap. The dog would shiver beside them. They kept their own counsel.

Even the servants did not gossip, although the neighbouring domestics did their best to get information. All that could be elicited was that it was very quiet, with good and plentiful food and that the lady and gentleman were very genteel. Everyone knew that. Eventually the dog died.

Not very long afterwards, observers noticed the doctor calling—it was he who had the brougham—and word went round that the old gentleman was ill. Very shortly afterwards there was a quiet but exceedingly respectable funeral. And the old lady lived on in that huge house alone until she, too, passed away and the place was sold. Why that old couple should have lived their secluded lives in such a large house is incomprehensible to people of the modern age, but it was well understood then. They were living in the manner to which they were accustomed and which they considered befitted their position in the world.

There was another retired gentleman with a very red face and white bushy beard, who resided in that road and with whom lived his quite considerable family of boys and girls—all grown up, or at least in their twenties, but none of whom seemed to have acquired the habit of matrimony. This was apparently not the case with the bearded gentleman, for he caused a terrific scandal by marrying his housekeeper. And the family at once left home *en masse* and all got married except one son, who died a bachelor for reasons which will become apparent. Nobody in the road spoke to the newly married man nor to his bride. She had long been an object of suspicion and was graded, in the fashion of those days, as 'no better than she ought to be'. Her ascent to legal wifehood made no difference. She and her husband were persistently CUT. They did not care. They remained for years until he died and his widow sold up the house and confirmed everyone's worst suspicions by marrying a local publican. . . .

And in another house there had been a family who held to the Ancient Faith. They were the only people of their race in the road them—now there is a synagogue nearby. They did not stop long. Their name was that of a famous composer very popular in Victorian times. They gave parties, they made considerable noise. They were, of course, ostracized. The daughter of the house (there were three sons as well who were given to loud patterns in their clothing) was a handsome, attractive girl, a regular Rose of Sharon. She caused male heads to turn and earned the dislike of every woman in the vicinity. She dressed in flamboyant manner and high colours suited her type of beauty. She was always in the extreme of fashion and every woman was certain that she 'made up'. She was 'fast' —and this was social death. But when the Undesirables moved out another family bought the house and moved in. Here, again, the master of the house and head of the tribe was of the Ancient Faith but a very different type of man. He was quiet, respectable and well behaved. He was of French birth and had the manners and courtesy always connected —and often so wrongly—with Frenchmen. His wife was so English it could hardly be believed. They were complete opposites. He was small, neat and dapper and quick in movement—though he never took a decision quickly in his life. She was an enormous woman, who had been a beauty and still had great charm. She had been married before and there was one daughter. By the French husband there were four children, three girls and a boy. The Victorian boy watched their arrival, surveyed the young people and came to a slightly adverse opinion. He did not know that Fate was upon him. But the lady of the house, whose girth prevented much activity, liked to sit in the bay window of the front room and, secure behind lace curtains, watch the life of the road as it went by. Respectability was her god—and she watched especially her next-door neighbours.

Now the house next door contained the Private School which has been mentioned. It might be considered that such an establishment would not redound to the credit of this most exclusive neighbourhood. The reverse was true. It was run by a lady of such learning, such refinement and good appearance that the inhabitants of the Best Road were glad to send their children there. The lady who ran the school lived in the house, as did her parents and her brothers and sisters. Respectability reached to the zenith. There was little to proclaim it a scholastic establishment except a very discreet notice which referred to it as a High School, and gave the principal's name. Otherwise it was just like the other houses. The father of the schoolmistress was a wonderful old gentleman. He was the quintessence of Victorianism—Victorianism as understood today. This old gentleman, well advanced in years, was tall, slim and upright. He was wonderful to look at, with his head of silver hair and his beard like a patriarch. He always wore his frock coat buttoned up and was never seen in less formal attire. He was slow, deliberate and dignified in all that he did, but there was always a kindly smile on that handsome face with its fresh complexion and rosy cheeks. His eyes were blue and had a twinkle. He was so fresh and clean that he shone. Whenever that Victorian boy in after life wanted to conjure up a picture of the word Benevolence he would think of the old man. And to make the respectability more monumental, that man had spent his life in the Bank of England and had now retired on his well-earned pension. His wife was a little woman, who always dressed in black, wore silk aprons, bonnets and corkscrew curls and was as quick and active as her husband was slow and leisurely. She was birdlike in appearance and movements and kept the old man on the go. She had a voice with a snap in it which contrasted with his deep and measured tones. She would always find him little jobs to do—and he could be seen, by discreet observers, sitting in the shade, during the summer, in a secluded corner of the garden, shelling peas at his wife's order. He took his time over this—and would occasionally doze until his wife's sharp voice would be heard, "Have you shelled those peas yet, Jackson?"—when he would come to himself with a slight start and reply gently, "Shortly, Maria, shortly. . ."

They were the pillars of a church some distance off—and when they went there together on a Sunday morning you saw real Victorianism at its best. They had a large family—large in every sense of the word. All the girls and boys of that couple took after the father. They were tall and handsome. The two eldest went into the Bank of England, both played games well and both were Volunteers. The younger son, who did not live with the family, did not go into the Bank but into Music. It was feared he would come to a bad end despite the fact that he was connected with a Chapel Royal. He formed a habit of going backstage at Theatres and heads were shaken at the news. There was a time when rumours of a scandal filtered through but it passed over and it affected neither this eminently respectable family—nor the School.

The Headmistress was the eldest daughter and the premises were certain rooms in that large desirable Victorian residence. The pupils were mostly girls although some boys were admitted until they were eight or nine. The Headmistress had a great personality and was most impressive. She was tall, like all her family; she could have made an excellent model for Britannia with the eyes and gaze of a Pallas Athene— whom she much resembled. It was impossible to find anyone better fitted to turn out young ladies trained in the decorum and manners of the day. She had a regal, queenly way with both parents and pupils and it is difficult to say which held her in most awe—yet she was kindly and gentle for all her firmness. And she was fully qualified as a teacher of youth—she did not merely trade on her appearance. It was not easy to get into her school; parents had to pass a social test before their children were admitted. They all lived nearby, of course, but if they did not come of the most respectable families they did not get in. Children whose parents were in 'Trade' were not wanted—although there was one there whose father actually kept a shop, but he was in the main a nursery-man and the shop was regarded as a showroom for his goods. The school was always full—she could accommodate about thirty-five pupils—and the terms were, from the modern standpoint, quite amazing. A man and woman, brother and sister, who had attended that High School in 1904 when they were small, found one of the accounts in their Father's box room. The fees for the term, for both of them, not separately—were £3 16s. 0d. No charge was made for books or stationery but milk for that entire term came to 3s. The girl took a special subject—brush drawing—and this cost 7s. 6d., whilst the materials necessary for it ran the Father into the additional expenditure of 1s. 9d. With all the extras the total cost for those two for that term was £4 8s. 3d. and from that 11s. 3d. was deducted for the times the youngsters had missed school through illness and had consequently not received tuition. That will surprise modern parents. How the lady made it pay is most amazing but she did well out of it. She had staff, too, and extra instructors for special things like dancing which was taught by two maiden ladies of equal respectability to the Headmistress. They taught not only dancing—ball-room dancing, of course—young ladies did not learn tap and ballet then—but also deportment. They gave instruction in Court Etiquette and how to behave when presented at Court—though it is not on record that any of the young ladies receiving such instruction ever had to put it into practice. Still, they knew how to behave if called upon.

This Headmistress was go-ahead, too. She even introduced scientific subjects, or what passed for them in a most unscientific age. An attempt to teach biology by means of a sheep's eye in a saucer of water caused most of the girl pupils to faint, and a demonstration with mercury, popularly known as quicksilver, ended in disaster—but of a more en-joyable kind, for the mercury got spilled on the floor and caused much hilarity in pursuit. Those lessons were abandoned. But the girls learnt the elements of what they might be expected to know; few, if any, were destined for a commercial life. Botany was a great feature—and all the girls who went there were turned out as well-behaved, properly con-ducted young ladies with enough education to be good for them and not too much as to frighten the men. Few of them ever learned to spell correctly but that hardly mattered—there was always someone to ask. But they wrote well and clearly, they spoke correctly, they had accomplishments and their manners were excellent. Which was good education for a Victorian Miss. They knew exactly how to behave in any society in which they might find themselves and their morals had been carefully attended to. They all did pretty well. So the High School was held to enhance and not detract from the quality and tone of the Best Road.

That very English lady who lived next door held the Headmistress, her brothers and sisters in the highest respect. They represented all she would have liked to be herself. Her birth had been somewhat humble —she was country born—but she knew gentlefolk when she saw them. She who made little pretence at religion, nevertheless went to the same church as did her neighbours—when she could summon up enough energy. She made handsome gifts to its charities and spent largely at its bazaars. Her husband was of the Jewish faith but the children all followed their mother. And her idea of bliss was to watch her neighbours, and especially her next-door neighbours. She missed nothing of what they did. To her their affairs were of supreme importance. She would chat with them over the garden fence in the summer time and that was joy to her. Two of her daughters went to the High School, too, which made a link. The Highly Respectable Family, or members thereof, would come to tea with her and she would go to tea with them. She did both in style—donning her best clothes and mantle, her jewellery, and putting on some rather grand manners. She would also be allowed to see the dancing class in action and sit outside on the landing where an assistant mistress was stationed, to prevent the girls going headlong down the staircase as they backed out of the room when learning their Court Etiquette. That was also a red-letter day to this very dear lady. She and her husband were as ill-assorted a pair as one could wish to see but they got along. She who adored respectability also loved 'professionals' and all to do with the Theatre, to which she was a constant visitor. When the Victorian Boy grew up and entered the profession— to which he was destined—she was truly delighted. For she liked him and he liked her. They understood each other. But that perhaps is to anticipate and is another story, as Kipling would say. Suffice that the boy became her son-in-law.

There was not a great deal of moving in and out of that road. It was the final anchorage for many. But sometimes a house fell vacant, and then there was also great speculation as to what sort of people would take it. It was quite an event and the newcomers had to serve a pretty severe apprenticeship before they were accepted as a real part of the community. It so happened that in the late 'nineties, one of the best of the best houses did come on the market and was quickly snapped up. Into it moved a small family—very small for those days. Their arrival and that of their goods and chattels were kept under constant supervision from behind the lace curtains which draped all windows of surrounding houses—screens through which the viewer could see without being seen. And as the furniture was being moved in quite an astonishing number of Nannies and the lesser breed of girl who was employed to take the children out walking found occasion to pass that house on the same side, and to linger awhile. An equally astonishing number of domestic servants might have been observed *en route* to the pillar-box. All these close observers were under orders from the ladies who employed them and reported back in detail. Much ornate and good furniture was going in and it was hoped that the traditions of the road would be maintained. But the sight of the new residents gave rise to grave doubts. The gentleman was large and corpulent and had a most expansive way with him. Of dignity he had none. His clothes were a shade too smartly cut, far too new and resplendent. He wore a lot of jewellery in the form of rings and tiepins, and his watch chain was far too conspicuous. It was of solid gold but so massive it could have held a battleship to its moorings. He was always smoking very large cigars when seen going to or returning from whatever business it was to which he gave his attention. And he seldom, if ever, walked to the station, as did the other gentlemen. He had a hansom. He was outsize in all respects—and so was his wife. Her clothes, although of good material and cut (the watching matrons admitted that), were brighter and cruder in colour and not in the taste which typified the road. Her hats, too, were far from pleasing to them. The verdict, a damning one, was that she was not quite ladylike. Women in those days were not spoken of as being 'smart'. The word was 'stylish'. This lady had a bit too much style in not the right style.

The family was completed by a small boy, aged about eight or nine. All the children of the Best People in the Best Road loathed him the moment they set eyes on him and instantly resolved on his destruction. No other course seemed to them possible, for he wore suits of velvet with lace collars, white socks and black shoes with a bar across and showed bare legs between the knickerbockers of velvet and the white socks. His hair was long—and in ringlets. It was like Little Lord Fauntleroy, the detested of all decent, normal, dirty little boys. He was seen to carry a violin case and rumour spread round like wildfire that he was an Infant Prodigy. That was the final straw and the boys of the road got together. Those who object to the 'comics' of today may be surprised to learn that the boys of the late Victorian Age read very similar publications, the chief differences being that they were home-produced and knew nothing of Sex—for all boys then considered girls objects of horror. But they devoured those 'comics', then called 'penny bloods', and would play games based on their reading. There existed already in that Best Road the machinery for coping with this new situation. For the Road possessed a 'gang' of which the Victorian boy who figures herein was founder and captain. For reasons best known to himself this gang bore the awe-inspiring title of 'The Ever Victorious Band of Revenge'. It had six members besides himself, two recruited from lesser roads but eligible because they were hefty and pugnacious and went to the same school. The Band was in a rather languishing condition for there was little cause for revenge in the ordinary way. It flourished around November 5th when householders who had given it or any of its members offence were likely to find their letterboxes full of Chinese Crackers in a full state of explosion or a cannon cracker living up to its name in their front porch. But this was June and the Gang had nothing on hand. So here was a heaven-sent job for them. They met secretly—in the area of the Victorian Desirable Residence, screened by the ferns. They were harangued by their Captain and reminded of their Vow. They all took a Vow on joining. A plan was formed and the members established a watch on the enemy so as to choose the right moment for offensive—very offensive—action.

Meanwhile the whole road was agog over the newcomers. There were three servants in that house—none too many—and a Nannie who never left the horrid boy. This was noted by the Band of Revenge who went into conference about it. So far nobody knew what business or profession the family followed. They had moved in on a Thursday. On Sunday (yes, on Sunday) they gave a house-warming. This was not at all to the liking of the Best People, who all went to church or chapel on a Sunday and kept it as a day of rest and quiet. A crowd of guests came, mostly arriving in dogcarts and traps of a sporting cut and build. The ladies and gentlemen attending the party were overdressed, loud and noisy. As the night wore on, there was music and dancing. At one period there was a wailing of catgut and horsehair which was put to the discredit of the Infant Prodigy. The house-warming went on until a very late hour indeed—the house must have been red-hot by the time it was over. The guests departed, disturbing the peace of a Sunday night—or early Monday morning—with shouts, vulgar laughter and the clatter of hooves. As early as possible, discreet enquiries were made of the tradespeople. The servant system of information had not yet had time to get working, but the tradespeople knew. The information they imparted caused a tremendous flutter amongst the Best People who passed the word around with speed and were in and out of each other's houses hot foot. Ordinary

Upper left: "Pa". *Upper right:* Uncle Peter—who made the Germans speak English. *Lower left:* Uncle Charles. *Lower right:* Uncle James

"A Safe Escort"

The "Arm of the Law."
The Bank.

"Point Duty" Piccadilly Circus.

The Mounted Constable.

The Victorian and Edwardian Policeman; when the man in blue was
on the beat and when it was possible to cross the road—also when
nobody got coshed and could sleep quietly in their beds

etiquette of calling was suspended. It appeared—what *do* you think?—
the gentleman of that house was—a Bookmaker! This was a staggering
blow—one not to be borne. It verged on regional disgrace, the fair name
of the Best Road was sullied. On the arrival home of the men folk they
were told the dreadful news. The males did not appear to be so shocked
and upset as the females. One man, the head of the Victorian house here
concerned, said that the man causing all the trouble was probably a
Turf Accountant. This might have softened the blow for there were
already several ordinary Accountants in the road. But nobody called
on the newcomers, nobody acknowledged them in the street, although
the lady and the gentleman who accounted on the Turf showed every
desire to be friendly. All they received in return to their bows and smiles
was a frigid stare. It was the children of the road—the Ever Victorious
Band of Revenge in particular—who rescued their parents from their
predicament. They led that reputed Prodigy a dog's life. His every
appearance was greeted with boos and hoots, with stone-throwing,
salvoes of slap-bangs (a kind of firework wrapped in a twist of paper
which gave a satisfactory explosion on meeting the earth) and, if possible,
bodily violence. The Band of Revenge was joined by other boys from the
far ends of the road, for word had gone round of the sport. Even some
of the girls were admitted—they were useful as sentinels and givers of
alarm signals. The wretched boy, who had tried friendly overtures and
had been very nearly killed, dare not venture forth without his Nannie.
Then the little avenging savages would circle round the pair with whoops
and yells and insulting cries. Strategy was resorted to, planned in that
area by the Victorian Boy. A section of the Band, the swiftest runners,
would so infuriate the Nannie that she would lose her temper and pursue them. The rest then closed in for the kill. With howls of victory, they
assaulted that imitation Fauntleroy, inflicted every possible indignity
upon him, pulled his ringlets, threw his hat in the gutter and kicked it
about and on one occasion carried off his very lace collar as a trophy,
rejoicing therein as a Redskin might over a Paleface scalp.

It is admitted that the parents had the good sense not to lodge complaints with the parents of the savages—not that they knew from which
houses they came. The Nannie did complain to a policeman but that
wise man gave it as his opinion that boys will be boys but if he caught
the little devils they had better look out. He took good care never to
come within range when a raid was on. The usual method of the police
for dealing with bad boys then was to give them a cuff over the ear with
an empty glove. But as those whose beat lay amongst a lot of naughty
boys took the precaution of filling the fingers of that glove with marbles,
this seemingly gentle corrective was most salutary. It must also be

D

admitted that the parents of the avenging boys did nothing to restrain or check their offspring. It was not long before the Turf Accountant, his wife and the Prodigy moved away—violin case and all. It was just as well, for a plot was hatching to seize that boy, shove him in one of the coal cellars and burn his violin and case. No doubt the operation would have been successful. But the flight of the Family saved the boy.

Most of the Victorian families which once inhabited that best road have long since moved away. Of the children who played there and grew up, some have made their mark, some vanished into obscurity. Some, of course, went abroad, and one amassed a considerable fortune in South Africa, where his brother and sister prosper today although he has passed on. Another is an eminent Q.C. There were not very many children but mostly they did well. And of course the greater portion went into Business. Some went into the Professions. One is a Coroner today and yet another entered the Theatre, as his breeding led him, and today he writes this book.

One family still remains of those who resided there in Victorian days. One of the old people has gone but only very recently—he celebrated their Golden Wedding and reached a ripe old age. And the remnants of that family cling to the old home, those who did not marry and launch out on their own. Their house, which was one of the newer buildings adjoining the Big Houses—but it was big enough in itself to hold about three families today—was notable for its flagstaff. This had been erected to celebrate the birth of a son born to the original inhabitants of the house. He died in the 1914-1918 war—a war which took heavy toll amongst those who had spent their youth and childhood in that Best Road. But the present owners of the house, when they moved in many years ago—long before that disastrous war—kept that flagstaff. It was seventy feet high and a landmark all around. The head of the house was as proud of it as if he had actually erected it. A man of integrity and meticulous correctness, he applied for and obtained permission to fly the Union Jack at the masthead and the St. George's Cross at the jib. And on special occasions (personal as well as national) those flags were flown, being raised at 7 a.m. and struck at sundown. One of his daughters, who still lives in that house, was O.C. Flags and woe betide her if anything went wrong with the hoisting. But she became expert. The flagstaff was dismantled and taken down a bare two years ago. It had become unsafe.

Rentals in the road varied slightly. That of the particular house shortly to be entered was £60 a year, considered very high then. The rates were around £6. That house had fourteen rooms, besides a scullery, bathroom, innumerable cupboards and landings, an immense coal cellar, a larder and wine cellar in the same proportions and a very extensive garden—and there were naturally what are referred to as the usual offices. It seems incredible and fantastic today, but there it was. That road is still there, almost intact, but it is no longer a Best Road. The houses mostly remain, but like the rest of the world they have shrunk, inasmuch as they are now mostly divided into flats and hold as many as four or five families. Like the neighbourhood in which they stand, they have descended the social scale. There is no longer serenity, peace and dignity there; most of the houses are unkempt and decaying and the inhabitants take no pride in them at all. Why should they? So many of them are birds of passage, students of all nationalities, races and colour, coming from overseas. And those who are not are largely of what is still called the Working Classes. Yet the rents of those houses, wholly and in part, are much bigger than in the days of the glory.

But a landmark or two holds fast. Just round the corner, in the first bisecting road, the pillar-box in which the Edwardians and Victorians posted their letters is still there. It is the same box, of different shape to those of today. It contained the correspondence of several generations and it still bears the monogram 'V.R.' It was rather more than a letter-box, it was a rendezvous. Youths waited there for the girls to whom they were 'paying attention'. The young man would wait, balancing himself on his walking-stick, until his loved one appeared from round the corner in her large hat, her flowing skirts and rustle of petticoats. When they no longer met there, the romance was either at an end or they had received the necessary parental approval and the lover could call at the house. Domestic servants sent to post letters lingered awhile in the summer dusk (last collection 9 p.m.) and maybe had a few whispered words with that 'follower' who was as a rule 'not allowed' but who was, as on this occasion, always just around the corner. The love romances of those domestics were quite exciting, breathless affairs, moments snatched for a fleeting meeting, a wave of the hand as he passed the house, a few words at the door (for often the chosen swain delivered goods for the tradespeople) or the tiny glimpse of happiness at the pillar-box—planned, because the maid would ask permission to go out to post her letter—and would run up the street in her black dress, with her white apron and streamers flying around her. And there was the long-drawn bliss of 'the evening out'. That old pillar-box, still sturdy and strong, was not only part of the postal system of this country, but a wayside shrine for lovers' meetings. Once it held masses of postcards bearing the faces of the beauties of the stage—today it probably contains innumerable football pool coupons.

CHAPTER THREE

The Box Room

THERE was considerable activity in the Desirable Residence (which will now be simply called 'the house') because it was 'The Third Thursday'. That meant the three ladies who lived there were officially At Home. At least two of them were, the two unmarried sisters who were still entirely of the Family. Their married sister, who had of course another name but who lived with them, was simply their helper. She had no At Home Day of her own because she was not actually in her own house—she was of the family and she was not, according to the somewhat complicated etiquette of Victorian Days. It was the Third Thursday —which meant a lot of rush and bustle for everyone and a lot of guests, too, because the two ladies who were officially at home had many friends. So from middle afternoon the brass knocker on the front door had been almost continually in action—the bell was silent for the very good reason that it did not ring. The servants were all on duty and there was great activity and stir all over the semi-basement, first and second floors. The chatter of female voices resounded on all sides, there was a clinking of cups and saucers and a lot of shrill laughter. Everybody seemed cheerful, even the servants, who knew the knack of the whole thing and by long service had no worries—except a Boy who was at that moment in a room in the semi-basement, known as the Breakfast Room. He was standing at the open door of a large cupboard therein—the one nearest the door—which contained his toys. He was, that day, a little tired of them all. He was lonely for he was still in quarantine. He would have been at school and out of the way of his elders, but he was recovering from an attack of measles. Normally, he would have revelled in every moment of being at home because he disliked school very heartily, but now that the excitement of being an invalid (it had been a mild attack) and the bedridden centre of attraction was over, he was beginning to find time hang a little heavily on his hands. He could not go out—he was not yet allowed to play with other children—he had to entertain himself. He was the son of the married sister, who did not participate officially in the At Home Day but only as a helper. If it had not been the Third Thursday his mother, his two aunts—her sisters—who were completely devoted to him, and the servants would all have been at his beck and call, to play any game in which he chose to indulge. Not that he worried very much about adult participation. He was an imaginative lad, tall and big for his nine years, with plenty of good firm flesh, rosy cheeks (pale from his illness at that moment), a shock of dark hair which had a tendency to curl in front and showed flecks of chestnut, and brown, rather dreamy, eyes. He could and did amuse himself for hours—but that day it was difficult. Despite the size of the house in which he lived, he had no playroom of his own. What did that matter—he used the whole house and nobody denied him. Not in the general way, that is—but this was 'The Third Thursday'. It meant that the house had been invaded by a pack of women. That was how he saw it. There were occasions, during his holidays, when he would submit to being dressed in his best clothes and going into the drawing room, there to be admired and spoken to by the visiting ladies. This caused him acute embarrassment. They asked him what he considered completely idiotic questions, such as how he was getting on at school, what was his favourite lesson and if he were being a good boy and what was he going to be when he grew up. (He had not given this much serious thought, there was so much to do in the present.) And some would either ruffle or stroke his hair (little knowing how near to death they were) and occasionally a misguided and gushing lady— exclaiming that she had known him from birth—would even kiss him and make him feel simply terrible.

He endured that sometimes to please his mother and his aunts—but only if the day happened to be wet. He did it largely because he could not resist the rolled bread and butter which was also served on those occasions. It was his only opportunity of getting any, unless a few pieces were left over, which was seldom. He simply loved it but he never saw it at any other time except on At Home Days. He presumed in his mind that this was governed by some law. It was just ordinary bread cut very thin, then spread thickly with butter—and rolled up. That was all—except that it was remarkably well cut and spread and the elder of his two aunts did it, allowing nobody else the right. But to him it was the true ambrosia of the gods. He did not want any of the immense selection of cakes, the fancy cakes, the cream pastries, the jam sandwiches, the petit fours, the cream slices, the little scones, the Madeira, the seed, the currant, the

Tennis cake, cherry cake, gingerbread, the sponge-cake which had little ridges along the curved top—perhaps to enable the slices to be accurately judged—or any of the other delicacies. He liked them all but he could get them at most times. He did not worry much about the varieties of sandwich, the thinly cut ham sandwiches, the cress and the tongue. And he certainly did not want any tea to drink. He could resist the many varieties of biscuit (even the sweet ones with icing on them, made to resemble dominoes, to which he was addicted), none of them mattered on these occasions. He put up with the idiocy of the adults, the pawing and caressing, so as to get a few pieces of that rolled bread and butter. It was worth it. He liked bread and butter at all times—but this was his greatest treat, and one which, oddly enough, he was never given.

He was a strange lad, rather given to plunging into mental games. He could disassociate himself entirely from his surroundings and transport himself to wherever he wanted to be. The habit endured for life. His body was present but his mind was in realms unknown to his companions. On one occasion, when taken into the At Home Day company, he had just returned from a visit to some rather grand friends who lived in a Castle—actually a castle—in Yorkshire and who had in the normal way a butler and a footman. He had watched these men when he first met them, and during the stay friendship had grown. He had marvelled at their dexterity at their job. And on this At Home Day he became a footman. He carried round the trays of cakes and eatables, offering them silently and deferentially as he had seen those menservants do. He did it very well. He dropped nothing, he made no slips. The ladies exclaimed at his wonderful behaviour and were loud in their praises of this remarkably good little boy. He paid no attention—it is doubtful if he heard them. He was not a little boy at all at that particular moment. He was a footman in livery. Of course, nobody knew but himself. He did not, however, hand round the rolled bread and butter. He hoped it might get overlooked. There he was defeated by the housemaid. When he had had enough of being a footman he became a guest—and he helped himself as freely as he could to that mouth-watering dainty.

He was an observant lad, he noticed how the ladies folded their long kid gloves back over their hands when eating, how they curled their little fingers and he took note of the jingling bracelets and bangles—many of them were hung with imitation coins (it was a sort of sub-fashion) and he was acutely aware of the perfume they used. He did not like perfume much—except eau-de-Cologne and lavender water. They were all right because men used them. He would, when trapped, listen to the conversation, of which he could make little, nor did he want to, but he noticed how the subject changed when the servants were out of the room and how some ladies would moan that they were 'without', and he knew they were short of a servant when they said that. Another would give a lively account of the latest malpractices of her 'beauty'—he gathered this was meant to be funny—whilst some praised their 'treasures', which meant they were pleased with their servant, or servants. He also observed how, on the instant, the conversation changed when the housemaid brought in a fresh pot of tea or more eatables. It changed as if by magic, there was no awkward pause. He thought, even then, that it was remarkable. Sometimes trapped in a corner, he would try and make head or tail of what was being said. But it did not seem to add up. And often a lady would look at him and the conversation would sink to a whisper. Or perhaps his aunts would suggest that he would like to go and play. This invitation he always accepted but it had its drawbacks. He had to get out of the room gracefully and he had been well drilled in his manners. He could not, of course, go to each of them and bid them adieu, so—feeling his position acutely—he would make for the door, adroitly and almost imperceptibly avoiding clutching hands which meant an eventual caress or kiss and, having reached there, make a little bow, go red in the face and feel a complete and consummate ass. He was always glad to get out—if there was no more bread and butter rolled up.

For the scene was never static. Ladies were always leaving or arriving —and this meant that he eventually got spoken to by them and had to make some sort of reply. Two At Home Days, when he had been got into the Drawing Room, he had thoroughly enjoyed. Once was when he had been able, unobserved, to consume nearly a whole plateful of rolled bread and butter before he was seen and the other occasion was written in letters of fire—for one of the visiting ladies had a fit. It was terrific!

But on this particular At Home Day he could not get out, he could not see his 'chums', as the grown-ups called them, never the boy, and he could not play about the house. His fabulous quantity of toys were useless for the moment. He was an outcast and might be a carrier of infection —and many of the ladies had children of their own. He had indeed been told to keep out of sight. It might not sound much to ordinary ears but to him it meant close confinement. He was not wanted in the kitchen where there was enough to do, nor in the long passage between the kitchen and the Breakfast Room, for servants went to and from carrying trays and silver teapots. The scullery was as bad, for into it were being carried relays of tea cups, saucers and plates. He could not play on the stairs for fear of observation, nor on his favourite landing, the first one, because that was in full view of arriving and departing guests. His beloved Little Room was closed to him, for it had changed into a sort of service buffet—and the Dining Room, well, that was next to the Drawing Room and was an additional cloakroom that day, for it was wet.

The second landing, by the main bedrooms, was also taboo, for guests went up and down stairs to leave their things—and for other, more intimate, purposes. The landing above it offered little scope that day although as a rule it had great possibilities—for again, he might be seen. What was he to do—where was he to go? And then light dawned on him. And a smile. He made up his mind. He ceased at once to be a small Victorian Boy and he became Jim Hawkins. He was going to explore a pirate's cave, a treasure trove. Softly he crept up the staircase—the first flight. He must at all costs escape observation. He was under orders to that effect but he had recreated the scene entirely. The guests were not guests—they were the pirates and he must outwit them. He wormed his way up the first long flight, went past the drawing room and along the chief passage—the entrance hall in reality—up the next long flight like lightning and he met nobody on the way—and so to the next landing. Here he paused and took his bearings, for the mysterious treasure cave was near. He had not come unprepared. He had donned a belt out of his toy cupboard and in it was a sword—of steel but pointless and without blade—a couple of pistols and a very serviceable Japanese dagger—capable of real damage, which he had acquired during a holiday. The pistols were not revolvers (he had some toy ones made to resemble revolvers but these were of cast iron, they did not revolve like the much better toy pistols of today). His theatrical blood gave him a sense of character—he had chosen two wooden pistols which fired actual metal caps—such things were used on sporting guns even then, old guns, but still serviceable, which were muzzle-loading with gunpowder, shot and wadding and discharged by caps. These pistols looked very like those in the hands of Jim Hawkins as he threatened Israel Hands if he came a step higher, and were therefore greatly esteemed. In his hand he carried a gun—it was not a rifle although at that time a modern toy. It had a hammer and it even had a ramrod. Of course, it could be a rifle if so desired, but just now it was what it most resembled—a musket. That boy would never have undertaken any expedition unless properly equipped and organized—the habit lasted into manhood and still survives. Here he was, anyway, safely past the enemy and on the threshold of the Cave. He surmounted the last flight of stairs on hands and knees, with great caution and fully on the alert. And at last he stood before the Cave of Treasure which was on the top floor, one of four rooms. And it was—the Box Room.

He had joyous thoughts about this adventure. There was nobody about—he could rummage as he wished without interference—the whole household was fully occupied. He could do as he liked. Yet he did not rush into that room. There might be a bloodthirsty pirate on guard—grisly things might be encountered. He approached it warily on hands and knees, putting his ear to the ground to listen. There seemed no sound, no danger. His musket slung on his back now—it had a sling—he held a trusty pistol 'fully primed' in one hand and with the other he very slowly pushed open the door. There it was—before him. The heaps of treasure, all the lumber, the throw-outs, the discards which made a Victorian Box Room one of the most delectable places in the world—a place of Magic.

Some folks called it the Lumber Room, in this house it was always the Box Room. The name is immaterial but there was a reason for that reference to Boxes, because the hard core of the contents were boxes —trunks, portmanteaux and the like, which were worn out but could not be thrown away—they might come in useful. That was the open sesame of the Box Room of that Possessive Age—a thing might come in useful. You never knew. So upstairs it went, into the Box Room. In that house the room held many boxes, which were no longer thought fit for use on travel. Those in use were kept on the landing below. But although those old discarded boxes took up much room, they also saved space, for they were all crammed with other discards. None of them was empty. Nobody travelled light then—the fashion forbade it —one had to have many changes of dress on holiday or one 'lost face' —also much more was habitually worn. There was no stuffing a few things in a fibre suitcase or into a nondescript kind of bag of some canvas material—where the contents must become creased—or into a kind of civilian haversack or kit bag, either. They were properly packed in a proper kind of receptacle. A trunk, a portmanteau—the word 'suitcase' is comparatively modern—and even, by the old-fashioned, into a carpet bag. All those things were solid, heavy and made to last. And last they did. Weight did not matter, there was plenty of help, of manual labour. But when they had served their time and got shabby—shabbiness was abhorred—they went into the Box Room. And still they paid their way, for into them went old winter curtains of serge or even plush, summer curtains of light material, which had been superseded but 'might come in useful'. Old clothing went into the trunks as well—again, it might be useful and could be given to necessitous people and poor relations; and some were filled with old underclothing—and that was of linen and voluminous. Again, one might contain old boots and shoes in not too bad a state of repair. Ladies' boots with buttons, gentlemen's lace-ups and sometimes buttoned too—shoes for all purposes: satin shoes worn at dances, walking shoes, tennis shoes, and what were called sand shoes.

These were of two kinds—they could be of white leather or white canvas, with brown toecaps of leather and a brown leather backing to the heel, or they could be of some sort of canvas, full of tiny dents or pinholes —still with brown leather toecaps and heel backings. Quite a number of plimsolls, too—male and female. Ladies played lawn tennis in black plimsolls as a rule, unless they wore white dresses, when the plimsolls like the stockings were of white. Those stockings were not silk, but cotton or lisle thread. There was no such thing as nylon, of course. There were not so many boots and shoes as there were other things because they had a market and this was a commercial age. They could be exchanged at the door in a deal with men who called, who would give a plant or a pot of musk, or a 'pot fern' for such things, according to their value. The pot ferns were always the same, small with leaves like bits of tape, spreading at the end. There was a brisk traffic in old jam jars and bottles as well. Rag-and-bone men constantly perambulated the roads and did a brisk trade of their own and shabby, dirty men crying 'Any Old Iron' abounded. They either pushed a barrow or drove a small flat cart and would sometimes reinforce their shouts by ringing a bell. But whether they had a barrow or a cart, there was always an old iron bedstead on it—either whole or in part. They were a race of their own. In this house the servants were allowed to deal in the bottles and jam jars as their 'perks'. And despite the rag-and-bone men, there was usually an old iron bedstead in the box room, but it would be dismantled, lying against the wall with its top and bottom end against each other and its side girders and cross slats of steel all neatly tied up—just in case. . . .

And there was nearly always a child's cot, of black painted iron, a small edition of the bedstead and usually in good repair if a little chipped. The brass knobs on both were no longer polished but otherwise they were in good order. And as well as the beds you could find a baby's cot, still draped in its muslin with its little canopy and sometimes a cradle with rockers on it.

But there must be some sort of order in this survey, so a return must be made to the bags—the trunks can wait until later. Those carpet bags were dreadful things. They were indeed made of carpet—Brussels, as a rule, and had a hard bottom with a brass nail at each corner. They were long in shape—the cricket bag is their exact modern counterpart —and had two handles in the middle of the top which you gripped in your hand—they were of leather—and quite likely one of those handles would come unstuck at the wrong moment, with disastrous results to contents and temper. This presented a nice problem for it was impossible to carry the bag by one handle only, so it had to be shouldered, which was not consistent with the headgear or neckwear of the period. At the best they were awkward to carry, they swung in front, they got between the legs and they bumped into the unsuspecting calves of people walking in front. Also they crushed the things they carried within them. They were despised things, giving their name to a species of politician who would go anywhere and do anything—a 'carpet bagger' was a term of reproach. They were not popular bags and yet most families had at least one. Their one real use was carrying cricket things. And most men played cricket.

There were Gladstone Bags in the box room—but they were useful and were, in a sense, the ancestors of the expanding cases of today. They were named after the great statesman—the Grand Old Man—so one presumes he used them, or perhaps he did not. And as a rule there was a school box. That was of white wood, with iron protections at the corners, square and very strong. The initials of the owner and sometimes the full name were on the lid in large black letters. They were fastened either by a padlock or a mortice lock—and the keys always got lost. Incidentally, there were many bunches of keys in the box room, too. Those school boxes, which held a surprising amount, had a kind of enclosure all down one side of the interior—a sort of shelf or elongated cupboard, a box within a box. There was an iron handle at either end. These boxes were taken to boarding school by boys and girls alike. Sometimes more than one generation used them, so strong were they. It was only a matter of changing the name or initials on top. And when the children grew up and left school, the boxes went to the box room, ready for the next generation. The Victorian Boy had one, although he had never been to boarding school. It was a birthday present from an Aunt whose knowledge of boys was evidently culled from school stories. She thought every boy should have a school box and she had her own ideas as to what boys' pockets contained—gathered from the same source. She thought every boy carried a lot of string, several knives, a whistle, a mass of sticky sweets, some straps, a top, and either a frog or a white mouse. The Victorian Boy never disillusioned her. He was no fool. This same aunt—it should be mentioned that she was one of many aunts by adoption, and no relation at all—was always asking him what he was making—a rabbit hutch or a railway engine? He regarded this as adult idiocy for he was never making anything at all. He could not do so. He was no good at that. But he bore with the lady—for she would sometimes part with a brand-new five-shilling piece . . . which in his eyes covered a multitude of gaffes and grown-up sins. . . . In some of the old trunks there were samples of china and earthenware—old cups and saucers from services which had long since come apart in the hands of domestic servants—but—they might come in useful. There were ornaments of all kinds: once pairs, now in single blessedness through smashing—the worst kind of domestic and the most dreaded was the 'smasher'. All sorts of table fittings and utensils abounded—salad bowls sometimes whole but mostly in sections, wooden bowls of polished wood which had lost their china and detachable linings, cut glass ones slightly cracked. There were many old cruets and their bottles—one or two always missing, mustard pots which had lost their lids, mustard spoons which had lost their pots—salt cellars, old epergnes, tarnished and odd forks and spoons, but seldom knives, knife rests which had become twisted and were no longer serviceable and old napkin rings of metal or bone—now and again an ivory one. Old plated entrée dishes, sugar bowls, either china, glass or metal, fish slices from which the plating had worn off but which made quite serviceable short Roman swords when transmogrified by the Boy's imagination—and once he found an odd thing with a flat spade-like fixture pierced with holes and a kind of mandible above, which did not work. It was an implement for serving asparagus but to him it became a mattock—he could use it when he was a Royal Engineer—who in those days carried small spades like swords beside them. In some trunks old bed linen was stored, carefully folded with sprigs of lavender between the sheets, which never saw the light again and grew yellow with age—and old blankets, too, which did come in useful. The Boy saw to that when he played Red Indians and he was able to extract a sheet, too, which made a fine tent, and was never detected.

Rolls of old carpets stood around the walls like columns and rolls of old stair-carpet, too; they might come in useful some day. There were quantities of stair-rods, of brass, and the Boy found a use for these. Under his magical command they became javelins or any weapon he chose to make them. There were old mirrors, mostly cracked and in wooden frames which had their angle altered by two wooden screws which held them in place. They stood upon polished stands. The Boy gave them a wide berth, he was already superstitious and dreaded lest he might break one, being certain that seven years' bad luck would ensue. Old rugs of all kinds abounded, so-called Persian, wolfskin, bearskin and sheepskin. All these were treasures to the boy, he could wear them when a Polar explorer, an Esquimo or an ancient Briton. He regretted the absence of a leopard-skin rug, but no such thing was in the Box Room. There were doormats, of course, which had no great use, but there were old metal trays which could produce thunder, be converted into shields (the odd-job man was quite expert at this), or could be toboggans when used down the top flight of stairs—but once only; that game was stopped after he had half stunned himself at the end of the run. Quite a large variety of chairs and tables had been kept, the former mostly with defective legs or the cane of their seats in a hole. They were always going to be mended one day—but that day never came after they reached the Nirvana of the Box Room. There were hat boxes—which included a man's hat box of curious shape intended for the carrying on travels of a tall hat, and a whole lot of women's circular hat boxes. All these were packed with odds and ends of silks and materials and bits of ribbon, which actually did come in useful at times.

Several old clocks languished silent and pointing with fixed determination to different hours. Probably some boys would have thought it heaven to take them to pieces but this Boy was no mechanic and loathed machinery of all kinds. And on a special shelf stood a wonderful mixture of articles—china ornaments, knick-knacks, bronzes, novelties (the use of which defeated all beholders), odd brass things, some pictures —a weird collection of junk which represented in every case gifts received by various members of the family and loathed on sight. So up they all went to the Box Room, kept handy in case the donors came to call or to visit. Then they were taken out, cleaned, washed and furbished, put downstairs in a place of honour until the donors had gone—and back they went to the banishment of the Box Room. Married couples relegated all their distasteful wedding presents to the Box Room but followed the same procedure and always without mistake, for no bride ever forgot who gave her which, as it were. But they thanked their stars for the Box Room. There was also, in this one, a stuffed barn owl in a glass case, leaning a little forward and peering through his boot-button eyes. He always appeared to be watching and could be quite disconcertingly real in the dark. A stuffed canary, too, in another glass case, sat on a twig against a background of very improbable imitation flowers but very realistic ears of corn—a most unusual setting for any canary in this country, at any rate, and he also kept his eyes unwinkingly on the beholder. Both were in an excellent state of repair, for the cases were never opened and the air never got in. How they got there was a thing nobody in the house could explain. Not a soul ever remembered how they came into the family, but there they were, right up to the last.

That Box Room contained many things of an athletic and sporting nature—a sure sign of an athlete in the house—and he will be met in due course. There were Indian clubs of all sizes, from little ones with rather bulbous ends—highly esteemed by the Boy as useful weapons for games—middle-sized clubs, right up to those of truly gigantic size —with which the Boy staggered about when being Hercules—and one pair were of black with silver bands running slantwise around them. There were dumb-bells of wood and iron, size and weight various, and an assortment of straight pieces of wood with knobs at each end, called, one believes, barbells. There were quite a lot of old fencing foils and masks, but their number rapidly diminished when the Boy came to live there because they were of immediate use—the foils were rapiers and the masks knights' helmets; they did not fit well, but that did not matter—imagination made them perfect. Several pairs of boxing gloves hung on hooks—not much use then as being too big for small hands. And there was one solitary golf club—a cleek. Evidently the game had been considered, even tried, and abandoned. It was not nearly so widespread in popularity in Victorian days—at least in and around London. There were Clubs, of course, and men in scarlet jackets played on public courses in Richmond Park and at Chingford. Nowadays golf seems to be everybody's game but that Victorian Family ignored it—the Boy himself never played a round in his life although during his youth and early manhood he played most other games. There were several old tennis rackets—one or two as used by men but most of them suitable for women—and they had a fishtail handle—which was then considered 'the thing'. One of the ladies of the Family played tennis, and the Athlete would sometimes—but rarely—stoop to it. It was Lawn Tennis then, not the swift and amazing variety of today. Some old dinner-bells, minus the clappers, could be discovered and these had their uses to the Boy, for they became maces as used by knights in armour. To take a detailed inventory of the contents of that amazing place would occupy more space than can be given to it. But its great charm was that when you began to poke about you always discovered something. You would unearth articles lingering on from the youth of the Family, things which gave a hint to their tastes and habits as they grew up. These box rooms contained a sort of biography of the inhabitants of the house. And they went back even further—possessions held dear by grandfathers and grandmothers, even great-grandfathers and great-grandmothers, still found haven there—odd trifles, fans, letters, daguerrotypes, old writing desks, trifles ageing but redolent still of the once-young people who had carried and used them, not thrown away because of sentimental reasons —found again and exclaimed over during periods of spring-cleaning— and put back with a sigh, for they had almost assumed the aura of heirlooms. But to a boy who searched closely there might be something better than mere sentimental trifles. Few things in that room were useless to him in some game or the other—some old coal-scuttles, of which the inner portion had worn out whilst the outer survived, suggested nothing to him, but one of brass which bore a remote resemblance to a Roman helmet he had tried on, to find it a very bad fit indeed. A long-discarded (or maybe not so long at that period) wicker crinoline had him guessing, but it finally became a cage in which he might be imprisoned by savages preparatory to horrible tortures and lingering death. The type of savage varied—they might be Red Indians, Zulus, Dervishes—popular at that particular time under notice as there was trouble in the Sudan—or Papuans. He had recently encountered that name place and, being sensitive to nomenclature, it fascinated him. He knew little of Papuans or their ways although he had seen a picture or two in a travel book, drawn by someone who had never set eyes on one—and they seemed promising. At any rate they were savages, and, he hoped and believed, cannibals. Of course, he escaped in the end, by superhuman ingenuity and bravery, and fought his way to the seashore, where the British Navy, in wide straw hats and beards, effected his rescue. Once when that Box Room had been 'done out' and somewhat rearranged, he had struck a real Golconda. He got access to a large box which had always had too much stuff on it for him to open before—if indeed he had been aware of its existence in this crowded place. In it he found, of all things, two large model yachts fully rigged. At least, not quite yachts, for one was a two-masted schooner and the other a very trim, strongly built, somewhat bluff-bowed vessel which might have been a trawler. But they sailed splendidly when he got them down to the bath and when, eventually, he launched them on a pond where boys could sail boats, they were amongst the largest craft there and certainly the most seaworthy. He did not risk them loose on the open water, although they would have sailed across all right—subject to breeze—he kept them on the ends of balls of string, tied round a piece of fireword (he got a lot of splinters, but who cared?) which he paid out as they ploughed through the main. They were now amongst his treasures. And on another occasion, under a pile of rugs, he discovered an old air gun. He had an air gun—a 'Daisy' which cost 3s. 6d. and was cheap at the price—but this was a heavy, solid affair, a breech-loader and obviously of immense power (the suction proved weak), but also immense weight. He found great difficulty in manipulating it as a gun should be manipulated—indeed, it turned on him once and cracked him across the skull, raising a tremendous bump and stunning him for a few moments. But he would not part with it—he knew what it was: it was not a rifle at all. It was a Gatling Gun—such things as machine-guns were then new implements of war. He found a way of fixing it to his mailcart and it made a very excellent machine-gun indeed, in all but shooting power, but that mattered little—the idea was all, the execution nothing. For this Boy, like all children, had the imaginative faculty developed, perhaps slightly more than most. But he shared with all children the power of recreation. Give a child a toy and he or she will play with it for what it is at the first go off. Then their ideas change—and the toy alters its form to suit the new requirement. A ship becomes a train in the twinkling of an eye and a train a caravan of camels crossing a desert. The child is content, he sees it as such and all is well. Very few toys remain in their own form for long—they are transformed as their owner wishes. That is the real and joyous gift of Youth—'Let's Pretend'. It is not so easy in after life.

This Boy had a great faculty in that respect. He once found in that lumber room a circular piece of wood which had probably started life as the bottom of a barrel. How it got into that room is nobody's worry now. He knew what it was. It was a shield, indeed it was a target or targe. He bored holes and fixed up handles of string. He got some of the steel studs which bootmakers then sold and which covered the soles of navvy's boots—they can be seen on mountaineers' boots today—and he hammered them into that shield which thus became heavily armourplated and the envy of all other boys who saw it. He got the nails out of the lumber room, too—they had been in the soles of an old pair of boots once used for climbing, and he also found an alpenstock, complete with spike—quite a large alpenstock of rough oak with the bark adhering. It was no alpenstock—he knew that—or it ceased to be one directly it came into his possession. It was a spear, or a pike—it was a bill used at Agincourt, and frequently it was that very lance with which Sir Lancelot unhorsed six knights in succession. His inspiration for the 'Target' came from the novels of Scott—he had read some—and from illustrations of a story about Rob Roy in some old annual printed long before he was born, the name of which is forgotten. But the memory of the pictures remains. There was Rob Roy, his claymore flashing over the heads of six or seven English soldiers, in their tunics and tricorne hats and pigtails. They may have been well-disciplined troops but they lacked initiative for they all thrust with their bayonets at the same time and apparently aimed at the same place and the intrepid Highlander had no difficulty in taking all the points on his studded targe. That had been a splendid day of discovery. He had also rummaged in a couple of old chests of drawers but drawn blank although they were full of odds and ends, like a theatrical wardrobe—but there was nothing he wanted.

There was one object there which he had passed up as useless. It was a dressmaker's dummy—the ladies of the house made a lot of their own clothes, or at least one of them made her own and also some of her sisters'. Those dresses were built and tried out on this dummy. Its body was of female shape and red. It had no arms or head, these deficiencies being supplied by knobs which made it more portable. It had no legs, or rather, it had one—a straight one in the middle fixed to a circular base. And that leg was covered with a wire skirt—or just the

Upper left: Poor Frederica—mother of the Victorian boy. *Upper right:* The large Victorian lady—the baby on the lap is the Victorian girl who married the Victorian boy. *Lower left:* Walter—husband of Frederica and Father of the Victorian boy. *Lower right:* Uncle John

Upper left: Fred Leslie in *Cinder-Ellen Up Too Late. Upper right:* Nellie Farren in *Ruy Blas. Lower left:* Sir Charles Wyndham as "David Garrick". *Lower right:* Fred Leslie in *Cinder-Ellen Up Too Late*

outline of one. The Boy could see no use in this, so far as he was concerned.

But on that particular Third Thursday, it was to come into its own. He rummaged and ferreted freely, nobody was about to come and see what he was doing. He found an old meat chopper, and that was a promising start. This could be either a tomahawk or a battle-axe. And then in a cardboard box of some antiquity, and hidden away from casual glances, he found a couple of ornaments of such appalling ugliness that they almost took his breath away. The general scheme was a terrible shrimplike pink, as hard as iron. They tapered up from the base to a bulbous centre and had two circular handles like arms on both sides. Above the swelling they tapered again to narrow necks and suddenly sprouted into a fringe. There was a great deal of gold paint mixed with the pink but the real horror was that on the centre of the bulge was superimposed a picture of a blue volcano, on a green ground, in a full state of eruption. They made him grit his teeth. The backs were devoid of any decoration at all, which told him, young as he was, that they were of no value. He set up this pair of atrocities and pondered. Evidently they had been hidden from sight as things almost obscene. He decided on their destruction—but how and for what reason? He became aware of the meat chopper in his hand. Everything was clear at once. They were dogs of Hurons in full war paint—no doubt about that—and he was Uncas the Mohican. He smashed those vases in a thrilling mortal combat. He put the pieces, or as many as he could gather, back into the box. He shuffled the smaller bits under an old carpet. He felt it was a job well done—he had avenged the Family Honour! And then, beneath a pile of old curtains which had recently been moved and placed on a flat trunk, he made his Great Discovery. It was nothing less than a full-sized bow and arrows in a quiver. At some time one of the family must have taken up archery and dropped it again. Here was a treasure indeed —here was joy and romance! Uncas faded. Jim Hawkins was far away. Here was Robin Hood in all his Lincoln Green. He seized that large bow (far too big for him), he fitted an arrow with considerable difficulty. He looked around for a target. The dressmaker's dummy came into its own. This was no dummy. It was, of course, the Sheriff of Nottingham and had stood there all those years for just this supreme moment. He riddled it with his arrows—it was one of the best and most satisfactory games of his life . . . and the bow was a favourite weapon for years, for he was allowed to keep it. That was a wonderful Third Thursday in the treasure cave of the Box Room.

CHAPTER FOUR

Cabinets and Cartes de Visites

THE Boy had a grand time. No wonder a Box Room was such a favourite place, crammed as it was and yet never completely full. Today, if any box rooms exist, they could never be so full. Things are not made so solidly and well. But then, in Victorian and Edwardian Days, nobody bought inferior gimcrack things or badly made articles. They bought things to keep and to last, they did not hanker after change—they liked comfort and things they knew—their suites of furniture, their ornaments and their fittings became old friends, ageing as the years went by less rapidly than their owners, so soundly and solidly built were they. And even when broken or superseded, they were not flung away. They went upstairs to the Box Room. They became lumber. Now they are becoming of value again—for antique, second-hand and junk shops are full of the contents of old lumber and box rooms—at a pretty stiff price.

But the Boy had not yet done with the Box Room. He sought for further treasures. He remembered the first discovery of those fencing masks, which had resulted in a spirited reproduction of the lists at Ashby-de-la-Zouch—an added feather lent a knightly touch, and the Boy was of course the Disinherited Knight. He recalled the discovery of two very useful cricket bats—their presence had puzzled him because none of the male members of the Family (the adult ones) knew or cared anything about cricket. The game held little interest for Scots. But the Boy, being English by birth and fatherhood, loved the game and as one of the bats was the right size for him, used it to advantage. The other he kept until he grew into it, which did not take long. This day his search was rewarded by the discovery of a small table with a loose top—which could be an excellent raft for a shipwrecked mariner—and some bamboo poles of varying lengths. To him they were not bamboo poles, the longest were lances and the shorter ones assegais—he knew his Rider Haggard well and his joy was further heightened when he found, in the drawer of a hitherto untapped small dressing table (probably sent there during a partial refurnish), some old knife-blades minus their handles. He could fix these to the bamboo poles and all was complete. This was to be a Red Letter day, obviously. Clambering over some old trunks he found some pictures piled one behind the other with their faces to the wall. He had them out and examined them. He liked pictures, but some of these revolted him. They had possibly been received from time to time as presents—there were quite impossible landscapes always dominated by a church tower against a sunset—water-colours, most of them, and gifts of the artists as like as not—but all pretty terrible.

But on this wet afternoon he sought still further. He played for a while with an old worn-out perambulator, very heavy and with solid rubber tyres to its wheels. It was, for a time, a Roman Chariot which enabled him to use the shorter bamboo poles as javelins. Then it became a ship at sea, in a heavy gale. He got into it rather perilously and made it rock about. Very soon it was overturned and he fell out—a realistic shipwreck but the end of the game.

Then his eyes fell on some things which always gave him pleasure. They were photograph albums—Family Albums. They were of all sorts, some fairly slim, some thick, some plain, others ornate. The plain and slim ones mostly held views of places once visited or of mere acquaintances, the thick, ornate ones were filled with the Family Portraits and old and trusted friends. Those albums were quite handsome affairs in their Victorian way. They were mostly leather-bound and many of them embossed. Some were bound in velvet. They had thick pages with gilt edges. The pages were board, not paper, and there was a frame aperture in the middle into which the photo slipped. Some held only one photo per page, others were double-sided. There were albums which looked like Bibles used in churches and cathedrals, with brass ornamentation and even padlocks and keys. They were as solid and respectable as the people whose photos they held. Some had their pages ornamented, some were content with black or red rulings along the side. One album in the Box Room had each page illustrated by a scene from a Shakespearean play, in colour, which rather dwarfed the photograph and was provocative of contrast because the serious-looking people always seemed to get into the pages illustrating comedy, and lively young things appeared beneath the counterfeit presentiments of Hamlet, Macbeth and Lear. Not that anybody cared.

There was one album in the Box Room very much esteemed by that

Boy. It was the thickest and most solid there. As an album it was dis-
appointing because only half of it held portraits, the other half was a
disguised musical box, and when the book was opened it stuttered
through 'The Bluebells of Scotland' in a very high and tinkly key. The
Victorians delighted in that sort of mechanical toy—the Boy remembers
one house which contained a comfortable-looking chair upon which
people would seat themselves with an expectation of ease, only to find
that as soon as they sat down that rather lively air 'Weel May the Keel
Row' was struck up as from some invisible orchestra. They were always
puzzled at first and wondered from whence the music came, and then it
would dawn upon them that it was their own doing. They would put
on a sickly smile and suffer acute embarrassment, not knowing whether
to remain seated and musical or to get up and stop the noise. It was a
fine quandary for they did not know how long the tune would last and
whether, if they remained seated, it would go on and on in vain repetition.
They usually solved the problem by getting up 'to see how it worked'.
And they were very careful never to sit in it again. The Boy recalled one
old gentleman being most offended and saying 'Damn and Blast the
thing' very loudly. He liked that. He also remembered when that musical
album was kept in the Drawing Room and how he would offer it to
visitors whom he did not like. They would take it with effusive thanks,
open it—and promptly be confounded. He liked that, too. But it got
defective and spasmodic—his fault for overworking it—and as nothing
not in perfect condition could be tolerated in the Drawing Room, it
was banished to its last and lofty home. He always played with it and
regarded it as a miracle of mechanical ingenuity.

There were a lot of albums and a lot of photos in the Box Room.
There were the old, out-of-date and demoded photos showing the family
from youth until grown up. The more modern photos were in the Drawing Room, the Valhalla, as it were, in albums, in frames and sometimes
in receptacles which looked like albums but were not. They were species
of files. Instead of opening them bookwise, you pulled off the top half
and found the photographs stored inside.

Family Albums and their contents are always regarded as funny by
succeeding generations. The young people of today who laugh so heartily
at the outmoded photos of their elders will appear just as funny to the
generation which succeeds them, always supposing they leave any such
pictorial record behind them after growing out of childhood. A wedding
group perhaps and some snapshots—which seldom survive. But they
will be laughed at. Doubtless Elizabethans thought pictures of mediaeval
ancestors screamingly funny and they in turn amused Carolian descendants who would be objects of mirth to Georgians, whose fantastic

attire was queer and laughable in the eyes of Victorians. It was only when the costumes got the aura of history that they ceased to be amusing. And that takes time.

But the moderns, unless professional stage or film folk, will not leave anything like such a pictorial record of themselves for their descendants' amusement as did the Victorians or Edwardians—and the former easily outdid the latter.

It must be admitted that even to people in their late sixties and early seventies—at the time of writing—Mid and Late Victorian Fashions did not represent the best period of sartorial art. The women somehow contrived to look regal and splendid but the men most certainly did not. They, poor creatures, had swung from grace and colour to clothes of shapeless drab. It got a bit better in Edwardian times. . . .

Those photos in the albums in the Box Room not only marked the changes in the appearance of the Family but also the changes in the fashion of clothes and the progress of photography. The specimens under review dated from the early seventies down to the 1890s and even later —some of them well into the 1900s—but they display the period and the life thereof with great force. There were a great number of professional photographers in those days and they all seemed to do well. People had become very photo-conscious and were constantly being photographed.

Many people in those days spoke of photographs as 'Likenesses'. You had your 'Likeness' taken, and that was just what the Photographer did. He took a photograph of what he saw through his lens. He took a great deal of time over it, too, retiring and emerging from beneath a black cloth, altering his focus and sometimes even shifting his rather rudimentary lighting—he was concerned not so much with the best aspect of his sitter in this respect but with the absolute necessity of having no shadows. That would never do. Then, having got it all fixed up, he took a pretty lengthy exposure. Most photographers exhorted their victims to 'Smile, please', often with unhappy results. But there were subjects who would not, or could not, conjure up a smile—and were the better off thereby. Photographers in general did not bother about Art, and did not expect the sitter, who so very often stood, to be at ease. Although they might ask for a pleasant expression of countenance when the exposure was made, they did not trouble too much about it. What mattered was to show the subject exactly as he or she appeared to the photographer. The gentleman with the camera stood no nonsense. He was in command and could be—and often was—despotic and ruthless. No good telling him you had a 'best side', such things meant nothing to him. In those Victorian days there was no question of lounging about or lolling (Mrs. Wilfer's horror of that idea will be remembered by all

Dickensians), of hanging over the side of a chair, of getting into an easy or even recumbent position. Being photographed in Victorian Days was not a matter of enjoyment, but of fulfilling a Duty one owed to one's relatives. No Victorian ever shrank from such a duty. Although almost every picture shows a lurking agony of mind, this is overridden by an expression which denotes the fixed determination to go through with it, to face this ordeal with courage and resolution. To many people, a visit to the dentist presented less terrors than a visit to a photographic studio —and a visit to the dentist was pretty grim then. There is hardly ever a glimpse of relaxation or even cheerfulness. Maybe it is these old photos which spread the idea amongst succeeding generations that the Victorians were a severe, unsmiling, unrelaxing race living colourless lives in dull surroundings. It was not so in reality. They merely seem a stiff unbending generation because of the way in which the Photographer treated them. Some of these gentry made some concession to what they perhaps considered Art and Good Taste. In addition to the ornate tables and chair, and the few heavy volumes which usually represented the 'properties' of their studios, they 'went into production' as people of the Theatre would say. In addition to the ordinary plain cloth which formed the background for most pictures, they had a grey backcloth which had in sepia the outline of a rustic village upon it, dominated by a church spire. In front of this they put a 'property' stile and customers who so desired (who were always most unsuitably dressed for rural rambling because best clothes and most elaborate gowns were worn for the Photo) could be photographed leaning across this stile gazing ahead in a contemplative attitude—the whole representing something entirely untrue to nature or the character of the 'sitter'.

But these efforts into illusion were highly esteemed. Photographers who specialized in the 'likenesses' of children had quite a number of 'props' which ranged from toy horses, guns and dolls to 'profile' boats and cardboard or papier mâché rocks. Young gentlemen of tender years who were members of Her Majesty's Royal Navy according to their attire (or some of their attire, because even boys wore kilted skirts for several of their early years) could be and were pictured in the act of pushing off the boat with an oar, gazing the while straight into the lens —or sitting on a rock with a spade in their hand. In this pose they usually wore a sailor cap with the riband of H.M.S. *Victory* or other ship of the line round it—their sailor blouses of navy blue with collar and singlet, black silk handkerchief and whistle lanyard (maybe they were all little bo'suns), their kilted skirt of dark blue, their full-length stockings and their button boots. They were supposed to be at the Seaside in summer. Or they might wear a sailor hat with some unknown badge on it, but with rank badges on their arms. That is how the Victorian Boy is pictured in an illustration herein. In his case the lanyard and whistle were missing—both had been confiscated on account of the noise. He was about 3½ to 4 years old and registered a protest at being given a wooden spade. Such things were for girls, he maintained. He is also shown at 2½ years, not in sailor's clothes but holding a boat, to show that he was a scion of a maritime race and a son of Britannia. In both pictures he looks slightly resentful and that is not at all surprising. Those smaller toys often led to tears when the 'likeness' was taken and the child found he had to give them up. He or she had been under the impression that they were gifts and there was usually a scene. These Victorian children strongly objected to being victimized and things were made no easier by the fact that the dicky bird mentioned by the kind gentleman with the camera had not materialized. The children felt, very rightly, that the whole thing was a gigantic swindle and testified to the same in the usual manner. But that photo of the boy holding the boat is not without interest, for the photographer who took it—or rather the firm—had studios in Regent Street and branches all over London and proclaimed themselves 'Photographers of His Highness Akbaloddowla, ex-King of Oude'—and printed that potentate's signature in native calligraphy!

That Victorian Boy examined all the photos he found in the Box Room (or as many as he had time to gaze at), for he was very interested even then in family history—with him the Family was something of importance, and he liked to know what his relatives who were dead and gone, or whom he had for some reason never seen, looked like. He had a wide selection. For the portraits in the box room were those which were out of date or of people who were dead. He was interested in the photographers, too, whom as a race he hated for he abominated having his picture taken. It was a shocking waste of time which could have been devoted to games, for one thing, and it entailed being dressed in his best, which no normal boy, then or now, really enjoys. There were at times consolation, for it meant having tea out at a teashop, then considered a treat, and a bus ride to and from, which was not so bad. But he thought the balance was on the debit side, taking it all round.

One of the portraits was noteworthy because it provided amongst that collection now being inspected by the Boy the one cheerful-looking likeness of the lot. The Boy had divided those pictures of the people who actually lived in that house, and those he knew, from those who were dead and whom anyway he did not know. He believed he had actually seen the original of this particular likeness, but that man had never lived in the house although he was a close relative. But he had, of course, visited. He liked his looks, too.

The Victorian gentleman made an excellent subject—the least self-conscious and dogged-looking one of the lot. He had a lot of hair which he wore fairly long and brushed out over his ears, he carried a pair of pince-nez on his rather wide and purposeful nose, a very strong clean-shaven mouth, but his equally strong chin was draped underneath by whiskers which stretched from ear to ear, with a fringe-like effect, a mode fashionable to the time. He was a good-looking fellow with a quizzical expression which not even the photographer could subdue (he may have increased it). He was a Scotsman and held the view that his race was the best in the world. His business took him to Germany long before the German Empire arose from the defeat of France, and there he controlled a mine, with very great success. All through his career there he steadfastly refused to speak one word of German, either to customers or employees, although he knew the language perfectly. He pointed out that they were Foreigners and must learn to speak his, the dominant, tongue. He made them do it, too. He married a beautiful and graceful Norwegian girl of whose language he was quite ignorant and never tried to learn at all. But he made himself understood and he made his bride speak English, which she did with a delightful Scots intonation. They were very happy indeed and had a large family, who were completely bilingual but who regarded themselves as 100 per cent British. That was the sort of man who represented this country in Victorian times. There was no nonsense about him. To him there was nothing in the fact that he might be regarded—and indeed was—as the foreigner in a foreign country. He did not hold with that. He was a Scot, a British subject of Her Majesty Queen Victoria, and that was good enough for him. It had to be good enough for the natives, too. And believe it or not he was immensely popular and greatly respected. The Victorians may have succeeded in arousing dislike amongst the other races but they always commanded respect. Nobody dared push them about.

Amongst the photos which interested the Boy very much were several of a Victorian city merchant, who also hailed from Scotland. What held the Boy's attention was the fact that this man was his maternal Grandfather. He had never seen him for the gentleman was dead before the Boy was born. But his influence was still strong in that household—he himself had never lived in the house—and he was spoken of almost daily. In all the portraits this man has his legs crossed. It does not look as if he was usually in the habit of sitting thus, but the earliest portrait of the lot—taken in the early sixties, one would imagine—shows him in that pose and so, always afterwards, he repeated it. He was that sort of man. His dress changes hardly at all down the years, it was always the morning coat, high-cut waistcoat, shapeless trousers and heavy boots of the period, superfine material obviously but no fallals. Always, too, he sits by a table and in three of them an unopened book lies thereon. He did not like change. This was the way his portrait should be taken and doubtless he overbore the photographer. He was that sort of man. The portraits are all good ones. They show a man of immense determination and strength of will. The forehead is high with the hair already receding therefrom but long at the back and sides. The mouth, large and very firm, is clean-shaven but there is the fringe of fashionable chin-whiskers. The eyes are rather full, with a steady, direct gaze, but they obviously hold imagination and belong to a thinker as well as a man of action. The brows are heavily marked. He looks elderly to modern eyes but in the portraits he was only in his forties. This man came down from Scotland to London at a time when the railway went no farther than Carlisle. He took his wife and his eldest son—the only child then —by coach to that city. He had seen a chance of business in respect of a new scientific process as regards steel. He took immediate advantage of it. He had drive and power and an acute business sense, but he also had an obstinacy and impetuosity which at times landed him out of his depth. But he always won through. He went into partnership with an Englishman and he made a fortune rapidly. In due course the Englishman retired and became a landed proprietor. But the Scot kept on. He had taken a large house in Canonbury—then a very high-class and exclusive suburb in the north of London—and he set about raising a family. Altogether he had seven children, all, except the eldest boy, born in London, but all regarded themselves as 100 cent Scots. His wife, whose name was Mary, his being John—was a quiet, gentle soul who bore a respected Scottish name. Her ancestors had been Covenanters and one had suffered martyrdom in the Solway Firth, of which this lady was immensely proud. She was completely dominated by her forceful, irascible and impetuous husband, but she did not mind. In those days a man was master in his own house—also she had sworn to love, honour and obey him. She would not have dreamed of doing otherwise so they got along very well together. She was of Lowland and he of Highland descent. To the family, he was 'Pa' and she was 'Ma'. Both exacted and received implicit obedience. Pa's word was law which allowed no appeal. With him a command was a command. Ma was obeyed, too, but it was possible to reason with her, she would hear arguments and had been known to relent. Pa believed in corporal punishment and administered it with a slipper. Once the entire family, except the eldest boy, went to the house next door, where the children were great friends of theirs— which friendship endured as long as a member of either family was left alive. There was a servant there who was a natural born story-teller.

They loved to listen to her and this time they stopped far too late. She held them enthralled around the kitchen fire until long after the proper bedtime. Then, realizing the lateness of the hour and the enormity of their crime, the children crept home, hoping that Pa would be out. But Pa was not out. Silent and grim as Fate, he was waiting on the mat, slipper in hand. And as the panic-stricken children fled past him, they each got a hearty smack with the unerring slipper, and one of them, a daughter who was the slowest and most muddle-headed of them all, got a double allowance because she was last in the line. . . .

Pa took an interest in his family of three boys and four girls. He would, from time to time, examine them to see how they were progressing with their education. That daughter who had received the double slipper-smack had a slight impediment in her speech and a burning desire to recite. Pa would demand a recitation. Always in a confused state of mind, she would stand up filled with awe at the sight of Pa in attentive pose, put her hands behind her and try to say her piece. Despite her love of reciting, she always got hopelessly confused, would go purple in the face and get so tongue-tied as to be completely incomprehensible. 'What does the child say?' the impatient Pa would exclaim and it only made her worse. So the slipper would come into play. He was sure that would cure the drawback and, marvellous to report, to a large extent it did.

Pa had a large interest in a mine in Spain, to which he—and later his eldest sons—paid frequent visits. It prospered amazingly. But after Pa's death the shares declined. The vein of ore seemed to be worked out until the shares were worth only a few pence each. The eldest son sold them. Later their value rose to stupendous heights. Had those shares been held by the Family, it is doubtful if this book would ever have been written.

Although Pa could speak several languages fluently, he had a very poor opinion of foreigners. So when abroad he spoke only English, relapsing into the vernacular only in moments of great stress or annoyance —and by so doing creating confusion in the contumacious foreigners. Conversely, when a foreigner came to this country to see him, he would show the greatest hospitality and insist on speaking to that man only in his own language. He did not mind foreigners individually, but he could not stand them collectively. So to a Spaniard, for instance, in this country he would speak only Spanish. Had he met him in Spain he would have insisted on speaking in English only. He felt that this kept them in their place.

His wife had a brother who was a minister of the Established Church of Scotland and whose manse lay in a very beautiful but then remote part of Galloway. The brother was very strict and severe in his observance of the Sabbath Day. All blinds were kept pulled down, there was no cooking done and a minimum of work by the domestics. There were many prayers. It was incumbent on all people at the Manse—the family and visitors—to attend the Kirk three times a day. Some got away with one visit only to their own Kirk for morning service. That was a necessity. It was a bit of an ordeal. The Minister, a brilliant and good man, was not a very good preacher and went on for rather a long time. The Kirk lay in the hollow of a hill, with a burn running beside it. In warm weather the effect was soporific. Swallows would get in and swoop, twittering, over the heads of the congregation, who did not dare watch them because the Minister would observe it. The Manse party, sitting right by the pulpit, did not dare do other than remain wide awake—although some of the lesser people at the back indulged in forty winks.

Everyone sang the hymns, which were accompanied by one of the Manse family on a harmonium. She always set the key too high, so the result was rather more varied than impressive. In the afternoon certain of the Minister's family had to attend the Wee Free Kirk down in the village, to show there was no ill will. And in the evening one or more had to accompany him to some outlying village in his immense parish which entailed a long drive in what was known as a 'governess cart' drawn by a pony with its own ideas about pace and time. The Boy, who often spent his summer holidays there later, liked these drives. He adored the rugged country and on one memorable occasion they saw some Red Deer. Ma did not mind this sabbatarian ordeal, she was used to it. But Pa objected. Consequently, he never stopped at the Manse, as Ma did. So as not to give in, he put up at the village inn. There was no bad blood, they were all on the friendliest of terms. Pa was regarded as an eccentric and it was considered that his long residence in London was the cause of his apparent softness. That suited Pa all right. But for all Pa's strictness with his own family, he was always scrupulously fair. That applied to home life and to business, where his integrity was unimpeachable. His word was his bond. He looked impressive and he was impressive. He believed in Family Life and Family Pride. Although he jibbed at the austerity of the Manse, he had his 'sittings' at the Presbyterian Church near his London home. He would go there once on Sundays and saw to it that his children went too, and he frequently examined them on their Scriptural knowledge. His family loved and respected him and he stood as an example to them. If he was pleased with them, he gave them pennies, a coin which had considerable purchasing power then. He kept them in every comfort in the large house with its spacious rooms and very large garden. He gave them the best education possible. Ma never sat in judgment on the children except for the smallest trifles. All matters of discipline were referred to Pa. But Ma could be wheedled into keeping quiet about small delinquencies. Neither Pa nor Ma ever set foot in a Theatre, although Pa took the Family to see the sights of London and to the museums; he was great on museums. Now and again they visited the wonders of the Crystal Palace and Pa never missed the opportunity of taking the children to see any foreign royalty who passed through London—the Lord Mayor's Show, military reviews and any big national event which happened. He saw to it that they were kept conversant with current history, too. When they did not go to Scotland for the summer holidays, they went to the seaside, mostly to Herne Bay, for a month, and Pa came down for weekends and as often as he could. He was a great reader and within his limits a cultured man. He took great pride in Scotland and once removed a daughter of his from her school because the geography book used therein described his native country as a wild, bare and barren land, containing little but moors, wastelands and mountains. It cannot be said that he was a friend to his children, but they held him in the utmost respect and affection and his example was followed to the best of their ability—his influence remaining with them always. Yet he could unbend and be a charming companion—if they were good! He was a typical Victorian, who believed in stability. He hated debt, he hated scandal, he hated dishonesty. About him was that Victorian indomitability which made this land rich and powerful above all others. He believed in the Family—and he was a member of an ancient Scottish clan. His own grandfather had fought for the Young Pretender at Culloden Moor and although badly wounded got away alive and evaded capture. Indeed he lived to pass his century and to cut some new teeth in his ninetieth year. They bred men in those days. A glance at those photos of Pa seemed to bring the '45 very near. He himself died in 1875 at the age of fifty-two, his life's work accomplished, leaving his Family well provided for.

Ma mourned her husband. She was a sweet-faced woman with a gentle and rather yearning expression. She wore her hair parted in the middle and low over her ears and always a Paisley shawl fastened by a cameo brooch. She shared few of her husband's tastes. She never went about to any extent. She stayed at home, ran the house and watched over her husband and her children as a good Victorian wife and mother was expected to do.

She just gave herself up to the Family. She died three years after her husband. She was then forty-seven, never very strong, and had had seven children—which was regarded as a rather small family in those days. Her last photo shows her as retired from active life and looking rather elderly, although she never reached the age of fifty. All her family loved her and she loved them. She loved her husband and never recovered from his loss. She was always referred to as 'poor Ma' but she would have resented this. She thought she was a very lucky woman—she had never lost a child. The Victorian Boy would pore over her photo and wish he had known her. He felt he would have loved her too. And he was recently considerably moved when his little grand-daughter saw a photo of his own mother—her great-grandmother—and made the very same remark. . . .

CHAPTER FIVE

In Loco Parentis

WHEN 'Pa' died the eldest son took charge of everything. He was then twenty-five years old and unmarried. He assumed the reins of the business into which his father had naturally placed him. He was now Master of the House and on him devolved the duties of looking after his 'Ma' and his six brothers and sisters. He moved them all out of the big house in Canonbury and into one not much smaller but more modern and convenient in another suburb of North London. The road in which that house stood—the house itself was destroyed in the Blitz —was then a lane with hedges on each side, or perhaps semi-country road is a better term—and new houses were arising throughout its length. It was being 'developed' but it was an eminently respectable residence in an eminently desirable neighbourhood. Now it is a busy main thoroughfare verging on a slum, up and down which traffic rattles and buses hurtle. But there the Family lived until they moved into the house which is the opening scene of this story.

This intermediate house was tall and much like the one already described but not quite so large, and although modern in those days, not quite so convenient. But it had the great advantage of being near a Presbyterian Church. That meant much to the womenfolk of that family who were all devout churchgoers. The Church also was the hub of their social life. They were original members of that Church—it was only a little tin chapel then. It grew to a large, important place paying a high salary to its chosen ministers and it still flourishes today. Two of that Family attended it to the day of their deaths and their funeral services were held there, with the Victorian Boy as chief mourner—a middle-aged man and paying the bill.

They were in that house for three years until 'Ma' passed away.

Having placed her in the Family Grave next to her husband, the eldest son moved the Family again—this time into the Last of the Big Houses in the Best Road. He now stood *In Loco Parentis* on his own.

He was a very remarkable man, and was uncle to the Victorian Boy. He had owned the alpenstock, and used it, too, the boxing gloves, the Indian clubs, the dumbbells, the barbells, the foils and the masks. He was expert with them all. He was a superb gymnast and the founder of a great amateur athletic association. Athletics rather than sport was all in all to him—but they had to be amateur. He was a good oarsman and quite a useful tennis player—he did not take that game very seriously. Nor did he play much football—he left that to another member of the family. Despite his love of amateur sport, in his later years he took the keenest interest in professional football and became a keen supporter of the Tottenham Hotspurs.

He was truly Victorian and had all the characteristics. What he did, he did well. He was probably the best amateur wrestler of his time. If he took up a thing, he mastered it. He created a superb butterfly collection, perhaps the finest private collection in the country. That achieved, he started something else. He did not know what it was to be either idle or bored. He was a pioneer of cycling, but cricket meant nothing to him. He could speak four European languages besides his own and write them all perfectly grammatically. His accent in them all was impeccable. He knew a lot of Latin, too. He had travelled all over the world but was a miserable sailor. The mere boarding of a boat was enough for him, he had been known to be ill before it left harbour. Quite characteristically he took no precautions against sea-sickness. He faced it and let it take its course. Once, and once only, did he manage to cross the Channel without being ill. That was when he took the Victorian Boy to Hastings for a weekend. There was a trip from there to Boulogne and without any warning the Uncle decided that they would go on that trip—the Boy should stand for the first time on foreign soil. He was like that, and the Boy's delight can be imagined. It was a complete surprise. He had not expected a sea trip at all, knowing his Uncle's weakness in that respect. But his Uncle had decided in his own mind that the Boy ought to start his travels and did not consider himself. It so happened that the sea was as smooth as a park lake on a windless day. As a rule that made no difference to the tendency to *mal de mer* on the part of the Uncle. He kept the tightest hold on himself. He stood amidships and kept his teeth clenched. The Boy is now of the opinion that but for his presence the Uncle would have been sick even then, but the thought that he might lower himself in his nephew's estimation made him exert his really terrific will power and concentration. He was not going to be beaten that time—and he was not. The Boy was and is a first-class sailor. They had a wonderful day at Boulogne and sent home postcards to astonish the Family. And the voyage back was achieved safely, as well.

Despite his travels, the Uncle had a true Victorian contempt for all foreigners, especially the French, and he regarded Portuguese and Spanish as hardly of human status. He had some esteem for the Germans, their thoroughness appealed to him. He had seen the outbreak of the Franco-Prussian war and his prophecy of a German victory, discounted when he made it, nevertheless came true. He admired Bismarck but he despised the Kaiser. But he regarded Germany as a menace to this realm —he saw the danger of her victory over France. He died the year before the first World War broke out but he had seen it coming, quite clearly.

Fortunately a number of photographs survive, at various stages in his life, to enable a visual picture of this man to be realized. Today of course he would have been a complete Back Number, on account of his Victorian ideas and attitude to life. He had been brought to London from the wilds of Galloway, where he was born, by his Pa and his Ma, when he was two years old. His younger brother was born shortly after the small family had settled in London—and that was at Kingsland, a northern suburb and very different then to what it is today. From there, in due course, they moved to the big house in Canonbury, for success came speedily to Pa.

The eldest son—his name was James and from now on he will be Uncle James—was given the best education his Pa could afford. Being a Scot he lapped it up. The softer Southern air did not sap his desire to learn, a quality inherent in the sons of 'Caledonia stern and wild'. Also he had a marvellously retentive memory. His education cost the merest fraction of what it would take to keep a boy at a grammar school now, but this Victorian lad learnt far more in shorter time than do the boys of today. He liked learning for its own sake and he went on learning right up to the time of his death. He had very little boyhood, as it is understood today. He had hardly any toys and was brought up to take a serious view of Life. He was found tasks to do in his short holidays. There is a picture of him taken whilst he was still at school—probably at about twelve years of age. He wears a high-cut, buttoned-up little jacket, a white collar and bow-tie, awful trousers and heavy boots. In his left hand he holds a most uncompromising-looking round, hard hat. The right hand rests on an 'occasional' table. The whole thing is as stiff as the cane-bottomed chair which stands beside him, but which serves its purpose of giving an idea of his height. No boy would ever have stood thus, save at the photographer's behest—and those men hated the touch of real nature. The face is set and determined, the eyes gaze

Upper left: The Victorian boy aged fourteen months or so. *Upper right:* The Victorian boy aged two and a half. *Lower left:* The Victorian boy aged between three and four. *Lower right:* The Edwardian young man —aged nineteen

Victorian and Edwardian Royalty

Upper left: The Duke of Windsor. *Upper right:* Queen Alexandra. *Lower left:* King Edward VII. *Lower right:* The Emperor of Germany—"The Kaiser"

right ahead, steady and level. It is quite certain that he did not like having his picture taken but he underwent the ordeal frequently in his youth, because he considered it his duty, on account of the large number of relations who wanted to see how he was getting on. Being a Scot he regarded relations as being important. He knew all about his family and could trace out a kinship which to an Englishman would have been non-existent. He knew all about Duty, too. For the whole of his life this man worked and took responsibilities. Was he not head of a family and the head and driving force of a flourishing business at the age of twenty-five? He was never able to do much in the way of relaxation. Yet there is one picture which shows him in a more nonchalant mood than usual —leaning stiffly against an elaborately carved cupboard, his right arm akimbo and his legs crossed. There is a velvet curtain as background. There is also an uncomfortable-looking chair and maybe he was wise to stand. His expression belies the studied easiness of the pose. He is as alert and watchful as ever. He might be on the wrestling mat (where he already shone). However, this picture and others of the period, roughly 1870–4, show that he had already adopted the form of neckwear which he favoured to his end. It looks like a black silk tie in a sailor's knot and so indeed it is. But he never tied that knot. It was ready-made and fastened by a loose end which slid through a hoop and was held by a pin fixed in the fabric, point downwards. That man never tied a tie if he could help it—he considered it a waste of time and his battles with an evening-dress bow were something to see, although he had them ready-made too. Probably he was not good at ties although clever with his fingers, but it is far more likely that he just could not be bothered. Nobody ever remembers seeing him in anything but a black tie. He did not believe in personal adornment in any way. He never wore a ring, a tiepin or any of the jewellery affected by men in those days. His very watch-chain was tucked away, only the crossbar of his Albert showing, and eventually he discarded that and carried his watch loose in his pocket. He soon discarded high collars too, and wore a variety known as 'Laydown', 'Polo', 'Loftus' or 'Shakespeare' collars, according to the taste of the haberdasher, but they were of starched linen and so was his shirt. He never wore a soft collar or shirt in his life, although they became quite fashionable in his later years. He considered them a piece of modern slovenliness.

The photos show him as he was, with his fair, sandy hair parted at the side, his short, well-trimmed moustache, broad brow, well-set eyes, finely chiselled features and firm mouth and chin. He had a fair, white skin, a ruddy complexion and blue eyes which despite their direct gaze had a twinkle in them which the ordeal of photography managed to

F

subdue but which was never absent in real life. They could flash anger but they could and did radiate kindliness and good humour. He was not a patient man and he did not suffer fools gladly. They were strong eyes, too—he never used glasses at all, a magnifying glass for a very small print such as one finds on maps, to which he was much addicted, was all he needed until the very end.

He was of middle height but his great spread of shoulder and immense depth of chest made him look shorter than he was. It was an amazing chest, the envy of less fortunate males and the despair of tailors. He was a man of immense physical strength and the muscularity of his legs made them appear slightly bowed. He walked with the spring of an athlete and was as light as a feather on his feet. He never learned to dance, he did not like it, but he would have danced beautifully. There was an air of determination and self-confidence about him which gave courage and support to everybody. He never admitted failure but once in his life when, a few years before his death, he tried to learn Russian and failed. He was very cross indeed about it. He blamed the Russians entirely and he was, of course, right.

His brusqueness was a cover for shyness; he had the excellent manners of his time and he hated slackness in any form. To be late for an appointment was unforgivable, and not to answer a letter on the day of its receipt was something quite out of the question. Yet he had little life of his own. He assumed complete responsibility for everyone connected with him when his Pa died in 1875 and he bore that little world, Atlas like, until he too passed on. At an age when most young men were 'having a good time' he bore his full burden of responsibility and never grumbled about it.

For very many years he had fourteen people directly dependent upon him—apart from employees and staff. As time went on they dropped to eight and then to five, which was the least number he ever supported. There was always a host of partial dependents who looked to him for the little luxuries that made life worth living, and he saw to it that they got them. He worked almost entirely for others. It never dawned on him that he was not legally bound to do so. It was his duty as he saw it. To his Victorian mind, a family was something for which one was responsible, even though one had not begotten it, and the responsibility was, he felt, his. He did not complain, it was his pleasure to give and he was certainly a glutton for that. He asked no returns—these people, his brothers, sisters, nephews and nieces, naturally looked to him and he never failed them. He never married—how could he? He had no time and perhaps no inclination. No wife would ever have stood for what he did and the small army he supported.

He seldom took a holiday. There had been one or two in his youth, climbing holidays in the Alps and a visit to Italy. He never forgot them. He had hobbies galore, but active hobbies. He put his duty to others before he put his duty to himself.

He was Uncle James in name and fact to the Victorian Boy. And Uncle James to a host of others who had no right to call him so. He was the Boy's guardian as well. To him he stood *In Loco Parentis*, for the father had died young. And when that Boy's mother, Uncle James' youngest sister, returned home with no support for her Boy or herself, he took them in without question. His home was their home, they were his people, so they came home. That was the sort of mind he had. Nor did he ever by word or gesture suggest that they were poor dependants. He would have died first.

Uncle James' body was as clean and well-found as his mind. Almost every sport save Association Football—which he liked to watch in later life—and cricket came easily to him and as a gymnast he was supreme. He was a member of several famous cycling clubs in the days when the Cycle Show (the Stanley Show, as it was called), organized by the Stanley Cycling Club, was to the Victorians what the Motor Show is today. He rode the old high bicycles, the penny-farthings, the 'kangaroos' and the 'safeties'. He had been one of those who wore the special bicycling uniform; they had little round hats like pillboxes, jackets, knickerbockers which fastened at the knees, and they blew little bugles at times. He was a regular attendant at the annual rally in Bushey Park.

But it was in Amateur Athletics where his greatest fame lay. He could fence expertly, if not quite in championship class, and it did not matter if the weapons were sabres, foils or singlesticks. He was a more than useful middleweight boxer and a celebrated referee at contests. His brightest jewels were Gymnastics and Wrestling. He was easily one of the best amateur wrestlers in the country either at Græco-Roman or Catch-as-catch-can (he preferred the latter because he was not a heavy-weight and Græco-Roman champions ran to tonnage). His grace and speed as a wrestler made one think of a Greek statue come to life.

It was to Gymnastics, and wrestling is part thereof, that he devoted what leisure he had and made them the greatest interest in his life. He was a Leader of the German Gymnastic Society in London, whose gym-nasium lay between St. Pancras and King's Cross Stations in London. It was very celebrated indeed. Not by any means were all the members German, although members of that race had founded it and formed the hard core. After all, *Turnverein* was their national sport. They were the champions of the world with the Swiss as their runners-up. Uncle James did not see why the British should be left out of this form of physical

training and sport. This country held all the sporting championships
—mostly because other nations were not playing the games at all—but
in Gymnastics it lagged behind. He showed that this race could produce
superb gymnasts for he became one himself, in every line, apparatus,
club, massed movement, bars, horse, rope-climbing—what you will.
To further the cause he translated a famous German text-book on the
subject—and in this he collaborated with another member of the German
Gymn, as it was called, one Oscar Knofe (pronounced Kan-o-fee).
The original author was Ludwig Puritz, who was the final authority,
and the book was called *Code Book of Gymnastic Exercises*.

Uncle James fostered the art of Gymnastics with Victorian complete-
ness. An International Gymnastic Competition was held in Brussels
and he was much affronted by the fact that no team was being sent officially—or unofficially—from this country to compete and uphold the
honour of England. He decided to alter all that—'To make other arrangements', as was his favourite term. He organized and took over his own
team of gymnasts. They competed at Brussels against the picked teams
of Europe. They won. They returned home in triumph and were fêted.
They gave a display in the Central Transept of the Crystal Palace and
showed the huge crowd which came to watch them how they had won
for England. Uncle James' solo contribution was to climb to the Very
Top of the great transept up a loose rope and to slide down head first,
holding by leg only, at breakneck speed, turning at the right second to
prevent his brains from being dashed out. It was probably the proudest
moment of his life. And it did much to advance the cause of Gymnastics
here.

But although the Family had to support him and his constant dis-
plays and competitions at the G.G.S., he never succeeded in converting
any of the male members thereof to gymnastics. They all went, in duty
bound, and they all praised, but left it at that. They were all bored, except
the two unmarried sisters, who found their own pleasure in making as
many acquaintances as possible and bowing to people they already knew.
The males sought the Bar, for there was a good one. The Boy was frankly
bored. He liked the boxing, if any, the fencing (he was to indulge in
both later) and the wrestling. But not the Græco-Roman form, which
he found insupportable. He was never any good at gymnastic exercises
other than with the gloves and foils, except that he climbed a rope well.
But the eldest sister of the Family married into a gymnasium, the captain
of which was the rival to her brother. This may have been enthusiasm
on her part but was most likely expediency, as will be seen later.

The devotion to gymnastics did Uncle James no good in the end.
It was a contributory cause of his death for he developed heart trouble.

But whatever he did, he did well. When in later years his heart troubled him and he had to give up any form of violent exercise and even cycling, he took up botany—the study of wild flowers. He would go every week-end for gentle walks of twenty miles or so, often accompanied by the Boy who was then growing up and almost a young man. He would collect his specimens from the fields, the hedgerows, the woods and ponds, place them in a tin box, take them home and, by the aid of his books, he would identify them. Once identified, he never forgot them. He and the Boy would spend weekends in the country. Uncle James would be busy with his flowers and the Boy with his birds—he had a passion for birdwatching fostered by Oliver G. Pike and Cherry Kearton at a time when this pleasant hobby was not so popular as it is now. Uncle James showed little interest in birds—although he would come home with books on the subject and shove them across the table to the Boy muttering, 'Here, this may be useful.' But the Boy picked up a good deal of knowledge about the flowers, for he liked to make his Uncle feel that he was interested—and he now occasionally staggers his grandchildren with his knowledge of wild plants. They went to places in the Home Counties—those were in the Edwardian days—and would stop at good hotels, taking long walks therefrom. Once there was a bottle of very good Burgundy at dinner. The Uncle called the waiter and asked how much there was in stock. The waiter asked the head waiter who asked the landlord who did not know. So he, Uncle James and the Boy went down into the amazing cellars below that old hostelry —said to be a Norman crypt—to find out. There was a matter of twelve dozen, it appeared. Uncle James bought the lot. He was that sort of man.

His contempt for foreigners has been noted but he was always cour-teous to them when they visited this land. He spoke to them in their own tongue unless that tongue was outlandish. He had the greatest contempt for all Greeks. He had to deal with them in his business. He refused to have anything to do with the works of Homer or with ancient Greek culture. He said it was not possible—he knew the Greeks and they could not have changed to that extent. Americans—or Yanks, as he called them—mildly amused him but he was devoted to the works of Mark Twain. He did not altogether believe in L'Entente Cordiale, but pre-sumed it could not be helped. He thought it a bit of luck for the French that if they ever fought Germany again they would have 'us'—as he said—with them. He was dead right in that. He did not consider it possible for 'us' to be beaten. He was pure Victorian in that.

Uncle James was a very good man but in some ways a very strange one. He paid for his sisters' 'sittings' in their Church but only a wedding, christening (and not always that) or funeral got him there himself. None of the male members of the family were churchgoers, but the females made up for it. Uncle James would keep aloof from social life. When not engaged in athletic activities or meetings in connection therewith, he would sit and read the whole evening. He could read with ease in a room full of chattering people. He did not much care for novels but he adored Dickens. He liked biographies, books on travel or the special subject which occupied his mind at the moment. He said as little as he could to the sisters who kept house for him and, although they loved, respected and admired him, they were also a little frightened of him. The one who was the housekeeper never dared ask him for money unless something very unusual happened. Nor, for that matter, did she have to. Every Friday morning, when he had finished his breakfast, he would put the weekly housekeeping money on the end of the mantelpiece in the Breakfast Room and walk straight out. He kept his money in his waistcoat pocket—it was real money then, not paper, and as there was usually a hole in the pocket and the sovereigns and half-sovereigns slipped through it into the lining and were mixed up with the innumerable odds and ends which he also kept in it—nobody ever had so many stubs of pencils as Uncle James—it was sometimes a job for him to get it. That made him irritable, and he was easily irritated by trifles although crises left him cool.

There would, of course, be occasions when annual Festivals like Christmas, Easter or the arrival of visitors to stay would make it necessary for extra housekeeping to be forthcoming. The sister in charge never asked him for this directly, but would discuss it in his presence with the rest of the family, in a marked manner. Uncle James never gave the slightest sign that he had heard or was cognizant. But on the eve of the event, just as he was departing for business, she would go very red in the face, splutter a bit (as was her habit) and say, 'Cash, James.' He would grunt in answer, put his fingers in the pocket where he kept his gold, dig around amongst the rubbish until he found what he considered enough—it was always far more than enough—and then, if in a good temper, put it on the mantelpiece—he never put money into anyone's hand. If, however, he was irritable, a far more likely thing in the morning, he would throw it on the table, or on the floor, and walk out. His brother, nominally a partner in the firm but in reality a quite useless passenger, got his salary and share in the same way. He would go into 'The Senior's' room—Uncle James was always The Senior at the office—and ask for it. Uncle James would take it out and throw it to him—he never gave a cheque, always cash. It would go on the floor but the Junior made no bones about picking it up. The right thing to do with bills was not to make any mention of them but put them beside Uncle James' plate. He would thrust them into his pocket without looking at them. But he always paid and never queried.

When the members of the Family went on holiday—which they did individually when they grew up—they saw to it, by discussion before him but never with him, that he should know all about it and where they were going. The date of departure was mentioned constantly. He took no notice at all but at bedtime on the eve of their departure he would grunt, 'Here, here,' and throw a very liberal sum towards them. One thing was Law. He must never be thanked. That he could not endure.

His family gave him birthday and Christmas presents every year—if 'gave' is the right word. They knew what he wanted and they would purchase the things and put them somewhere where they knew he would find them. He never showed the slightest sign of being aware of these gifts. Nor did he use them until some time had elapsed—he would not be compromised in that case, he thought. He spent nothing on himself. He was careless about his clothes. He would wear the same suit until it was tattered and so shiny that it reflected the rays of the sun. His sisters could never get hold of it to mend or press it—that was why there was always that hole in the pocket. They had to talk 'at' him about his shabbiness and the state of his wardrobe. He showed no sign of having heard but, after a period of this oblique criticism, he would go to his tailor and order four or five suits. He would then proceed to wear one—and only one of them—until it was in its turn fit only for a scarecrow. The others languished in his wardrobe, protected from moth by his sisters. When he died there was an immense accumulation of suits, all of superfine cloth, of shirts, collars and underwear which had never once been put on. For the journey to and from the City he wore a bowler hat or a straw according to the season. In the City he donned a very ancient top hat. That was eminently Victorian. He had no sense of the fitness of things at a time when men were meticulous in dress. If the suit of his choice happened to be a morning coat he would wear a bowler with it—a terrible solecism then but he did not care. His hats got as old as his clothes before he changed them, but, like his suits, they were always carefully brushed. Nobody ever saw him in a dirty shirt or collar or in bad boots. In an age when all men wore gloves as part of their attire, he never used them at all, even in the depth of winter.

He had a very hasty temper and he hated inefficiency. He could play havoc with people who upset him but he would never affront a guest. Once his two sisters inveigled him into playing tennis with them and a gentleman who was said to be in the championship class. That was probably the reason for Uncle James agreeing to play at all. But the man turned out to be an impostor, the veriest rabbit at the game. The sisters were terrified as to what James might say or do. True to his code, he played on. To him, of course, the man was contemptible. After each set Uncle James muttered, 'We shall have to make other arrangements.' This was his direst threat although it never materialized as to what those other arrangements might be. The game over—Uncle James vanished without one word to the offending and to him offensive partner.

Yet he was very patient with those who were in trouble—unless that trouble was physical. Let anyone start saying how ill they were and he had one sovereign cure. 'Get up and walk about,' he would snap. He followed his own prescription, too, until he was stricken down at the end. He would perform minor operations on himself with a penknife —one with a brown horn handle—and on anyone else who would submit to it. He once extracted one of his own teeth with this weapon. He did not groan or stop although his eyes watered with pain and his nose wrinkled up until he had dug out the painful molar. But he got it out at last. He did not like dentists. But in a case of really serious illness he could be as gentle as a woman. He adored children and they adored him, yet he had none of his own for he lived and died a bachelor. He did not actually play with children much but he understood them and they knew it. Probably he was one of those very lucky people who never quite grow up, for his knowledge of a child's mind was uncanny. He seldom played actively with the Victorian Boy, his nephew, but he would watch the game without seeming to do so, and would suddenly make a suggestion which was so absolutely right that the Boy would adopt it with acclamation and find the game much improved. At home, Uncle James was the most unsociable of men. He would seldom speak conversationally to any of his sisters there. But sometimes, without raising his eyes from his book, he would break into a conversation or argument with a remark of such pith and moment that there was no more to be said. He did this as a rule when the affair seemed inclined to be repetitive, a thing he could not endure. Yet he would go round to the houses of his brothers and sisters who were married and talk freely—and even make jokes. He did not like bad language and was seldom heard even to exclaim a mild 'Damn'. Nor did he like dirty stories or suggestive talk. He would soon put an end to that, even in male society. And in those days, of course, one did not talk that way before the ladies.

He could be, and was, a bit of a trial, especially to that sister who was the Housekeeper. He would come home from the office and there was always a meal ready for him in the Breakfast Room, of which he partook alone. The sister took a pride in making this meal as tasty and attractive as possible. As like as not he would remove the cover, look at the food, get up and go straight out of the house. At other times he would eat every scrap. It was no use asking him what he would like, he would not tell you. Once, however, it was observed that he partook freely of oatcakes. The result was a supply of oatcakes at every meal. He got sick of the sight of them and left them alone. They still appeared, so he crumpled them into powder. Still his sister did not take the hint. She served some more. With great ostentation he threw them in the fire. That was that. There were no more oatcakes.

He seldom, if ever, went to a Theatre but he did not disapprove of them. In the early 1900s he suddenly developed a passion for the Music Hall. He became a regular patron of the Tivoli, Oxford and London Pavilion, but never of the Alhambra, Palace or Empire. He would take his nephew to the Saturday matinées at the Oxford—taking him down to his office in the morning (he never took Saturday mornings off), giving him lunch and driving him to the music hall in a hansom—a form of transport he never used himself but which he knew the Boy thought wonderful. He knew, too, that the Boy had greasepaint in his blood from the other side of his Family. It was probably the advent of Harry Lauder which had first attracted Uncle James, as a loyal Scot, and he never missed him when he was in town. But it was not only Lauder; he had a high regard for Eugene Stratton, Gus Elen and, later, for Harry Tate. He considered Dan Leno a genius and said he was 'out of Dickens'—his highest praise. He viewed the acrobats and tumblers with a critical eye. He knew all about that, and club-swinging acts left him cold. He could do it as well, if not better. But he was seen to applaud Cinquevalli, and he hardly ever applauded anything—not even Lauder.

Although regarded by his Family as unsociable he had an immense number of friends with whom he was extremely popular. These were the cronies of his athletic days. He would suddenly turn into a quaint old inn in a country or seaside town, stand in the bar and say nothing. The proprietor would in due course notice him and there would be a shout of 'Why, it's Jimmie!' and a wonderful reunion would take place. Uncle James never smoked but he could do full justice to the wine of his native land and was a connoisseur of whisky. None of his Family ever dared call him 'Jimmie', by the way.

He liked wines, too, but he never knew how to drink them. He would go into a City branch of Short's and order one of their best ports —and wonderful port it was, something to savour and linger over. He took it down at a gulp. He took his medicine the same way. He knew a lot about chemistry and drugs and in the last years of his life, when he was an invalid, he would get much interest out of his prescriptions which he would discuss with his doctor, who was a brother Scot. He examined his own symptoms too, and was a very helpful patient, though never a patient one.

He was not an epicure but he did understand good food. He lunched well in the City. In the days when his firm had offices in Old Jewry, he would go to Birch's, drop in at Sweetings for sandwiches, sample what Pimm's had to offer or the best restaurants in Cheapside. When the firm shifted to St. Mary Axe and later to Billiter Street, he went to the City Arms, at the top of the first-named thoroughfare, where the cooking was superb and the proprietor a Frenchman—Uncle James acknowledged the French knew how to cook. He would go to the Ship and Turtle in Leadenhall Street, or to Crosby Hall, the old Royal Palace which still stood then in Bishopsgate and where royal food could be met with. He seldom went up West but when he did it was to Simpsons, the Trocadero or Frascati's. His nephew, when a young man, introduced him to the Hotel Florence in Rupert Street and to the D'Italie, too. He approved, and spoke Italian to the waiters. But perhaps the place he liked the best was Kettners.

He travelled down to the City each day to Broad Street and went Second Class with a season ticket. Only at the very end of his active life was he persuaded to travel First.

In politics he was a Liberal. Gladstone was his man. He had a poor opinion of Disraeli, whom he considered a Charlatan, but whose Suez Canal deal and whose making the Queen Empress of India he applauded. But he did not trust Disraeli, who was a Jew, and Uncle James never trusted that race although no anti-Semitic. He did not consider that a Jew could be English and so could not be fully trustworthy. No amount of argument would shift him. It might be advanced that a Jew was born in this country, to which he would reply: 'You may be born in a stable but you are not a horse. He is a Jew. Very well then.' That tag of his, 'Very well then', was final. It was no use going on. He did not think much of the politicians who succeeded Gladstone but he respected Lord Salisbury although that Marquis was a Conservative —but he did not extend the same feeling to A. J. Balfour. He was violently opposed to Joseph Chamberlain and especially to his campaign for Tariff Reform and Protection. He was a staunch Free Trader. But he was in favour of the Boer War—although it brought disaster upon him—and it took him some time to forgive Lloyd George's attitude to this. Yet he strongly favoured that Welsh statesman's attitude towards Landlordism, which was one of his pet detestations. He felt very strongly about the Leasehold System and although he never gave Socialism a thought he believed the Land should be free. 'You cannot increase it,' he would say, 'and so no one person should be allowed to have too much of it, to the exclusion of others.' But he was an Imperialist. He gloried in Kipling and in the amount of red paint on the map. He believed very sincerely—and probably quite rightly—that British Rule brought good to all who lived under it. He would never have believed that the British oppressed anyone. Had he lived today to see that Empire disintegrate, he would have disintegrated with it.

Despite his Liberalism and his jeering at Tories as reactionaries, he held to old-fashioned ways. He disliked the idea of women coming into the City—he disliked typewriters and it was many, many years before one ever appeared in his office—one is doubtful if it ever did in his lifetime—and certainly no lady clerk ever crossed the threshold. Letters there were written by hand and copied in the old-fashioned 'letter books' by means of damped tissue pages and a press. He wrote his own letters in a characteristic and flowing hand. There was a clerk in that office for many years, named Bob Read, whose copperplate writing was a thing of marvel. Very few people possess that art today although the author of this book numbers one or two—they are, of course, elderly—amongst his correspondents. It is dying and almost dead, killed by Mechanism.

Uncle James seldom went to Public dinners because it entailed wearing evening dress and that he disliked, although he looked very distinguished in it. Sometimes he could not refuse as he would be a Guest of Honour, but he always steadfastly refused to make a speech. He would be most embarrassed when a speaker referred to him, grunting and fidgeting in his chair. But one function he really did enjoy. That was the wedding of his nephew, the Victorian Boy, then an Edwardian young man—the Boy to whom he had truly stood *In Loco Parentis*. That was in 1912 and the Boy took the opportunity of expressing his thanks to his Uncle James—a thing he could never have done personally. Emotion and sincerity gave him eloquence. The Family and the guests, all of whom knew the truth of what he said, cheered and cried at the same time. It was their opportunity, too, which they would never have dared to take singly. Uncle James, his ruddy face a couple of shades deeper, wriggled about and muttered 'Nonsense', but he had moisture in his eye. His nephew knew that he was pleased, proud and gratified.

Uncle James liked that nephew's bride and their new home. He stocked the garden and took pride in it all. He would come over on Sundays and talk. That young couple, on their return from their honeymoon, gave a Housewarming, as was the custom of those days. Indeed, they gave two, one on a Saturday and one the next day. For they had many friends and the bridegroom was in the Theatrical Profession and most of his friends therein could only come on the Sunday. Uncle James, renowned for his unsociability, came to both events. He arrived first and was last to go. He beamed on everyone and spoke to everybody—a most unusual thing for him. He showed people over the house and pointed out its advantages. It was indeed a nice house. It had ten rooms and a large garden. The rent was £42 a year and the rates £6. The young couple had £4 a week income and were able to live in complete comfort—and to afford a servant. . . .

Uncle James was wonderful at figures—he could work things out in his head which would have taken an ordinary man a long time and much paper. He was greatly addicted to Algebra. He was a brilliant but erratic man of business. The financial depression following the Boer War brought disaster upon him and he was forced to give up that Desirable Residence in the Best Road which he liked so much. But he started again, his will was indomitable, and when he died he was once more in comfortable circumstances. This reverse in fortune was largely contributed to by the extravagance of those who were really dependent upon him, and it was his fault for not checking this, but he lacked the final ability to say 'no' at the right time.

His heart began to trouble him in his late fifties but he went on. Eventually he had to give up even his long walks and he fell back on gardening and, of course, became expert. But in his early sixties he had to take real care. Still he carried on. He had to spend two days a week at least in bed, with a telephone beside him over which he could conduct his business. He never deputed his authority and he was right—for there was nobody to whom he could depute it. His knowledge of his trade was unique. The Victorian Boy was not taken into the business, he having a horror of commerce and an inbred love of the Theatre which claimed him. Uncle James worked on to his end. Save those days in bed he took no holidays but he still paid for everyone else to have them. He asked no reward or thanks, but he was delighted to receive letters descriptive of their travels, which he would read to everyone and bore them stiff.

All his life he did what he considered his Duty. It never crossed his mind that he was making any personal sacrifice. He belonged to an age which believed in Family Life, and that it was right to help those who needed it. He took the greatest pride in his family and although he was father to none in fact he was father to many in deed. He never spoke of what he did or what he gave. After his death it was discovered that he had pensioners of whom nobody knew—including an old aunt in Scotland whom he had never seen but whom he had supported until she died. That was his code. He gave nobody his real confidence—the Victorian Boy came closest in that respect, perhaps—but he was a true product of his Age, proud of his country, his race, his credit and his good name. He never gave up, he never despaired.

He loved life and he did not want to die. The last few months of his life were agony. His heart was almost worn out, he had dreadful attacks, but he fought on and kept himself alive by the power of his indomitable will. He did not fear Death itself but he feared very much what might happen when he was gone to those who relied upon him for so much. He was very ill and in great pain, to him Death might have been a happy release—but there were those others to think of and he had spent his life thinking about others. So he fought on right up to the end, knowing that Death was in the room and reaching out for him. That Victorian Boy and another nephew were by his side during those terrific and terrifying last rounds and the Boy knew his presence gave comfort. Very gently he told his uncle that there was no need to worry about the two unmarried sisters, the Boy's aunts—he would look after them. But still that Victorian who bore so much on his shoulders fought on, but the last round came. Death closed in and delivered the blow, and when that Victorian man died, conscious and fighting to the last, it was the Victorian Boy's arms that held him as he passed through the veil.

That was a man who was a true son of that much-derided epoch. And when the news of his death was known, letters came from all parts in a shoal, all testifying to respect, admiration and some kind deed he had performed—never known or mentioned before.

It would seem that Shakespeare wrote his epitaph when he said of Brutus:

> His life was gentle; and the elements
> So mixed in him that Nature might stand up
> And say to all the world 'This was a man'.

A Victorian man at that—who stood *In Loco Parentis* to so many who needed his help.

CHAPTER SIX

A Victorian Family

THE description of the Head of the House may seem rather long to modern readers but the author is anxious to show a picture of Victorian life as he knew and saw it. He does not suggest such men as Uncle James do not live today—he is sure they do—but he wants to prove that they did exist in the days of Victoria and that men then were not the stern, unbending, joyless, humourless people who lived narrow lives and who were very often moral hypocrites. There were such people; there are today. But there were the other kind, too, who had their code —a code not understood in this age of speed and gadgets and therefore often sneered at. It had its points, it built up something which nobody else but the people of this race could knock down (and they are proceeding to do so—or so it seems). Neither Uncle James nor any of his Family—which includes those of the generation living today—would ever have tolerated the outlook on life expressed in the phrase 'I could not Care Less', which is the canker of our time and which will ruin the country. They, the Victorians, could not care more about everything they did.

Having dealt with the Head of the House, a title which in those days really meant what it said, it is time to examine the rest of the family whose belongings and discards went into the Box Room. Some of them have left their likenesses behind, others were victims of the Blitz which wiped out so much of the little remaining of their world, especially the bricks and mortar. There were six of them left, some noteworthy, some of lesser personality, but all typical of their time.

The next in line by birth to Uncle James was a boy. He saw the light of this world in Kingsland in the year 1852. Queen Victoria had been on the throne a mere fifteen years. This brother, whose name was

Charles, was of a very different type to Uncle James, although they resembled each other in features. Charles, however, took after his Ma, and Uncle James his Pa. He was of a much more gentle type, he had none of the immense energy or strength of will of his brother. He was very good-looking, very easygoing and he too could never say 'No' at the right time. He made what the rest of the Family, especially the female side, regarded as an unfortunate marriage, although he did not think so, and he had two daughters. Never a very strong man, he died in 1899. His elder brother immediately shouldered responsibility for Charles' family.

The next born was a girl—and she entered into that large house in Canonbury. She, too, in looks resembled her brothers and she had plenty of energy and will power. Hardly good-looking, she had clear-cut features and an air of distinction. She was fair, indeed she was sandy, tall, slightly angular as to figure and she had a temper. But she had a great sense of humour, too, and an innate kindliness. She was born in 1854, the year in which the Crimean War broke out. She was alive during the siege of Sebastopol, the charge of the Light Brigade, the Heights of Alma, Inkermann and all the mess and carnage of that muddled campaign. She was alive when Florence Nightingale lit her lamp and she lived to see the Blitz of 1940 onwards. Truly some of those Victorians saw some changes.

The girl was named Margaret but she was always called Maggie. She was the female head of the house, of course, and she spent her life bickering with her sisters. It was a considerable time before she got married—she looked like being an old maid, which was almost a social disgrace then for it showed that a woman had failed in her ambition and career, which was Marriage. But eventually a suitor came along. He was the small English gymnast who was captain of the gymnasium which was the rival of that of which her brother James was chief. He hardly reached to her shoulder. He was dark, immensely serious and had a walrus moustache. He was a very neat and accomplished gymnast on the apparatus but he could not compete in wrestling and the more physical forms with much hope of success, unless against rivals of his own size, and there were not many of them. He was no cyclist or footballer but he joined the brothers of his bride-to-be in a rowing club of which they were members. Living as they all did in North London, they rowed on the River Lea, which was a much more pleasant stream than it is now but which, of course, had not the dignity or status of the Thames. Because of his small stature this little man, whose name was Arthur, was made cox. He took it all with deadly seriousness. The crew won many prizes in the Lea Regattas and even competed in some of those on the Thames, and with success. So, greatly daring, they entered at Henley. They met with disaster. Their cox, whose sight was not too good although he would never admit it, steered them into the bank when they were two lengths ahead of their competitors in the heat. It was all over. They never went to Henley again—and they never used the same cox. Indeed, some of the crew never rowed again—the disgrace was too much for them. That little cox had a dreadful time; it was worse for him because his father had been a pilot at Gravesend and with that breeding he should have known better. But Arthur married the daughter of the house—his Maggie—and they lived a happy life although totally unsuited to each other. Victorians made the best of marriage and understood what give and take meant. It was in their view a sacrament for life and they mostly made it work out. Arthur was a man of tremendous gravity. He seldom laughed and he had no sense of humour. He thought it a waste of time. Such things as legends and romance he held in horror. To him, fact was everything and he cared for nothing else—save gymnastics. He had a sense of his own importance out of all proportion to his size and standing. In business—he was a kind of general produce merchant—he was as tenacious as a limpet, screwing the last penny and the highest possible price out of his customers, who would often concede him an extra farthing a pound, or whatever it was, to get him out of their office. He was a great walker and he took strides as long as, if not longer than, those of a man six feet in height. He was a very honest man and of complete integrity, his word was his bond—but he got no fun out of life at all. He never went to a place of amusement and he never went to Church, both of which were to him an utter waste of time, and money. There were wild rumours that he was an Atheist. He was most careful in his expenditure. *Per contra*, he lived in the biggest houses he could procure. They got bigger as the years went on and his fortune increased. He was well to do and at the end he and his family lived in a mansion in another Best Road in North London, an immense place with about twenty-five rooms and a lot of ground around it. It was far too large for them, but he liked it. Probably like most small men he saw himself as a giant. Possibly his lack of inches gave him a craving for size which he satisfied this way. There were two children, both boys. They had a Spartan upbringing on account of their father's austerity and their mother's hot temper.

At Christmas and on their birthdays they were given parties to which their little friends were invited. They were never very cheerful affairs. The trouble usually started at tea-time when some unfortunate urchin upset a cup of cocoa or glass of milk, or whatever beverage was going. For this the eldest son was always blamed although as like as not the

MISS MARY

MISS BESSIE

Left: Miss Bessie. *Centre*: The Victorian Boy. *Right*: Miss Mary

Note. This was the one and only time the Boy consented to wear the "bonnet"—to please his Aunts

Upper left: Uncle Mac—a Victorian seaside Entertainer. *Upper right:* A Victorian Scottish Minister—Rev. J. Stewart-Wilson, D.D. *Lower left:* A Victorian Parlourmaid. *Lower right:* The Victorian Boy at the Photographers. Age about three or four

poor child was right on the other side and end of the table. After this there would be games and things would liven up until 'Pater' came home. The two boys had to call their father 'Pater' and their mother 'Mater', at Pater's expressed order, which was rather curious in a man who despised Latin, Greek, the Classics and all such dead things. Pater acted on the party with rather stronger effect than the skeleton at a Roman Feast. He iced and froze those parties as that ambassadorial Tite Barnacle in *Little Dorrit* had iced and frozen foreign Courts. Mater had done her best up to then, to give her credit, but she could not cope with the frigid atmosphere created by her spouse. He probably did not mean to do this, but he succeeded. His one contribution to the Festivity was to work the Magic Lantern. For this he demanded—and got—complete and utter silence, and can anyone imagine little boys enjoying themselves under such conditions? The slides were shown on a white sheet in such silence as could only be matched in the grave. Not even dumb people could have achieved it, for the children were scared to move. It was more of a religious rite than an amusement. There was a large stock of slides but no new ones were purchased. The same ones were shown on every occasion but as few boys ever came twice to one of those parties that did not matter very much. If any child exclaimed or asked a question it was immediately told to be quiet. As they did not know what they were looking at the show went on with deep and increasing boredom until all the slides had been exhibited or the demonstrator burnt himself severely—which sometimes happened and cheered things up a lot. The last slide formed the climax of the show, for it actually moved. It was a kind of star and on a little handle being turned it altered its pattern several times. The Victorian Boy who saw it *ad nauseam* was reminded of it in his advanced middle age when he observed a very modern diagram being shown as a preliminary sort of announcement and sign on his television set. It was very much the same as the Magic Lantern Star, only that was more varied and full-blooded, as became its Victorianism. After the star, the show closed down (as the B.B.C. says about itself) and the magic lantern was put away until another festive gathering came round. The two boys who owned it jointly never got a chance of a private show, let alone the joy of working it themselves. And no party ever ended without Pater taking some small boy out of the room, holding him firmly by the arm, and administering a 'good talking to' him in an adjoining room. The unfortunate lad, by word or deed and in either case quite innocently, had offended Pater's ethics. That did not make for gaiety either. And when all the guests had gone one or both of the sons of the house usually got a good hiding for some misdemeanour during the gathering.

G

They had little in the way of toys—of which Pater did not approve. They did not get many treats unless Mater relented or their Aunts took them out. The Victorian Boy, some years their senior, would tell them stories, give them little books about the Greek heroes or King Arthur's knights and even write them original adventure stories in little note-books, all of which things had to be carefully hidden from Pater. The Victorian Boy was always a Romantic and he found an answering chord in the elder of these two children, who was so unlike his Pater that it was hardly true. There were some physical resemblances but there it ended.

To this Victorian City merchant, this Arthur, this Pater, life was real, life was earnest. His wife played the piano pretty badly—like all Victorian ladies she had acquired accomplishments (more or less), and he would occasionally come into the Drawing Room and listen to her, unless he was very busy indeed on his ledgers and papers which he often brought home from the office in a shiny little black bag—attaché cases and brief cases were then unknown. He did not know one note of music from another but he possessed a piano and wanted to get his value out of it. Those Drawing Rooms (there were a procession of them, for the couple and their brood were constantly moving into bigger premises) always seemed the same—they were stiff, cold, cheerless and pallid with white paint. Nor did the furniture nor its position alter in any of the houses. It hardly seemed worth while moving at all. Arthur did not smoke and he never touched alcohol unless very unwell. His fetish was Physical Fitness and he was not a very good example of it. He was muscular in his way but he was very small-bodied and as he took his long strides he also seemed to roll a bit. There was no athletic grace about him off a gymnastic apparatus. On those he was neatness itself. He ate a lot of some early form of cereal known as 'groats' which to the onlooker seemed as unappetizing as its name, and he consumed much brown bread and butter, with Demarara sugar spread thereon. He re-garded anything which lent colour to life as 'stuff and nonsense'. He did not get on very well with his eldest son, a lad who had inherited his mother's quick, blazing temper and had hair of such a violent red that it was quite startling. That boy had a vein of imagination and an appre-ciation of beauty which was always frustrated. He had rebelled against gymnastics, which made a breach between him and his Pater. But he found his niche in the First World War—for which he volunteered as soon as it broke out. He proved to be a gallant and clever soldier. The younger boy was of a different type, a much quieter and watchful lad who managed to keep the peace and still be the best of friends with his impulsive and explosive elder brother. He was a good business man from

his earliest days, but he was gassed in the 1914–18 War and did not survive
it long. The impulsive one took his risks and came through. Indeed he
lives yet.

The Family went away every summer for a holiday at the seaside
and Pater's Mater went too—a perfectly dreadful old lady—on whom it
is true the modern idea of Victorianism might well have been formed.
On the face of it she got on well with her daughter-in-law Maggie, who
called the old lady 'Mater'. In reality there was no love lost at all. But on
this occasion Maggie played for safety. Grandmater, as the boys had to
call her, sat in a chair all day, wearing her black silk dress, embroidered
black or lavender apron, a lace cap on her head and a shawl. She was not
at all bad-looking but she could say more unpleasant things in an apparently pleasant manner than would seem humanly possible. Maybe she
sat and thought them up. She was never at a loss and so delicately and
withal deliberately were they delivered—with such art was the poison
dropped—that it was some time before the recipient realized that he
or she had been insulted and then it was too late to do anything about
it. Nobody liked her except her son, who thought she was marvellous,
and he was, according to his lights, a very good son to her. Her grandchildren were wary of her. Her daughter-in-law performed marvels in
the way of keeping her temper. The Victorian Boy did not like her but
was neutral. She had once, for reasons best known to herself, presented
him with a new, bright, shining five-shilling piece—a fortune to a boy
—and he remembered that. Perhaps she liked him. He did not know
and it cannot be said that he cared much.

They nearly always went to the same place for their holidays, and
that was Deal. There was little or no sand for the children to play with
or upon, but lots of pebbles to make life hard. However, there was the
shipping to watch, although the pleasure of that soon palled on the
little ones, but Pater derived much satisfaction from surveying it, possibly inherited from that pilot sire of his, who had also, one suspects,
taken Pater to Deal as a small child and thereby made it the only possible
holiday place. Nor was Grandmater the only extra passenger on these
holidays—which could never be described as jaunts. A friend of Pater's (a
German), who was a member of his gymnasium and a renowned gymnast,
came along with his sister. The man was nice but very ugly and his sister
was probably the ugliest woman who lived and would strike terror into
the hearts of children seeing her for the first time. She spoke English very
badly but that did not prevent her from saying the most unpleasant
things. She even outdid Grandmater in this respect, but there was a
belief that she did not really understand what she was saying. Therefore
she got away with murder, and revelled in it, too.

There were only two variants from the annual visit to Deal—once when they went to Felixstowe, which Pater regarded as modern and frivolous and where a series of disasters befell them, and he accepted that as retribution. Another time they went to Hunstanton, which the children enjoyed so they never went there again. Holidays were not really for enjoyment but for furtherings of physical fitness.

Maggie managed to get satisfaction out of her married life and it is believed that the chief reason was because she was not an Old Maid. She still waged war on her Family, but she had the greatest affection and respect for her eldest brother James. She did not forget to ask him for money for purposes which did not appeal to her husband and from whom it was impossible to extract it. But Uncle James never refused. He would also buy anything for the two boys if she asked him.

It was the habit of this Victorian Family—it was common to all and is probably the same today—to disagree violently among themselves and have the most violent quarrels. They might not be on speaking terms for months—although Uncle James stood aloof from all this. But let an outsider take a hand and speak ill of any of them, or attempt something which was considered wrong, and he or she met a common front, closed tightly and embattled, all disagreement and feuds lost in the common cause.

Maggie had few hobbies. She read a lot. She had once played what had passed for tennis, but her main idea was housework. She attacked her house as she attacked her foes, her glinting steely blue eyes aflame, her mouth tightly closed like a rat-trap and all over her the will to win. She was very social minded but she voiced her opinions freely and loudly and would give offence. There was a closely cherished family legend that once when on holiday at Whitby (before her marriage) she had told a fishwife there that her wares were not fresh. The fishwife's reply was instant and to the point. She slapped Maggie across the face with a sole. And as Maggie was a Lady nothing could be done about it, so the fishwife had the last word—or more properly the last action—and was left victor in the field.

She was extremely fond of the Theatre as were all the womenfolk of her tribe. Later in her life she would come to see her Victorian nephew act and actually enjoy it. And on one memorable performance she persuaded her austere husband to accompany her. That stern puritanical man saw his first, and, it is confidently believed, his only play. He came as a duty because his wife pressed him to and because all the rest of the Family were going too—or all who were available. He did not enjoy himself, or so he said. Indeed, he highly disapproved. For the play he witnessed was the late Stanley Houghton's *The Younger Generation*, which dealt with the revolt and ultimate victory of the young members of a family, aided by a mature and good-natured uncle, over a stern, rigid and strict Father . . . much the same sort of man as himself. He was horrified and scandalized—he said he did not know why such plays were allowed to be performed. His discomfiture was made worse because his elder son saw it too. His wife reported she had actually seen him smile broadly—and that at a scene his nephew-in-law played. This must have been wishful thinking, for Arthur had no sense of humour. He told that young man, grudgingly, that he supposed he had acted well, but he was no judge. Anyway, he said, it was a wicked play and no good would come of it.

Maggie, that Victorian matron, had a fine sense of Family Pride. In common with her clan, she considered her own maiden name the best in the world and her own family the salt of the earth but she would never have admitted this to anyone. Although she had changed her name on marriage, inwardly she still clung to her maiden name and believed in it sincerely. That whole family, when discussing other people, did so with a tolerance befitting those of superior birth. They never said so but their attitude and tone showed it. If scandal arose amongst their friends, well, they were sorry for them, but then, what could you expect from people who had not the good fortune to belong to their tribe? Maggie was an uncompromising customer to the world at large. Her idea was that the world must subscribe to her code and behaviour, not she to it. She would alter her customs and habits for nobody. She always carried her umbrella—in summer time her parasol—in something of the manner in which Mr. Punch carries his stick. It went across her body, clutched tightly by a bent arm, its handle protruding beyond her shoulder. That she gave people terrible pokes, knocked off hats, and endangered eyes was nothing to her. She had always carried it that way and she always would. She did, too, right up to the end.

She quarrelled perpetually with her two unmarried sisters, especially with the younger of the two, who greatly resembled her in looks and character, except that the young one was much better-looking. If she went to their house—which she still called 'Home'—she took wicked delight in insulting their friends. All these sisters were very charitable in a spasmodic, undisciplined way. They had a string of poor retainers who called round and were presented with parcels of odds and ends of broken victuals which were referred to as 'the pieces'. On one occasion Maggie was at 'home' and found an old lady on the mat, of a very untidy and rather shabby appearance. She eyed her askance. 'If you have come for the pieces,' she snapped, 'it's the side door. How dare you!' She slammed the sacred front door with a resounding bang. It transpired that the visitor was a very rich but eccentric lady who was a pillar of the sisters' Church and who had called round on very special business connected therewith. This led to a fine old row and Maggie owned she was in the wrong. But it is believed she was secretly delighted, all the same.

Arthur died during the First World War. He served as a Special Constable and the people on his beat had to be very careful. The slightest infringement of the many new rules imposed under the Defence of the Realm Act, and he was on them like a ton of coals. He was The Law and they had better remember it.

Maggie laid him in the Family Grave and settled down to widowhood. It did not alter her life much except that she no longer had an account at the Army and Navy Stores, in which her husband had perfect and unswerving faith. He was sure you got the best of everything from there. So he had an account there and when buying things you had to quote the number of it, so that it could be charged up. Sometimes friends in need of something which could be best obtained at that famous shop were allowed to quote the number. Often they got it wrong and one wonders what happened then. . . .

Maggie's greatest triumph was the fact that she had got married. She had achieved the ambition of Victorian spinsterhood. She was not left on the shelf. It was not too hard for that to happen to a girl with no special appeal. The Victorian young ladies had not the same free and easy chances of meeting young men as their modern descendants and yet one thinks the proportion of marriages was greater then. It was certainly more enduring. The luckiest girls were those who had brothers. Of course, the brothers despised them as being mere 'girls'—the weaker and inferior sex. They could never see anything attractive in their own sisters at all. They knew them too well. Other people's sisters, yes, but they were not 'girls' in their sense of the word, they were young ladies, of infinite attraction. They really belonged to Womanhood, which was then regarded by most decent males as something to be worshipped, adored and protected. No brother felt like that about his sisters—they were just little horrors and a nuisance, not worthy of respect or protection in the general way. But they stood by them against outsiders and would never have told even the most slightly *risqué* story in their presence.

Uncle James thought little of his sisters' abilities or mentality but he looked after them like a father because it was his duty. Brothers were a blessing to Victorian girls because they had young men friends whom they brought home and therefore the girls got to know them. And very often those young men took a very different view of them to that taken by their brother. The advent of a young man was watched by the young ladies as if they were cats watching a mouse. He was assessed and summed up, and at bedtime, when these girls gossiped whilst 'doing their hair' (and doing their hair was a job then for it was always worn long and there were no bobs or shingles to say nothing of poodle or urchin cuts) —he was a possible husband and as such of immense and consuming interest. Had he been 'smitten'? they wondered. They did not use the phrase 'attracted'. Would he become 'sweet' on one of them and, if so, which? There was no ill-feeling between them about it at this moment —the affair was too open. But they would soon find out. For if the swain was at all smitten he would constantly come round—or as often as he could get an opportunity. And it would soon be clear as to which young lady had done the smiting. For he would then begin to 'pay attention'. The girl thus singled out was proud. Perhaps she liked him, perhaps she did not—but hers was the triumph. Her sisters on the whole took it well. There might be disappointment but it was choked down and a feeling of triumph—of moderate triumph—prevailed that at least one of the family had made a capture. The young man would then begin to pay 'marked attention'. He would send flowers. He would always manage to be at the same dances to which that girl went—and he would monopolize the little dance programme, pink, blue or white, having its own little pencil of the same colour attached by matching silk cord tied in a little fluffy bow. He would snatch the 'supper dance'. If his attentions were welcomed, the girl would see that he got it, too. All she had to spare for less-favoured young men were some of the 'extras'. Young ladies then were chaperoned at dances, either by their mother or some more mature female relative or a married friend. None of these attentions passed unmarked and the girl would be told that she was making herself conspicuous by dancing so much with the same man— for nothing escaped observation by anyone in the Argus-eyed days of Victoria. She would say she did not mind and perhaps she would blush (Victorian young ladies could blush), and it was realized that, in the parlance of those times, this might be 'a case'. But the young couple were not able to see much of each other alone. If he and she had reached what was known as 'an understanding', they would find romance in accidentally meeting when out walking—by his being at a pillar-box when she went out to post the letters and by turning up in a most lucky fashion when she suddenly decided that it was her job to take out the dog for its evening stroll. Victorian dogs got a lot of exercise when there were unmarried girls to whom attention was being paid. It soon became clear to all beholders that the young man 'had intentions' and it was hoped that these were 'strictly honourable'. Mother watched the situation carefully and would report to Father when they went to bed or when the Family was out of the room. Probably the father was pleased at the idea that he might be relieved of a responsibility and expense—for hardly any young Victorian lady of the real Middle Class worked for her living or even for pin money. It was Father's job to feed, clothe and look after her and he did it. Sisters would do their best to help this affair when it became 'marked attention'. There was great *esprit de corps* whatever private heartburning there might be. If the young man was really in love and ardent and had reached this 'understanding' with the object of his affection, he asked to see the Father, who received him in state. The nervous youth would then apply for permission to be engaged to the girl of his choice. If his position was satisfactory and his family and character such as passed the rather strict code of the Family with which he desired to ally himself—he was given permission and received into the bosom of the Family as the girl's 'intended'. Their engagement was 'announced'. There was a good deal of embarrassment about what to calf him in his official capacity. The word 'fiancé' was foreign, not easy to pronounce and a bit lah-di-dah, a thing to be discouraged by all people of breeding and all Victorian middle-class families knew they had that, of course. And rightly, for they mostly knew not only who had been their grandparents but their great-grandparents and often their great-greats as well. Young ladies of the Middle Class did not 'keep company'. They did not 'walk out'. And they were not 'courted'. They had attention paid to them and they became engaged. The young man was usually referred to as 'the intended'. Now the couple could see each other alone, and go about together to dances, theatres, concerts and the like. Engagements were not very long and the intended soon became the bridegroom and the young lady his white-clad bride with her wreath of orange blossom and her bridesmaids, had her day of glory at the Church her Family attended. Then another young couple settled down and started a family —and a box room of their own. Sometimes if the couple were very young—and they often were—or the young man had not sufficient means at the moment to justify marriage but had prospects which in father's eyes seemed good enough, an engagement was not sanctioned at once but the young couple were allowed to have 'an understanding' with parental cognizance. This conveyed all the benefits of an actual betrothal but not quite so much being alone together and more maternal supervision.

Tennis clubs were great hatcheries of weddings—and often a gentleman paying attention would join the club for his loved one's sake. But the great formation centre of such romances was a Church or Chapel. There young people and their families met, there the young folk took part together in the various activities of the place of worship. The swain would attach himself to the girl's family, carry prayer or hymn book, and the whole affair was watched by the entire congregation who took the greatest interest therein right up to the time when the couple stood before the Altar.

The code of morals, or what are now called the Conventions, were much more strict, nor was it a bad thing. Under their steadying influence the young people had the time to get to know each other. Conventions simply meant good manners and decency. The Family life kept a rigid moral code. Some young ladies kicked over the traces, as they have done through the ages, but in Victorian times they had good cause to regret a discovery. Strange as it may seem today, the young Victorian and Edwardian male, in search of a wife, expected and demanded virginity and chastity in the woman of his choice—and he got it. The girl did not expect it—but, odd as this may sound, she sometimes got it too. When a Victorian couple exchanged marriage vows they fully intended to keep them—and in ninety-nine cases out of one hundred they did so. They regarded marriage as a sacrament and for life. They did not look upon a marriage ceremony as a licence or a trial trip, with speedy divorce if there was the slightest disagreement or disillusionment. They looked upon it as something which had to endure and they made the best of it —they made allowances, they indulged in give and take and mostly they grew to understand each other and became the best of friends and real helpmates. They did not expect the first careless rapture to last for-ever—or for life, which in their case was the same thing—and because this was not expected, very often that first love endured. The husband expected a good housekeeper, a companion, a mother for his children and one who would be loyal and faithful to him and the progeny, whom he could trust and who would be his well-loved mate on their journey through life. He and she had taken a vow and a man's word then meant a great deal. He had, before God, sworn to love and cherish her, to cleave to her forsaking all others and to endow her with all his worldly goods. He meant it, too. She had sworn the same and she had also sworn to love, honour and obey. That word gives offence in these days. It did not mean that the woman was a slave who had to carry out the husband's lightest wish. As he understood it, it meant that there should be a High Command which, in matters of urgency, would take a decision which his wife must support as well. Victorian husbands seldom issued a command. They discussed matters with their wives and weighed their words. They left the management of the house to them and the upbringing of the family—with themselves as the final court of judgment. They gave their wives their love, and their respect—they did not consider women their equal in all things—very often they considered them as being superior, to be put on a pedestal and worshipped—and very often it was the husband who obeyed, if the wife was a clever woman. They had been taught to be chivalrous to women. The Victorian husband gave his wife his name and his protection. He gave her everything she wanted within his means. He took a pride in her for she redounded to his credit. He did his best to provide her with every comfort—certainly she had a lot of children as a rule, but he would provide domestic staff to do the hard work. He did not expect her to betray him or his confidence. He had a horror of scandal and a terrible fear of divorce and the social ostracism it entailed. That the woman came off worst in these cases he knew—but a divorced man was not looked upon with trust and was not welcomed in most homes—unless he was a very much-wronged character. Both husband and wife, in those days, had a great respect for their good name because it involved the Family as well. Nobody would lay down any statement to the effect that all Victorian or Edwardian wives were models of perfection or all Victorian and Edwardian husbands plaster saints. Not at all. But by and large there was a stricter sense of morality and duty. Those Conventions must be observed—and they were. Therefore there was very little slackness and looseness of character. One was proud of having a character, from the Head of the House and his Consort down to the humblest domestic servant; from the Chairman and Managing Director down to the office boy. To succeed was essential—to get the sack disgrace. Therefore one did one's best, at work or at home. Nobody ever said 'I Couldn't Care Less'.

Despite the code of procedure which governed young couples, there was a lot of romance. One had to do the right thing and say the right thing. At those dances mentioned above, a girl was not expected to dance more than twice an evening with any one young man, or people talked. Sitting Out caused active searching by chaperones. But some young couples who were attracted to each other managed to pay court in some degree of secrecy. That was usually when the young man was in no position to have even an 'understanding' in the eyes of parents. But somehow these youngsters met and sometimes the young man would give the girl a ring which she dared not wear openly but suspended by a ribbon round her neck, dangling it on her bosom, free from prying eyes and often succeeding in hiding it from the eyes of sisters, if any, with whom she shared a room. And when they discovered it, the romantic sense appealed to them and they seldom gave her away.

Along with that belief that the family must not be let down was the feeling that one's Class must not be let down. And the Middle Class regarded themselves as the mirror of the virtues. They read novelettes about the shocking behaviour of the Upper Ten and the Smart Set—

they read of the High Families in 'Modern Society'. But they were different, these decent Middle Class people. They must behave accordingly. Above all, the girls must be ladylike and the boys gentlemanly. That applied to speech and deed. Thus the love-making period was difficult to classify in speech. Middle-class couples did not even 'court'. That belonged to the lower classes. They did not speak of their 'boy friend' or their 'girl friend'. So a budding affair, although most closely watched and privately discussed, had no actual name. It was just that 'So-and-So' was paying much attention to that 'What's-her-Name Girl'—do you think it will be a case? And when engaged, they were, as stated, shy of the word fiancé, and the good English words 'Affianced' or 'Betrothed' also seeemed to them a bit lah-di-dah. So 'intended' crept in. It was all very respectable but true romance and lasting love was mostly its life's blood.

The code of morals was strict. It came from the Top. It came from the old Queen herself—the widowed ruler of so vast an Empire and such a conglomeration of races, she who kept the memory of her husband always with her and who endured that fierce light which Tennyson mentioned without a blink. One followed an example in those days—and Queen Victoria set one.

CHAPTER SEVEN

Background to Spinsterhood

THE next children born to that family—also in the Canonbury home—were two daughters, one arriving in the November of 1856 and the other in the April of 1859. These two were the spinsters of the Family. They never married. That acted as a bond between them and they were indeed a couple of spiritual Siamese Twins, utterly unlike in face and manner, but always together and practically inseparable, except when they took a holiday. That they did alone and each according to her own taste.

They fought constantly—they often came to physical violence in the form of pinches, shoves and sly yet vicious kicks—yet there existed a firm bond of comradeship between them and indeed a deep love and holding bond of sisterhood. They had their own friends, entirely different sets of people, and neither got on very well with the friends of the other. But they travelled down life's road together, only once separated and then not for long.

Their Christian names were Elizabeth Symington and Mary Wilson but they were always Bessie and Mary and, to their vast host of acquaintances, they were always Miss Bessie and Miss Mary.

Miss Bessie arrived just too late for the Crimean War, which finished in the March of her birth year, so that little Victorian girl did not worry her head much about War. For one thing, she was far too young, and although there were plenty of distant wars in her long life, it was not until the First World War broke out that she realized much about it and she was quite hazy then. For this was the daughter of 'Pa' who was always the slowest of them all, the one who got the double dose of the slipper and who had the impediment in her speech. She was of entirely different type to the rest, quite one on her own. She possessed, of course, certain of the family characteristics, but by and large, in looks and methods, she was different. To begin with she was dark and stout whilst the others, with one exception, were fair and slim. The men were burly but never fat. She had a different-shaped face, very full and round, she had a dark complexion and dark eyes, heavy eyes which were, however, always wide open and staring, and although by her appearance she should have been easy-going and phlegmatic she was really extremely nervous and highly strung. The tongue-tied impediment improved as her years increased, but she always retained a sort of hesitance before speaking and had a curious habit of over-aspiration, as if determined to speak clearly. Some words she never mastered at all. She always said 'skukkle' when she meant 'scuttle' and 'bokkle' for 'bottle'. She had immense energy but her mind never quite caught up with her body. She never quite got anything right, unless it concerned her fingers or what is now known as Domestic Science. She was a superb needlewoman in every branch of that art, she could make a bridal robe or a loose cover with equal dexterity and her darns were invisible. As a cook she was a *Cordon Bleu*, she could have turned out a banquet as well as any famous Chef. Sometimes one finds a good cook who fails at certain dishes. Miss Bessie failed at none. It did not matter if she was frying a steak or bacon, boiling a fowl, roasting a turkey, cooking a chop, dealing with any sort of game, fish, soup, or sauce, making a *soufflé* or a plum duff—it was perfection. She had a method of making little meat pasties, the secret of which she imparted to one other person only, the girl who married the Victorian Boy. To mere men they were miracles—the meat was rolled and covered with a transparent paste of such lightness that you could have wrapped Titania in it, and then she fried them. To eat those pasties was to know pure gastronomic delight. And the beauty of it was that they were not regarded as special delicacies but as a way of using up the joint. And it must be recorded in all fairness that the girl who learnt the secret learnt it thoroughly and carried on the art. Miss Bessie could cook Scotch collops as they should be cooked, and she stewed steak in a way all her own. Her steak-and-kidney puddings and pies were food for the gods. Her sauces might have caused Escoffier a pang of jealousy, her very melted butter was different to that made by anyone else and her bread sauce —well, the girl to whom she taught that art is the only one allowed to make it for her grandchildren. Her vegetables never lost their colour, and were never soggy or wet, her beans retained their flavour and their very scent. Even potatoes obliged her by being quite gay and lively food. She served mashed potatoes in a way which the Victorian Boy adored. They were squashed in a masher which forced them through a wire gauze like a myriad tiny worms; she served them white and steaming and they were delicious. Her salads were for epicures, and although the Victorian Boy has since eaten pancakes in the best restaurants in many countries and has had them served under many different names, he never found one to equal those of his Victorian Aunt Bessie. She was a Cook amongst Cooks. True, she lived in the days of plenty when even the now seemingly wild demands of Mrs. Beeton could be and were met with ease. But this was a Cook, nevertheless. She got very hot and red in the face, she breathed heavily and she sweated a bit on the upper lip whilst she cooked. It was no use talking to her at such times, she was under the spell of complete concentration. But she smiled with pride when the meal was served and partook heartily of it herself. It was just as well that few people then went on diets—they would have had a terrible time resisting Miss Bessie's dishes.

She was, too, a perfect housekeeper. She took over that department when her elder sister Maggie married her small gymnast and she ran the house and succeeding homes as houses should be run. The servants adored her—for she worked alongside them and set an example. They never shirked their work when she was in command and she never lost her temper with them. If a new girl was no good, she was treated with patience and then quietly told her failings and discharged.

Miss Bessie was very devout. She sang in the choir of the Presbyterian Church where the females of her family worshipped. She did not know one note of music from another, she had no voice at all, but she liked singing in the choir. So because she and her sisters had been original members of the congregation, were such pillars of all the church's activities and such regular worshippers, she sang in the choir for years.

She played tennis and was not a much better player than she was a singer. But she was always asked to make up a set because people liked her so much, and when the Club gave entertainments or strawberry teas she took charge of the catering—with immense success. She was really of a very gentle disposition and liked to give pleasure but she found much difficulty in expressing herself. She had much in common with Mrs. Nickleby—which allusion all Dickensians will understand. She seldom finished what she had begun to say but would wander into byroads of irrelevance into which even her own family found it impossible to follow. She would make remarks which did not seem to connect. She said to a friend, as a comment on the winter weather, 'It's cold enough for a bath.' She meant to imply that the sensation of stepping outdoors into the frigid air was similar to that of plunging into an icy bath. Some refurnishing was going on in the family and she declared that she would 'Buy the pictures at Maples. They are so good for bedsteads.' That took a good deal of working out. What she really meant was that Maples were such excellent universal providers that everything could be left to them. She was very strict in the matter of morals and exceedingly puritanical. She hated anything which was not 'ladylike'. She had never been known to swear and in moments of very great stress she would cry out 'Murder, murder, bullocks' kidneys'—a most astonishing remark to which nobody at all ever had the clue. She had not an ounce of tact, but imagined she was a diplomat. But she never spoke to wound. She had many habits which irritated—she would go round a room re-dusting it after it had been 'done'—she would alter and move about all the articles on a table laid for a meal—she had to improve and put the finishing touch. But her worst failing was a constant, unreasonable opposition to everyone else's ideas. Someone had only to say 'I shall go to the Exhibition tomorrow' to have her reply, 'Oh, I shouldn't if I were you.' It did not matter what it was, a declaration as to the purchase of new clothes, buying a bicycle, going for a day in the country, to the dentist, the doctor's, to get engaged or married—it was always the same from Miss Bessie, 'Oh . . . I shouldn't, if I were you.' When pressed for a reason, she had not any. It was—in her estimation—not wise to do it. She thus implanted seeds of doubt which often spoiled a long-cherished desire. Yet in spite of her primary opposition she would often join in the plan, carrying her doubt with her and rather marring the occasion.

She had tremendous courage, resolution and fortitude. The family met with very serious reverses in fortune. They had to give up their Victorian home. Money became a problem. Miss Bessie, who had never done a day's work outside her own house, who had lived on a high standard, immediately put her shoulder to the wheel. She got a job in charge of the linen room of a famous restaurant. How she got it is a mystery but perhaps her entire difference to the rest of the applicants, her tremendous gentility and the patent honesty which shone from her face, impressed the foreign proprietor. She ran that linen room as she had run her own home. She hated the surroundings like poison, she was contemptuous of the foreigners and their open immorality and she kept herself rigorously aloof from them all. But she did her job magnificently and never made a slip. She made great improvements in the table decorations and the flowers, she turned out the napery as it had never been done before. She earned the respect of all the staff from the manager to the lowest kitchen hand, amongst whom she was the only Briton, and a Scot and Presbyterian at that. She kept expenses down and appearances up. The Chef would send her up little delicacies and she would send her thanks. But secretly she thought she could have cooked them better and she was probably right. As soon as things got a bit better in the family finances and another home—although lodgings—was prepared, she left that job, at her brother's orders. The proprietor begged her to stay, offering her what was, in his estimation, a fabulous salary. But she went and she shook the dust of that place off her feet—for she regarded it as a sink of iniquity—and it must be admitted that there were 'private rooms' there—and she wiped it out of her memory for ever.

That period spent in Soho was the only time in which Miss Bessie was separated for long from her younger sister, Miss Mary, who must now enter the story. They were complete opposites but quite inseparable. They might have been twins, they were so much together, and yet they were so very different. Miss Mary was born in 1859 in Canonbury. She was a very fierce and warlike person and maybe the state of the world at her birth had something to do with it. Maybe also the fact that her birthday was in April and she was a real Arian. In 1859 England had cause to believe that her erstwhile ally, Louis Napoleon, was planning an invasion of these shores. He had created a great arsenal at Cherbourg and was building up a big fleet there. But England was watching. So was the Poet Laureate, Alfred, Lord Tennyson. He wrote a bugle-blast of a poem which echoed from coast to coast:

> Form, form, riflemen, form
> Ready—be ready to meet the storm.

This gave such an impetus to the Volunteer movement, which assumed such numbers and efficiency, that if the wily French Emperor had really considered an invasion, the resolute front displayed against him made him think again.

Into a world of turmoil—outside these islands—was Miss Mary born and she was able to cause plenty of turmoil herself. She was slender, and fair as a lily. She had real golden hair, like ripe corn, and her eyes were a deep sapphire blue. She carried herself with perfect poise—but all women of her period did that. Her features, although aquiline, were classical and wellnigh perfect. She was a tornado, utterly unlike Miss Bessie the calm, a person of fierce scorching rages with a whiplash for a tongue, indeed a real shrew. Later an Army Reservist who did the Garden and had seen service in China was heard to observe that if Miss Mary had been sent out to deal with the redoubtable Dowager Empress of the Celestial Land—only he called it 'Dow-agger'—there would have been no need for the Army to trouble. She could be, and was, violent in thought, speech and action. At times it was surprising that she escaped actions for slander or being bound over to keep the peace, such wild, sweeping statements would she bring, such amazing and surprising charges would she level at opponents. Yet under it all there was charm, courtesy and a warm, generous, easily touched heart.

School group of young Victorians at the High School in the Best Road. The Head Mistress is in the centre of the third row. Many of them are still alive

Top left: Victorian Milk Can
—unhygienic but nobody
died

Top right: A Victorian
Sovereign purse—and
sovereign

At left: A Mail Cart

Miss Bessie, the sister, was the perfect housekeeper. Miss Mary could not darn a sock, hem a handkerchief or boil an egg. To make a pot of tea and a bit of toast was about her limit and then the toast was likely to be burnt.

But then it was generally understood that she was 'clever', that she had brains. She herself fostered this idea. Perhaps she even believed it, but there was no foundation in actual fact. Her domestic job was the shopping. She considered herself very good at this and she was, too. She had her own methods which were effective if irregular. She did everything at top speed. She always jumped to a conclusion and nearly always the wrong one. In the end she would persuade the other side that she was right and they were wrong. She had a way of making a statement of such wildness and absurdity that the senses reeled. But she did it with great authority and nodded her head. 'Oh, yes!' she would say, 'that's a fact. Everybody knows that.' If she wanted a thing to be true, then true it was. She would invent conditions on the spur of the moment to get things her own way. People travelling with her would discover to their own astonishment that they were just convalescent after a long and dangerous illness and must not suffer the slightest inconvenience. By that means she got attended to out of her turn, made fellow passengers vacate corner seats and even persuaded guards into giving her and her companions a first-class carriage to themselves, despite third-class tickets. She did it at public gatherings and other places of resort. She always succeeded. She was quite unscrupulous in such matters and would utter complete fabrications. It appeared that she always knew someone in authority and would quote a name made up on the spur of the moment. She did this with such confidence that even the underlings she battled with—who had never heard the name—were shaken and never quite sure. She seemed so assured—she was so obviously a lady—and a pretty one—and they gave way. But she must now pursue her way jointly with her sister Bessie as she did in life. . . .

H

CHAPTER EIGHT

Victorian Spinsters

UNLIKE Miss Bessie, Miss Mary did not play tennis. Nor did she sing in the choir. She indulged in no outdoor sports—except very long walks—because she had a very delicate skin. She was actually a skin short, which gave her a wonderful complexion but upon which the sun must never shine. So she was always veiled and in summer carried a parasol. To make up for the lack of tennis and singing, she was a keen politician. She took sides as violently in this as in everything else. She was the most zealous of partisans, and her politics, like those of her Family, were Liberal. To say that she understood anything about it would be to overstate grievously, but she was perfectly sure that the Tories were wrong and wicked and the Liberals right and holy. That was enough for her. At election times she worked like a beaver for the Liberal Candidate in her constituency and never once in her long life was she on the winning side.

Because of her 'brains' and 'cleverness', she was a most active member of the Literary Society of her Church, which she called 'The Lit'. She was very critical of the efforts of others, unless she approved of them personally. She was always quite unfair. There was one man who had a good deal of self-confidence and bounce but very little else, whom she was convinced was a 'genius'. She said so to everyone and she told him so to his face. He agreed with her, to her great delight. When her Victorian nephew grew into an Edwardian young man and entered the Theatrical profession he also showed a tendency to write. He used to write 'papers' for his Aunt Mary to deliver at her 'Lit' meetings. She claimed those papers as her own, quite shamelessly. He would also, with his fiancée who was a beautiful singer, help to illustrate those 'papers' with recitation, song and little acted scenes. Much kudos accrued to

Miss Mary. It must be admitted that the choice of the subject was usually her own and would mostly be the works of some obscure poet or author about whom little was known. That she knew was held up as an example of her cleverness. Those 'papers' of Miss Mary's were quite occasions in that church hall. She usually managed to start the evening with a row, falling foul of one of the Committee—grown men whom she had known in their youth and whom she still regarded as boys—and to whom she referred as 'Young So-and-So' although they would be in their forties. When quite an old lady she decided she would become a *raconteuse*. She cut stories from newspapers and periodicals and pestered her friends to tell her 'new' ones. They were all of complete cleanliness, of course. She would tell these stories from the platform at 'The Lit' and get away with it. She did not tell them well, having no sense of timing at all, but then few of the members could have done better. It is probable that she regarded herself as a 'genius'—a title she was fond of bestowing, as above.

She and her sister Bessie were keen theatregoers. They went to all the shows, mostly in the pit at matinées. In the earlier days of their play-going there were no queues, just a shapeless crowd lumped against the entrance ready to fight it out to the last gasp. Somehow or other Miss Bessie and Miss Mary, though frequently late arrivals, always managed to get into the front row. Although it does not sound likely, Miss Bessie was the spearhead in these manœuvres. She looked a perfect lady and she could make her usually placid face quite expressionless. Without seeming effort, she would progress through a tough crowd right to the very front, with head erect and eyes looking straight before her. She would be followed by her sister Mary, who made considerable use of her elbows, parasol or umbrella. But it was Miss Bessie who cleared the way. She did it by the simple process of kicking the ankles of the people before her. As they gave ground and stared angrily around to see who had done it, she slipped into their place, her sister behind her. Miss Mary consolidated the ground thus gained. Miss Bessie looked so innocent, so unconcerned, that nobody ever suspected her. Accusations were hurled against people who were guiltless, and in the scuffling that often occurred the sisters made further progress. They did this in all sorts of crowds, not only outside theatres, and it never failed.

These ladies, once inside the theatre and seated in the front row, spent far more time staring about them to see if there was anyone there they knew than in watching the play. They had a tremendous number of acquaintances and would gaze around hoping to see one. If they did, their cup of happiness was full. Sometimes they did not know the person's name, but that made little difference. The one who had spotted the acquaintance (it might be only someone they knew by sight) would nudge the other and say, "Look, there's Mrs. Err-err-err." Then they would both stare hard and try to catch the lady's eye. This being achieved they bowed and would get a bow and a smile in return. That gave them great joy and thereafter they watched 'Mrs. Err-err-err' to the detriment of the play. If no acquaintance were visible they did give some attention to the traffic on the stage and often knew quite a bit about it when they came home. One man could compel their entire attention and that was Lewis Waller. Even 'Mrs. Err-err-err' had no chance with him. And on the musical side, Hayden Coffin held them entranced. Their great heroes were Tree, George Alexander, Charles Hawtrey, Wyndham, H. B. Irving and Martin Harvey—as they went down the years. As regards actresses they esteemed Ellen Terry, Mrs. Kendal, Julia Neilson (who they said was really beautiful), Marie Tempest and Mrs. Patrick Campbell, and, later on, Irene Vanbrugh. They fulfilled the best traditions of British Theatregoing by eating steadily the whole time they were in the playhouse, and on one occasion, when seated in the upper circle of the Haymarket Theatre at an important first night, Miss Mary dropped a tin sandwich case which rolled down the stairs and upset everyone. Miss Mary was concerned only with the trouble of getting it back. They were great supporters of the Gaiety in the times of Fred Leslie, Nellie Farren, Florence St. John and Sylvia Grey, and would talk about them often. But apart from Gilbert and Sullivan and the Gaiety they did not patronize many musical shows unless Hayden Coffin was playing. Then they went. They would have died rather than enter a Music Hall. They did not applaud much. If very thrilled they would hammer on the floor with their umbrellas. But if anything offended them and their ideas of propriety they would hiss loudly. They adored amateur dramatic performances because they knew nearly everyone in the audience—they did not worry much about the play or the poor players. For the same reason, when films became popular, they had little use for them. One could not stare at a 'Mrs. Err-err-err' in the dark. It is doubtful if the cinema would ever have held their attention. When Miss Mary was an old lady she went to see a film in which her nephew appeared. She could give no clear account of it at all afterwards, but on leaving she had met a friend she called 'Mrs. J. L.', so the day was successful. She was also taken to see her great-niece, whom she adored, make her début in pantomime at Drury Lane. She spent a great deal of time gazing around her and then, her attention drifting to the stage, she suddenly recognized her great-niece thereon. She stood up in her stall, waved violently and called out 'Coo-ee'. She was promptly pulled down by her great-niece's mother, who was properly scandalized. Toole was a favourite with these ladies, as was Edward Terry. They had a favourite play, *The Birthplace of Podgers*—quite forgotten now but written by John Hollingshead who founded the Gaiety. They knew that almost by heart. Strangely enough it was the vague Miss Bessie who seemed to retain more of a play than Miss Mary. During conversations about the Theatre—and people really discussed it then, there being no television —she would suddenly quote lines from a play she had seen, needless to say not the one under discussion—but certainly a quotation, rather in the manner of Mr. F.'s aunt in *Little Dorrit*, and she could cause quite as much consternation.

They had enjoyed *Liberty Hall* and would always laugh at the memory of George Alexander cutting sandwiches. It amused Miss Bessie, the expert in such things, most of all. They revelled in seeing their nephew act, and in their opinion he was the best actor in the country. They loved him dearly and they had, to a large extent, brought him up. They lavished on him all the love which would have gone to their own children. He could do no wrong from babyhood to the end of their days. They had in a way the gift of perpetual youth, for to them people who had been young when they were young remained young forever. Their brothers and their brothers' friends were always 'The Boys'—even when in their sixties. Their sisters and their childhood friends were to them always 'The Girls'. With them, time could stand still. They were, of course, Victorians and therefore from today's standpoint 'Back Numbers'. To them, the Male was the master. The man always knew what to do, he must be followed and obeyed even against their own judgment. They always did exactly as their brother James told them and then they obeyed their nephew when he succeeded his Uncle. He often had trouble with them. He would take them out for a day in the country, which they adored. He had to treat them rather like a flock of sheep and herd them. They were not good travellers. They would stand on a platform waiting for a train. When it came in and there was a perfectly good and almost empty compartment right opposite them, they found it necessary—unless under his strict control—to run wildly up and down looking for a full one, into which they would crowd themselves. Taking them out for the day was a little wearing but he would often do it to give them pleasure. Their attitude to men was completely Victorian. But if they did not like a man—woe betide him. They did not like their nephew's Father and that man had cause to know and rue it. But they adored his boy and spoilt him, making great personal sacrifices for him at the time of their hardship. He had enough of his Uncle James in him not to forget that and he was able to do something towards repaying their kindness in later life.

In due course, when his own daughter arrived, Bessie and Mary became her abject slaves. She was the Wonder Child who could do no wrong and she did as she liked with them. They loved all children and all children loved them, but those of their own family naturally they loved most of all, although the Victorian Boy was an easy favourite. He was orphaned young and to him went all their frustrated maternal instincts.

They abhorred anything 'fast', they deprecated anything unladylike. They both dressed quite well but Miss Mary was the most 'stylish' of the two. She could carry colours; Miss Bessie wore darker things and liked a blue dress with white spots thereon. When Miss Mary went off in the morning on her shopping expeditions, many eyes regarded her from behind the lace curtains, to see what she had on, and many male heads turned. A French gentleman living a few doors away was a great admirer of hers—he considered her quite beautiful. He was to become Father-in-Law of the Victorian Boy. He bowed deeply and treated her with the greatest respect when the children of the family became friendly. She treated him with kindly condescension as became a Scottish lady unbending to a foreigner. Both she and her sister were intensely Scottish although born in Canonbury. To accompany Miss Mary on her shopping foray was quite an experience. She would go from shop to shop 'pricing' things. There were regular shops at which the Family dealt, there were others at which Miss Mary made occasional purchases. She would compare not only prices but also goods. Useless for a provision merchant to hold a large slab of bacon in his hand, regard it fondly and say, 'Fine piece of bacon, that.' Miss Mary would immediately tell him that his rival across the way had much better bacon in stock and would draw upon her very vivid imagination as regards the competitive price. She nearly drove the shopkeepers mad but they were all anxious to serve her. They wanted the custom of this family which bought largely and paid cash. Miss Mary carried with her either a shopping basket or a string bag, into which she placed articles wanted at home urgently. The rest were sent up by van, cart or errand boy. No lady need carry anything home if she did not want to. Shopkeepers deemed it their duty to deliver the goods and they did so in every sense of the word. There was no extra charge for this. It was part of the service. Nowadays this service is seldom forthcoming. Why it is impossible for deliveries to be made nobody knows.

Miss Mary carried some things, had others sent home. They got there in good time because shopkeepers knew that they got their living and their assistants' wages from the customer. She also shopped at a large confectioner's. They sold bread, all sorts of pastries and specialized in cream gateaux. They also sold light refreshments, cakes, ices, coffee, tea, lemonade and they had a licence for liquor to be consumed on the premises. They did a roaring trade. Ladies who would not have dreamed of entering a public house—such things were not done—dropped in there during the morning, making quite a journey so to do, to recover from the ardours of shopping by partaking of a little drop of 'something'. Maybe it was a glass of stout, or a Guinness, a glass of port or sherry—and sometimes something a bit shorter and stronger. The place was a gold mine. There was nothing derogatory at all in having a drink in there, but if any of those ladies had been seen entering or leaving a real public house—it would have been social ruin. The firm had a hall adjacent which was a centre for social gatherings and dances, marriage receptions and the like and the catering was splendid. Miss Mary would drop in —to her nephew's delight if he were with her—for she bought many cream gateaux. She did not imbibe any strong refreshment—although she was by no means a teetotaller—but she would have some coffee and would buy the boy a special confection only obtainable at that place. It was a kind of basket made of ice wafer with a handle made of angelica and filled with some form of cream—not ice cream proper but of the same consistency, and pink—which was perfectly lovely to eat and never met with elsewhere. The shop still flourishes but maybe the goods have changed.

There was also near that licensed caterers another little café which that Victorian Boy appreciated. There were no milk bars then, and the Aerated Bread Company was in its infancy, but there were little cafés, just the same—before the white shop fronts of the Lyons' enterprise spread far and wide. The one Miss Mary patronized was on the first floor, over a shop devoted to a different business altogether. It made no display save a discreet little hanging sign. It was near a famous public house which is still a fare stage and not far from an equally famous prison now devoted to female convicts. It was full of atmosphere. You went up some steep steps and pushed through a beaded curtain and were immediately presented with North London's version of the Orient. There was a lot of glassware about, Japanese prints on the wall, and Chinese figures everywhere. There were joss sticks for sale and sometimes one burned to increase the atmosphere. The staple drink was coffee. With the coffee were served biscuits which never seemed obtainable elsewhere. Some were white and round, a cross between a sweet and cheese biscuit, and the others resembled miniature sponge cakes but were harder, crunchier and very nice indeed. The Boy liked going to that café and having those biscuits. He kept the semi-sponges to the last. And sometimes he got cream with his coffee. Those were the days, indeed. . . .

Going shopping with Aunt Mary had its points though there were bad moments when draper shops had to be entered—moments not only of boredom but of acute embarrassment. The only bright spot was that sometimes there was an overhead railway along which the money rolled, screwed up in wooden balls, and change and receipt came back the same way. To work one of those would have been joy indeed. The Boy never achieved it. He regarded them as miracles of mechanical skill. They almost made up for the horror of being spoken to by the shopwalker or the young lady attendant. But Aunt Mary was very good. She never hurried by a toy shop and there were several on the route, if they walked. One sold toy soldiers separately—a penny each. That shop was never passed without a purchase.

Neither of these two sisters ever married, and in an age when marriage was the ultimate ambition of womenkind that might have been considered a great failure, but it is doubtful if either of them cared. Certainly not Miss Bessie, who was the complete virgin. To her any thought of carnal passion or sexual embrace was completely abhorrent. She could not understand it at all. Yet both had known Romance. They had attracted young men. Miss Bessie perhaps had only one real heart-stir. She would sigh when she recalled it in later years. He had, it appeared, been tall and handsome but—it could not be. For in the parlance of these two ladies this young man, who shall be called Charles Winter although that was not his name, 'had a weakness'. They would drop their voices when they said that and stare at the person who received the confidence. If the confidante did not quite understand, they would amplify the information by saying simply 'He took.' What they meant by that was that the young man was not of a sober disposition, that he liked the bottle, that he got drunk. They were far too ladylike to say such a thing but whenever this was the case about any of their friends that was the euphemism they employed: 'He has a weakness—he takes.' It was a by no means common failing then. Miss Bessie had not married the young man with the weakness, however taking his ways may have been. There she showed that innate good sense of hers which was so seldom expressed. In the garden of that Victorian House was a very hideous affair. It was made of earthenware, massive and solid, and was roughly in the shape of a very dead tree trunk. It was of a vile red-brown colour and it had holes where branches might have been before they decayed and fell off, and a hollowed-out top. That top and those holes were filled with mould in which flowers fought for existence and seldom won. It seemed to blight everything. This thing was called 'Charles Winter's Grave'. Why, was never clear. Had he proposed to Miss Bessie beside it; had he presented it to her as token of his affection or had she, in a flash of imagination far beyond her usual range, metaphorically buried her heart and her romance in this thing which symbolized her lost and only love?

Miss Mary had several love affairs which reached the 'understanding' stage but never got to marriage. If the men had only known, they had narrow escapes. Only Petruchio would have stood a chance with this Victorian 'Katherine', who was useless in the house although highly decorative. Yet she loved children and had a most uncanny understanding of them. She knew their minds, she could invent games on the spur of the moment which were exactly right. She knew what the children wanted and what they thought. She was always the centre of a group of children when any were around. Miss Bessie loved them too, but was a bit shy —although much more reliable. Although denied Romance themselves, Miss Bessie and Miss Mary took a delight in watching it in others. They would be the first to see any budding attraction, especially at their church. They would announce that a certain young man was 'after' a certain young lady. They would watch the affair closely and if they observed the two taking a stroll together would nod their heads and say 'It's a case.' They were nearly always right. They were not above doing a bit of match-making themselves and were successful at it.

To Miss Bessie and Miss Mary, churchgoing meant a lot. It was the hub of their lives and most social events radiated from it. They were most critical of the sermons. Otherwise they stared about them a good deal and took stock of the congregation, every soul of which they knew. They were parted in church for many years, for Miss Bessie sang in the choir, or was at any rate a member of it—and Miss Mary did not. So Miss Bessie had the best view, for the choir was perched in the gallery. On their walk home they would compare notes of the dresses and hats worn, of the general demeanour of the people present, on what they had observed in the progress of the various 'cases', whether their friends appeared to be in good or bad health and especially about any strangers that might have been present. They would speculate on who they might be and why they had come. Sometimes they would attend evening services at other places of worship than their own to hear a preacher who was reputed to be good. They travelled quite long distances to do that. They seldom went to a Church of England—they had nothing at all against the Episcopalians but they thought on the whole the preaching was poor. There were in their day some wonderful preachers in the Non-Conforming Ministry and doubtless there are still. When a sort of peripatetic preacher appeared in their district who had a 'name', they would take their nephew, much against his will, to hear him. But he was to thank them for the opportunity of having heard Dr. Parker, the Rev. R. J. Campbell (neither of them peripatetic, of course) and an evangelist named George Clarke, who was a Congregationalist, if memory serves. He came from America and he wore a frock coat of excellent cut and he looked—and preached—like an actor, and a very good actor. He was a good-looking man and his photographs sold well. And there was the Rev. Mark Guy Pearce—whose appearance was as wonderful as his sermons. One of them, concerning oysters in the North Sea, lingers in the Boy's memory yet.

The spinsters were inseparable in their churchgoing and also in their devotion to church work. They both devoted much time to the various activities and especially to the work of the Mission which that church ran in a rather slummy district not far away. Here the church's section of the Boys' Brigade had an annual display and inspection and some retired general would don his uniform and come down to inspect the lads. He was regaled with an excellent tea prepared by Miss Bessie and with conversation by Miss Mary—who never did any real work. She would often take the Boy with her, who was much impressed with these old soldiers and would stand stiffly to attention and wriggle with pride if spoken to—as he always was. He was not allowed to join the Boys' Brigade, although he wanted to. Socially, it was beneath his station. But he envied those inferior lads their smart pillbox caps, their belts, their white haversacks and their hammerlock guns. He knew the drill backwards. The two ladies were prominent at the Rummage Sales held in that mission hall. Again Miss Bessie looked after the catering. The Boy enjoyed those—but often he regarded the rubbish to be sold in the light of treasures. He proved quite a good salesman, however, and once persuaded a grim-looking burly man, accompanied by his wife, to buy two old dress shirts, very stiff-fronted, for twopence each. The man turned out to be a coal-heaver.

Miss Mary was most active on committees. She was on every committee possible in connection with the church and never kept her views to herself. She went beyond that in committee activity. She was on the local British Women's Temperance Association, although anything but a teetotaller, the Women's Liberal Association and many more. And when, late in her life, the League of Nations came into being, she got on the local committee for that—and even succeeded in being elected the local delegate for central meetings. She understood little about it—but she could—and did—talk. Miss Bessie seldom opened her mouth in public but was always on a sub-committee which did the practical work. Miss Mary also attended what were called 'Working Parties'—needlework was the job—but she did no sewing. She could not sew.

After their childhood, they took their holidays separately, for the tastes of these two ladies ran in different directions in this respect. Miss Bessie liked seaside resorts but they had to be at some distance. She never patronized Brighton, Hastings, Eastbourne, Folkestone or the handy and popular places. She preferred Stonehaven, Tenby, Aberystwyth, Llandudno, Ilfracombe and Swanage. She would stay at a nice hotel and do a lot of walking. She would pick up a few friends and take trips with them. In the evening she invariably sat in the hotel drawing room —nearly always the only person so to do. That was her idea of a holiday and she did it. She may have had a hazy idea that it impressed the others. She was seldom able, on her return, to give any clear description of what she had seen or done, but there was usually just one thing which had struck her above all others and she would mention this with great impressiveness. She gave no description of it—she just mentioned the name and stared at the person with whom she was in conversation. She was never more impressive in this respect than after a visit to Swanage. All the following winter, when she was asked where she had spent her holiday she would reply 'Swanage' and then, after a slight pause, with unusually clear enunciation and immense emphasis on the letter 'H', she would say, 'Tilly Whim Caves.' She would then nod at the person addressed. It was enough. The complete description of her holiday. Whether the caves themselves or their curious name had impressed her nobody ever knew. But if anyone mentioned Swanage she would always say, 'Tilly Whim Caves.' The memory stayed with her, as did 'The Great Orme's Head' after a visit to Llandudno—and again the 'H' was over-aspirated. . . .

Miss Mary did not go to the seaside, it did not suit her skin. She had always to protect that—with her veils and double-lined parasols. Miss Bessie had a skin which stood all weather and went brown by the sea with no preparatory red stage at all. So Miss Mary chose the country. She had a perfect army of old friends scattered up and down the kingdom, to say nothing of relatives, and she kept in touch with them all by long discursive letters which she believed were miracles of correspondence. She would go to tiny, remote and unheard-of villages in Leicestershire where somebody she knew lived and make the whole village wonder who and what she was. She got into the depths of Staffordshire, Yorkshire, Westmorland and Cumberland and would do the rounds of her relations in Scotland. She much preferred staying with friends to going to hotels. She believed she was very welcome. For a few days it is probable that she was—but she made a lot of work and was always inclined to argue and put people right. Her own happiest memories were of a time spent in Harrogate—for the 'Cure,' she said—and at the Gairloch in Scotland—she stayed at Hydros each time—and these, with a visit to the English lakes and sojourns at a village called Newabbey on the borders of Dumfries and Kircudbrightshire, were, to her, Heaven. She wrote long letters home of the most rambling nature and all sprinkled with the phrase 'I must tell you'—but she never did it clearly—and there were always floods of picture postcards to mark her trail. It was often a wonder to the rest of her family that her visits did not kill her friendships, but somehow these survived.

Like her sister, she had no tact at all, although she believed she oozed it. If there was a subject in a family which was taboo, that was the very subject about which she talked. On being told that it was distasteful and that they did not want to hear—and often she was told so quite bluntly—she would stop for a moment and then continue in a lower tone of voice. Nothing could deflect her from saying what she wanted to say. She was not going to 'lose face' by being told to shut up. The fact that her conversation matter annoyed and even hurt people did not affect her in the least. She was interested in what she had to say, to her it was news and that was that. Her dropped voice was the one concession to other people's feelings. Yet in times of trouble or sickness she was a tower of strength.

Miss Bessie and Miss Mary liked to see everything that was going on and their nephew benefited by that. For they took him with them if it did not interrupt his schooling and even sometimes when it did. They—and consequently he—missed nothing. Foreign royalties *en route* for the Guildhall found them in the crowds, and also any celebrities who were entertained by the Corporation of the City of London. And here that pushing enterprise of Miss Bessie's was most helpful. Lord Kitchener drove to the Guildhall after his re-conquest of the Sudan. The Boy wanted to see him badly for he thought he was marvellous. They got to Queen Victoria Street rather late and the crowd was dense. But Miss Mary saw some workmen doing something to a church before which there was a small yard and railings. She had a word with them. Those men erected for her a miniature grandstand of planks and the Boy saw his hero admirably. He also, for the first time, saw a woman faint— who went a wonderful shade of pea-green before she passed out. That impressed him almost as much as Kitchener. They took the Boy to the Crystal Palace twice a year, to the pantomimes, and often to the Theatre if suitable for him (and they were not narrow-minded), to the Egyptian Hall to see Maskelyne and Cook and afterwards Maskelyne and Devant. Incidentally he saw a minimum of three pantomimes a year—often four —one of them always being at Drury Lane, with which he had family connections. With those Victorian spinsters he saw volunteer reviews, assaults-at-arms, the City Imperial Volunteers (the C.I.V., satirized as Chamberlain's Innocent Victims) depart for and return from the Boer War—he wants to do those gallant gentlemen every justice, but he retains the impression that many of them were slightly inebriated on both occasions—it may have been patriotism, of course; to the Diamond Jubilee (in reserved seats in St. Paul's Churchyard provided by Uncle James); to the funeral of Queen Victoria—in Hyde Park on a bitter morning. Here they were in the crowd and Miss Bessie and Miss Mary were well wrapped up, and to defeat cold feet wore stockings outside their boots as well, which earned them a good many jeers of which they took no notice. And when the procession passed by—thanks to Miss Bessie's special powers of crowd penetration—they were in the front row.

They took him to regattas on the Thames, to all the museums, places of interest and the sights of London. They were all nearly killed at the corner of St. James's Street and King Street when viewing the Diamond Jubilee illuminations, but they got home all right. They never took him to a cricket match but they did go once to a Rugby Football match, probably because one of the 'Boys' was playing. The Victorian Boy believes it was London Scottish *v.* Blackheath. But there was considerable confusion caused by Miss Mary getting the heel of her boot between two boards. She was trapped. Maiden modesty prevented her removing her boot in public and quite a crowd got round to help her extricate her foot. He remembers little of the match. However, they took him everywhere and he saw everything. Even the immense and revelling crowds for Mafeking did not deter them. They were in the thick of it. There were regular trips to Hampton Court, to Epping Forest, to the Chilterns and even to Leith Hill and Hindhead—quite expeditions then. In later life the Boy often wondered how they survived, for the two ladies were never at any time traffic conscious. In the more distant days they were not in any great peril, although they crossed the road suddenly when the spirit moved them. They paid no attention to what was coming towards them or from behind them. In the days of horse traffic this could be done —but they were, even then, in constant danger of cyclists. They were often nearly run down but the cyclist usually managed to escape this, though he frequently came a purler and hurt himself. The spinsters would be most incensed with him and accuse him of being at fault. 'You lost control of your machine,' they would tell him severely. They always got away with it. How they escaped destruction in the days of motors defeats imagination. They still crossed the road in their own manner. In such things they were a law unto themselves. They were wrapped in the impenetrable armour of the old and celebrated Scottish name which they bore. They were, therefore, not as other people. Bye-laws and road regulations were not for them as they were not for Royalty. In the Second World War when Miss Mary was a very old lady (Miss Bessie had died in 1931) she refused to have anything to do with the

Black Out. It—and Hitler—meant nothing to her. When wardens came angrily she simply stated her name and expected them to apologize for their rude intrusion. But her nephew told her it had to be done and said he ordered it, then she obeyed. She thought it stupid, but she obeyed. He was a Man and she was a Victorian.

Both ladies were great cat lovers and all cats adored them. They always had one of their own and fed numerous strays.

In their old age they became members of a club which provided bowls for the men and croquet for the ladies. That they loved. And Miss Mary became quite a good croquet player—actually winning the club championship on one occasion. They were enthusiastic onlookers at the bowling matches and made friends with the visiting team. They always found somebody with whom they shared mutual friends. They were rather a nuisance but everyone knew them and liked them. They bored their friends stiff with stories of their wonder nephew and he had a great deal to live down. So he seldom accompanied them to their beloved club, although for a considerable period he paid their subscriptions.

Neither of them ever quite conquered a fear of what they called 'wireless'. In their day it was crystal sets and headphones. Miss Mary got along best. Miss Bessie always found it necessary to bend herself double in order to hear and it is probable she did not understand what she heard. For if there was something to which the others wanted particularly to listen, that was the moment she chose to make a great rustling of paper or other penetrating noise. Neither liked the telephone. Miss Bessie, if rung up whilst busy with housework, would always remove her apron before answering and go very red. She was also terrified of signing a cheque. When an account was opened for her and she had to go to the Bank, she suffered agonies of mind for several days beforehand and it took her quite a while to recover. Her nephew went with her— or she would have fled the ordeal. As it was, she sat still and sweated. Naturally, she forgot what was the specimen signature she had given, but the nephew remembered and told Miss Mary, who saw that Miss Bessie got it right.

Neither of the ladies ever swore, smoked or drank a cocktail. They never used make-up—save a dusting of powder at times. They never appeared untidy or badly dressed. They would have died at the thought of wearing trousers. They were modest and circumspect, they would never have looked at a doubtful picture—they hurried the Victorian Boy past nude statues and pictures in Museums, galleries and the Royal Academy—or listened to a *risqué* story or read a salacious book. But they were great readers of fiction. They gave handsomely to charity and they had a band of retainers of their own who called at the house and were given old clothing, old boots, and broken meats and stale bread. They were always thanked profusely (a few coppers went with the gift, as well), but as old garments, boots, bones and bits of bread were often observed dumped in the gutter near the house, it is doubtful if the 'pieces' were really appreciated. One old couple, however, never forsook them until death removed them. This was an old man and his wife, who were inmates of a workhouse and allowed out together on Sundays. Miss Bessie and Miss Mary saw them picking up cigarette ends in the road. So every Sunday they were told to call and they got a bit of tobacco for the old man, some tea for the old lady and a little sugar, sixpence each and some fruit. The nephew once contributed a pipe for the old man. This couple were really grateful. The old lady died first but the old man called until he, too, died.

They bickered continually, these two spinsters, but they understood and loved each other. They lived together until Miss Bessie died of a stroke in 1931. It was thought that Miss Mary would not survive her long. But she did. She had great vitality and a strong hold on life, which she loved. She clung to it and her relations. That nephew looked after both of them for years, and his wife helped him nobly and they both loved her as if she was actually of their blood and not just somebody who had married into the family. Miss Mary died in 1942, at the age of eighty-three. She outlived all her family but one—her eldest sister Maggie. So Miss Mary went into the Family Grave and was the last for whom there was room. She was reunited with that family she adored. She and her sister Bessie were together again. Both their funeral services were conducted by their own Minister, the Rev. H. T. Lewis, now in charge of a much more important church, but a good man if ever there was one. They were odd but remarkable women, utterly unselfish. Never once did they put themselves first. They always did their duty as they saw it and tried to live Christian lives. They had been brought up that way by Pa and Ma and that training abided.

Utter Back Numbers, of course—but true Victorians.

CHAPTER NINE

Very Tragical Mirth

Iᶠ the story of Pyramus and Thisbe as performed by the rude mechanicals at the wedding of Theseus and his bride Hippolyta was described in *A Midsummer Night's Dream* as very tragical mirth, so must the lives of the last two members of the Victorian Family be designated. They were a brother and sister but that was the only link between them. Complete opposites in all save name and the family characteristic of pride therein and of loyalty and duty, they were as unlike in manner and mode of life as they were in appearance. The elder of the two was a boy, whose name was John. He was the mirthful side of the tragedy—yet there was perhaps tragedy in his mirth, tragedy of a wasted life. His sister, the baby of the Family, was named Frederica, after that handsome Norwegian lady whom her Uncle Peter had married—the man who would speak nothing but English and who treated Germans in their own country as if they were foreigners. Frederica was the seventh child, but that mystic figure brought her no luck. She had not a glimpse of it in all her short life—she was the mother of the Victorian Boy of these pages, and he has not had a great deal of luck either—although his life-span has doubled that of his Mother's.

John, the boy, was born in 1861, in the home at Canonbury, the birthplace of Frederica, too.

To those young people who think that all Victorians were stuffy, straitlaced hypocrites, the figure of Uncle John will come as something of a shock. He was a strong, sturdy boy who grew eventually into a man of immense physical strength, with strength of mind in the reverse ratio. He was on the red side of family colouring, he was a chestnut inclined to ginger and had blue eyes. He was sent to a good school but absorbed little learning. He was not interested in that, but in having a good time and in Rugby Football; cycling and gymnastics had little appeal to him but he knew how to use his fists. He had to abide by discipline whilst Pa was alive, but even as a small child he would lure his sisters into trouble by his reckless ways. But Pa died when he was fourteen years of age and Uncle James became responsible. When John left school he was taken into the family business, which was a mistake. The trouble was that he was always let have his own way.

He was pure Victorian. He had all there was to have of that age, its virtues and its vices. He believed in his own family above all others, he was sure his name was the most illustrious in the world, was quite sure that his race was the salt of the earth and just as sure that all foreigners were objects of contempt tempered by pity. Although he was never completely sober, he never did a mean or dirty action, never broke his word, never did anyone any harm and would go out of his way to do anyone a good turn. He was immensely generous, his tips were princely but he never earned a copper by his own efforts all his life. His drinking was hardly a vice, as in other men, it was just his hobby, his way of life, and strangely enough it never interfered with his appetite, which was enormous, matching his huge frame. He never had a hangover because of the permanent state of alcoholism and in that maybe he scored.

Big in every way he had a remarkably powerful bass voice, quite untrained but yet musical. He liked to sing. He preferred songs of a maritime type and made the house shake when he sang them. He would get his nephew's fiancée to play the accompaniments when she came on the scene; she was an accomplished pianiste and singer herself, and he would oblige with a song about his 'Polly' which turned out to be a fishing smack or some small vessel which was 'Lying agin the quay'. He would bellow 'The Midshipmite'—a ballad of the Crimean War. Those were his favourites but he would give the Army a chance with 'Boys of the Old Brigade' and 'The Seventh Royal Fusiliers'. He sang when he felt happy and was liable to burst forth at any time, anywhere. He did not mind or care whether other people liked it or not. He did. He had good manners but it was difficult to keep him quiet, if he was enjoying himself. He would hail people who were at great distances from him and start conversations in a voice of thunder, like 'Cap'n Cuttle' in *Dombey and Son*. The best thing to do was to hurry to him and greet him, thus shutting him up. Utterly sure of himself and of his superiority over all other men—his brother James always excepted—he would be furious if his requests, which to him seemed reasonable enough however outrageous they appeared to others, were not dealt with at once. He and his family all went to Llandudno for a holiday—and when this

I

happened the whole town knew about it. They embarked on a steamer trip and it got rough. He did not mind, for he was a good sailor, but it was a little too rough for his beloved wife Maria, who was not at all fond of the sea. It blew half a gale, the pleasure steamer bobbed about like a cork; Maria and many other ladies were sick and scared. Uncle John took immediate action. He sent his compliments to the Captain and asked that the boat should be turned round and make for home. The Captain, very naturally, ignored the request. Uncle John sent a stronger message drawing attention to the state of the ladies and intimating that he would contribute a Five Pound Note as a salve to any feelings the Captain might have for turning back. The Captain sent back a message to the effect that no power on earth, not even the King (Edward VII), could make him put back. Uncle John sent his ultimatum. He told the Captain what HIS name was and bade him turn his rotten little boat at once or else he—Uncle John—would come and do it for him. It took half the crew and all of Uncle John's family and friends (he was treating half the visitors at the hotel to the trip) to restrain him from putting his threat into action. His son and the First Officer got him down into the Saloon and there whisky produced a more mellow effect. He sent the Captain a bottle of whisky as he went ashore at the end of the trip. On the same holiday they took another steamer trip up a river, on a very small steamer indeed, which stuck on a sandbank. There was a village with an inn adjacent. Uncle John organized supplies and it was a very hilarious lot of trippers—and ship's company—which finally arrived at the journey's end.

John was, on the whole, a well-dressed man, unlike his brother in that respect. He was most particular about his linen. The local laundry in the good suburb in which he lived did not suit him; he heard of one which operated from the City. Once a week he took all his shirts and collars (all with starched fronts as to the shirts and high as to the collars) up in a portmanteau and nobody was supposed to know what was therein. He would have felt degraded had anyone known he was carrying dirty linen. It was collected from and returned to his office. One day, as he got out of his first-class compartment at Liverpool Street in what was then the rush hour—though nobody nowadays would have recognized its gentleness—at about 8.45 a.m., the portmanteau flew open and all the dirty linen was strewn over the platform. Collars entwined themselves round the legs of hurrying City merchants, shirts flew about in the breeze in the most embarrassing manner. Uncle John, his face expressionless, kept straight on his way. Disregarding the attempts of the few who had seen what had happened to apprise him of the fact, he took not the slightest notice of anything or anybody. He cast off and forsook that linen and wiped it from his mind. He went into the refreshment room and had a pretty stiff drink. He never brought his washing to town again. He had to replace all that was lost, but prices were as cheap as the materials were good—and anyway, he had saved his face.

But it put him off railway trains. For years afterwards he travelled down to the City by private bus. A number of gentlemen hired one collectively and it would call at their houses and pick them up, driving them to the City non-stop, dropping some at their offices and others at a central spot, collecting them in the evenings and delivering them to their homes. It was, of course, a horse bus. The gentlemen were all friends and the driver and conductor were treated like old retainers and did very well. The passengers wrapped themselves in travelling rugs in winter, read their papers, chatted and smoked—which was not allowed inside buses even in those days—and it was very pleasant indeed. In summer they rode on top. The only disturbing factor was Uncle John's habit of dropping into song—but they knew and understood him. The return journey was not accomplished with the speed of the outgoing one. A habit was formed—when Uncle John joined the little community —of stopping at a pub which they christened The Half Way House— though its regular users knew it by another name. Here the gentlemen would drink sherry and bitters or gin and bitters—mostly orange or peach—to get an appetite for dinner. Cocktails were unknown. The driver and conductor stuck to beer. Uncle John stuck to whisky—he needed no *apéritif*. There were a great number of these private buses in use in all parts of London. It worked out—refreshments included— at slightly less than the first-class return fare by train and was much more pleasant.

John and Maria lived in a very nice road, just off the Best Road in their particular neighbourhood. The Best Road was an affair of great mansions each standing in several acres of grounds and in many cases backing on to two reservoirs. There was a little bridge which carried the Best Road over the stream which joined these great lakes and it was quite rural. One might have been miles from London instead of a mere five. The reservoirs were veritable sanctuaries for wildfowl. It was all very rich, seemingly stable and enduring. Today council houses cover the site of those mansions. More people live there, of course, but they pay far more in proportion than did the Victorian mansion-dwellers. They do not believe it, but they do.

John and Maria had a nice house, with front steps, a side entrance and a matter of ten rooms and a box room. It was of course overcrowded with furniture and nick-nacks. There was scarcely room to move. One room, a very pleasant one, where letters could be written but seldom were, contained a large number of books—sets of Dickens, Thackeray, Mark Twain, the classics and, later, all of W. W. Jacobs' books were added as published. Uncle John was a voracious reader of all kinds of literature. He was particularly devoted to magazines and illustrated periodicals, as were all his family—the trait which exists in the survivors today. There were many such in those days and they all went into the house. Uncle John read them all, from cover to cover. He took many of them to the office where they filled in the time nicely from 9 a.m. to 6 p.m. There was nothing else for him to do there, but he attended with great regularity and punctuality. Having read each one through he would mark it heavily with a cross in pencil. On being asked why he did this he explained that, if he did not, he might read them all through again. It was pointed out that surely he would remember having done so, but he thought not and that he would probably read it all again and find it fresh. He did not want to waste his time that way, he said, so he marked them. He would look at each paper before he started on it and, if unmarked, would give it his undivided attention and seem to derive much benefit although he never remembered a single thing. His nephew tested this. He removed a marked periodical and substituted one of the same issue, unmarked. In due course Uncle John picked it up, found it did not bear the cross and read it all through again with apparent interest and enjoyment. It made not the slighest impression on his mind at either reading. He got on well with most people but he had a contempt for the Greeks, with whom his firm did much business. This he shared with his brother, James. What he disliked most about them was their names. They were, of course, endowed with the great classical names of their race—amongst them Epaminondas, Sophocles, Euripides, Themistocles. And these, together with their surnames, equally outlandish to John, were not easily pronounced by him. So he would distort, mispronounce and generally make game. The Greeks would smile and pretend to be amused, but one imagines that had he been in their country he would have felt a knife at his ribs. He did not care about them—they were foreigners and fair game.

John did not get on very well with his father-in-law. This old gentleman was also a Scot, but the complete opposite of Uncle John. He was astute, cautious and rich. He watched the pence and never spent a halfpenny more than absolutely necessary. He had a nice house on the verge of Epping Forest to which he retired and although he lived very carefully, he lived well. His house was run according to rule. But when his son-in-law came to visit, all the rules were broken. Uncle John, well aware of them, set them at naught. He had not been averse to his daughter Maria marrying this man. It got her off his hands and John's family was at the time well-to-do. But he ruled his family with a rod of iron like a patriarch of old—and he looked like a patriarch himself. So he did not think much of this erratic, unreliable son-in-law, who seemed to have no sense of reverence for anything, who made so much noise that every dog within hearing barked and who continually bellowed music-hall songs—for John and his Maria were great patrons of 'The Halls'.

Maria, wife of John, was a pretty girl, with a fresh and rosy complexion and she bore a resemblance to Marie Lloyd. She had the same sort of face and figure, the same white teeth peeping from the upper lip and some of the vivacity. She was like her mother but had her father's sturdiness. She was also much smaller than her immense husband. Although Scots by blood there was little of the Scots girl about her speech. Her accent she derived from the city of her birth, London. She dressed well, if rather flamboyantly as regards colour—but she could carry bright hues and had a trim figure. In the phrase of the day, she was stylish. She had nothing much in the way of intellect or brain, but a good deal of common sense and business aptitude inherited from her Father. She was a magnificent housekeeper and cook. She kept her house like the proverbial new pin—it was as clean and shining as she was herself. No speck of dirt or dust was allowed. She was tremendously houseproud and would work herself, very hard indeed. She swept, she dusted, she 'turned out' and she cooked; she kept the domestics up to the mark. And then she would suddenly sit down on a chair and say in an argumentative tone, 'I MUST sit down—just for five minutes.' Nobody was trying to prevent her, she was completely her own mistress. It would not have mattered had she sat down for hours, but she was too domestically restless for that. Friends wanting to annoy her, if they caught her sitting down, would tease her and ask her if she had dusted the coals. She did not actually do that, but every summer she let the coals run out completely and would then have the cellar scrubbed right out, before the new supply came in. Not many housewives went as far as that. John's family considered he had married beneath him. They thought Maria would have been better off as a publican's wife. Perhaps she would—but she married a man who kept the publicans going, anyway.

But John and Maria were devoted to each other. If she had few brains and no intellect, he had so fuddled his that they stood level. Both of them loved the Theatre and the Music Halls and went constantly. They were great diners-out, Frascati's being a favourite haunt of theirs, and the better Soho restaurants. For a time they became addicted to Canuto's, which was near King's Cross Station, and to the Hotels Florence and D'Italie—called by them the 'Dittaly'. They shared a contempt for foreign ways and people but not for foreign cooking. Anything which smacked of education or culture was to them ridiculous. They did not understand it, so it was absurd.

John had been abroad, which had served to deepen his contempt, for he had had difficulty in getting whisky. As the business which John attended but did little else had a large overseas connection, many foreigners came to the office. Whilst they were waiting to see the Senior, Uncle James, John would entertain them in what appeared to be a bright and breezy fashion but which was covertly insulting. One very important customer was very deaf. It was John's delight to go out to him, smiling affably, offer him cigarettes and even cigars, and all the while under his breath call him all the most dreadful names he could think of. It was fortunate that the old gentleman could not lip-read, but even so, John's heavy moustache would have defeated that. The old man considered Mr. John a very nice gentleman and said so. . . . Had Maria been a different sort of woman with a stronger and more determined mind, she might have guided her easy-going, self-indulgent husband. But perhaps not.

John had been a great Rugby Football player in his youth. He had played for the London Scottish, he had achieved amateur international status. He did one really remarkable feat. Things were going against his fifteen and a score was badly wanted. John determined to score. He seized an opponent who had the ball. He held him in such a bear's grip that the man could not get rid of the ball, which was lodged between the bodies of the two men. And having thus collared his man, John ran with him right over the line and touched down in triumph. There was some bother about this unorthodox manner of scoring a try but after discussion it was allowed . . . for John was certainly carrying the ball if he also carried his opponent. The try was converted and his side won. It caused quite a stir. Caricatures appeared of the redoubtable man and he had them framed, being most proud of that which appeared in *Ally Sloper's Half Holiday*. That, he felt, was real fame.

He gave up Rugby when he got married and settled down to enjoy married life and his hobby of drinking. He and Maria had one son who was the apple of their eyes. The boy was very delicate, which was surprising, for apart from John's potations, his constitution and strength was that of an ox, and Maria never ailed either. But this boy had no health at all. He was rather like little Paul Dombey, for he had every childish ailment—and almost every other—in its most virulent form. An ordinary cold in the head with him assumed almost the proportions of pneumonia. His greatest foe was asthma and it was terrible to see his struggles with it. His parents kept him in cotton wool; they overdid the care. They had not the slightest idea of how to bring up a child. He slept in an airless room, overcrowded with furniture and so carpeted and curtained that it was stifling to see. He was fed wrongly, he was pampered and might have been utterly spoiled. It was no fault of his. He was taken to theatres and restaurants at night when he should have been in bed. He was, because of his ill health, never sent to school. He tried it once but it made him ill. His education was casual, half-hearted and intermittent, supplied by a succession of Tutors. He was often far too ill for even that sort of teaching. It was a marvel he managed to learn as much as he did but he had intelligence and quick wits. A little less coddling might have been better for him, but he survives today—to read this book. His parents bestowed on him a nickname to which he objected strongly and discarded as soon as possible. Probably only two people recall it now—he himself and that Victorian Boy, his cousin. He was christened John, after his father, but was always called Jack—except for that nickname. He had a decided talent. He could draw and paint. His tastes lay in seascapes and ships, his idols were W. R. Wyllie and Stanhope Forbes. But he never had proper training and his talent, which was very considerable, was wasted. He was eventually taken into the Family Business for which he had no interest at all. He loved the Theatre and the West End. He married a Gaiety Girl of great beauty and she makes him a splendid wife. But he came through it all, had a family himself, conquered all the drawbacks and carries on like the true Victorian he is.

But Uncle John was a real character. He was, to all intents and purposes, the exact type of man whom Harry Tate featured in his wonderful sketches. He was the natural born swanker. It was not stupid, affected swank, but supreme and overwhelming self-confidence. He had developed the complete Ego. He was He and that was that. With absolute faith in the wonder and power of his name—a belief which no one but the members of his family shared—he considered it a key to all doors, enough to settle any row or argument, to constitute the final Court of Appeal in all disputes. Frequently embroiled in such things, he would be heard declaiming 'My name's Mackintosh.' (That was not the name but it was that of another old and famous clan.) This, in his view, settled everything and supplied the last word. He never stopped to consider his actions—enraged, he worked like lightning at reprisals. Once, in a provision shop with his wife, a large dog ran between his legs and nearly threw him over. He aimed a kick at the dog, got his foot under its stomach and lifted it into the crate of eggs standing on end against the counter. There was no lack of eggs then, at all prices—twelve a shilling was a fair one. The dog upset the crate and the eggs cascaded on to the floor, smashing gloriously. The dog fled, unhurt but yelping. Its owner took up cudgels on its behalf, the shopkeeper wanted to know who was going to pay for his eggs. There was a great noise and above it soared the voice

of Uncle John, stating in godlike thunder, 'My name's Mackintosh.'
He strode from the shop. Nobody stopped him. He went on his way,
unhurried, unruffled and smiling. Justice had been done, he felt, his
assaulted dignity had been restored. All was well with the world. And in
point of fact he heard no more about it.

He was, indeed, a formidable figure of almost six feet of solid manhood, not fat, despite his drinking, barrel-chested like an ox and of really
remarkable physical strength. He hardly knew its limits himself. He could
crack nuts between his finger and thumb, tear up packs of cards with no
effort at all, lift immense weights with apparent ease and do things which
professional strong men found difficult but which were, to him, child's
play. He would lead people on to boast of their strength and then, to
show them, he would punch his fist through the panel of a door. It never
hurt his fists, which were like lumps of granite, but it did the doors no
good. It mattered not to him where he did this, in his own house or in
those of other people. It gave him great satisfaction, in which the owners
of the doors did not share. They were not amused—but there was never
an argument.

Like all really strong men he could be gentle and tender. He loved
children and they loved him—perhaps realizing he had never grown up.
He hardly ever started a row but, if one blew up, well—he was in it.

An easy-going soul, he would nevertheless take quite unreasonable
and instant dislike to complete strangers. A telegraph boy, or some sort
of messenger, upset him. The boy had done absolutely nothing to earn
the dislike. But there was something about him which revolted Uncle
John. They passed each other every morning in St. Mary Axe, in which
the office Uncle John frequented was then situate. And every day, as
they passed, this Victorian gentleman, casually looking the other way,
would swing his arm and his big stick in the boy's direction in the hope
of catching him in some painfully vulnerable part of his body. He would
frequently succeed. Hit or miss, he would pursue his way without taking
any notice. After a very little while this rather slow-witted boy became
aware that he was actually the chosen target for the blows of this strange
man. The extraordinary thing was that the boy could easily have crossed
the road or gone another way round. But he did not do so. He maintained his route. As he approached his assailant, who never gave the
slightest indication that he was aware of his presence, the boy would go
pale and look terrified, mend his pace and dodge aside to evade the
swinging stick. There appeared to be some dreadful fascination in the
forthcoming danger. It went on for a couple of years and the boy never
altered his course nor did Uncle John ever miss making his attempted
and frequently successful assault. He could not explain his dislike for

this boy when questioned. All he could say was that he considered him a —— and he used his sole word of reprobation. It was an invention of his own—a composite word which started with the old-fashioned term for a sexual pervert, with the word 'bones' tacked on at the end. Uncle John never used foul language—drunk, sober or in the midway stage. For nobody could ever say he was completely drunk or sober. He just used this one word which he considered fitted every occasion.

He was quick to avenge a slight or insult, real or implied. Sometimes in these revenges he eschewed violence and had recourse to strategy. He was once annoyed by the landlord of a public house, which was a regular house of call for him on his way home from the office. He was affronted and placed in something of a difficulty. It was awkward to withdraw his custom as it was the only pub between the station and his home. So he called just the same and had his drink, or drinks, and as he left would manage to abstract something from the counter, put it in his pocket and take it home in triumph. He annexed small bottles of Apollinaris water, crown cork openers, corkscrews, matchstands and matches, and on one occasion a syphon of soda—these always stood on the bar and customers could have a 'splash' free—and once, some Heart Cakes, for which he had not the slightest use. When he had accumulated enough of these means to wipe out the insult, real or imagined, he took no more.

If the modern generation does not know what a Heart Cake was, it was a particular make of cake, a sort of Madeira quality, made in the shape of a heart with a cherry on top. They were seldom, if ever, met with outside public houses but therein they were plentiful, usually piled neatly in a circular glass jar with a top to it. One presumes they were eaten, but when and by whom remains a mystery. Perhaps parents bought them for their children, who in the early part of this period were allowed to go into bars. The writer cannot say for certain, but although he saw many heart cakes, he only saw one sold and eaten on two occasions—once when purchased by a gentleman for his dog and the other time he bought and consumed one himself, out of curiosity. It was rather sweet but quite pleasant. It was also quite fresh so there must have been a demand. It was probably regarded as part of the victuals which Licensed Victuallers had to keep in stock. But in any event, heart cakes were of no use to Uncle John. . . .

On another occasion John took more drastic and open action although along the same lines. His wife Maria had had a row with the provision merchant with whom she dealt and she was much aggrieved. She told her husband, who at once took over the matter. He went round to the shop and, having no use for subtleties, stated his case roundly and rather rudely. He called the manager by his favourite term of abuse and also informed him that he himself rejoiced in the name of 'Mackintosh', a fact of which the manager was already aware. The manager was tough and not impressed. He refused to apologize, withdraw or set anything right. Uncle John announced that his custom was therefore lost forever, none of his family would ever deal there or darken the doors again, and that ruin must speedily ensue. Even that failed to move the manager. So Uncle John left, with great dignity. Outside the shop, he paused. He must be revenged. So he took from a hook, where it was hanging, an Ostend rabbit. They were then highly esteemed. They hung in rows in provision shops, minus their skins, very naked and very dead and all appeared to have their arms akimbo and their hands behind them. They were excellent eating, all the same, despite the purplish blue of their complexion. So Uncle John took one, to show his complete contempt for the shop, its manager and all connected with it. He took it as a protest against injustice, put it under his arm and walked away. But the manager had seen him. 'Hi—put that rabbit down!' he yelled and went in pursuit. Uncle John had no intention of surrendering his loot and equally he did not want to fight the manager for it in the middle of the local High Street. The rabbit was his by all the laws of justice. So no surrender! He took to his heels, hotly pursued by the younger and far fitter manager. Uncle John's Rugby days were over and the constant absorption of whisky is not conducive to good bellows or fleetness of foot. But he sprinted, all the same. The manager gained ground. Uncle John's mind once more caught up with his body and he observed he was in a bit of a spot. There must be no question of surrendering the rabbit—that was too ignominious. The manager was at his heels when he saw a pillar box. He dodged the manager round it and—he pushed in the rabbit. He posted that rabbit, unaddressed and unadorned. Then he ran on. The manager paused, baffled. Should he pursue the fugitive or should he stand by the letterbox and his rabbit, so as to recover it when the postman next cleared the box? He had little use for Uncle John now. If it came to physical violence he knew well enough he had no chance. If he gave him in charge they would both look ridiculous. So Uncle John escaped, the rabbit remained in its unusual burrow and what the manager did was never known.

John was seldom defeated but he suffered ignominy once when he joined a lawn tennis club. He and Maria attended in state and he played his first game, a double, with a lady partner. They won. Uncle John, to show his athletic prowess, leapt the net, caught his toe in the top, fell heavily and was confined to the house for weeks with a wrenched ankle. The tennis club never saw him again.

There were times when his imagination soared on its spirituous wings beyond his control. He returned home one evening rather muddy and announced that he had killed a man. It so happened that his brother James and the Victorian Boy (now a young man) were calling at the house. John gave complete and seemingly authentic details. He had been set upon whilst taking a short cut across some waste land. There was a scrummage —there were several assailants. He had smitten one and the man had fallen whilst the others fled. Uncle John had examined his prostrate foe and found him dead. So he had come home. He was quite positive about it. Knowing his strength, his brother James was uneasy. 'Think he's really done it?' he whispered to the Boy, who had his doubts. They went to the scene and found no body but lots of footprints in wet clay which might have meant a struggle, also a man's cap. They went back, really perturbed. John was not concerned, he was having his meal. The others knew that if this had really happened the police would soon take action. Very shortly afterwards there was a loud knock at the front door. The servant entered and announced that a police sergeant was there asking for the master of the house. Even Uncle John went a bit pale. The Victorian Boy took command. He went to the door and there stood the sergeant. He braced himself for an awkward time. The sergeant beamed. 'Good evening, sir,' he said. 'I've just called to see if you would care to buy some tickets for the Police Minstrels.' He was astonished at the generous response. No more was ever heard of the manslaughter.

There had been a distant connection belonging to the same clan and of the same name, who had been a Judge in Scotland and had had a title conferred on him—a life title only. It was enough for Uncle John. He inherited that title, in his own mind. He told everyone that he was really a Lord but never used the title because of the expense and bother in keeping it up. He was most convincing about it, as he was about everything, and lots of people believed him. He would enlarge on his present expenses and the amount of poor relations he had to keep. He instanced the Victorian Boy who at that time was the only one of the family keeping himself and not dependent, as was Uncle John, upon Uncle James. But the Boy did not mind. He knew Uncle John and he knew his Uncle was fond of him.

John was probably one of the champion consumers of alcohol. But he was no secret drinker. He hated to drink alone. He must have a companion. He did not sleep well. He would rise at dawn and wait for the milkman, and they would have a drink together. When they moved to another part of the district he discovered to his joy a way of evading the loneliness of the night and the lack of drinking companions caused by the necessity on their part for sleep. He discovered about a mile away an all night tramway stable. There he resorted with bottles of whisky in a bag.

He became most popular with the drivers and conductors who frequented the stable, and when he died he became a legend.

He was really a throwback to the feudal age. He would have made a magnificent Lord of the Manor, scattering largess to the serfs and tenantry. As it was, he gave ticket collectors on railway stations half-crowns for no reason apparent to them or himself. He would hand bus or tram conductors half-crowns for a penny fare and wave away the change saying, 'That's all right—anyhow'—in his best Harry Tate voice and manner. On holiday he pervaded the hotel, he entertained everyone, staff and visitors alike. He and his family would go by 'fly' to local beauty spots. Not that he cared much about such places but it was a way of spending money and entertaining, and there was always an inn handy, which meant drinks. The driver usually returned from these trips very exhilarated but nobody could say that John was drunk. He was—just himself. He adored travelling in carriages. He preferred them to trains, on which in his day there was hardly ever a dining car and no train could be stopped in order to get a drink. Flasks did not hold enough for even a moderate journey. But carriages could be pulled up—and were.

When his brother James died he attempted to run the business. Naturally he could not, but sufficient survived to keep him going until he too passed on in 1915. During the First World War whisky was hard to come by—his world was ending amidst the guns and slaughter.

He created a sensation at the very end. The undertakers could not get his coffin down the stairs in the usual way, feet first, and had to, in their own phrase, 'up-end him' and bump him from stair to stair. . . .

Despite the fact that, in his sisters' parlance, he 'had a weakness', most certainly he 'took' in no small measure—he was a good and honest man. He never did anyone any harm, he lived a clean life from start to finish. He loved his wife and son dearly. He really imagined he was doing his duty by them. His crippling extravagance should have been curbed by his elder brother—but James always found difficulty in saying 'No'. Apart from his drinks, he spent little on himself but he loved to give to others and he was happiest when giving pleasure. He would take his wife, his son, his Victorian nephew for long rides for the pleasure it gave them, driving to Epping Forest in a landau. The boys would sit with the coachman, and learn all about horses and harness—bearing reins, bits, belly bands, kicking straps and the like—and would sometimes be allowed to hold the reins. There would be lordly meals at the Royal Forest or High Beech hotels and Uncle John delighted in their joy. For he was very much a child himself, a creature of impulse, who knew and cared little of the ways of business or responsibility. But if help was needed, he was there. He frightened young suitors who tried paying attention to his orphaned nieces out of their wits and many of them fled. But he did it because he thought he ought to and held that they were no good if they ran away.

He was a Victorian; he loved his family, his country, and he did his duty—so far as he was able to observe it through the roseate clouds which enveloped his mind. Poor Uncle John, there have been many worse men who were total abstainers, but very, very few kinder and better-hearted souls than this character of mirth and tragedy, who once fell through the bottom of a four-wheeled cab, as they do in pantomimes—and ran quite a distance before it stopped. But that was Uncle John all over.

CHAPTER TEN

Poor Frederica

IF Uncle John had been a comedian, as indeed he was, then his youngest sister, the baby of the family, was a complete figure of Tragedy. Poor little woman, she never had any luck. She never had the sunshine with the shadow and if for a little while the sun did indeed show her its radiance, it was so soon obliterated that life seemed the darker for its brief spell. Frederica was one of those people who are born to love and be loved, who achieve the former but hardly ever the latter, who ask so little of life but receive even less, who take the buffets of fate and the slings and arrows of outrageous fortune on an armour of loyalty and self-sacrifice and who hoard the few grains of happiness they may have garnered close to their hearts, seeking to make it immortal. Frederica's life was short and it was unhappy. It was full of pain, physical, mental and spiritual. For many years she hardly knew a day's health or any peace of mind. Yet she bore her sufferings proudly; she came of a proud family and it would never do to let them down. She fell head over heels in love with a handsome, dashing young man—and maybe he loved her. Neither of them got any happiness out of it although she loved him to her dying day and never for one moment admitted there was a fault in him. She was born in the Canonbury family home, the last to enter the clan and the second to leave it. Her birthday was 9th June, 1863. It should have augured well for her, for it was a year of National Romance. It saw the wedding of the Prince of Wales—afterwards Edward VII—to the beautiful Princess from over the sea—Alexandra of Denmark. It was a tremendously romantic affair and people were still talking about it when little Frederica slipped into life on 9th June. Little of the romance of that year surrounded this last child of her parents, although it may have accounted for the fact that she was herself a true Romantic—with all the faults and qualities of those uneasy people. Even the date of her birth seemed unpropitious, for the 9th June (unrecorded in her case save in the Family Bible, on a gravestone and in her son's memory) is marked in the diaries as the day on which Charles Dickens died and on which the Alexandra Palace was burned down—a fact that son always remembered when many years afterwards he became manager of the rebuilt Palace. Although those things did not actually occur on the actual day on which Frederica was born, they were events which happened on succeeding birthdays. Obviously not a lucky day, despite the fact that June is the month of the roses. There was little luck and few roses, although plenty of thorns, for little Frederica.

She was never a strong child and she did not resemble any of the rest of the family—except in her determination to do her duty and never tarnish her family name of which she was also very proud. She was a very gentle soul, who disliked violence, who was easily attracted and as easily repelled. Rudeness, harshness, and roughness repelled her, kindness and understanding brought out the best in her. Give her affection, give her just a little love and she opened her petals to it like the rose of her birth month. She was very sensitive and very proud—two qualities which so often go together. She might be, and she often was, in the deepest distress but she would never ask for help. She would do all she could, often more than that of which she was physically capable, to keep herself going and maintain her independence. She kept her secrets from the world and so often missed help which would have been willingly forthcoming.

Being delicate and the baby of the family, perhaps she was a trifle spoilt. Even majestic, rigid Pa may have unbent to her, only a trifle, maybe, but still unbent—and Ma was more lenient and tender to her than to the others. She was a favourite with her brothers and sisters, they all loved the little lastcomer. But she always seemed a bit 'fey'—in all her portraits that can be seen there is the faraway look in the eyes so frequently observed in those of people who have not long to live, who are already gazing into what lies beyond, trying to pierce the veil. She is slim and graceful in her pictures, not pretty perhaps but attractive. One sees the gentleness, the repose, the suggestion of the desire for affection and love. She had little enough of it. She attended a good school, as girls' schools went, and she acquired quite a bit of knowledge. She was possibly the cleverest of all the sisters, despite Miss Mary's claim. For she was what was known as 'accomplished'. She could paint well for an amateur and she drew very well indeed. She was excellent at needlework and embroidery of all kinds. Her crochetwork looks more like real lace than that of most women's. She had considerable taste, she dressed well and wore her clothes with style. She could play the piano very well indeed, she could read music at sight and she could sing in a pretty soprano voice which, if not strong, was true and always dead on the note. Also she was all of her life completely stagestruck, although she never played a single part even as an amateur. She played and sang at church concerts and was a valuable accompanist. She took part in Tableaux Vivants, which were very popular then. They were, from the modern point of view, a rather dull and exceedingly static type of entertainment, but people liked them and they gave a lot of fun to those participating, for there was a chance to 'dress up'. Usually, they either illustrated well-known pictures—never classical subjects which would have demanded some partial nudity—and songs. The Victorian Boy remembers seeing a representation of 'Twickenham Ferry', in two scenes. He was extremely critical of the way in which the ferryman held the punt pole. He had spent much of his youth on the Thames and children are observant. He liked that song and does still. It had something of what 'Orsino' calls a 'dying fall'. Frederica was not in that set of Tableaux Vivants, and to the best of the Boy's remembrance he never saw her in any at all. He would remember had he done so for she was his Mother.

But she would act little scenes with him, teach him recitations and poems and many Shakespearean speeches and he, who had the Theatre in his blood from his paternal side, just lapped it all up. She taught him to sing and until his voice broke he had a nice one, but lost it on breaking and could never sing a note afterwards. But as a lad he sang solos, to his Mother's pride and joy. And with all this, she was a good cook and housekeeper.

But even as a girl she had little luck. Her Pa and Ma died when she was young but Uncle James replaced them nobly and she adored him. She was always getting ill and had very little reserve strength, only immense spirit. She would get very tired indeed. But she played a little gentle tennis, and, greatly daring, she rode a tricycle. She danced well and was in great request at such functions. She was very circumspect and never danced many times with the same young man—she was no trouble at all to her chaperone. Well-brought-up ladies then exhibited maiden modesty which became them very well—and was an additional attraction to young men, as the girls knew very well.

Frederica had many young men 'after her', as they said then, one of them a dashing blade, with red hair and a red Vandyke Beard (he greatly resembled Captain Kettle, a fictional hero of Victorian and Edwardian days who wrote his letters with a revolver cartridge so as to be ready for anything and was quicker on the draw than any cowboy), and this particular 'Captain Kettle' fell heavily in love with Frederica. He was not a sailor, he was in the Insurance business. He was actually

Upper left: Maskelyne, the Master of Magic. *Upper right:* John Philip Sousa. *Lower left:* Colonel Cody—The Real "Buffalo Bill". *Lower right:* Ellaline Terriss and Seymour Hicks

Sylvia Grey

Julia Neilson

the eldest son of that resident in the Best Road who had so far forgotten
himself as to marry his housekeeper, whereupon the red-bearded hero
and the rest of the family left home. He proposed to Frederica five times
and five times she refused him. So the hero cast off the respectability of
Insurance and went into the Theatrical Profession. He rose very high
in it. He was of a rakish, pushing, buccaneering type with great assur-
ance and what was then called 'the gift of the gab'. He became First
Lieutenant to a great Theatrical Manager, an American, who had half
his interests in New York and half in London, who shared those two
cities in his heart and whose name was Charles Frohman. The rejected
of Frederica became the chosen of Frohman, travelling all over the world
for him and doing remarkable things. He always cut a figure, he was
always picturesque. His opera hat worn at an angle, his gold-headed
cane, his red-lined opera cloak and his keen face and jutting beard—in
an age when few men were hirsute about the face in his profession—
were familiar in every big city the world over. Years afterwards he met
Frederica's son, the Victorian Boy, who was entering the Profession.
On learning who he was, he bade him stand quite still, walked round
him several times and surveyed him from all angles. Then he put his
arm round the Boy's shoulder and took him to lunch. He helped that
Boy a lot. He told him he took the greatest interest in him because he
(the Boy) might have been his own son. He never had a son, he died a
bachelor, faithful to his Frederica. The Boy often wished that man had
indeed been his father.

But Frederica met her Fate. He was the handsome dashing young
man already alluded to, with great charm, a most attractive personality,
a good, if theatrical, background and immensely popular in whatever
society he found himself. He could speak several languages, he had a
good and classical education and seemed likely to do very well. He also
appeared to be very much in love, and probably was, so far as his weak
nature allowed him to be. He swept the girl off her feet with a whirlwind
wooing. There was no doubt of his being 'smitten'—his attentions
were 'marked' from the first meeting. Her sentimental and loving nature
responded ardently. They were soon 'engaged'. And the bad luck started
at once.

A cycling craze was sweeping the country. Frederica was of a cycling
family or, at least, her brother James, who stood *'In Loco Parentis'*, was a
famous and pioneering cyclist, and Walter (for such was the successful
suitor's name) liked cycling too. He wanted to enjoy it with his Frederica
so he bought what was called a 'Sociable'. A 'Sociable' was a horrible
and dangerous contraption with two large wheels and one small one,
on which two people could ride, one behind the other. The one in the

K

rear, who sat a little higher, steered the machine by means of two levers —they looked like inverted stirrups, set in little metal cups. Walter and Frederica rode about on this 'Sociable', but one fatal day it got out of control when descending a steep hill. It threw its riders on to a heap of hard, jagged flints piled by the roadside for road metal. Frederica, sitting in front, fell undermost. She was badly hurt, stunned and very badly cut about the face and body. Although she escaped facial scars, her nose was broken. It was reset but it took on a Roman shape, which rather suited her and gave a touch of character to the face. But that accident laid the seeds of her death although it was not realized at the time. That was the end of the Sociable. It lingered for years in a covered passage in the Desirable Residence where the Boy found it, rode it and had a bad fall. Then it was destroyed.

In due course the couple were married at the Presbyterian Church at which the womenfolk worshipped, although Walter was Church of England. The honeymoon was spent at Folkestone. They went on a day trip to Boulogne and the weather turned rough. Walter was a good sailor but Frederica took after her brother James. She was horribly ill and prostrate for some days. But a record of that trip survives, for in Boulogne (the roughness started on the return journey) they purchased a couple of dolls, a French fisherman and presumably his wife, in correct costume, and those dolls are still in being. Walter and his bride had a very good start in married life, plenty of presents, and possessions of first-class quality and they took a very nice house in a beautiful county. And there the Victorian Boy was born.

He entered the world on the evening of an April day in the year 1888. Frederica and Walter had been married in 1887, the Jubilee Year of Queen Victoria. It should have been lucky for them but was not. The arrival of that boy caused a great stir in the Family. He was the first male child of the second generation—Charles had had two daughters. There were no telephones then so the news came to the Desirable Residence by telegram and there was much excitement. It was a Wednesday evening (if there is any truth in the old jingle about children and the day of their birth it has been largely right in that Boy's case) and Miss Bessie was at Choir practice. When she returned and heard the news she wanted to start right away to see Mother and child. She had to wait until next day. By report the Boy was big and lusty, weighing nine pounds. At once he became the focal point of the Family, who all went down to inspect him, with Miss Bessie running the house for her sister Frederica. When his days were still few the child was christened by a Bishop, his father being Church of England. This was not altogether pleasing to his Presbyterian Aunts—the Uncles did not care—but the fact that a

Bishop performed the ceremony and that they all had tea with him in his Palace went a long way to smoothing things out. Up to now the Boy has not noticed any particular advantage that has accrued owing to so eminent a cleric having soused his tiny head with water and blessed him. Perhaps it has still to come, perhaps it will work Hereafter. But he was hardly born before his Mother fell a victim to rheumatic fever. She suffered terribly—she had some sort of electric treatment. The attack crippled her, one leg shrank shorter than the other. Blisters were applied to the sole of her foot which caused excruciating agony but did little or no good. But she recovered, her heart slightly affected and with a limp which lasted the rest of her life and necessitated the use of a stick.

The year 1888 was barren of anything of national or international importance which might have had any bearing on the Boy's life. It was an uneventful year but his own life has been very eventful—which just goes to show, or perhaps does not.

But there was one thing which makes him believe in prenatal and birth influence. Whilst he was preparing to make his entrance into this world, his father read to his mother the works of Charles Dickens, which they both loved. And the love of Dickens was passed on to the son, in full measure.

Two years after the Boy's birth, a little brother arrived, said to have been a very lovely child. But the bad luck worked on. That second boy was not destined to live—he had been dropped by a careless nursemaid, who left the house quickly—saying she had had a telegram from her mother who was dangerously ill. She was of course allowed to go, but later when Frederica was bathing her baby she observed that the child screamed when touched. A doctor was fetched and the baby examined. The truth was discovered. The telegram was discovered too—handed in at the town in which they were spending their summer holiday. The maid had sent it to herself.

There is often much discussion as to how much can be remembered of extreme childhood. That Boy just faintly recalls his little brother and the fact that he was very attached to him. He would give the baby his toys and try to interest him. He remembers one occasion very clearly. He had a little celluloid ball—yellow on one side, green on the other, and it had tiny shot inside to make it rattle when it bounced. He liked that ball and he wanted his little brother to share his joy. The baby was sleepy and reluctant and, of course, did not understand. But the Boy was determined that the baby should enjoy the ball. The baby had its mouth open so the Boy put the ball into it. It was a tight fit and the baby nearly choked. It was rescued in time and the Boy got into a lot of trouble which he did not think fair, for he had meant well. But nobody seemed to understand. He also remembers a field at the back of the house with what he now knows to be Red Devon cows in it. He remembers his playroom and a large wooden cannon which fired wooden cannonballs by means of a spring—they travelled quite a long way—and a Christmas Tree decked with coloured glass balls. He seized one of the attractively bright and shining spheres and it cut him badly because it broke in his little hand and pieces of the glass of which it was made had to be dug out by the doctor. All those things happened before he was four and he does not remember them from hearsay. Many years afterwards he went back to look at that house and it was all just as he recalled it. He also remembers another nursemaid—a Nannie—who helped his Mother to look after him. She was a believer in the dictum that children should obey promptly and implicitly and that they should go to sleep the moment they were put to bed. She thought that the mere fact of saying 'Go to sleep' would immediately induce slumber. As an aid to repose she told the Boy stories whilst bathing him in a tin affair—with one of the ends high up so that it could be leant against as a backrest—before the nursery fire. She told stories of a vile beast which she had invented—and she had a remarkable power of descriptive narrative. This thing was half beast and half bird, so that no matter where you went, you could not escape it. It had a long red neck, she said, so that it could reach round corners. It had a long sharp beak, but the beak had teeth like a tiger. The front half was bird and the front legs had talons, the back half was beast, yellow with black stripes. She knew its name. It was a Turkey Tiger. It prowled about all night looking for naughty children who were still awake. It made no noise at all. You never knew when it would spring. No use climbing things because it could fly, no use hiding under the bedclothes because it could reach with its neck and claw the clothes off. It lived on naughty little boys who did not obey their Nannies. It gave the Boy agonies of fear. His Mother was ill again and he did not like to tell her. But his Aunt Mary came to stay. He told her. She talked to that Nannie and the inventor of odd zoological characters must have thought that she herself was being assailed by a Turkey Tiger. No more was heard about it. But Nannie had odd ways of preventing little treats. Bananas were then not the cheap and popular fruit they afterwards became. They were quite new delicacies. He asked for one for his supper. He was told 'No, certainly not.' He was informed certain facts concerning Bananas. They were, it appeared (according to Nannie), 'Gold in the morning, silver in the afternoon and lead at night'. It appeared this was true of all fruit, for he got the same answer when he asked for an apple, orange or anything else. He had to be content with a glass of milk and a sponge cake. Those his Nannie had brought up on a tray. She was not going downstairs again for fruit—hence the legend. She never let him have any until his Mother got to hear about it.

The loss of the second boy made his Mother ill again but when she recovered she lavished all her affection on her firstborn. Those two understood and adored each other. Very few mothers understood boys as did Frederica. They moved frequently. She had to go to Westcliff because of her health—the ozone was prescribed. The Boy liked living there, in a tall Victorian house which still stands facing the Shrubbery, as it was then called. And from Westcliff he had the only outing he ever remembers his Father giving him. The two of them went by boat from the end of the pier to Clacton-on-Sea—or it may have been only Margate. It was, of course, a paddle steamer. And before they went his father bought him a toy which, apart from a little walking-cane, was the only one the Boy ever remembers receiving from him. The Boy chose a toy lifeboat. This was a big adventure for him, his first sea trip, and he was taking no chances. He read fairly well even then and had many books—given him by his mother and his aunts—and knew all about shipwrecks. He went aboard with confidence, clutching his lifeboat to him. He asked his Father if the Captain would not be glad to know there was a lifeboat on board, and his Father agreed with him. He does not remember much about the trip except that he enjoyed it and apparently went to sleep in the Saloon on the return journey, for he awoke to find himself alone. He was going in search of his Father but a steward took him in charge until the Father was found. . . . His age was five.

That dashing young man was not a good Husband and not a good Father. He did not understand children. He was stern with his son, kept telling him he must make haste and grow up into a man. For Walter the Father was weak and easily led. He could not say 'NO'. He was far too popular. His wife, far too gentle and sweet, far too much in love, had no influence over him. She was as clay in his hands. Her Walter was not a bad man at heart and he had only one besetting sin. He was a gambler. He was not a successful gambler, either. He plunged and he always lost. His schemes, however promising, always went wrong. He took to the Turf and it is said that he never once backed a winner. Soon there was no money at all. There was trouble at Westcliff and a flaming row between Walter and his two sisters-in-law, Mary and Bessie. The breach was never closed—he told them to leave the house and they did. They never spoke to him again. But they would come down to see their sister and their nephew, to whom they gave a splendid time. Uncle James now came to the rescue. The little family went to live at East Molesey. Here there was a brief period of happiness. Walter loved the river and was a good oarsman. Frederica loved the river too and so did the Boy—

—who adored the boat they had and the regattas and especially Molesey Lock—a very different East Molesey and Lock then to what it is today. They were there during the memorable floods of 1894-5 and the hard, bitter winter which followed it. The Thames froze over, you could walk across to what was then Tagg's Island—and carts were driven across the ice at Kingston Bridge. The Boy enjoyed the floods—for they had to live on the first floor. The mess and destruction meant nothing to him, the excitement was terrific. He was very sorry those floods had gone before the frost came. What a time he could have had then! As it was he learned to skate on the Long Water when it was frozen to a solid block of ice. He knew every nook and cranny of the Palace and was friends with all the attendants there. And in those days a squadron of cavalry occupied the quarters just inside the gates, which was a tremendous attraction. Some of Walter's schemes turned out well for once and, for a while, the sun shone.

But East Molesey was far too near to Hurst Park Racecourse, Sandown Park and Kempton Park. The old lure of the Turf reasserted itself. The father's money went to the bookmakers in a steady stream. To the little family, it was disaster. The Boy went to school for the first time at East Molesey and he did not like it at all. He remembers the Head Master well—a fearsome figure with a bellowing voice, a sudden pouncing manner, and a vast drooping moustache. He disliked school from the word 'go'—from the day he went to his first school to the day he left his last, his education finished—or maybe beginning?

But the dark times returned—debts accumulated and could not be met; Uncle James came to the rescue again. They moved to Surbiton, to a house far too big, and there the Boy was sent to school, to an establishment for the Sons of Gentlemen, where the tone was so high as to be almost out of reach, where good manners, 'posh' pronunciation and sport were esteemed above mere learning—although the curriculum, when it got a chance, was strictly classical. Here difficulties overcame Walter, and his poor Frederica suffered. Often there was a mere trifle of money in the house, more often none at all.

Frederica went through Hell. Delicately nurtured, delicate in health, she fought against circumstances she never dreamed could happen. Often she went hungry so that the Boy could have enough—he knows that now—and sometimes there was not really enough for him. But she gave him all she could. She gave him what joy she could. And she would somehow find enough to take him to the Theatre. She had done that at Westcliff, where he saw plays long forgotten—*Bootle's Baby* amongst them—and pantomimes which he reproduced on his return home. From Molesey and Surbiton his Mother took him to the County

Theatre, Kingston, where he saw all sorts of plays and dramas, some of which he understood, others being beyond him—they ranged from Sydney Grundy's *The New Woman* to *Two Little Vagabonds*. Sometimes they went to the Assembly Rooms at Surbiton and saw the small companies perform. He saw *Proof* there, *The French Maid*, *The Gay Parisienne* and many others. They always went in the cheapest seats but neither cared. To be in a theatre watching a play—that was heaven. Frederica would have sacrificed a meal to go to the theatre and often did so. But at last the inevitable came. There was a final breakdown. Walter and Frederica parted. She never saw him again in her life.

So she was faced with that dread of every married woman—the necessity of returning home; a wife with a husband living but unable to support her and the child she took with her. For a widow it is not so bad—but under her conditions it was horror. The Boy remembers the journey home. To him it had no dread, for he loved that Victorian House to which he was going and his Uncle and two Aunts who lived in it. He had his store of toys there and the happiest memories—indeed, to him, whose childhood had been so nomadic, it was really Home. He remembers the journey to Waterloo, the bus ride to Broad Street and the fact that his Mother bought him a ham sandwich there which he found delicious. What it was costing his Mother—this journey and the prospect before her—naturally never entered his mind. But they were at once made to feel that they had come home. Uncle James never alluded to any misfortune. Frederica was his sister, the Boy his nephew—this was his house, so it was their home. He shouldered the extra burden willingly. And so there they lived for some years. His Mother got what happiness she could. Her position was awkward—her return had in some sort to be explained to friends—she was of no importance in the house save that she was one of the Family—she was a married woman living apart from her husband—a difficult thing indeed in those days. There was, however, very little friction, save occasional outbursts from the fiery Miss Mary. Frederica was a creature of the background and she faded into it.

She got her joy from her Boy. He went to a new school and being blessed with a quite remarkable memory he found little difficulty in learning, save mathematics, which meant nothing to him. He refused to learn algebra, in which he said he did not believe—which staggered his headmaster. But that man let him learn History instead and thereby laid the foundation of a means of livelihood. The Boy, because of his memory, shone at examinations. He took many prizes and Frederica had her pride at the Annual Prizegivings—when she smiled sweetly but rather pityingly at other Mothers whose boys were empty-handed whilst hers bore five or six handsome volumes and some certificates. Sometimes he sang at those affairs, and even played in Shakespeare, and she would sit and cry quietly for joy.

She got pleasure at home, too, in playing the piano. She played all sorts of music; from her the Boy learned all the Gilbert and Sullivan operas, the current musical comedies, the popular *opéras bouffe* and the Music-Hall songs—for she always acquired the annual Francis Day and Hunter volume of popular Music-Hall songs. He learnt ballads, too. And if he was playing elsewhere in the house and heard his Mother strike up a song he liked, he would race to the Drawing Room and sing it with her. He sang, amongst others, 'The Holy City', 'Tatters', 'Daddy' and a song about a highwayman who was obviously Claude Duval. He liked that one. The sentimental songs would make his Mother weep—she was very sentimental—and sometimes he would weep, too. It was catching.

But despite all her emotional crises he never saw her faint. It is a popular belief that Victorian ladies, faced with a difficult situation, fainted or swooned. The Boy lived amongst a collection of Victorian females and knew many more. He never saw any of them faint. There was far more likely to be mutual recrimination and a flaming row. Those he remembers, but a faint—never. The only faint he saw in those days was the woman in the crowd when Kitchener was to drive by. Its singularity impressed him.

Frederica understood boys. She never intruded on them, she never demanded their company or thrust herself upon them. She never interfered in her son's games; if he were with other boys she kept aloof. Sometimes when he was coming home with his little friends he would see her—hovering—in her black cape and her ebony stick, with the little smile upon her lips. All boys of spirit until in their very late teens are embarrassed by their parents. Frederica knew that. So if he was with boys whom she did not know well she took no notice. She knew better. If the boys were those who lived in the same road and who were often in and out of the house, that was another matter. They knew her and loved her and she would go home in the midst of them, listening to their ceaseless chatter—accepted by them as one of themselves. She never got a holiday but she did not mind. Her Boy would go and stay with relations in Scotland and she got pleasure out of receiving his letters. She would hear him his lessons, she would play with him when he was alone if he wanted her to do so—but she never interfered with his own games. She made him all sorts of gadgets—a serviceable bandolier when the Boer War broke out, belts, revolver cases, frogs for his swords and was always full of ideas and suggestions. She looked after the large garden, so far as her strength allowed, and really had 'green fingers' with flowers and plants. They seemed to respond to her. She never talked of her husband or of her woes. She never complained and she fought desperately against illness. She made her own clothes and looked well in them. Everyone liked her and many called her 'Freddie'. That name, however, was never used in the Family. They were not people for abbreviations or pet names—only the son of John was called by his because his Father and Mother did so and Miss Bessie, of course, was never Miss Elizabeth, and her sister Margaret was Maggie. But although thousands of men called Uncle James 'Jimmy', he was James to his family and the Boy was always called by his own name—which was the same as his Father's—but he had his Uncle James's name as well.

Frederica found peace and a certain happiness in that Victorian house from which she had been married and to which she returned. But it was not to last. The Family Misfortune struck hard and the house was given up. For a time the Family was dispersed, living with other relatives. But Frederica was stricken down with the most fell disease, that which everyone dreads. She must have suffered from it for a long time but bore it herself in silence. She wanted to give no trouble, she knew the worries which beset her beloved brother James at that time and would not add to them until at last she collapsed: she could do no more. Even then, in the midst of financial disaster, James showed his sterling character. He did not send his youngest sister to a hospital; somehow he found the means to maintain her in a Nursing Home where she could have some privacy, some comfort and see her relatives, friends and her son. During that financial upheaval the Boy was sent to the kindly sheltering Manse at Newabbey for his summer holiday. He remembers it today and what a happy time he had. His Aunt Mary was with him. But the holidays drew to an end and he was then told his Mother was ill. He had to travel home alone, there was nowhere for Aunt Mary to go, so she stayed on at the Manse. He travelled home all alone in that Express, a very lonely, rather forlorn little figure. He knew now his Mother was ill but he did not know she was dying. But some sense of foreboding smote him. He would have loved that journey and the importance of being 'on his own'. But a sense of evil to come swept over him and he sat quite still in his corner, neither eating nor drinking all the day, although he had ample refreshment with him. He just sat there and thought.

He had written two or three times a week to his Mother and had her replies. He was not going Home, either, he was going to stay with Uncle John and Aunt Maria and, although he knew them well, their house was not home. To him the future seemed hopeless. Uncle James met him at St. Pancras. He was living with his sister Maggie. The Boy felt very lonely and not a little frightened. But he put a bold face on it.

Next day he was taken to see his Mother. She lay on a bed filled with water—she was already almost a skeleton. He knew what was coming then—he did not have to be told. She could hardly hold him in her arms but her joy was wonderful.

Each night, on his way back from school (he had a four-mile walk to and from school each day) he went to see her for a few precious minutes, to try to cheer her up and the mere sight of him helped the suffering, dying creature. Then back to his homework, in an atmosphere utterly foreign to him, but every night his Uncle James came to help him, as if he had been his Father. His Saturdays he spent with his Mother and Sundays, too, for as long as he was allowed to stay. He was approaching thirteen. He got his meals as and when he could and was more than a bit neglected, but he never said a word to his Mother—to her he was always happy.

But one day he went to see her and his Uncle James was there, too. The poor woman could hardly speak and her brother had to lift her arms to put them round her son. He, the Boy, held her closely and could feel her bones. But she smiled at him and spoke to him and he understood what she said though her voice was a mere weak mumble. He heard her ask her brother to look after him—he heard the brother promise—a promise nobly fulfilled. He heard his Mother's faint whisper asking him to kiss her and he did so, again and again, clinging to her, for he loved this gentle, understanding Mother of his with all his heart and soul. Then she lay back, exhausted and almost at her end. He felt his Uncle's hand gently leading him away. At the door he turned and saw his Mother's large dark eyes—eyes which seemed so large now they were about to close for ever—fixed on him hungrily. He went back and kissed her, again and again. She lay back, she closed those eyes but there was happiness in that smile on her bloodless lips. It was the last the Boy saw of her as his Uncle took him away. The next day his Aunt Maggie told him, very tenderly, that his Mother was dead. He heard it in silence— and he went to an empty room. Mercifully they left him alone. He could not cry. His grief was too deep for that. In his heart was a blind, surging rage against something he could not understand, against what seemed to him to be terrible cruelty and injustice—that his poor Mother should be taken like this—that everything should crash—that there should be grief and suffering amongst those who had been so kind and so good. The relief of tears never came to him at all. When he grew up he was able to realize the real tragedy of that poor woman, dying there in her early years, bereft of all she had known—in a little room which was just round the corner from that Best Road where she had known happiness, from whence she had gone as a bride with the man she loved—the man she never saw again after they had parted. No doubt he wrote but she kept her counsel. She had nothing but her son, her family—and her life—and that was taken from her. Her mind must have been as agonized as her body as she lay there waiting for the end. But the Boy knew nothing of that at the time, nor did any thought of his Father cross his mind. He never saw him again either and never heard from him until, long after, news of his death came from abroad. He made a good end, that much can be said. . . . But at the time a bitterness came into the Boy's mind, to give birth to a childish resolution to try to stop suffering and grief and to try to give happiness; in his poor little way he took a vow to that effect and prayed he might be given strength to keep it. He believed in prayer and does still. . . .

He stood beside his Mother's grave in a very ancient cemetery when she rejoined her Pa and Ma and those who had passed on. It was bitterly cold and the clergyman had a sniffle. The Boy noticed such things. He did not cry even then. But he thought of his Mother—no thought of what was going to happen to him crossed his mind for he had heard Uncle James promise—and he could see her quite plainly as he had seen her last. He went back to a cheerless house—not Home to him in any sense—and everyone was kind to him. That night when he went to bed, the tears came to help his loneliness. . . .

Frederica, the loving and unlucky, had died in 1901. She was only thirty-eight when she left the world which had seemed to promise her so much but had given her so very, very little. . . .

CHAPTER ELEVEN

Interior

Having gazed at the photographs of the Victorians who composed his family—and whose stories he has now committed to print—that Victorian Boy in the Box Room went to the landing and, hanging over the banisters, listened to sounds from below. Gusts of laughter and conversation reached him and the sound of the closing, at intervals, of the front door. He knew that another Third Thursday was pretty well over and that he could descend in comparative safety. And he knew where he was going. He would avoid the Drawing Room where one or two old friends might linger—he would avoid his Mother and his Aunts—he would make for the Kitchen. There was a reason for this. The remains of the feast would be down there and he could take his pick. Nobody would have grudged him, he could have had as much as he had liked in the Drawing Room, but there was a more adventurous air in the Kitchen —as if one was getting it surreptitiously—and that was far more sporting. Also, he would not have to wash his face and hands, none too clean from rummaging in the Box Room, and that appealed to him most. The great thing about the servants was that they did not mind your being dirty. So he decided on descent. He slung his gun on his back and fastened his sword to it. The pistols he had had in his belt he withdrew and placed inside his sailor blouse, which was where he and all children then carried things too big for their pockets. The blouses fitted round the waist by elastic—and his was further secured by a belt. It was an ideal receptacle, as handy as the pouch of a kangaroo. He did this to keep his belt clear because he was not going to walk downstairs—he was going the quick way—he was going to slide down the banisters. It would take a few seconds only. And off he went, savouring a joy few children know today when flats and bungalows prevail. He shot to the first landing, then

down to the second and then headlong down the long flight to the hall.
There were still voices in the Drawing Room, so he shot by, down the
three little steps on to the last landing and then accomplished the last
flight, head foremost, his usual way with these straight and speedy
polished banisters. He checked at the bottom and swung round his
legs to land on the mat without a stumble. He was expert at this game.

And he found himself in a long passage which ran the whole length
of the house in the semi-basement area. The level of the Best Road outside was higher than the back gardens of the Best Houses, so this ground
floor was semi-basement. He went down the passage to the Kitchen door.
Outside on the wall was a long row of bells on 'C' springs, the bells
which rang—or did not ring—when the inhabitants of the houses wanted
to summon their domestics. The servants knew which were which—they
soon learnt them—and as the bells were not electric there was no board
with the circular discs to indicate from whence the bell was rung. It
had to be memorized and it was. The servants knew the sound of each
bell, although to a stranger they might have all sounded the same. The
Kitchen door was now on the Boy's right and the Side door or Tradesmen's Entrance was on his left. The passage was papered with a fairly
dark but shiny paper—which could be sponged down—and it was lit
by a solitary gas burner over the Side door—which had a fanlight and
a hanging gas bracket at the foot of the stairs with two branches each,
with a burner on the end. This bracket could be raised or lowered by
pulling it down, or pushing it up—balance was kept by two vase-like
metal containers which had little holes in them and were filled with small
shot, and hung on chains which went over pulleys and thus maintained
the balance. The jet over the door was solitary and had an opaque white
globe. And just by the Side Door was an immense and deep cupboard
under the stairs tapering to a point because naturally the stairs descended.
That cupboard was no place for small boys to enter after dark. It contained all sorts of junk and useful things—candlesticks old and new, oil
lamps ditto, brooms, dustpans and brushes, pails, even Uncle James'
bicycles. It was the Box Room of Below Stairs indeed, but had not the
same entrancing variety of contents. But it was grim and dark and deep
like a wizard's cave. Old boots and shoes abounded, old hoops belonging
to the Boy (iron hoops, of course—wooden ones were suitable only
for girls), baskets filled with odds and ends (it had shelves as well), a
wringer and the knifeboard, on which knives were cleaned by rubbing
them on some composite material on which a red-brown powder was
sprinkled. The tin which contained the powder had a perforated top
and bore the likeness of the Duke of Wellington. No stainless steel then.
But still, a Boy should avoid it after dark. One never knew, especially

when the memory of Turkey Tigers lingered . . . there were no such things, of course, one *knew* that—but . . . why run risks?

There was a large iron hat and coat stand by the Side door on the opposite side to the cupboard and a mat whereon feet should be wiped, and young feet seldom were. That wiping of feet on mats showed a good deal of character—Miss Mary never wiped her boots like other people, she jumped up and down, thereby exhibiting her spasmodic nature, but not removing much mud. Miss Bessie would remonstrate on muddy days, 'Oh, Mary!' and sweep up some practically invisible mud with a dustpan and brush as a remonstrance and lesson, which was never taken to heart. The Kitchen door, opposite the Side door, was grained. The Kitchen itself was a very large and light, airy room. It looked on to the back garden through a large window which ran right across it and reached from the ceiling down to the height of an ordinary person's chin. So there was no restriction in seeing out. It was protected by thick iron bars, as were all the windows Below Stairs. Beneath the window and running the entire width of the room was an ironing board. This was also very broad. When not in use it hung from its hinges which were fastened to the wall against which it laid flat and out of the way. When wanted for ironing it was lifted up and three legs, which folded against it, instantly fell into position—and there it was, steady and strong. It had other uses for the Boy besides ironing—he did not do that, of course. But to him this board was a grand thing. He would get the servants to fix it for him, he would climb on it by means of a chair—and there he was on the deck of a ship, outside a prison preparing to rescue his comrades, inside a prison waiting to be rescued (the very iron bars had their place in his scheme of things) or, at times, he was on a stage. His performances —when he could be prevailed to do them in public, which was easy after a visit to the pantomime or theatre—were much appreciated by the domestics, who said he was as good as a play. It was his habit, when alone, to accompany all his games by narrative, invented by himself as he went along, and spoken aloud. Grown-ups would sometimes listen stealthily—for when engaged on this creative work of his he would become silent and terribly embarrassed if he thought anyone heard. But one servant—whose name was Louisa and who was with the family for years until she married a man whom she described as 'A Mariner'— thought it all marvellous. 'Mark my words,' she said, 'one day he'll write down plays and books all out of 'is own 'ead.' She was also amongst the prophets.

But ironing on that board was not a hard job—it had so much space that two worked at once and then had room. To the moderns it might have seemed laborious for there were, of course, no electric irons. The irons used were heated in front of the fire or on a gas ring—and that gas ring was almost the only form of gas-heating in the house, used only for irons or to boil a kettle quickly. The irons had little stands to fit them quite nicely, patterned with perforation, on which the irons stood when hot and a cloth of some thickness by which the handles (which naturally got hot) were held. There was a constant succession of irons being heated —they were used in relays. Their temperature was tested against the face and with a moistened finger and they were rubbed on soap to make them smooth. And the users were quite expert at judging the temperature and it was rare for anything to be scorched, although most of the ironing cloths bore imprints of over-hot irons.

The side of the room opposite the door was mostly occupied by the Kitchen Range, which stood between two immense cupboards in which were kept a variety of things like tablecloths, ironing cloths and all sorts of domestic necessities—all Victorian houses were rich in cupboard room. But the Range was an affair of terrific importance. It was of iron (or it might have been steel) and was all black except for the edges, which were of polished steel. It had to be blackleaded (Nixey's Zebra brand in black and yellow packages was the popular stuff) and the steel edges were scoured with emery paper. A vast amount of work, but there was time and labour to do it. The Range was inset in the wall. The actual grate was in the centre and capable of holding a large fierce fire and giving off great heat. It had a kind of grille in front which enabled the fire to be poked and it could be closed in with an iron door, beneath which was a space to allow for draughts. Beneath it was a receptacle into which the ashes fell, which could be taken away for emptying. About two-thirds of the way up the recess was a rack running the whole length, upon which plates were kept warm. The rails were of polished steel—hand-polished. Behind this was a series of dampers whereby the heat of the Range was regulated. On either side of the fire were ovens. The flat top of the Range had many circular holes on it, each of which had a little circular cover with a bar across—if you wanted to take it off when hot you did so with a small iron pick—if the pick was not lost. Otherwise you used the small steel poker. The circular hole over the fire was the means by which the coal got into the grate and also on which things were boiled—all the holes were used for that and some of the kettles of the period had a sort of bulge or extension in the middle of their bases, which went right down into the fire and made them boil the quicker. The Range was a thing of the utmost importance, not only for cooking but because it regulated and supplied the entire hot water system of the house. All Kitchen Ranges were temperamental. They could make the water boil in a jiffy or refuse to make it even lukewarm.

You never knew. For some people it would do nothing, for others it could not do enough. It seemed to have favourites, to take violent likes and dislikes. It was no respecter of persons, it would not oblige the lady of the house, if she lacked the right touch. Many an indifferent servant kept her 'place' because she 'understood the Range'. The question of hot water in general and baths in particular were controlled by this Range. The Victorians did not take as many baths as people do today because they had not the same facilities. A good house had a bathroom, a poorer one often none at all. When that Victorian Boy and his parents lived in a very good villa at East Molesey in the best position, opposite the Lock itself, that house contained nine rooms and a box room but had no bathroom at all. The bath was in the Kitchen, let into the floor in front of the Range. If you wanted a bath, you took off the wooden cover, heated water, poured it in, turned everyone out of the Kitchen and had the wash. There was a plug through which the water could escape but no pipe to bring it in. Imagine the conditions attendant on bathing. Yet that villa let at a good rent, was never vacant, had a large garden and excellent cellarage. Nor was it an old house, either. Baths could be taken in bedrooms in tin baths, hip baths and what were called sitz baths— and they were of painted tin, in some of them one end curved upwards to make a back-rest. The water had to be carried up in pails and the bath had to be emptied by the pails afterwards, for it stood on the floor opposite the fireplace. Some of the hearty and strong men of the period always took their baths cold. There was this about it: they were sure of getting them then.

To use the bathroom one was dependent on the Range and its be-haviour. Baths were therefore taken once a week and needed a good deal of organization to keep up the hot water supply, for naturally the tank soon got emptied and families were large. So there was a good deal of waiting even if the Range was in an obliging mood. It usually happened that if the water was hot there was a race for the bath and it was first come, first served. . . . Sometimes in big families Bath Night was split over two or three days.

The Range burned summer and winter for gas was not used for cooking—with the exception of boiling kettles on a ring, as mentioned —it was suspect in that respect and so it was for heating, but it was used for lighting universally, and often reinforced by oil lamps. The Kitchen in the Best House was lit by gas. There was one burner in the middle of the room. It descended from the ceiling by a long pipe, which turned a complete circle in the middle for reasons best known to the gas-fitter, but usually regarded as something to do with pressure. The light con-sisted of a flame of gas which was tulip shaped and had an arc of rather

Fred Terry and Julia Neilson in the early motoring days—one sat high in the world then

A Soldier of the Queen—Boer War

beautiful blue just where the flame left the actual burner, in which golden specks danced. The main colour of the gas tulip was a rich yellow. There was no globe over it in the kitchen unless it was a wire one such as used to be seen in old-fashioned theatres. As this gas-burner hung directly in the centre of the room and therefore over the middle of the table, the turning of it on and off and the lighting of it was quite a performance, but nobody ever dreamed of having its position altered. The kitchen table was a large one and stood in the centre of the room. It had a white deal top which was constantly scrubbed and scraped, as butchers do their chopping-blocks, and it had a tablecloth of shining American cloth, as a rule of white and blue or white and green, although sometimes the cloth was plain white with a coloured pattern running round the edge. This cloth lasted for years. It was washed over daily but it never seemed to split until it had done long and yeoman service. Occasionally a small piece of the rubber veneer would flake off at the corners, but even that erosion took a long time. In the first place its quality was magnificent, as was true of most things in those days—it was made to last and it did.

The servants lived in the kitchen and asked nothing better. They had no such thing as radio, they knew nothing of the films—so they read novelettes, they sewed, and they gossiped. They made their clothes and all servants wanted to own a sewing machine. Sometimes they were induced to buy these on the instalment system by specious salesmen calling at the back door. They would get into arrears and the employers would have either to help them out or make the man take it back again. The most popular present from employers to a servant leaving to get married was a sewing machine. But they could always find some work to occupy them, cleaning silver, polishing, odd jobs to save time to-morrow—and some of them were on duty to answer doors, fetch coal and, of course, answer the bell when rung. The cook had her own arm-chair by the fire and would rule the kitchen like an autocrat. When there were two servants only, the senior was the boss. Their baths were spasmodic—if the water happened to be hot one night, they would ask, or be told, to take a bath. But like most of the working people of those days they did not seem to set much store by washing. Yet they were a strong, healthy race and many lived to a good old age.

On the opposite side of the room to the Range was the Dresser— and what a dresser it was! It ran up to the ceiling, it had shelves and hooks, it had drawers, it had cupboards. All the crockery was on it— save the very best dinner and tea sets, which were stored elsewhere. But there were scores of plates, cups, jugs, slop basins, sugar bowls, saucers, sauceboats, vegetable dishes and vast platters for joints, some of them with depressions at the end into which the gravy ran as the joint was carved, finding its way, through little grooves, like juicy rivers. There was always a large pair of scales, sometimes two—one, such as may still be seen in greengrocers' shops, made all of metal and the other such as can be observed in provision merchants—of china, and coloured. The scales delighted the Boy, who played with them a lot. And that was often their chief use, despite the fact that all purchases were supposed to be weighed and that most families had the scales for this purpose.

Then there were the meat covers—made of white metal but polished to look like silver, with ornate handles which took a deal of cleaning. There were a lot of these, from huge ones large enough to cover the most gigantic turkey or joint of beef, graded down to tiny ones sufficient to cover a chop. They all had to be kept clean, inside and outside, after use. Nobody uses such things now, for food has no distance to travel from where it is dished up to where it is served. But in those days dishing up was a complicated affair—meals seldom being simple—and porterage from the kitchen to the dining room was quite a journey and often upstairs, too. The meat and fish or poultry had to be kept hot, so the covers were absolutely necessary. There were soup tureens of various sizes, bread boards and an incalculable number of things not used today. The drawers were full, too, with an enormous number of skewers, of both wood and metal, corkscrews of all kinds, some with little brushes to dust the lips of the bottles and remove the crust of age, a tin opener or two (but not many, for very little tinned food was eaten). The openers were usually made in the form of a bull's head, the blade being the lower jaw, presumably because the most usual form of tinned meat was corned beef and ox tongue, although this particular Victorian family liked its tongue in glass jars. Tinned pineapple chunks were popular, and they were cut larger than today, but perhaps the most popular were the pineapple slices, in rounds with dark marks where the cores had been. Peaches were in some demand, but there was nothing like the variety of tinned food, nor did people want it. They got it fresh and cheap. There were also in those drawers a great number of little skewers of wood, very rough and often with shavings on them, by which the butcher secured his little bill to the joint. These were kept, but nobody ever seemed to do anything with them. The little accounts were illegible also. In these drawers were hammers, nails, pincers, pliers, a saw for use on meat bones (broad in blade and square at the end), screws, gimlets, screwdrivers, a lot of picture cord, hooks of all kinds from which pictures were suspended, tin-tacks bought in a little rough paper bag, like a sugar bag, which usually burst so that the tacks got everywhere, staples, old door-handles and finger-plates which might come in handy but never did, worn-down knives, old keys which had probably never been used, wooden spoons of various sizes for various uses—nothing was ever thrown away. There were huge quantities of curtain rings, and hooks, screw-on ends of brass which went on the ends of curtain poles, small fittings of all kinds, including wooden acorns off the ends of cords by which cloth blinds were pulled up and down, those thick padded iron-holders to prevent burning of hands, old pairs of gloves used for wearing whilst cleaning the grates or the house in general and quite a lot of corks. Of course, nothing could ever be found when wanted without the whole drawer being rummaged through—and very likely not then. Somebody had always seen it and knew it was there, but . . .

Behind the door hung the string bag—not made of string but home-made of some odd piece of serge, fastened with a piece of tape through the top. Into this went every piece of string which came into the house for future use. It was a law that string round parcels should never be cut, but always untied. That law was more honoured in the breach than in the observance but the string always went into the bag. When some-body had recourse to the string bag, to get a piece of string wherewith to tie a parcel, they were rewarded with much string indeed but in one glorious, unsolvable tangle. A natural law had been at work which compels any piece of string to get inextricably involved and mixed with any and every other piece of string near it. No human hands could accomplish such confusion or such marvellous knots as this natural—or it may be supernatural—law can achieve. Perhaps the airmen were right when they spoke of gremlins—those little people had great affection for string bags and were most industrious in them. After frantic searches for a piece which was clear and an even more frantic attempt to solve the tangle, a demand would be made for the ball of string known to be in the house but as elusive as the afterwards famous Scarlet Pimpernel. Much time was wasted and tempers lost over the string bag, the only saving grace of which was the moral rectitude of anti-waste.

The kitchen table had a drawer in which lived the cutlery, spoons and forks used by the domestics. These were not of plate. The knives had black wooden handles and the forks the same (the forks were mostly two-pronged). The spoons were of inferior quality, Britannia metal or sometimes even lead. These knives and forks had not only to be washed but also polished.

In the corner stood the Meat Jack. It was quite large and its shape was like half a cone of white metal, stood on end. It was made of block tin, with a semi-circular base which stood on three legs, and in the middle of its floor was a circular depression into which the gravy ran as the cooking proceeded. The job of the Meat Jack was to roast meat, game or poultry. The roast was suspended by a hook from a clockwork affair shaped something like a mace such as used by the knights of old and this in turn was hung from the top of the jack. The jack was then placed in front of the kitchen fire, its open side facing the blaze. The clockwork gadget was then wound up and this caused the object roasting to revolve at an even pace and then, with a click, turn back again. Thus every particle of it got properly done. And whilst it was roasting, it was constantly basted in its own juice. Only those who have tasted things cooked that way know what roasting really is. Meat cooked in ovens is not roasted but baked. It took a good time to roast this way and a good deal of cleaning up afterwards, but it was worth it. The kitchen walls were covered with some kind of grained and varnished paper and its floor was covered with oilcloth, but there was a rag mat before the fire, thick and heavy. The furniture was wooden, ordinary chairs and a couple of Windsor armchairs—of wood but cushioned. On the walls hung a cheap mirror and tradesmen's almanacks, with highly coloured litho pictures more often than not of Her Majesty Queen Victoria . . . which was usually honoured by some sort of frame but generally originated from the butcher who always seemed the most loyal of subjects. There might be a text or two, if the family was pious, with a flower design and a white frame. Of course, the servants could hang up any pictures they liked, so long as they were decorous. Underneath the dresser on a flat shelf lived the saucepans, frying pans, cooking dishes and, as a rule, a very large fish kettle of block tin, large enough to take an entire salmon. People bought and cooked entire salmons in those days of large families. They did not cost very much. Sometimes there was a special sort of tripod stand with little shelves for saucepans and kettles but it usually got knocked over and was discarded. From hooks in the dresser also hung such things as nutmeg graters, bread graters, lemon squeezers, tea strainers and other implements of that kind. The fender to the range was of black metal with a polished steel top, which broadened out to a circle in the middle, on which things could be placed to keep warm.

But there were things in that kitchen not to be met with now. They were called Fly Papers. Flies were very plentiful then and had to be kept under, so there were destructors of all kinds. There were square brown sheets of thick paper, with pictures of flies printed in black on them. These were put into soup plates with a trickle of beer over them —or sometimes sugar and water. The flies came down to drink the beer or the sweet mixture and were poisoned—or that was the idea, though many flies did not seem to care much. It was believed that the poison was arsenic and a celebrated murder case revolved around this type of fly-killer. There were also large sheets of thick white paper covered with a shiny, glutinous stuff which was very sticky indeed. Men sold these in the streets, wearing tall hats with a sticky sheet tied around it, always full of flies. It was certainly more effective than the arsenic mixture. There might be a thing like a reel of cotton suspended from the central gas jet by what appeared to be a piece of string which passed through the reel, knotted at the lower end to secure it. Again, this string was very sticky. Flies alighted on it and never got off again. It was cleared of the dead bodies by the simple device of taking it down, pulling the string through the reel and suspending it again. Flies never seemed to take warning from the corpses of their kind. Perhaps they did not care. There were also little paper cages, which were hung up, called fly cages. How these were of use passes comprehension, for if a fly was foolish enough to enter there was nothing to prevent it going out and nothing to slaughter it. But there were quite a lot in use.

Altogether the kitchens in those Best Houses were bright, airy, comfortable large rooms, and kept very warm—too warm in summer, for the range supplying the hot water never went out. There was a lot of work in them, the range and the fender alone meant the vast use of elbow grease.

After the kitchen one came to the garden door. That was the only way out into the garden from the house so it meant that visitors had to go right through the domestic regions and even get a sight of the scullery. For the scullery was next to it. This was a large room, with distempered walls, mostly of pink or yellow and the distemper came off on one's hands and clothes. It had a large sink under the window, and the window was also protected by iron bars. Next to the sink was an immense copper for the family wash. The wooden circular top to this from time to time served the Victorian Boy as a useful shield, being held by pieces of rope tied round it, but it was never very secure in the grip and not entirely satisfactory. There was a little grate in the copper by means of which it was made to boil. Water came into it from a tap. There was another large dresser against the wall. opposite the window, on the flat part of which knives were cleaned on the knifeboard. There was a mincing machine kept there, but used in the kitchen. There was a wringer and a mangle, for nearly all the washing was done at home. Opposite the copper was the domestic lavatory and two large cupboards. In one the vegetables were kept in greengrocers' circular baskets, in the other were the pails, mops, brooms, scrubbing brushes, soap (soap for cleaning purposes, not toilet soap), flannels, rags, and such like. The domestic soap was yellow and in long square bars. You cut off what was wanted, like so much cheese. The name of that soap was 'Primrose'. It can still be obtained but it is differently packed. There was nothing like the variety of soap powders and detergents available nowa-days—in fact, there were very few indeed, the best known being Hud-son's Extract of Soap. There was a pot of beeswax, greatly esteemed for polishing purposes, Monkey Brand, Sapolio, blacking and black-lead and the boot-cleaning paraphernalia, and metal polish, as well as furniture polish, which was a kind of greyish-yellow cream in stone bottles. All of which combined to give the cupboard—and the scullery—a complex-haunting aroma not to be met with today—that full flavour which scented Victorian housekeeping. The scullery was constantly being scrubbed out, and it had a stone floor. On that stone floor the Boy learned to spin tops, instructed therein by the male odd-job man—or youth—who in that household was always called 'William', whether it was his name or not. One of these Williams was an expert top spinner and imparted his art to the boy. There were peg tops and whip tops, the former requiring more skill. You wound whip cord round the grooved portion of the peg, you threw it with a jerk, holding on to the string, and the top span like a Dervish. William could do wonders with spinning tops. He looped the string round the peg, jerked the top in the air and caught it on the palm of his hand, still spinning. He could get his hand under a spinning top and make it come on his palm, also still spinning—there was nothing he could not do. And the Boy was a willing and successful pupil but he could never do the loop trick. Whip tops were whipped with a small whip to keep them going.

William—there were three of them in this house during the period under observation—always considered it part of his duties to 'help the young master'. It was a welcome relaxation from his work of carrying coals, cleaning boots and windows, doing all the odd jobs about the house and generally making himself useful. It did not matter if the William was seventeen or sixty—and there were Williams of both ages —he of the seventeen years was the top expert—they were always ready for a game, and when any of the Family were heard approaching William and the Boy would disperse severally with conspiratorial air. The Boy found plenty of uses for the scullery, which he liked, besides top spinning. He began what was then called Science at school and took some interest in it. Borrowing certain materials from the school 'lab', he informed his Family he would show them how to make chlorine, which his Family thought very clever of him. He succeeded beyond his wildest dreams and the smell did not evaporate for days. And having been provided with a retort by his Uncle James, who was of a scientific turn himself on occasions, he told the Family he would show them how to distil water. Again they watched, although they should have known better.

Not much water was distilled but there was certainly a lot of broken glass. Scientific experiments in the scullery-laboratory were thereafter banned.

Washing Day was the gala day there—and the Boy kept clear of it. He was and is allergic to the smell of washing, steam and wet clothes. But Washing Day—a Monday in that household—was a busy day. The good lady who obliged by doing the wash arrived early and did not leave until she had finished her job—the time varying according to the size of the family and the wash. She received half a crown and her food, also constant refreshment, sometimes in the form of glasses of ale—most families kept a small barrel of draught ale in the cellar—tea and a snack of bread and cheese at mid-morning. The servants all had to lend a hand, except the cook, and even she did so at times. Large circular wooden wash-tubs were brought in from where they were kept outside, also zinc oval-shaped tubs were filled, and things were put in to soak. The copper fire was lit and work began. These washerwomen not only scrubbed and rinsed, they also did the mangling and wringing. There was always a mangle and a wringer in the scullery, things seldom seen in houses today. The mangling was hard work, with the wheel to turn and thick material to go between the wooden rollers. Sometimes the washerwomen did the ironing, except for handkerchiefs and delicate pieces. They worked amazingly hard but they never slacked. Sometimes they were large and strong, sometimes thin and seemingly frail—but both sorts seemed quite tireless. They became family retainers, working for the same families for years and becoming practically a part of it. There was one who worked in the Best House who had about the ugliest face possible to find on a human being. It would have earned her a fortune on the stage—she would have needed no make-up at all for the Weird Sisters and would have made the others seem quite handsome. As a pantomime 'Nasty' she would have been without equal. She had a large and shapeless body, a few fangs for teeth and a plentiful supply of warts—her hair was of a dull reddish hue and going grey. If a Phrygian cap had been placed on her head, Dickens would have found his ideal 'Vengeance'. Yet she was a gentle, lovable soul and children, who do not always judge by exteriors, adored her. Despite her looks she had found a husband and had a family. When at last she could work no more, one of her daughters succeeded her. But that ugly dame was a wonderful laundress. She shrank nothing—and some of them were champion shrinkers—she spoiled nothing and when she had finished with them, clothes looked new. The Victorian Family were much attached to her and she to them. No doubt that applied to others for whom she also worked. She would 'oblige' by giving a hand at Spring Cleaning to her favourites and she polished as well as she washed. She was quite contented with her half a crown a day although in that household she got extras. She was what was known as a 'Treasure'. Her daughter, although good, was not so expert or tireless as the old lady.

Finished clothes were put into clothes baskets and then into their appointed places. If fine, drying was done in the garden, but if wet it had to be done in the scullery, and there were hooks in the walls to which lines were attached. This was not popular with anyone and those who have had experience of drying clothes in the confined space of modern houses will appreciate it. The drying overlapped into the kitchen where clothes horses, fully laden, stood before the fire. There were hundreds of clothes pegs, always at hand, kept in baskets. They were wooden and forked, and went over the garment or object to be dried, thus holding it on the line. Clips were not in use. Washing Day meant confusion, steam and heat, to say nothing of that peculiar odour which soap, water and clothes distil. The only individual to enjoy washing days was the cat, who would sit on the heaps of clothes, dirty or clean, and be constantly shooed off, until it jumped on top of the very warm copper, curled up with a sigh and went fast asleep.

The scullery was where the washing up of dishes was done, too. The sink was shallow, there were none of the deep ones in use today, and a lot of splashing about was unavoidable. The lighting was gas; there were four burners and these had wire globes, not glass.

The scullery looked out on to a tiled court, and the tiles, which were red, had to be constantly washed down and cleaned with red ochre. Opposite the scullery window, on the other side of the court, at some distance away, was the dustbin. This was not the movable zinc affair of today but a large, square brick box built against the wall. It had a sloping wooden lid which was lifted for the purpose of putting in the rubbish. In front was a little wooden door, which lifted up on slots, rather like a portcullis, and this was the method by which the dustmen cleared away the contents. They came round with open carts with two wheels, drawn by horses, and the carts had high sides to them. To deposit his load of rubbish in the cart the dustman climbed a little ladder. In that Best House the dustmen came right through the passage from the side door, into the court, bringing a large basket like an upright pannier with them. They then opened the small door and forked out the rubbish, which they deposited in the basket. They carried it through the house again, up the side steps, right down the front garden, up the ladder and shot it into the cart. Often they had to make several journeys. They wore rough clothes, corduroy trousers strapped at the knee, enormous boots with nails, a kind of loose shirt over their waistcoats but not tucked in, which was of coarse thick material, coats open and rather cut away at the front, a handkerchief round the neck and a leather hat fitting tightly to the head with a flap over the shoulders. Sometimes they had a bit of excitement by finding a rat, which they killed expertly. Dogs loathed them and unless chained up or locked in would fly at them. And the barking never ceased until the dustmen left. Cats fled at the mere sight of them. They were strong rough men and surly, but still gruffly polite. Often they were rewarded with a twopenny tip and they touched their caps for it. It bought a pint of beer. They shouted 'Dust-Oi' as they came along, and sometimes rang bells. It was all very un-hygienic—not even the carts had covers. Bottles were their perquisites and any bits of scrap they found—they put these in a sack at the back of the cart. They did not get a fraction of what is paid to dustmen today. But it cost them so little to live.

The Boy liked the tiled court, despite the proximity to the dustbin. He could play there when the garden was still too wet. And on the floor of the scullery and the tiles of the court he learnt to roller skate, on a pair of large and heavy skates he found in that dark cupboard beneath the stairs, relics of probably the first roller-skating craze. Ice skates, which screwed on to the heel, were kept in that cupboard, too. Every member of that family could skate, and did so on every opportunity. The parks near the ends of the roads had lakes and not very far away— a penny bus fare—there was a sports ground with a large asphalt entrance to it, about as large as four or five tennis courts. When it was cold enough the enterprising owners flooded it and turned it into a good rink. It was always crowded with skaters—at 6d. a time.

It was, however, always considered a pity that the entrance to the garden lay through the domestic quarters and by the side of the scullery and that the first thing visitors saw was the dustbin. But the peculiar construction of the house and the different levels made no other way possible. One or two residents installed iron staircases to the first floor, which was expensive and entailed structural alterations and looked pretty bad. In the Best House, they made do with the ordinary door. It was kept locked and bolted at night and had a chain to it, but although the house was 'locked up' every night with a regular routine, in all the years the Family lived there, some twenty in all, there was not even an attempt at burglary. . . . And nobody was afraid of opening the door at any time in the night—for nobody was ever coshed when they did so. The policeman on the beat prevented that. . . .

CHAPTER TWELVE

Still Below Stairs

BEFORE the stairs in the Best House are ascended there is a good deal yet to observe. One or two details have to be fitted into place, and the question of the Domestics, a very important part of every Victorian and Edwardian household, must be considered. There were the mouse-traps, which were kept in the scullery cupboard. These were of the old-fashioned, wooden variety, like little cages out of a menagerie. They had a sloping door in front beyond which a piece of wood projected which, when the trap was set, was lightly held up by a little hook, the other end of which went into the trap and held a piece of cheese or bacon rind. The idea was that the mouse entered the trap, nibbled the bait, which released the door—which slammed down—and there was the mouse, safely caught. Often the mouse got off scot free, if the trap was ill-adjusted. But if caught, its tail was always shut under the door and the poor little wretch was in pain as well as imprisoned. It could see liberty beyond the bars, perhaps its own friends and relations. . . . In the morning it was put, trap and all, into a pail of water until it drowned and then it was thrown into the dustbin. There was also a type of circular trap with the bait in the middle. These were like metal dishcovers, flat and round, with holes pierced through the sides, through which the mice crawled to get the bait. They could reach it when halfway through the hole and, when they bit, springs closed on them and broke their backs. It was the more humane of the two but it did not catch so many mice.

Most kitchens had an egg boiler—one of those hour-glass gadgets in which red sand poured from one bulb to another in just the right time to boil an egg. A good cook ignored them. She knew by instinct what was the right boiling time.

In the very late Victorian and in Edwardian times a knife-cleaning machine came into being, a circular wooden affair on legs with apertures into which the knives were thrust. A handle was turned and the knives were cleaned—it was made by a firm with the name of Kent and saved much labour. That was before the days of stainless steel. Knives in that era took much cleaning, but they had really sharp blades.

The servants kept a lot of their own possessions in the kitchen, nearly always their workboxes. Every woman then worthy of the name had a workbox. Some were plain, some ornate as to the woodwork, but all had the interior lined with padded satin and they held all the paraphernalia for needlework—and ninety-nine out of a hundred women were expert with their needles. Even Miss Mary had a workbox but nobody ever saw her use it. . . . There was usually the end of a candle handy, for waxing the ends of thread and making it easy for it to pass through the eye of the needle. There was a lot to do in those houses and any amount of elbow grease required. There were very few labour-saving devices. Until the Bissell arrived, all carpets were swept with brooms (carpets lasted much longer in those days, by the way, before vacuum cleaners took off the pile) and the 'pieces' were taken up by hand, with dustpan and brush. But the idea that domestic servants were driven, overworked slaves is quite a fallacy. Good domestic servants were treated well and with respect. Indeed, they had a high idea of themselves and they knew their worth. They were prepared to work, and if they found what they considered 'a good place' they did their best to keep it. But they maintained their independence and could 'give notice' if dissatisfied. Mistresses simply hated receiving 'notice'. Equally, of course, if not satisfactory, they could receive 'notice' too. The most precious possession of a domestic servant was her 'character'—her 'reference'. If she forfeited that she was indeed lost. All that remained was 'steps' or a factory—and domestic servants looked down upon a girl who worked in a factory. In these days when only One Class is insisted on, it is well to remember that the lower castes were just as class-conscious as the upper and had their own social gradings as well. A girl engaged in 'service' saw nothing degrading in it. Most likely she came of a line of ancestors who had all been 'in service'—on both paternal and maternal side. There were, of course, bad mistresses, but they either got 'notice' given them or had to put up with bad servants. The average worked out. The girl in service who wore a 'uniform' was quite happy, independent within bounds of good behaviour and never saucy or impertinent. She 'knew her place' just as much as she hoped to 'keep her place'. Indeed, where several servants were kept, the etiquette below stairs was far stricter than above them. The girl in service had not the faintest idea that she was engaged in a Science. To her, it was a job. Now it is Domestic Science. She wore her print dress and her rough apron in the mornings with her little cap on her head. She flirted with the tradesmen who came to the door and often found her husband that way; very few good domestics died old maids. In the afternoon, she changed into her black frock, with a smart apron and an even smarter cap, sometimes with streamers, and very nice she looked—and knew it. It was not such a bad life as it has been made out to be. Of course, not all employers were ideal, but neither were all the maids paragons, or 'treasures'. They worked hard during the morning and there was quite a lot of running about in the afternoon, but at night, unless the family dined late, there was not much to do. They washed up the dinner things—supper usually waited until the morning—and they answered the bell—and if the family or the best part of it were out, that did not ring much. If the family entertained, that made a bit more work, but they looked upon it as seeing a bit of life. Many girls preferred a house in which there was a lot of entertaining to one which was quiet. Otherwise they sat in their kitchens, did their needlework, read their 'smart novelettes' or *Modern Society*—they seldom read a newspaper—and gossiped. They talked a good deal about the Mistress, who was referred to as 'She'. They ate a good deal, they drank a lot of tea and even more cocoa, which was a great kitchen drink. As regards freedom, they had one afternoon and evening out a week and every other Sunday. Friction sometimes arose when the mistress, to suit her convenience, asked them to change their day—but that was seldom, for she had more sense and, if more than one servant was kept, it did not arise. In some households (such as the Best House) after long service they also got a whole day a month. The proviso was that they must be in at ten o'clock, unless special permission was given and a good reason shown. That rule was really for their own good. There were no cinemas, no dance halls, and not many amusements within their reach. They were prone to 'get into trouble'. Another rule was that no 'followers' were allowed—'followers' being young men who came courting. That was blinked at when the girl was well known. They saw quite a lot of young men, those tradesmen's messengers, who all had an eye for a nice girl likely to make a good wife. And there were the rather more superior young men who came round from the grocers or the provision merchants to take orders, which they wrote in a book. These men, who had quite good jobs, often found their wives amongst the girls who opened the doors and gave them the lists—and they opened their own shops, of which their ex-servant wives became the efficient mistresses and often good business women, for they knew how to serve.

Each girl was expected to come to her job with a print dress or two and a black dress. But often these were provided by the employers, there being an understanding that they were to be paid for out of wages —and if the girl was good, this got overlooked. Their caps, aprons and the little white cuffs or wristlets were given them as part of their Christmas or birthday presents. A housemaid, or 'general', got £14 to £18 a year in ordinary middle-class houses and a cook from £18 to even £25 a year. They had their keep and 'all found'. And they were, more often than not, far more comfortable in service than at home and infinitely better off. The most dreaded type of girl was the 'smasher'—that had then not the same meaning as in modern slang—the one who wreaked havoc amongst the glass, crockery and everything breakable and who would come to her mistress with the plaintive story that 'it came apart in me 'ands, mum' or that 'the cat done it'. Sometimes they were made to pay but if the smashing was habitual they got their notice. Very cheerful girls, who constantly sang about the house, were perhaps not over-encouraged, and impertinence, pertness and head-tossing were not tolerated. There was discipline, and it was no bad thing. A girl was expected to be clean, honest and willing—great stress was laid in references on 'willingness'.

More often than not domestics and the families they served were very good friends and the girl, after marriage, would come round 'to oblige' at busy seasons, such as Spring Cleaning or at times when her ex-mistress was 'without'. They worked hard, they had to work hard, it was a hard-working age and people did not expect to get on if they did not work. And everyone wanted to 'get on' and 'better themselves'. They had no taxation to worry about and not until Edwardian times did they have National Health Insurance. What they earned, they kept. By and large, they were strong, healthy girls. Some 'got into trouble' and then they were dismissed, returned to their families (if any) with their goods in the little tin trunk which was their usual luggage. They had 'lost their character' in both senses of the word. That was then very serious. Mostly they were very honest, though there were some black sheep who pilfered, who stole the spirits and put water in the decanters, or who conveyed food home to their relatives. If caught, they too lost their characters. Those Policemen on the beat were supposed to have a soft corner for cooks, who were alleged to regale them with rabbit pie —why always rabbit, nobody knew, except that it was very cheap. But it is doubtful if anyone ever saw a policeman in a kitchen whilst on duty, minus his helmet, consuming this provender. . . . It was a favourite joke in the 'comics' and with music-hall comedians and always got a laugh.

The giving of a reference was a responsibility on the employer and the lady of the house had to be fair in this respect. She usually was so, for having got rid of what she considered a bad maid, she did not want the girl to be without work. Sometimes the references were a bit kindly but the lady salved her conscience by saying to herself, 'Well, although she did not suit me, she might suit other people who are not so particular.' Written references were suspect, of course, and always had to be confirmed. Where possible a prospective employer would ask the late employer personally and this saved trouble all round, for much could be said which was not possible to put on paper. Some employers who regretted a good maid leaving were vindictive—but usually overdid it and the girl did not suffer thereby.

Ladies in search of servants got them either by personal knowledge and recommendation or through the agency called a Registry Office. These establishments were usually run by middle-aged ladies, sometimes by sisters, who did a thriving business and fulfilled a useful economic function. They were the forerunners, in their field, of the Labour Exchanges and far more personally efficient. They took a personal interest and knew what they were handling. It was their job to find maids for mistresses and mistresses for maids, and they did it. The lady finding herself 'without'—the popular phrase meaning without a servant—went to her local registry office and 'registered' her want. She gave full particulars of the job, wages, evenings out, other servants kept (if any), all the good points, and she also stated what she expected to find in anyone working for her. She paid 2s. 6d. registration fee. In due course the lady in charge of the office produced a succession of applicants for the job, for servants registered with her, too. When suited, the employer paid the office another fee, sometimes 7s. 6d., sometimes 10s. (in some rather lordly offices it was £1), the fee being dependent on what was wanted. The value of this system was that the lady of the Registry Office knew all about the employers on her books and their peculiarities. She found out from her knowledge of them, from what previous maids had told her, and she also, with great tact, 'pumped' clients about each other. She could —and did—warn maids about idiosyncrasies on the part of mistresses. *Per contra*, she knew all about the maids too, and would give good advice to those who wanted them. She knew who was likely to suit whom, and she did not make many mistakes. It was to her advantage to give mutual satisfaction. Sending a bad maid reacted against her and getting a good maid a bad job had the same effect. She gave the maids useful advice and also would give diplomatic guidance to mistresses, so neatly done that they were often unaware of it. There were a lot of these Registry Offices and it must have been quite a paying game in the days before domestic service became Domestic Science. The beauty of the system was—which should delight Socialist hearts—that the employer paid and the employee got the service for nothing. A few Registry Offices remain today but the scope is limited—they deal mostly in what are known as 'dailies'—a description which is often quite literally true. . . .

Good employers looked after their girls and got good results. They kept the girl 'in her place'—and without discipline nothing can be achieved—but mainly they were kind and helpful. They got the girl's confidence. Some made the mistake of being too friendly and familiar with their servants which always made trouble. There were additional difficulties in the cases of young girls just starting work and a good deal of responsibility devolved on the mistresses, who really had to teach them their job. They had to get them to understand method and punctuality—all sorts of things—and above all, thoroughness, which was esteemed above 'willingness'. They had to protect the girls against the touts who called at the side door and persuaded them into purchases on the instalment system which they could not afford. That often led to constant dunning and eventual pilfering. But if the girl told her mistress she got help at once. Naturally there were housewives who put upon domestics, who treated them badly and overworked them, and showed them no consideration at all. If the maid was any good, she gave notice and the lady got a black mark at the Registry Office too. According to modern experts, the evil was always on the side of the employers. It was not so, by any manner of means. The maids had many faults; there were pilferers, slatterns, bad workers, late risers, slovens, and girls who drank and got into trouble, who 'Borrowed' their mistresses' clothes, who left dust in corners and swept it under the mat, who did not use 'elbow grease', who 'smashed', who forgot, and left impressions of dirty fingers all over the place.

Perhaps the worst employer was the poacher, the woman who enticed good servants away from the houses of her friends, by promise of easier and better conditions and more wages. Some loyal girls would report this to their mistress; some, less loyal, would give 'notice' and go to the tempter. This form of poaching was one of the great social crimes; successful or unsuccessful, it was never forgiven. Also, it seldom worked out for the poacher, who could never be quite sure of the loyalty of the 'poached' and feared to lose her. The girl, on her part, felt too secure and got uppish, so nobody was any the better off—for it usually led to 'notice' on one side or the other. The lady addicted to poaching found herself in a false position. She did not like meeting the lady whose servant she had suborned, at 'At Homes' or other social functions. She knew that all her acquaintances were aware of what she had done; the bereaved mistress saw to that. Long friendships were thus broken, and it even extended to the husbands, who were members of the same clubs or political associations and found themselves estranged. . . .

On the whole, things worked pretty well and it took a World Revolution to break up domestic service. The girls who wanted to work got on; those who did not, paid the price. The girls did not have luxury, but they never had had it so did not expect it or miss it. More often than not their lives in domestic service were far more comfortable than at home, with better surroundings and much better food. They knew their position in the world and fulfilled it. They got small wages but the money went much farther. They did not use make-up, silk or nylon stockings, flash clothes, and they never went to a hairdresser's for hair-do's or perms. They used hair-curlers and tongs in the privacy of their rooms. They did not try to emulate the folk who were better off or in a superior social position—and such things were clearly marked then. Maids there were who had been known to copy a hat worn by their mistress. They never did it twice.

For the greater portion of the period under review there was no National Health Insurance or pension scheme at all. But if the girls got ill, the family doctor attended them, at the employer's expense. It was not so bad. Most of the girls had accounts in the Post Office Savings Bank. And it should be noted that when they left to get married, although their husbands' earnings were small compared with today, they did not have to continue to work in order to make both ends meet. The good girls became one of the family and often took a hand in bringing up the children where no Nannie could be afforded. They got very fond of each other, the maids and the children, and the attachment was lifelong. Maids of long service would often speak their minds freely and have attention paid to what they said.

So much has been said recently about the slavery and degradation of domestic service, either by people who were ignorant of the facts or by those with an old grievance. There were bad cases, but there were far more good than bad, and the servant was always free to leave.

The old-fashioned domestic servant was no serf and would have been very angry had she been so described. Some people, who should have known better, employed the terms 'skivvy' or 'slavey' as of reproach—the same sort of person who jeered at a black-coated worker as being a 'clurk'. They were the people who had lately come from that class themselves and who, by their efforts to hide it, made it all the more apparent. Such things are very obvious today in the new-found equality of the classes, when One Class so often becomes No Class at all. The Domestic Servant was no slave but a free member of the community doing a good job and mostly doing it well. This statement—or the opening part of it—

The Boer War "Buttons" which all loyal Britons wore in their coat lapels. The Victorian Boy collected them—they are photos of the Generals, of Queen Victoria, of Kruger and Cabinet Ministers. Pinned on this green plushed piece of cardboard, made by his Mother, the now Old Victorian Boy still has them today

Upper left: Hayden Coffin. *Upper right:* Willie Edouin. *Lower left:* Sir Charles Hawtrey. *Lower right:* Sir Charles Hawtrey and Dagmar Wiehe

will probably bring a storm of protest. It is written from personal know-ledge and observation. It is written by one who was, with his wife, an employer of domestic servants. They have been married for forty-three years. During that period one maid stayed for five years and left to get married. Another stayed for thirteen years—before she too married, and she still keeps affectionate contact with the family—and a third served for seven and a half years until the labour restrictions and call-up of the Second World War took her away. That accounts for twenty-five and a half years—with three maids. They had, in the intervals, one who nearly set the house on fire, another who drank, a third who was mentally defective and refused to leave her bed, and another with far too long and intimate a following of followers, who entertained them in the house, using her employer's goods—when they were out . . . and ever since the middle of the last war they have had to rely on casual labour, which accounts for roughly eleven years. The facts speak for themselves. . . .

In that semi-basement, at the other end of the long passage to that where the kitchen and scullery was situated, were the Pantry or Larder, the wine cellar and the coal cellar. These were, all three, large and com-modious, if dark. The pantry and the wine cellar had windows masked by close-meshed wire netting. The pantry was always full to overflowing, for one could get everything one wanted at a fraction of today's cost. The wine cellar held wine, if the family was so disposed, and most of them were, and also a small barrel of draught beer, sometimes cider as well. There was no gas in either of these places, so candles had to be used. The coal cellar which, as described, lay below the front steps, was simply enormous. It could hold about ten tons of coal. This had to be taken in scuttles to all parts of the house, of course, and it was a dirty job digging out the coal and carrying it about. But at least that coal was under cover and not—as in modern times—kept outside the house, so that those bringing it in get very wet in rainy weather and bring into the house not only coal dust but mud and bad tempers. In that Victorian coal cellar, a candle was always used. Nowadays one needs an electric torch, and gets water down the back of one's neck from the sloping roof of the shed whilst trying to extract the last remnants of a scanty supply without knowledge of when more is to come. The coal cellar in the Victorian house normally held four tons, and the cost of the whole lot was about one-third of the cost of one ton today, and the size and quality so much superior as to be incredible to those who did not know it.

There remains one room on that particular floor of the House. This was called the Breakfast Room and rightly named, for the Family not only breakfasted there but had all their meals there except on very high

M

and mighty occasions when the so-called Dining Room was actually used for that purpose. This was semi-basement but still remained a light and airy apartment. It looked out upon the rockery or fernery and area previously described, and its bay windows were guarded with iron bars. The windows themselves had lace curtains and the recess in which the window stood had also heavy plush curtains to pull across it in cold weather, which worked on rings and were, at ordinary times, looped back with heavy sashes. The windows also had Venetian blinds. In the recess stood a large stand of bamboo, which held an assortment of plants, mostly ferns, according to the taste of the Family. The room itself was large and oblong. At the end facing the window were two large cup-boards—it will be noted how well off for cupboard room were Victorian houses. The cupboard nearest the door held the Boy's toys and was always quite full. To him it held treasures more priceless than the Crown Jewels. Here were his soldiers; he had well over a thousand of them, representing all branches of the British and Colonial Army. Every regiment was there, from the Household Cavalry to the Bengal Lancers, from the Foot Guards to the West Indian Regiment. He even had some Ghurkas. He had artillery of all kinds, and a mountain-battery, with a gun that not only fired little lengths of steel as shells but which took to pieces and could be loaded on the backs of mules. The gunners wore white helmets, blue tunics and white breeches, and puttees. He had toy battle-ships and naval guns with crews and a detachment of marines. He had the then up-to-date soldiers made by Britain (11½*d*. per box), and the older, flat leaden affairs which came mostly from Germany and were not at all so good. He had Zulus, Arabs, the Camel Corps, Red Indians and some cowboys. He had four forts of various kinds and importance. The cupboard also was an armoury, for this was no pacifist lad but a boy who adored military things; which he did not appreciate so much when actually amongst them many years later. He had toy guns, mostly of the hammer variety, more like muskets than rifles, but to set against that he always had a Daisy Air Gun, at 3*s*. 6*d*., which fired pellets and darts, and was Heaven! He had all sorts of pistols and revolvers. He had toy swords which, when bought, had belts, and sabretaches attached, but these, with the sheaths, always got discarded. The swords were blunt and had no point, the blade being squared off at the end. But he had better than that. He had some old long French sword-bayonets which to him were the real thing, and they were undoubtedly genuine. He had a more modern sword-bayonet, too, also of French manufacture, which was, he decided, a small-sword, and some old foils which were rapiers. He had helmets of all kinds, one of steel, and also a breast-plate, which he soon outgrew. There were air pistols, loaded by a spring which when fired protruded from the barrel and did not look real at all. But the dart so fired had penetrative power, which made up for it.

There were games of all kinds, horses and carts (no motors, of course), improvised shields, a variety of clubs; one extremely useful article in that respect, which was of oriental origin, had come to be used as a copper-stick and been begged by him as a weapon (copper-sticks were used to stir up the clothes in the coppers and made splendid clubs), catapults, bows and arrows, both toy and real ones found in the Box Room, various balls, his lances, spears and javelins, daggers (some very serviceable), bags of marbles, lucky boards, conkers, two large wooden cannons painted bright red, bandoliers and revolver holsters, a couple of axes, and some hammers which he knew were maces—one of them a large wooden mallet—toys without end. And on the shelf above were school satchels, and a lot of books of various kinds. His cricket bats and stumps he kept in his bedroom. They were sacred. His boats, of which he had quite a fleet, were not kept in the toy cupboard but in the airing-cupboard, handy for the bathroom. There was usually a football there, too, and an assortment of 'compo' cricket balls—he had sometimes a real one which was kept apart and treasured. That cupboard was the centre of the Boy's world.

In the other cupboard were kept linen tablecloths, tray-cloths and mats—the best of all kinds—the best tea-service and silver tea- and coffee-pots and the plate-basket which held the silver and which Miss Bessie cleaned herself. Also the things wanted for the breakfast-room table; the accessories like cruets, glass jam-dishes, table napkins and rings. Each of the family had two napkin-rings of their own, one of ivory with their names engraved thereon and one of silver, bearing their initials. Some of these still survive and are in use, as are some of the salt-cellars and the knife-rests of silver. Also in that cupboard was a large oak and silver salad bowl, with a porcelain lining (removable), and a very handsome salad bowl of cut-glass. There were biscuit-boxes, too, some silver, some cut-glass; and one, which had a cruet, jam-jar and sweet-dish to match, was made of glass of a lime-yellow hue, which looked very cool and fresh and had delicate ornamentation. The Boy thought it an object of beauty. He had a glass of his own with his name engraved on it, done whilst he watched at an Exhibition. He took great care of it, but a clumsy maid broke it and he never got another. Between those two cupboards was a sofa. It was long with one end curling upwards and away like a breaking wave. It was of mahogany and very highly polished. But it was upholstered in horsehair, very black, very shiny, very slippery and very uncomfortable. There was a kind of bolster, also of horsehair, which went across the curve where the 'wave' ascended from the frame. The

main seat was like a mattress and had buttons on it. It was neither ornamental nor inviting. It might have decorated a morgue with some degree
of suitability. If anyone lay upon this sofa and neglected to put a cushion
under their cheek, the result was a sharp pricking and the stamping on the
countenance of a pattern in angry red, like a nasty rash. The sharp pieces
of horsehair could penetrate clothes. Nobody ever used it except children,
who found a painful delight in printing patterns on their faces and hands
and looking like a bad attack of measles. It harboured the dust, a smart
blow would bring forth great clouds. The Boy knew the right use for this
thing, with the penetration possessed by childish minds. To him it was
not a sofa at all. It was a ship. It was whatever kind of ship he required it
to be. Wearing his steel helmet, shield and sword, as he stood against the
prow, it could be a Roman galley or a Viking Longship waiting to swoop.
It was Drake's *Golden Hind* or *Revenge*, or it was a Spanish galleon to be
captured. At times it was a First Rater, a ship of the line of eighty guns,
chasing craven French ships off the seas and sweeping them for England—
not Britain, England. It was all according to what book or story he was
reading at the time. It was often a pirate ship or a smuggler's. He would
mount thereon his cannon, fore and aft—the latter being a stern-chaser.
Of course it was the *Hispaniola*, with the Boy as practically every character
in *Treasure Island*. Occasionally it was an ironclad or torpedo-boat
destroyer, or just—a gunboat. It had a season as *Condor*, the small craft
which brought Lord Charles Beresford fame at Alexandria and now and
again it was a *dahabeyah* trying to get up the Nile to rescue Gordon, a topic
still fresh in conversation in that Boy's childhood. But it was never a
mere sofa.

   The table of that room was very large and fourteen people could be
seated around it. The lighting was a central chandelier of gas, with an
ornate steel cover and a circular plate of opal glass above to prevent the
whitewashed ceiling from blackening. There were two gas jets, wall-
brackets, on either side of the fireplace, with glass globes—again opal
glass but with little bright stars on them. The fireplace was on the left of
the room facing the window, with a real hearthstone, which meant more
cleaning, a low steel fender, which had to be polished and emeried, and
steel fire-irons which caused more work, too. The mantelpiece was of
marble but covered by a fitted board which bore a dark crimson valance
of plush. There were a lot of ornaments but the central object was a
clock. This was of ormolu, covered with a glass case, like half a bubble.
The clock, the dial of which was round and appeared to be the top of a
small barrel, was the very uncomfortable lounging place of a literary gentleman of the late 17th or early 18th century, who reclined more gracefully
than one would have expected and gazed pensively into the room. His

left hand supported his chin, his right hand, extended and resting on a small column, held his quill pen. Before him, on top of the dial, lay his tablets or a book. There was rich ornamentation over all. Nobody knew the identity of this man, who was certainly not Shakespeare but an author of some later date. The clock was undoubtedly French, so the author was held to be Molière. If so, he showed remarkably little sparkle. That clock had never been known to go. Its hands pointed persistently to ten twenty-five, so it was right twice a day. It was held to be an object of beauty. On either side of it was a china dog, of the greyhound breed, but of a curious tint, a kind of flesh-pinky-yellow. They sat on blue china cushions and they had as companions two china canines which were, judging by their ears, some species of spaniel. They were white with large red spots and gazed impassively into the room. They had no cushions but had chain collars fastened by large gold padlocks.

At either end of the mantelpiece was a set of lustres, also in glass cases, which gave off melodious chimes when dusted every day and reflected the light like diamonds. And scattered about were small ornaments, put there to get them out of the way until a rightful place could be found—and never moved again, except for cleaning. Fixed to the wall was a large mirror, a half-circle, with a thin gold frame. There were two mahogany and horsehair armchairs and sixteen small mahogany and horsehair chairs. On the right of the room was a large buffet, with three tiers, called a dumb waiter. This, too, was mahogany. It could carry an immense amount of food and did so, for in those days people lived well.

On either side of the fireplace was a bell. It had a circular boss of white china, edged with gilt, and a white china lever to depress for the purposes of summoning the servant. Neither of them ever worked, so there was a handbell, like a muffin man's, to ring when required. The carpet was Brussels and the walls covered with a grey paper bearing bunches of red flowers, but time had toned down the red and the effect was quite pleasing. There was a red mat before the fire.

On the whole, despite the horsehair furniture, it was a cheerful room had it not been for one picture. The pictures in the room were large steel engravings with boxwood frames. One depicted the Coronation of Queen Victoria, with the young Monarch sitting serene and calm whilst the Archbishop held the crown poised over her head and a crowd of picturesque notabilities all round, staring about them. Another was the christening of the baby Prince of Wales—afterwards Edward VII—chiefly memorable for the figure, in the foreground, of a very slender, elegant young man in some sort of Hussar uniform, with long hair, who bent over the infant with a wondering seraphic smile and a well-shaped hand extended in benediction. There was the meeting of Wellington and

Blücher at Waterloo, of which the Boy highly approved. But the depressing picture was of a rather terrifying and quite inexplicable Biblical subject of which a venerable figure in the centre was undoubtedly the Almighty Being, with a blaze of light and angels all around Him. He pointed inexorably to His right. In the darkness surrounding His aura were all sorts of people in Eastern attire, registering deep despair, not to say horror. It may have been the expulsion of Lucifer and his Dark Angels but nobody seemed to know. It was in the style of Gustave Doré and might have been his work. The Boy puzzled over it, and for quite a long time it formed his mental picture of his Creator. That Figure greatly resembled the old gentleman from the Bank of England, previously described, who lived a few doors away, but he was much more kindly and benign in his appearance. Still, the likeness was good enough to give colour to what the Boy had heard about God having made men in His own image. He saw nothing blasphemous in the thought. It was pure childish logic.

The Boy, that picture apart, liked the Breakfast Room, partly because his toys were there and partly from the many happy memories of cosy and good meals. It was best in winter when the fire gleamed warmly and he had come home from school to a packed tea-table. There would be both muffins and crumpets—why are there no muffins today?—brown and white bread and butter, toast, fancy pastries, two sorts of cake, three or four sorts of jam, some potted meat in a little white jar and, perhaps for him, a plate of cold ham—real York Ham, which Miss Bessie cooked and which always had a dusting of finely powdered breadcrumbs on the outside. He thought it was sumptuous. He had it off a plate which looked like Crown Derby and which he thought very beautiful, and the tea was in a white cup with green linear decoration. This cup was not round but square, and had a little overlapping ridge to it, flat at each corner. Tea tasted much better that way. In his milk-drinking days he had a white beaker surmounted by a bull's head made of china and he never broke it. Meals in the Breakfast Room were always things of pleasure and at Christmas time a gargantuan feast. The food was always hot, for the kitchen was next door. In *décor* and equipment it is today a Back Number, but it was a place of cosiness and comfort and had the real taste and feeling of Home.

It was in this room, too, that Miss Bessie would, every year without fail, make one of her most famous remarks. 'Second Sunday in February,' she would say. 'Have tea without gas.' Then she would gaze around with a smile. She was right, too. But she never let a year go by without saying it.

CHAPTER THIRTEEN

Living Room

FROM the semi-basement to regions above, one ascended a long staircase lit by a large window also protected by iron bars. That staircase was a favourite with the Boy because its balustrade gave a lovely run when sliding down the banisters. He knew every bit of that balustrade, every mark upon it. It was polished and stained like mahogany and about two-thirds of the way down were one or two rather large reddish marks which he hoped might have been bloodstains but were really only a bit of carelessness on the part of the original polisher. The stairs were covered with brown linoleum with a key pattern, in red, white and yellow, at the sides. The Boy did little to wear out that oilcloth. He went down the banisters. That delight remains in the mind of those who experienced it but cannot satisfy it in modern dwellings. Middle-aged and elderly men who find themselves in large public buildings with long staircases often gaze longingly at the balustrading—but do not dare. . . .

This staircase led to a landing which was a favourite playground of the Boy's. It had a large window, on the shelf of which he had a big glass bowl. It was not like the circular narrow-necked goldfish bowl, but rather more like a glass urn. He had placed stones and bits of rock in it, some sand at the bottom, and he managed to get some weed to grow. Originally he had some goldfish but they proved much to the liking of old 'Dick', the immense tabby cat who lived to be twenty years old and who scooped out the rather foolish fish with delight. So the Boy stocked it with newts which he caught in a pond in the corner of his School's playing-field. This pond teemed with newts, both the small lizard-like and olive-coloured variety, and the larger black-backed orange-stomached kind. The boy brought his captures home in a jam-jar and put them in his bowl. Old Dick inspected them and decided against them. Yet those newts vanished. One at a time they went, leaving no trace. Nobody knew how they disappeared, but they did so in a very short space of time. They were never found dead, either in the bowl or about the house. They just vanished into thin air. The Boy was puzzled. He replaced the stock several times but the same thing always occurred. He now believes that human agency may have had something to do with it. Neither Miss Bessie nor Miss Mary viewed the newts with favour and declared they were poisonous. Uncle James pooh-poohed this idea, but for once did not shake the ladies. The Boy appealed to his Mother for support but the utmost she would say was that they were pretty to look at but made her shiver. The breaking of the bowl by a servant—and it may not have been an accident —put an end to any other fishy or reptilian activity. He did attempt to introduce a grass-snake into the house but met with no success at all.

This landing, which was as big as a modern flat, was slightly below the level of the front hall, to which a flight of three steps led. The house was on a series of different levels, which gave it character. The Boy regarded it mostly as an ocean and would navigate its surface, using a little flight of steps, which lived in the corner, as a boat. It was nearly always sunny there and he liked to watch the dust dancing in the sun-beams. But this landing had its own Room, down one step, and this was called alternatively the Morning Room or the Little Room. It was the chief living room of the family, it held the core of the whole house. The term 'Little' was comparative only to the other rooms in that house; by modern standards it was a big room. It was here the Family sat together, it was the centre of the household every day but Sunday. It was a light and cosy room with three large windows, all with lace curtains and Venetian blinds, one of which looked to the front of the house, down the long side passage, the other across the red-tiled court to the house next door and the third on to the garden itself, right into the branches of a large plum tree which grew there. In blossom-time, when that tree had decked itself with the little starlike flowers which come so early, to look from that window was like gazing into the heart of spring. Before the window stood a largish box, with a green serge cover, and in that box was a large and varied assortment of odds and ends of all sorts of materials, from heavy plush to gossamer muslin and fine silk. Miss Bessie stored them there. 'They will come in useful,' she would say with her little nod. She was right. Skeins of wool and silks for mending lived in there too. It was a fine kneeling-place for the Boy, from whence he could see the whole garden and a considerable area of territory on either side. It was his Watch Tower. The Little Room was not papered. Its walls were painted apple green with a thin gold line round the middle, the green being slightly lighter above the line than below it. And the walls were covered with sporting prints in black frames, showing desperate finishes to races, with horses travelling at high speed, the front legs straight out in front and the back legs straight out at the back. Jockeys with whiskers sat bolt upright, using the long stirrup, and plied their whips. Gentlemen in high-hats looked on, sometimes holding up a hand, either in astonishment, despair or maybe triumph, according to which horse they had backed. There were hunting scenes in which men in 'pink' took amazing tumbles, or hauled horses from ditches. One set of prints represented some sort of a nightmare steeplechase across country by moonlight, in which the riders were obviously military men for their uniform trousers showed beneath their night-gowns. They had night-caps on their heads. They were all a source of delight to the Boy who knew them by heart. But before he went to live in that house, he would, when arriving for a visit, go round looking at them all and studying them again. Maybe it was his Father's gambling spirit stirring in him . . . but he took no harm.

In the window facing the front was Miss Bessie's sewing machine, which Miss Mary was not allowed to touch—which was a wise precaution—but upon which Frederica was allowed to work. Miss Bessie did wonderful things on this machine. She ran up curtains, loose covers, dresses—all with the same facility. She did the mending and darning, too, until Frederica returned home to help her. A needle was useless in Miss Mary's hands—worse, it was a thing of danger. But then, of course—she was clever! This window commanded a view of the side door and was of strategic importance.

In the window looking towards the house next door was a large bamboo stand with several shelves. On this were kept magazines, periodicals, and newspapers *en route* for the Box Room. The lowest shelf was reserved for the Boy's reading matter which must not be touched without his permission. On this he kept the current and most recent issues of *Chums, The Boy's Own Paper* and, later, *The Captain*. There also reposed the current copy of *Books for the Bairns*, edited by W. T. Stead, those useful little illustrated volumes, first issued in pink and later in blue covers, which gave so many children their first glimpse of and liking for the Classics. They were a penny each. A modern 'comic' journal does it in strip-cartoon form, at a dearer price. Stead did it far better in a more comprehensive way. The Boy remembers scores of them and can still see the illustrations in his mind's eye.

The Boy took in all the comics of his day—*Chips, Comic Cuts, The Funny Wonder, Scraps, The Big Budget, Funny Cuts, Ally Sloper's Half Holiday*—all that were issued. He had all the Penny Dreadfuls as well. These were the equivalent of the so-called comics of today around which so much controversy rages as to whether these affect children's mentality.

The Boy was a voracious reader of such things—often known as 'Bloods'.
He read *The Magnet, Deadwood Dick, The Union Jack, Buffalo Bill,* and lots of
others. The difference between the 'Bloods' of the past and the comics of
today was that there was no sex and little crime in the old ones. They
were tales of bloodthirsty adventure for the most part. Later, detective
fiction made its entry; when Sherlock Holmes had blazed the trail and
'Nick Carter' and others arrived. But Buffalo Bill was the Thriller King
and has never been surpassed. The Boy actually met him in person, and
still has a signed photograph of him as memento. He never forgot that
meeting. There was a weekly paper called *The Regiment,* devoted to
military affairs, with vivid illustrations and funny anecdotes, which he
liked very much. It had a blue cover but it died long ago. *Chips* was the
favourite comic because of 'Weary Willie' and 'Tired Tim', those
wonderful creations of Tom Browne's, from whom so many other
comic duos sprang. But *Chums* was his favourite of all.

The chief feature of the Little Room was the table. This was again a
very big one. It was circular and a thing of beauty. For it was a complete
section of a mahogany tree, cut from the actual trunk, in full girth. It
was beautifully polished. The edges had been turned and recessed and
decorated. It was of great thickness. It stood upon one single, solid
column, from which four branches radiated as feet, ending in lion's paws
just beneath the edge of the table, and keeping it steady as a rock. It was
a lovely thing, strong and shining. The Boy could, and did, slide right
across it on his stomach. Twelve people could sit around it with ease. In
the centre of it lay all the current magazines, periodicals and newspapers.
The Family were great readers. On that table lay *The Strand,* a new
magazine then, now, alas, deceased, *Pall Mall, Windsor, The Idler, The Wide
World, Pearsons, Chambers' Journal, Blackwoods', The Cornhill;* all the reviews,
including W. T. Stead's *The Review of Reviews,* which was the original
Digest, and covered the outlook and cartoons of the world and from a
picture in which the Boy formed his idea of The Devil. The many illustrated weeklies, *The Sketch, The Tatler, The Sphere, The Graphic, The
Illustrated London News, The Bystander, Black and White, The Spear* (for a
time only, it did not last long), *Illustrated Sporting and Dramatic, The
Queen, The Field, The Lady, The Lady's Pictorial,* and many more. The
glossies were sixpence then. *Punch* was there, always. Then there were the
cheaper weeklies and monthlies: *The Penny Pictorial, The Golden Penny,*
both amazing pennyworths, *M.A.P., T. P.'s Weekly, Cycling* (for Uncle
James), and a lot of women's papers, too. *The Weekly Scotsman* was read
from cover to cover by the females of the Family and was their Bible.
Years later, when the Victorian Boy had grown up and got a little
publicity, his name was actually mentioned in that paper and his Aunts

swelled with pride. That it had been in all the others, including *The Times*, meant nothing to them. *The Weekly Scotsman*—that was fame indeed! There were also current copies of whatever fortnightly publications were being issued, for the Family always 'took in' all these. The Boy remembers being thrilled with *Farthest North* by Nansen. They started with *The Flag to Pretoria*, but it was such a long time getting there that family disaster fell before it arrived and the series was, for them, never completed. But the Boy somehow managed to keep up the series issued by *Black and White* and has them bound today.

All these things were to be found on the centre of the table. When they were a fortnight old they were sorted out and put on the bamboo stand for a like period and then up to the Box Room, there to await the process of binding, which never happened to them. But a previous generation had achieved binding, and every copy of *Punch* from No. One was in that room, in bound volume form, and the Boy learnt much contemporary history from them. He still thinks of nations in the terms of those old cartoons, so vividly drawn and of such fine draughtsmanship. His mental pictures too of the statesmen are formed on them as the cartoonist saw them.

The penny periodicals did not achieve elevation to the Box Room, they were given to the servants. The newspapers which came into that house were *The Times*, the *Daily Telegraph*, the *Daily News*, the *Daily Chronicle*, the *Westminster Gazette*, the *Star* and sometimes the *Echo*, also the *Manchester Guardian*. It was a Liberal household but it read some Conservative papers like the *Daily Telegraph*, too. No vulgar papers like *Pick-Me-Up*, *The Pink 'Un* or *Sketchy Bits* ever entered the portals.

There was a Turkey carpet in this room and a rug to match inside the door and another before the fireplace—which stood opposite the door. The grate here was of polished steel and the fender and fire-irons matched it. Under the fireplace was a tray with slotted compartments for catching the cinders. The value of the divisions was not apparent but they made more work. The fender was quite a beautiful thing of cut steel. That fireplace must have used much emery paper and elbow grease. The Boy liked to lie before the fireplace and watch the fire on winter evenings. He would note the difference of colour in the smoke as it ascended the chimney, how it changed from a dark grey, which always reminded him of old socks, when the fire had been heavily replenished, to a light blue when the flames got the upper hand. He was always enchanted by the little puffs of smoke which came from pieces of coal about to catch fire, and how jets of bright flame would spit forth for a few seconds and vanish again, until the lump was well alight. He lost interest in it then. He liked to see the beginning of things, which may have been the historian budding in him. The coal was kept in a steel scuttle shaped like a knight's helmet and its main object in life was to prevent anyone getting coal out without spilling it. There was a mantelpiece with a clock, a small silver clock with a chime to match, and some china figures to flank it, and the mirror was exactly like the one in Tenniel's drawing which Alice got through. The Boy often climbed on a chair to look at the room in it and to wonder if he could do as Alice did. That was in his very youthful days.

On each side of the fireplace, bookshelves ascended to the ceiling. These contained hundreds of books of all kinds, foreign as well as English. The Boy was allowed access to them all. No bar was put upon his reading, a fact for which he has always been profoundly grateful. There were all the classics, there were many periodicals in bound form, which included Kingsley's *Hereward the Last of the English*, and the Boy remembers the illustrations today. There was *Livingstone's Travels* and Stanley's account of his discovery of Livingstone, both profusely illustrated. All these were drawings, not photographs. There was a history book upon whose pictures of battles, and Kings and Queens, the Boy still relies. There was Victor Hugo, Balzac, Shakespeare, Dumas, Scott, Thackeray and Dickens—the Boy read Dickens at an early age. He never cared very much for Thackeray.

He never tired of those books. The shelves had leather strips with scalloped edges upon them fastened with brass nails and there was a valance too on the mantelpiece with little plush balls dependent therefrom, green in colour.

In front of the bamboo stand stood the Boy's rocking-horse. It was a noble steed of dapple grey with most expressive eyes, and open mouth and flared nostrils. It had a grey mane and tail. It did not work upon ordinary rockers but moved to and from on some kind of iron pistons on a wooden frame which enabled considerable speed to be worked up. Mounted on this, the Boy was all sorts of heroes. He might be a Knight of the Round Table—he had made early acquaintance with Mallory by means of *Books for the Bairns*. He was almost convinced that the table in that room was the original Round Table itself and he called his own chair thereat 'The Siege Perilous'. The chairs were of mahogany upholstered in brown leather. His favourite knight was Sir Gareth. He liked the name— such things have always appealed to him. He liked Sir Gawaine too, and Sir Lamorak and Sir Palomides; but Lancelot, Percival and Galahad made no great appeal, nor did Tristram. King Arthur left him a little cold. He had as lance a long bamboo pole with an old knife in the end; he had his swords and his daggers and he had his steel helmet into which he fixed a plume. He became possessed of an iron shield, thin but still iron, which had been part of a sham trophy of arms in some decorative scheme.

On this he painted his own coat of arms—rather complicated blazonry in which the tressured lion featured. On his steed he re-created Chivalry, jousting, tournaments and desperate combats with recreant knights. He was sometimes unhorsed but he always won. He would also be the entire Light Brigade. When the 21st Lancers covered themselves with glory in the Sudan he paid them the honour of a place in his games. In the early days of the Boer War he was one of French's cavalrymen—and also a Roughrider and a Mounted Infantryman. He re-enacted Jameson's Raid, he was with Dundonald's Horse at the Relief of Ladysmith, with Mahon at Mafeking. He led charges in the Indian Mutiny and sometimes he was Nicholson himself. He was also a cowboy and a Red Indian. He would become a victorious general riding through London and acknowledging the plaudits of the multitude. He was of course Buffalo Bill—and Dick Turpin. When the smash came and the family moved he gave that horse to a relation. He felt like the Arab saying farewell to his steed. It never wore out and he has always regretted parting with it. How his own grandson would have loved it; but there would have been no room for it in the modern home.

There was another great family institution in that Little Room—the Roll Top Desk. Like most things in that house it was very big and of mahogany. It stood against the wall facing the window. Its top came down and fastened. It was not of the roller-blind kind, it was all solid. The desk was more than a desk, it was a treasure house, a source of infinite delight. It was part of the Boy's life. Its supports were columns of drawers which never stuck when pulled out, for cabinet-making was an art in those days.

In those drawers were all sorts of things, countless Ordnance Survey maps which were the property of Uncle James the cyclist. They fascinated the Boy, who has always loved maps, and he pored over the details they gave of battles, tumuli, camps, etc. There were maps of foreign countries and *Baedeker* Guides. In one drawer the Boy kept his stamp album, which had been started by the Mother when she was a child and held some rare stamps indeed. The writing part of the desk was flat and covered with leather, the middle portion having a brass ring sunk in it whereby it could be lifted up and more treasures disclosed. Here were blotting-paper of all kinds and colours, sticks of sealing-wax, red and black, all sorts of notepaper and envelopes, some plain and ordinary, some of extra quality and embossed with the address of the House—printed in black. There were sheets of foolscap, ruled and unruled, mourning paper—black-edged with envelopes to match. These mourning edges were of varying thickness, according to the nearness in friendship or kin of the deceased. The use of this paper was essential to the conventions. If a friend died you wrote to his widow or next of kin on black-edged paper and naturally you used heavily-edged paper if a death occurred in your own family. There were black-edged cards for attaching to 'floral tributes', ordinary visiting-cards—of course engraved—every member of the Family, except the Boy, had these, and the little copper plates by means of which the engraving was done were kept in that desk too. Such cards played a very important part in social life in those days. The die for the notepaper was kept in the desk, and there were pieces of indiarubber and ink erasers of all shapes and sizes. The desk held quite a collection of paper-knives— which the Boy used as daggers—and there was black, blue, red and green ink in the ink-wells. There was also a selection of what were known as travelling ink-wells, which were supposed to travel quite safely and not to leak. They were like small square boxes, covered with imitation leather. They opened by pressing a little 'push' outside which released the lid. Inside was a china ink-well, fitting tightly in a hole. Sometimes a bottle was used instead of the well. But if the well, then on the underside of the lid was a circular rubber pad which fitted the top of the well exactly and prevented the ink from spilling. Or so it was confidently believed. They were not always square, some were fanciful. The Boy had one made like a small orange and some were like cricket balls and the Globe itself, maps and all. There were circular glass ink-wells, of which the tops turned in right down inside almost to the bottom, leaving a hole for the pen and nib to enter and about half an inch of ink at the foot. You filled these up and the ink rose between the two walls of glass, leaving just the residue at the bottom which was always there, for, as it was used or evaporated, the level between the walls sank to replenish it. That these could be upset was proved by the Boy. Ink was usually supplied either in stone bottles or small glass square-shaped bottles—which curved up to a central column which, in turn, was corked. Along the edges, where the curves met the straight side, was a groove in which a pen could be laid. Fountain-pens, then in their extreme infancy, and not at all satisfactory, eventually ousted the travelling ink-bottles and will be superseded in turn by the ball pen. The fountain-pens of that time—and the Desk had some—were inefficient and messy affairs, which had to be filled with little glass tubes with a rubber teat on the end. Ink was sucked into this and then squirted into the fountain-pen, the head of which had been removed. The fountain-pen lived up to its name, for the ink often flowed far too freely and made a nice mess. Facing the seat where the user of the desk sat were numerous pigeon-holes and drawers. The drawers held nibs of all sorts— from broad 'J' to Waverleys—and some quill pens too. In those drawers were some pens much used by the Family. They had black or red wooden holders and the wooden part fitted into the metal end, of which the nib was an actual part. The nib was not separate and pushed into position. These pen nibs had a little dent just before the actual point was reached and the idea was that a certain amount of ink always remained there and thus saved constant dipping. Little round boxes of red wafers—used for sticking letters before envelopes arrived—reposed in those drawers, there was a lot of sticking-paper off the edge of stamps, paper-fasteners of various kinds but mostly brass, which were put through holes in the top corner of documents to be kept together and then had their split-ends flattened out—they are still in use.

Aunt Bessie kept a lot of Recipes in these drawers, which she had cut out of newspapers and magazines. There were rubber bands and always a plentiful supply of stamps bearing Queen Victoria's head—red, green, violet, mauve, blue and yellow according to their value. Postage on letters then was one penny up to four ounces and one halfpenny for a postcard. There were many more deliveries and collections than there are today, when postage costs 150 per cent more than it did. And very seldom did the Post Office make a mistake.

Other drawers held a collection of little black shiny account books, which cost one penny and would fit into the waistcoat pocket, in which Uncle James kept some sort of expenditure accounts of his own. There were the Post Office Savings books of the Family—postcards, tie-on and stick-on labels, old, broken penknives and special knives with a bulbous end but very sharp blade which were used for scratching out blots and making erasures (they mostly scraped a hole in the paper), stump-ends of pencils and whole pencils, relics brought back as small change in the pockets of the Family from abroad. There were cents, pfennigs, coins from Spain, Holland, Belgium, Denmark, Italy and Switzerland. The Boy discovered an Italian five-lira piece which he was allowed to keep. It looked big and important. On a shopping expedition to the West End at Christmas time, it was changed for him at a money-changers in Charing Cross and appeared to him what seemed riches, which he spent in the adjacent Lowther Arcade. Quantities of pencil-cases reposed in the desk drawers, and one was impounded by the Boy. It was shaped like a gun— the barrel being of silver and the butt of cornelian, the lead emerging, if you could get any to fit it, from the end of the barrel, propelled by a little trigger, fitted in a groove, which ran up and down. There were old collar studs and round boxes originally filled with pills but now with samples of metal and semi-precious stones like onyx, agate and some little freshwater pearls, which did indeed look like pills. Above the drawers were a double row of pigeon-holes, which held notepaper, envelopes, etc., for immediate use and quantities of scrap paper—old envelopes, halves of old letters and the like. Uncle James was always making notes thereon, putting them in his pocket and never looking at them again, so far as could be ascertained. The Boy did his homework at that desk and the scrap paper came in useful then. There were flat rulers and some heavy, solid ebony round ones. These were not rulers to the Boy but truncheons, either Field Marshals' or ordinary policemen's, according to the game. The desk held a large magnifying-glass which on sunny days would produce satisfactory fires, if nobody was looking. But the great thing about the Desk was that it contained a Secret Drawer. The Boy had been told about it but, search as he might, he could not discover it. One night, just before bedtime, he was searching again. Uncle James put down his book to watch him—and then—oh! the joy of it— that man leant over, did something with his hand and the front of the support of one side of the row of drawers leapt out—and there was the Secret Drawer. The Boy could not as yet see how it was done. His Uncle appeared to have touched the side of an arch which stood between the two nests of pigeon-holes, crammed with paper, receipts, etc. His Uncle pushed it back before he could discover how it worked and invited him to have another go. But the drawer was lost to sight. The Boy could not see where it was, even when using that magnifying-glass, so excellent was the cabinet-work. But he had watched his Uncle's hand. He tried pulling the various projections—no good; and then he tried, one after another, the little partitions between the pigeon-holes. And at last—click!—the drawer sprang open again. The Secret was now his. In the drawer were treasures indeed. There were a lot of seals bearing all sorts of mono-grams and crests and some quite plain. One was a kind of hub, with an agate seal top and bottom and six spokes screwed in—which could be unscrewed and used as seals themselves. There were two handsome fob-seals, gold and bloodstone. The Boy gloated over them. Then he turned to the drawer again. Under some old letters, at the bottom, were two coins—golden coins. One was a genuine spade guinea and the other a half -sovereign which had lain in there for a score of years or so. Uncle James, who understood children, smiled at the Boy's excitement. But from upstairs came the voice of Aunt Mary, summoning the Boy to bath and bed. She was officiating, for his Mother had gone to the Theatre with Aunt Bessie. He turned a deaf ear to the call, Uncle James conniving. But the voice above grew more and more pressing—not to say sinister. It added a rider, 'Don't be long because of the time.' And then, very peremptory, 'I'm waiting.'

The Boy sighed and put back the treasures. It was no good, the voice above sounded with the regularity of a minute gun, getting more and more threatening and abrupt. Uncle James said: 'Better hurry—she's getting cross. You know where the things are—they will be quite safe.

Upper left: Sir George Alexander and Irene Vanbrugh in *His House in Order. Upper right:* Mrs. Patrick Campbell. *Lower left:* Mrs. Kendal (Dame Madge). *Lower right:* Sir John Martin-Harvey

Upper left: Eugene Stratton. *Upper right:* Sir Harry Lauder. *Lower left:* Harry Tate. *Lower right:* Gus Elen

And—er—ah—hum—you needn't put back the half sovereign. You can have that.' Could anything have been more wonderful? But Uncle James was like that. What did bath and bed matter now? The Boy had half a sovereign, the secret of the drawer and tomorrow was Saturday, a whole holiday from school—a whole day with that desk and its secret. The desk did indeed play a large part in the Boy's life. He showed his friends that drawer popping open but he would never show them how it was done, despite their entreaties. He took good care they did not find out, either. . . .

As stated, the Boy did his homework at that desk, sitting in the large revolving chair with the circular back, waist high, heard by his Mother or his Aunt Mary. When it was Arithmetic, he was helped by his Uncle James, if that man was at home, for to him sums were as nothing. To the Boy they were as mysterious as the secret drawer—more so, for he had the secret of that but never of Sums. He has not found it yet.

He stuck his stamps in his albums—he had three altogether—at that desk, and he wrote to stamp dealers for sheets on approval. He wrote to his friends and he also wrote what he then considered to be the most important letter of his life at that desk—it was to his great hero, Lieutenant-Colonel R. S. S. Baden-Powell, defender of Mafeking in the Boer War, to whom he sent a letter of praise and congratulation when that small post was relieved and what he considered to be an excellent report of the great doings in London by which the Relief was celebrated, and of which he had been an eye-witness. He posted it with care—and he hoped. He never got an answer, but he did not mind very much. He had written to 'B-P', and if that man ever read the letter he would know how much the Boy admired him. Many years afterwards he met Baden-Powell, now a Peer and Chief Scout. They did quite a big job together. The grown-up Boy told 'B-P' about that letter and the great man was quite apologetic about the non-reply. He explained that he had received tens of thousands. But that Boy, now a man, got a letter from 'B-P' at the conclusion of the job they did—and has it still. They met often after that.

On top of the desk was a microscope and a set of compasses which both lived in walnut boxes with blue satin linings and were the property of Uncle James (the Boy was allowed to use them), and a pair of scales similar to those then used in Post Offices, with a slightly tilted tray on which letters could be weighed and a set of weights up to four ounces. All but the very smallest were round, with their weight stamped in the middle, and the smallest was a little upright affair rather like a pawn. When not in use, they stood in little circles which held them, with violet plush at the bottom. They were nice to play with but on no account must the weights be lost! They never were.

N

Also in that room was the Boy's personal bookshelf, of plain wood, with a green serge curtain which pulled across. Not that it contained all his books; some were downstairs in the top cupboard, others up in his bedroom. But here were his Hentys, his Manville Fenns, his Ballantynes, his Kingstons and his Fred Wishaws. Perhaps his favourite of all was by that author. It was called *Harald the Norseman* and was about Harald Hardraada, the gigantic Norwegian king who was killed in battle at Stamford Bridge in Yorkshire when he invaded this country. The Boy almost knew that book by heart.

He had a lot of natural history books, too. He esteemed one called *Wild Sports of the World* which told of adventures with wild beasts as well as of their habits and habitats and had exciting coloured plates. And of course he loved the Jungle Books too. A volume of Kingsley's *The Heroes* had an honoured place, and a slim volume of Greek mythology, called *Old Tales of Greece*, by Alice Zimmern, of Girton College, which he acquired in 1897 and learnt almost by heart. He still has it now in his vast library, in excellent condition. He had Harrison Ainsworth—he liked *Guy Fawkes, Old St. Paul's, The Lancashire Witches* and *Jack Sheppard*. Does anyone read Ainsworth today? If not, they miss a lot. On the shelves were *Three Men in a Boat, Treasure Island* and *The Black Arrow* by Stevenson, *A Prisoner of War*, by G. Norway, *Ronald Bannerman's Boyhood*, by George Macdonald (The Kelpie always thrilled), books by Gordon Stables, Fenimore Cooper and Baring-Gould—*Grettir the Outlaw*—*A Thane of Wessex*, by Charles W. Whistler, Alfred S. Miles' *Fifty-Two Stories for Boys, The Cock House at Felsgarth* and others by Talbot Baines Reed and other school stories later by R. S. S. Warren Bell. The Boy disliked *Eric, or Little by Little*, in whom he did not believe, and the same applied to *The Swiss Family Robinson*. He had *The Water Babies* and *Westward Ho!* and many of Rider Haggard's, which he adored—his favourites being *King Solomon's Mines, Alan Quatermain, Nada the Lily, The People of the Mist* and *Montezuma's Daughter*. He liked the books of Captain F. S. Brereton, especially *With Shield and Assegai* and *With Rifle and Bayonet*—the illustrations by Stanley L. Wood made them spring to life. He got his Hentys and his Breretons as school prizes, for his school, a sensible one, allowed boys to choose their own books from the publishers' lists—with reservation as to price. But he cajoled extras out of his family as Christmas and Birthday presents. He got his Ballantynes the same way. He still has all those prizes and confounds his grandchildren with the sight of them—neither of whom has ever won a prize—schools do not seem to be generous today. Gulliver was in the general books of the house and he read it for pure adventure, knowing nothing of its satire.

His Family were great readers and subscribed to a library. He read many of the books and made early acquaintance with *The Prisoner of Zenda* and the works of Stanley Weyman. He acquired those books, as he did those of S. R Crockett, the Scottish author his Family admired very much. The Boy thought most of his books were marvellous—*Men of the Mass Hags*, *The Grey Man*, *Joan of the Sword Hand*, *The Red Axe* and *The Black Douglas* being his favourites. He was on holiday at the Manse in Galloway when Mr. Crockett and his family visited it. The Boy quickly became friendly with the children and led them in games of which the Covenanters were the heroes. Crockett was the first author the Boy met. His autograph, with which Mr. Crockett described himself as the Boy's friend, might have been a turning-point. . . .

Other favourite books were those by Kirk Munroe: *Through Swamp and Glade*, *At War with Pontiac* and *The White Conquerors of Mexico*; *The Story of Robin Hood*, by William Heaton, which had been the only school prize his Father had won, or the only one which had survived (it is still in existence); both the *Alices* (in first editions); *The Three Musketeers*; *Tom Sawyer* and *Huckleberry Finn*; *Helen's Babies*, which is the complete understanding of childhood; and a book which dealt with the adventures of two Saxon lads, a period he liked very much; the name of the book is forgotten but the story and illustrations are clear in the mind. He was distrustful of 'Pi' books, and part of his dislike and disbelief in *The Swiss Family Robinson* was attributable to that. He never managed to get through *Tom Brown's Schooldays* until he had grown up, probably because he disliked school.

He read and re-read his Annuals—bound with the coloured plates in them—of *Chums*, *The Boy's Own Paper*, *Young England* and *Chatterbox*. He usually, in sentiment, found himself on the losing side and was inclined to espouse lost causes, but one book drove him out of his inborn respect for Crown and Country and ranged him upon the side of the French Revolution. This particular book appealed to him because a boy was the hero and the teller of the tale. It was called *The Reds of the Midi*, by Felix Gras, translated into English by Catherine A. Janvier. It was the Boy's first glimpse of what led to that tremendous upheaval and it held him spellbound. He first read it in 1896. He has it still. He thought the description of the sufferings of poor little Pascal and his family by the Aristocrats, and what that boy did in the Revolution when he marched with the Reds of the Midi, was one of the best stories he had ever met.

However, *A Tale of Two Cities* swung him to the other side—but he understood the Revolutionaries. There was another book which he liked, albeit it was sad. Despite the fact that he was a bit of a rebel and more than a bit tough, he had a vein of sentiment in him. This book came from the Home of Sentimentality—America—and was called *Timothy's Quest*,

by Kate Douglas Wiggin. Attracted in the first place by the cover which
showed a knight in armour escorting a damsel on a palfrey but slightly
deterred by an angel hovering above, he read it and wept over the woes
of poor little Timothy, the orphan, whom nobody wanted. It gave him
his first idea of American mentality, about which he now knows more,
and he also knows there are plenty of decent, honest, sentimental people
in that land, despite the Almighty Dollar.

The Boy liked Æsop's Fables and a book by Mrs. Prosser called *Original
Fables,* and he treasured, and still does, a huge *Don Quixote* with Doré's
illustrations. He read his fill—though not his fill, for he was never
satisfied—in the pleasant Little Room, which was the first in the house,
incidentally, to be lit with an incandescent burner—the fixing of which
required skill and a steady hand, for the mantles which produced this new
bright light were like the skeletons of small doll's night-shirts—delicate as
a fairy's robes; and they had to be placed on a little white fork which
supported them and must hang level, after they had been burnt. But
when they were fixed, all exclaimed at the brightness of the light as
compared with the old yellow glow of the gas. And that light, bright,
happy Little Room was the first to be so lit in the Victorian House. The
only drawback to the room was that the plumbing from the bathroom
and lavatory ran through it, thinly covered by boards, and strange
gurglings and groanings ensued. . . .

CHAPTER FOURTEEN

State Apartments

EVERY Victorian home, if it was of higher status than a mere hovel, had its state apartments—or at least, state apartment. In the poorer houses this was called 'The Parlour' or 'The Front Room'; where everything was kept fresh and clean, where the best furniture and show-pieces lived and which was only entered on very special occasions indeed and in which the family was never at ease. The Best Houses, of course, had State Apartments—two of them—and also a State Bedroom, to be met with later. In this particular house the State Apartments lay off the main entrance hall on the first floor and both on the same side of it, up the three little steps from the landing where that aquarium had been kept. They were known as The Dining Room and The Drawing Room. Not that the Family ever dined or had meals in the Dining Room, unless some Very Important Personage was present. But they sat there on Sundays, although they went down to the Breakfast Room for their meals. The Drawing Room was even less used—only for parties and the At Home Days. Nobody would have thought of sitting there for comfort and pleasure, that was not possible. Frederica would go in there at times to play the piano but it was by no means a living room at all. It is best to deal with it first. One turned a shining brass knob on the door and found immediately that one had to push pretty hard. The reason was soon apparent. It was not that the door itself was extra heavy. It was solid, like all the doors, but it bore what was known as a Portière. This was a heavy curtain of plush or velvet, the colour of which matched the *décor* of the room. This hung from a thick brass rail, which stood well away from the door on two arms and curved out at the end to cover where the door opened, thus preventing draughts. And indeed the first impression on entering that room was that it shut out Life itself for the place seemed of an unearthly stillness and airlessness. So might the tomb of an Egyptian King just unsealed from under a Pyramid have seemed when the excavators first set foot in it. Indeed the room was a Pyramid itself—a pyramid to Convention. It was a big room, with two large recessed windows on the left. They were seldom opened, except when the room was being 'done' and then only if fine. They were raised or lowered by sashline and there was a brass fastening in the middle which, on being turned, prevented them from opening at all either up or down. They had Venetian blinds, those favourites of Victorian times; indeed all the rooms in this house had them. They are not often seen today. They were made of slats of wood, brown and polished. These slats, which were quite thin and flat, fitted at each end into little ladders of webbing, which had cords to pull. The cords manipulated the blinds up or down. They could be made to lie flat against the window, effectively preventing light from passing in and making vision through the glass impossible; and they could be reversed as well. Or they could be worked so that the slats ran parallel with the windows, thus admitting light and air (if the windows were open), or they could hang at an angle so that sunlight was sent upwards or downwards. They were most efficient blinds and could be used for any emergency and would have made a perfect blackout had they been called upon to do so. They did so in the First World War, in houses where they lingered. They could be pulled to the very top of the window where they vanished under a little wooden pelmet or canopy, or they could be lowered to cover the entire window. They had certain drawbacks. If they were not raised right out of sight, but allowed to remain half-way across the top panes, care had to be taken to make them fast and keep them both level and even. If they hung slantwise or one was higher than the other, it was abhorrent to every good housewife. Indeed, when not properly fixed they made the house look slatternly and disreputable, like an unshaven man minus collar and tie. So much care was taken. All these wooden slats had to be taken out at least once a year, and scrubbed The little webbing ladders had to be renewed and a good eye kept on the cords. They were dusted daily. Although liable to go wrong, they were excellent as blinds and wonderful in excluding that Victorian bugbear, a draught. They had extra aid in this respect because along the ledge where the upper and lower windows met, where there was of course a crack, there lay a long thing like a snake or a very elongated sausage. It was full of sand and made of Turkey red twill. This prevented most effectively any air from seeping in. But even that was not enough. That Victorian desire for privacy must be remembered, and so in front of the Venetian blinds hung long lace curtains reaching right to the floor. An inmate of the room could see the outside world through them, but nobody from outside could see in. They were either white or coffee-coloured—according to taste or room *décor*. The coffee-coloured ones did not show the dirt. They could be looped back, if the weather was very hot and windows simply had to be opened, and this was achieved by sashes of silk, of a colour to suit the room, the sashes being hitched to brass hooks in the wall. But it did not often happen. And as a last and impregnable defence against intrusion and draught there were heavy brocade or velvet curtains which could be pulled right across the embrasure, running on rings along a wooden pole. They too could be looped back with little cords, like those used to close doors and gangways in theatres or cinemas. When closed they completed the hermetic sealing of the room from air, light and curiosity. That it was not possible by its very position in the building scheme for anyone to see into that room made no difference at all. The people inside could—and did—observe their neighbours in their gardens and could do so unseen. So long as they were not seen, it was not bad manners.

This Drawing Room was black and gold or perhaps yellow and black is better. The wallpaper was yellow with vertical stripes, shiny and matt, the shiny somehow seeming the lightest. Thus a satin-like effect was attained. The yellow, or old-gold, carpet was a square and did not reach to the walls, the surround being of dark-stained wood, highly polished. The chairs were of black-lacquered wood, with mother-of-pearl inlay and cane seats. Two larger chairs had yellow-brocade upholstery. A small settee, to hold three, was upholstered in old gold and stood slantwise across a corner on one side of the fireplace, behind it being a very large brass standard lamp with a very large shade, made of yellow pongee silk. This lamp burnt oil and one could see the wick curling into the glass reservoir. The immense fireplace, opposite the door, was of black marble with a curb to match and the hearth was tiled in peacock-blue tiles. The fire-irons and dogs were of brass, and there was a tray for ashes under the grate, also of brass. The coal-scuttle was solid and also brassy, like a Roman helmet. The shovel fitted into a slot in it. There were various sorts of scuttles in use in this house but they all had one thing in common, a reluctance to part with any coal at all. In the summer a screen stretched before the empty grate; it was in this case a rather handsome Chinese screen in three folds and had actually come from China. It had dragons upon it. Inside the curb were two curious-looking objects. They were a species of standard, each with an upright pole of brass and across which there was a crosspiece, about two-thirds of the way up. From this cross-piece hung a sort of banner, made of heavily embroidered material or *petit point*. Sometimes they were of beadwork. These are something quite out of date today, complete Back Numbers. They were complexion shields. Their purpose was to protect a lady's complexion from the heat of the fire. In cold weather, if she sat near enough to the blaze, she would place one of these banners between it and her face. For women wore their own complexions then. Apart from a light dusting of powder to take off shininess, no make-up was used. Rouge was 'fast' and nobody could either be or look 'fast' and remain a lady. And if she was not a lady, well, she did not get into the drawing room. There were some surreptitious sticks of what was called 'lip-salve' which ladies used, so they said, to keep their lips moist and to prevent them from becoming dry and cracked. If at times a little colour adhered to the lips, well, nobody ever knew; except perhaps the user and other ladies similarly guilty, who therefore could not say a word. But such things as making up openly and the public use of lipstick would have meant the complete banishment of any women guilty thereof from the visiting lists of her friends.

The mantelpiece of the fireplace was covered by a board in turn covered with yellow velvet and a pelmet descended from this to give decoration to the austerity of the grate. It had scalloped edges and gold-braid binding. The mantelpiece itself was crowded with ornaments of all sorts, and in the middle was a huge black marble clock which resembled nothing so much as a sarcophagus. It was probably a good timekeeper but it never went because the key had been lost years ago and nobody ever got another. There was an overmantel which went almost up to the ceiling and framed a mirror. That overmantel was of gilded wood, a cross between trellis and fretwork. It had little landings, alcoves or shelves which bore more ornaments, mostly Dresden or Sèvres—or near enough, anyway. There was a bell-pull on either side of the fireplace, of the china variety, here coloured yellow and encrusted with ormolu.

In the corner not occupied by the standard lamp was one of the chief objects of the room—The Cabinet. Everybody had a Cabinet. In this particular case it was of black lacquer with mother-of-pearl inlay like the chairs and quite a nice thing. Behind its glass doors were the treasures of the household and sometimes they were indeed treasures. You might find Queen Anne silver teapots, and milk-jugs which were family heirlooms. But the major display was of articles sent by friends and relatives abroad or brought home by the Family as travel trophies. Nearly everyone had relatives abroad because in those days the British Empire was a real thing and people went into what was called 'The Indian Civil'. They ran businesses in China, and all over the world—in 'The Colonies'. They sent presents home or brought them back with them when on leave. There would be curios as well, tropical shells, all sorts of things, silver ink-stands, trophies witnessing the athletic prowess of the Family; very numerous indeed in this case because of Uncle James, who had an amazing collection which no ordinary cabinet could have contained.

When Goss china made its appearance, it was to be found in the Cabinets. There were also christening-mugs and spoons of silver, although none of that family were born with the proverbial one in their mouths, and a baby's rattle of silver with a coral handle and covered with little bells. This had been presented at birth to the Victorian Boy, though he was never clear as to who was the donor and judging by its condition he had never been allowed to handle it. He was embarrassed by the sight of it, as are most small boys when confronted with facts of their babyhood.

All these treasures in the Cabinet were sometimes open to the Boy to take out and examine as a 'treat'. 'Treats' in those days were always being talked about but usually proved greater in anticipation than realization. But there were two articles in that Cabinet which the Boy esteemed highly. There were two little plain boxes of white wood whose lids slid off. One disclosed two perfectly little modelled Swiss Chalets, surrounded by a delicate miniature fence and with a little lake made of looking-glass in front of them. The other was better still. It disclosed a really splendidly-modelled brown bear, spectacles on nose, seated at a grand piano in the act of playing it. There was even music, with notes thereon, on the piano-stand. It was quite entrancing. The Boy would gaze at them and never damaged them. Eventually they became his. His own little daughter adored them too, but she destroyed the bear in an access of affection. But the chalets have survived to please the fourth generation, for Uncle James brought them from Switzerland. And although the tiny railings are broken, the chalets and the lake survive yet. The habit of keeping things is hard to kill.

Along the top of the Cabinet was a black silk runner embroidered with golden dragons. On this stood silver photo frames containing the 'likenesses' of dear friends and relations. You had to be 'somebody' to reach that eminent position, for the Drawing Room was the Victorian Middle Class version of the aristocratic Portrait Gallery.

Near the Cabinet was a large palm in a kind of openwork wooden bucket; ribs of black wood clasped by brass rings, with a brass handle on each side, standing on a pedestal which looked too small for it. Sometimes here might be a Flower Stand in the window recess which could contain ferns, aspidistras or plants—mostly musk and begonias. But the resultant earthy flavour made them unpopular in the best houses—and this was a Best House.

The room was encumbered with numerous 'occasional tables' all bearing ornaments or frames but all matching the general scheme. It was noteworthy that every ornament stood on its own special mat. Surfaces must not be scratched. That particular Drawing Room was the scene of innumerable At Homes, Receptions and Musical Evenings. No damage had been done, nothing had ever been broken, nothing had been spilled, no paint scratched. It was not the fashion then to stub out cigarette-ends on the piano or furniture, to grind them into the carpet or to make rings on tables with the bottoms of glasses. There was such a thing as decorum and good manners and a respect for possessions. And yet people got a lot of enjoyment from the parties, too. It was not easy to move about in that room, either, because the enormous amount of furniture. But there were plenty of chairs and no hostess ever invited more people than could be coped with; nor did people gate-crash with friends. There was one other article of furniture which was noteworthy and that was a species of chair or minor settee which was real Victorianism and may have been Georgian too. It was shaped like the letter S, with seats in the curves and the upholstered back to lean against. People therefore sat facing opposite ways, yet cheek to cheek. They were called 'Flirtation Settees'. Doubtless they were used for that purpose, but not in this particular Drawing Room.

The walls were crowded with pictures, which hid most of the wall-paper, and some of the pictures were good. They were of all shapes and sizes, all in gold frames and depicted a variety of scenes. No attempt was made to get them into anything like order or design. It did not matter if it was not easy to examine them. They were not there primarily to be looked at but to show that Victorians were cognisant of Art and gave it their support. The Best House happened to have a few good pictures; there were three animal studies by Sidney Cooper and a spirited seascape of a smack running before a stiff breeze, and some were not so good. There were church spires against trees and remarkable sunsets some Highland scenes, from which in those days not even English families could escape; there were some of the Marcus Stone variety—gateways to estates, and ladies drooping against pillars whilst tall, slim bucks bowed themselves away; and a couple of Darbies and Joans of the Dendy Sadler type. But one picture lingers most in the memory. It was large, fresh, bright and well painted. It showed Georgian beaux and belles promenading on the front at Weymouth. All those pictures came down once a year during Spring Cleaning. There was never any difficulty in putting them back into the right places; they had made their mark on the wallpaper which had not faded under their protection. There was their claim, fully marked. And up they went again in good order. Cushions abounded and there was a very large luxuriant black sheepskin rug before the fireplace over which it was easy to stumble. A mat or rug of some kind stood before every door in that house, except what were described as 'the usual offices'. Their only purpose seemed to be tripping people up and getting stuck under the doors but they apparently just had to be there.

The room was lit by a central chandelier dependent from the ceiling, containing four gas-burners inside rather ornate globes; in this case the globes were of thin yellow china, which were not easy to light, but once achieved, gave a lovely soft golden glow. There was a globe on each side of the fireplace too.

Athwart the corner of the room next to the door and opposite the fire-place was the heart and soul of this State Apartment—The Piano. No house could afford to be without a piano; even if, by a rare chance, none of the inhabitants could play. But that was a very rare event, for all young ladies had to be accomplished and one of the accomplishments was music, by which was meant the ability to play on the piano. Whether or no it could be said that the majority of young ladies accomplished this art is doubtful, but most of them could produce sounds which bore some resemblance to the notes and tunes on the sheet music which was so plentiful, and some could play really well. Music was an 'extra' at school. Some children went to a music mistress for further instruction, in other cases the music mistress came to the house. The cost of learning music was not very heavy. Old bills dug out of a box room prove that. One shows that the father of a young lady paid the music mistress, for tuition received by his daughter from 1st October, 1900 to 16th January, 1901, the sum of 8*s*. 6*d*. Another is a more elaborate account on a proper head-ing—and the address has before it the words 'Academy of Music.' The Principal's name was Christmas and he gave tuition in 'Pianoforte, Singing, Zither-Banjo, Mandoline, etc., etc.' His terms were 'In advance. One Quarter's Notice required before withdrawing a Pupil', and for the June Quarter of 1898 his pupil cost her Father 12*s*. 6*d*. Four shillings more than the music mistress; but this was an Academy, and therefore costly. Teachers coming to private houses charged a little bit more. Yet they all made a living out of it and did quite well.

Young ladies were made to practise, and if they did it regularly there was not very much in the way of objection from the neighbours because it happened in their homes too. It was mostly vocal practice which made trouble. It was socially necessary for a girl to play the piano but not for her to sing. There was no stigma of indifferent education if she did not happen to possess a voice. It was a sort of Victorian fetish that all girls could be musical if they so desired and therefore the most unlikely were forced to learn and practise. This did not apply to boys. Those who showed signs of being musical got lessons and persevered. Many people started to learn, few finished the course. It was also a belief that a violin was more suited to men for music than a piano. It was a complete fallacy and resulted in hundreds of violins going into hundreds of box rooms, to be used no more. A lot of men learnt to play the Banjo, when it was rumoured that King Edward VII—then the Prince of Wales—had received lessons thereon from James Bohee, a wonderful coloured banjoist, whose brother George was a vocalist and whose great song was 'A Boy's Best Friend is his Mother.' Banjos were not difficult to master and were very popular. They were gay and cheerful and when played in a boat on the Thames on a summer's evening, under the light of brightly coloured Chinese lanterns, they could sound very well indeed. A few struggled on with the violin and would have been better employed at almost anything else, and just a few men played the cornet, mercifully only a few, for it was not suited to Drawing Rooms at all. A few young ladies played the Guitar and quite a lot the Mandoline. This was considered ladylike and graceful. The Mandolines had ribbons which went round the girls' necks; the ribbons were of course of the most suitable colour, and the playing enabled them to display pretty hands and adopt charming attitudes. 'Finiculi, Finicula' was most popular. Most young ladies sang—even if they did not practise it—whether they could or not. So did most men. They sang ballads, and crooning was mercifully unknown. The Victorians attempted the notes, even if they did not always conquer them—they dodged nothing. Few people played the Guitar, because of a popular joke, 'You play the Guitar? Then Guitar way', which caused roars of innocent laughter but was not really appreciated by those addicted to that instrument. Nobody played the Saxophone. The piano in this particular Drawing Room was an upright grand, which was quite the general rule. It was of black wood and very shiny. The front had a screen of what appeared to be fretwork, behind which was quilted yellow satin. It was a Broadwood. The piano stool had a circular cushioned top which revolved on a screw and could be screwed up and down according to the height of the player; great effects were secured by this. Extra light was obtained for the player by means of two candle-holders which protruded from the framework of the piano on either side of the music-stand. They were of ormolu, curved and ornamented. Each held a wax candle and those candles were often twisted like corkscrews and sometimes enriched by blobs of gold paint as well. At their base was a little china disc-like saucer through which they passed into the holder, which prevented the wax from dripping on to the piano. And they had shades of yellow silk clasped about them by metal grips.

Along the top of the piano was another long silk runner with a heavy gold fringe. On this stood more photo frames, bearing photos of the members of the Family. This was their own domain. When the piano was wanted for playing, all these had to be taken off. There was an enormous amount of work in that room, which would have scared a modern housewife or 'help' to death. But it did not deter the Victorians. They regarded it as normal. They had plenty of time, plenty of help and plenty of money to pay for it. It will be noted that this Drawing Room did not boast a single antimacassar, a sad blow to the young experts of the B.B.C. There were very few in that house anywhere; they were Mid-Victorian affairs, when Macassar Oil was popular.

Next Door to the Drawing Room was the State Apartment next in order of precedence but not quite so exclusive, which was the Dining Room. As explained, meals were seldom taken there. It was, like the Drawing Room, of enormous size and the prevailing tint was blue. This was governed by a very handsome central candelabra of real Wedgwood, quite a beautiful affair, and many Wedgwood ornaments were in the room, and a lot of those attractive German earthenware articles, quaint-shaped vases, beer-mugs, which were, and still are, of grey and blue. There were Wedgwood ornaments and vases on the grey-marble mantel-piece, which had no valance, between German steins. The walls were blue and the mahogany furniture was upholstered in dark blue leather. A blue table-cloth with golden fringe covered the immense central table, and the portière over the door and long curtains across the window recess were of blue too. On that mantelpiece, in the middle thereof, was a most attractive clock. It was of wood and it was like a Gothic cathedral. It had a sharply sloping roof, it had gables, columns and spires and a most melodious chime. This clock actually went and kept perfect time; the whole house set their watches by it. The Boy loved the clock and liked to open the back, of openwork wood with a blue silk backing, and watch the little hammers strike the shining silvery spring of tubular metal which produced the chords which marked the hours. He never damaged it. The carpets and the cushions were blue too in that room, and the fireplace had blue tiles of just the right shade. Those bells on the wall had blue china bosses and handles. But they did not ring. There was a silver bell, in the shape of a Swiss cow-bell, to summon the maids. Some houses had speaking-tubes but they never seemed to work. The whistles got lost and the servants could never find them. It was best to ring the bell.

There was a massive armchair for Uncle James, also upholstered in blue leather, and two smaller armchairs and one little low chair, full-sized, as to seat and curved back, but with little stumpy legs as if it was deformed which the Boy always used. A gigantic sofa in blue leather ran almost the whole length of one side of the room. And opposite the window stood the sideboard. Like almost everything else in that room it was of polished mahogany. It was so vast that it was almost possible to live in it. It had shelves which bore pieces of plate, solid silver salvers, biscuit-boxes and a couple of wine buckets. On its flat top it had a Tantalus, always kept well charged and with little labels on chains round the necks of the cut-glass decanters, as if they were wine waiters themselves, saying what were their contents—sherry, whisky and brandy. There were also some ferns in Wedgwood plant-pots. In the vast cupboards of that sideboard were many things. There was a drawer below the flat top, and then the cupboard—or cupboards. Two doors opened, in the centre, and four compartments were displayed. One was a zinc-lined cellarette, in which were kept wine, spirits and *apéritifs*—gin, French and Italian vermouth, peach, orange and angostura bitters—and some very good port. In the next cupboard were some boxes of cigars and cigarettes. Both these forms of tobacco were in a shocking state of repair, for nobody smoked in that house, except Uncle John when he came to visit, and he had sufficient sense to use his own stuff. Nor were those cigars or cigarettes ever handed round to visitors, which was just as well, for they would only have caused embarrassment and nobody would have known what to do with them. They were just dried wrecks crumbling to dust. They were never thrown away. They shared the cupboard with a variety of glasses and tumblers, all of first-class quality. The complete array, from champagne to sherry, from port to spirits, the proper glass for any drink you wanted, and the drink to put in it was there. There was also a rather lovely cut-glass and silver claret jug, which still exists, alone of all that sideboard once held. In another cupboard were a variety of useful things like boxes of matches and boxes of sweets—which appealed to the Boy— and also glass jars of boiled sugars and twisted sticks of barley sugar. There was always a tin box of Edinburgh Rock, of which the Boy was not very fond but ate as a duty. In the last cupboard were dessert plates, some of Worcester and some of green Wedgwood, embossed by figures of fruit, and such things as corkscrews and nutcrackers and little spoon-like silver prods for peeling walnuts. Those cupboards had a distinct smell of their own, rather reminiscent of a stuffy bar parlour with a greengrocer's next door.

The drawer in that sideboard, with its curved front, held the household games. There were several packs of cards, both new and used. And a fair-sized black lacquer box with a gold design displayed, when opened, three compartments, that in the centre being rather narrow. The two large ones, right and left, held a pack of cards each. The centre compartment was filled with counters, white, black, red, yellow, blue and green. Some of them had been embellished by ink sketches of faces, very well done. The Boy regarded these counters as luck bringers if he got them in a game. There was Bezique, complete with markers, like little clock dials. There was a set of spillikins, a game very popular then but hardly seen now, demanding a straight eye and very steady hand. Bone or ivory pieces, very light and slender, cut to represent a variety of objects, swords, daggers, halberds, axes, lances, crosses, were all jumbled together higgledy-piggledy in a heap. Then they had to be picked out, one at a time, without moving or disturbing any of the others, by means of a sort of little bone hook which was, like golf clubs, ill-adapted for the purpose. The Boy was good at the game. In that drawer, too, were two sets of chessmen and a thing which looked like a ledger, but when opened disclosed itself as a draughtboard with men complete. The Boy learnt and played all sorts of games in that Dining Room. He played the ordinary childhood games of Snap, Happy Families, Old Maid, and Beggar My Neighbour. He also learnt and played Nap, Newmarket and Casino. He has completely forgotten the last two now; he never took any interest in cards when the Family left that house and is no good at any form of Whist and cannot understand Bridge at all. But he does vaguely remember that there was a Big and Little Casino, both of which were desirable things. There was a Cribbage Board in the drawer, too, and dominoes. The Boy never learnt Cribbage but he was all right at dominoes. He plays it now, and the same old juvenile card games, with his grandchildren. That drawer had everything wanted for a social evening of games.

On the sideboard was always what was known as Dessert, all sorts of fruit in large epergnes and special dishes with stands to them, mostly of Worcester. This fruit, unlike the tobacco, was constantly renewed, and it was eaten at all times of the days, except on Sundays. Then it really was Dessert. For on Sundays the whole family sat in the Dining Room, having meals as usual in the Breakfast Room but always going back upstairs afterwards. And after lunch that fruit was eaten as Dessert. There was a tacit understanding that on the Sabbath it must not be eaten at any other time, as it was on weekdays.

The pictures in that room were enlargements of family portraits; there was Pa and Ma and Uncle Peter, and also some enlargements of photos taken of a party climbing in the Alps. Uncle James figured in these. He had managed to squeeze in a Swiss holiday or two and had done some climbing. He never forgot those few brief holidays of his and the mountains were always near his heart. He had been born amongst the hills of Galloway, and their vaster brothers, the Alps, seemed to understand he was some sort of relation. There were photos of mountains too, the Matterhorn, the Eiger, Monch and Jungfrau and the view from the top of the Gornergrat. He used to tell the Boy about them and make him long to go there. He managed to do it and sent Uncle James letters back home describing the way he saw them; that was years afterwards, but it gave the Uncle much joy.

The windows, of course, had Venetian blinds and lace curtains. And in the embrasure stood what was perhaps the best piece of furniture in

the room. It was a really beautiful and elegant satinwood table, inlaid and
embellished with great taste and symmetry. It carried something which
will be welcome to all those who have the modern idea about the
Victorians. For here, on this table, were the aspidistras. There were many
of them and they were as fine plants as could be wished. They were in the
special care of Miss Mary, who had complete charge of them, taking an
immense pride and cherishing their broad green leaves with their curving
sweep and gleam. There were also a couple of variegated ones, white and
light green, the white being a little yellowish. Miss Mary watered her
aspidistras, gave them silver sand, dusted their leaves and snipped off
dead ones, and watched the pretty little bell-shaped blossoms of crimson
and yellow burst through the soil. She guarded new leaves as soon as they
appeared and brought them to maturity. When the plants got too big
for the large blue earthenware pots in which they stood she divided and
repotted them. She hardly ever had a failure and seldom lost one. They
were greatly admired. The Boy thought them very fine and could never
see anything comic or tasteless in them. He had his own uses for them.
He would bring his soldiers up to the Dining Room and place them
amongst the stems of the aspidistras, so that they became punitive forces
making their way through almost impenetrable jungle. Care had to be
taken, as the game was not popular with Miss Mary. There were other
objects of interest in that room. There were the big bronzes on the mantelpiece—most Victorian homes had their bronzes. These two depicted a
couple of Roman gentry having a good deal of trouble with their horses,
which were very high-spirited steeds. The men were ill-attired for their
jobs, wearing nothing but long flowing cloaks which must have impeded
their efforts and may have been the reason for the rearing of the steeds, by
frightening them as they floated in the wind. There were two brass
candlesticks which came from India, and represented cobras rearing in the
act of striking. These were brought to the house as a present for kind-
nesses received by a cousin who was then a junior in the Indian Civil
Service but who eventually reached the very top of it, and a knighthood.
He had often stopped at the house in his student days and this was his
tribute. It is a tribute which has endured. For that man was very kind to
the Boy at a time when kindness was needed, and a friendship grew up
between them which lasted until the cousin died at a ripe and honoured
age. The cobras still rise to strike and may go on for centuries. . . .

On one side of the fireplace stood that marvellous cabinet which held
Uncle James' equally marvellous collection of butterflies. On the other
side was a pillar chest of drawers which contained some odd things such
as samples of minerals, especially manganese, which was of great interest
to Uncle James' business, some pieces of lead which the Boy believed

Upper left and right: H. B. Irving—in the dual role in *The Lyons Mail.*
Lower left: Sir Henry Irving as "Becket". *Lower right:* Sir Johnston
Forbes-Robertson and Gertrude Elliott in *The Light that Failed*

Georges Hackenschmidt, the Russian Lion   Eugene Sandow   Madrali, the Terrible Turk

for years to be silver, some pyrites which he believed to be gold quartz, some flint arrow-heads and scrapers, for Uncle James had dabbled in archæology, several of those curled-up reptilian snake-like fossils, and the curious stone effects called millers' thumbs. It was quite a small museum and the Boy would display it to his friends, expounding the exhibits fluently, if not accurately. There was of course a large mirror over the fireplace and amongst the ornaments were some small blue and white fern-pots, the intention being to present themselves as Chinese. They were square with panels of china latticework which the Boy thought very ingenious. They were popular as fern-pots and you met them everywhere. They can still be encountered in junk shops today.

There remains the book-case, which was book-case and *escritoire* combined. The books were protected by glass doors and although there were not many they were valuable. For here were first editions. There was a valuable edition of *The Pilgrim's Progress*, illustrated with woodcuts, and the Boy would look at that very often on Sunday evenings. There was a splendid and spirited picture of the fight with Apollyon and some highly terrifying pictures of foul fiends. And in a drawer there also lived a Stereoscope which was the origin of what the cinema now describes as 3-D, and a lot more effective, even if the pictures did not move. You looked through two lenses at a double photograph held in a wire stand and you adjusted the thing to the right focus by shifting it backwards and forwards. Lots of pictures went with that Stereoscope, views of foreign parts, of Vesuvius in eruption, the Colosseum at Rome, Italian landscapes, Venice, the Taj Mahal, the Alps, our own Tower of London, the Parthenon, and pictures of many celebrities, the Queen—dear Victoria— Mr. Gladstone, the Prince Consort, the Prince of Wales and a series depicting a story concerning some Norse characters of the Viking period, with one or two links missing, so the tale was never clear. Nobody knew anything about them, or where they had come from, but the general feeling was that it might have originated with Uncle Peter's Norwegian wife. But the star turn of the Stereoscope was a picture mounted on a frame of thick pasteboard, but itself of transparency. When held up to the light and gazed at through the lenses it displayed Napoleon's Tomb at Les Invalides in all its glory and majesty, and in what today would be called 'Glorious Technicolor' too. It even reproduced the glow and glitter of the lamps and candles, for each had a pinhole through its top and the light itself did the rest and created an illusion. The result was quite astonishing to the simple minds which knew nothing about the cinema in any form, radio or television, but did see before their very eyes what the cinema now puts up as a novelty—3-D. That view of the Invalides was better than the real thing, so that Boy thought when he saw the actual place in Paris.

o

The Dining Room was a nice, comfortable apartment. It had not the stiff aloofness, the exclusive and best-behavioured atmosphere of the Drawing Room. And how did that Victorian Family spend their Sunday; that Victorian Sunday of which so much has been said and written and on which so much ridicule has been poured? To begin with, breakfast was at eight-thirty instead of seven forty-five, and sometimes it was as late as 9 a.m. There was always something special for breakfast on a Sunday too; very often kidneys and bacon, cooked properly and not overdone. Often two or three dishes to choose from after the porridge which took the place of today's cereal, and porridge is the original and best cereal of them all, tea and coffee, rolls, toast, bread-and-butter—and fruit. After breakfast Miss Bessie and Miss Mary would depart for Church and Uncle James would go out on his bicycle. The Boy would do whatever he wanted, so long as he did not make too much noise. That was the only restriction. Frederica would busy herself about the house or do needle-work. She seldom, if ever, went to Church. The Boy was taken by his Aunts, from time to time, under silent protest. He did not like it at all. To him it was confinement, similar to school, and confinement and repression were always hateful to him. He had to sit and listen. And after Church he would be forced to endure the horrible embarrassment of being spoken to by his Aunt's friends, who would tell him he was getting a big boy, and make all the inane remarks which so many adults who don't remember when they were young make to children. One worthy gentle-man, who had mutton-chop whiskers and a heavy moustache, patted the Boy's head as he conversed with the Aunts and said he presumed the lad would shortly be taking up Church work. The lad never did—and largely because of that head-patting. He had nothing against Church, as such, or against Church work. He was quite religious in his own way and so remains. But he had the strongest objection to head-patting gentlemen who did Church work and with whom he refused to mix. So do small things alter lives. . . .

Sunday lunch was a terrific affair, for this family did not dine late. It consisted of soup, fish, joint, sweets, cheese and coffee. After lunch everyone went to the Dining Room, where dessert was served and the family indulged in dozes. The Boy would look at the Sunday papers—the Family took them all in and he was allowed to read them. From his very start he was a regular reader of the *Referee*, that pale-yellow newspaper of sporting, theatrical, social and political contents. Later in life he met and knew most of the men who ran the *Referee*, Richard Butler, H. Chance Newton, George R. Sims, Arnold White, J. N. Raphael and Eallett, who looked after the perfectly wonderful 'Answers to Correspondents Column', who found out all the answers and kept one of them in type, so often was it asked. That was the question as to how old was Marie Lloyd. That Column was quite unique and no newspaper today of any kind has anything half so efficient, informative and amusing, because the answers were properly presented. When he grew up, the Boy, who learnt much from that Column, kneeling on a chair at that Dining Room Table, was able to answer many queries put to it and help it in many ways. For years indeed he supplied Fleet Street with free information, and two generations of Fleet Street reciprocated by helping him. The present generation has changed and the free information bureau is suspended. Nothing for nothing is the rule today and it may as well be general. But the Boy knew little of Fleet Street then. He looked through all the papers lying in the middle of that table, as the dailies did in the Little Room; the *Sunday Times*, the *Observer*, *Lloyd's Weekly News*, *Reynolds*, the *Weekly Dispatch*, *News of the World*, the *People*, the *Sunday News* and the rest of them. He always kept his *Ally Sloper's Half Holiday* for Sunday reading too. He would eat and enjoy his dessert but he would not doze. He would eat the sweets which formed part of the dessert. Miss Mary had a strange sense of economy as regards sweets, which were in those days as plentiful as they were cheap. Good sweets were four ounces a penny and very good sweets two ounces a penny. Miss Mary disregarded them. It was possible then to buy from certain shops what was known as 'broken chocolate', and also selections of slightly faded mixed chocolates which had lost their colour and gloss by being exposed for sale in the window and were therefore shop-soiled and very cheap. These were what Miss Mary bought for Sunday dessert; although there was always a box of good sweets in case visitors called. The Boy did not mind these rather stale chocolates. They were quite wholesome and edible and he never came to any harm. Sweets were sweets, that was his motto, and if the small chocolate creams were a little hard to start with, sucking soon brought them to their right texture.

At four o'clock the ladies of the Family went upstairs to Dress— although best clothes had been worn by those who went to Church. At five o'clock everyone descended to the Breakfast Room for an enormous tea, with muffins, crumpets and tea cakes in winter and always brown and white bread-and-butter and a remarkable selection of cakes. After tea Uncle James departed to call on other members of the Family—and the Aunts either went to Church again or out to 'pay calls', a thing to which they were terribly addicted and which to the Boy was his greatest horror if he got involved. He would dodge them at all costs and he would spend the evening playing games. Or he might drag out of a corner in that Dining Room a huge pile of fortnightly copies of *Beautiful Britain*, which had for some reason not got to the Box Room, and also similar copies of *The 100 Best Pictures* in colour. *Beautiful Britain* was not in colour but inspired him to make up his mind to see his native country. *The 100 Best Pictures* gave him ideas about Art. He fell under the spell of Watts and Turner. His favourites were 'The Minotaur', and 'Hope', 'The Fighting Temeraire', and 'Ulysses defying the Cyclops.' He asked to be taken to picture galleries as a result of those periodicals, and was taken to the best. He liked the Tate Gallery when it opened and the Wallace Collection. He had recollections, though more in the mass than in detail of the galleries and pictures at Hampton Court. The National Gallery was a bit vast for him. But he liked Holbein and Van Dyke from an early age and he found a charm in the Dutch school which still remains with him. Of the British he liked Gainsborough, Reynolds and Morland, with Constable as runner-up. He learnt the groundwork of these things on Sunday evenings. His taste might be bad but he knew about writers and painters all the same. He still likes the pictures he liked as a Boy and has never been able to understand Modern Art or Statuary. He would swop all the modern masterpieces for one Dying Gaul. The Boy played about the house, or he lay in front of the fire looking at those pictures. Sometimes his Mother played hymns on the piano in the Drawing Room and they sang together; 'Hold the Fort', 'Onward Christian Soldiers', 'All Things Bright and Beautiful', and 'Eternal Father' were the favourites. And the Boy would gaze out of that Dining Room window into the gathering dusk and watch the lamp-lighter go zigzagging down the road, leaving a trail of golden, flickering points of light behind him. Evening fell in a leisurely way in those days before Daylight Saving, rather sadly in autumn, rather suddenly in winter, very reluctantly and with a special glow in springtime and it seemed never to come at all in summer. . . .

Supper was at nine and the Boy sat up for it on Sundays. He could watch for his Family's return, peering through the slats of the Venetian blinds in winter when the silence of the road was only broken by the lisping feet of the pious, either going or returning from Church, or the rattle of the hooves of the doctor's carriage and pair . . . until he saw his Aunts coming, erect, side by side and arguing heatedly but with outward dignity.

Then—Supper—a good one, but nevertheless with an air of sadness for the Boy which had begun to descend on him from about tea-time onwards. That cloud which made enjoyment misty and damped all real pleasure was the fact that there was School Tomorrow. . . . That was the one and only bad spot about a Victorian Sunday as the Boy remembers it. And he notices that it still exists despite the plethora of chance for pleasure given by modernity; the easy transport, the motor-car, the gramophone, the radio and television. For he sees his own grandson immersed in and complaining of that same cloud.

CHAPTER FIFTEEN

Upstairs

THE Front or Main Hall from which the State Apartments opened
was long and rather narrow. It started broadly from the Front Door,
but narrowed off beside the ascending staircase. It had a Turkey Carpet
in it and several rugs, and the wallpaper was a mottled brown, with a
broad dado. There was a massive hallstand, of mahogany, with both
hooks and protruding bars for hats and coats, and a drawer in the middle
with a brown marble top, which contained hat brushes, clothes brushes
and hatpads—those oblongs of stuffed velvet used for imparting a
shine to silk hats. Some of the hat brushes were long and curved like a
blunted sickle, so that the dust could be got out of the rims of bowler
hats. On each side were stands for sticks and umbrellas. This accommodation was reinforced by a drainpipe which stood just inside the door.
This was literally a drainpipe with one end—that on which it stood—
covered in. It was for umbrellas on a wet day—and a very sensible
idea too. The front of the drainpipe was ornamented by painting—the
work of Frederica. There was a square mirror in the hatstand and the
divisions for the sticks held quite a wide variety of such things. In those
days almost every man carried a stick in fine weather and an umbrella
in wet. Uncle James was an exception. He would, on very wet days, use
an umbrella, always a disreputable one—but he never carried a walking-
stick. There were canes, Malacca and partridge, sticks of oak with
rough horn handles and of carved ivory, there were ashplants and rattans
and there was one especially beautiful. It was solid ebony, carved throughout its whole length, and its handle was a dog's head—probably a Saluki,
with staring eyes. The head unscrewed and somehow it got lost. . . .

A Barometer hung in the hall but it did not work and a very old
grandfather clock featuring Father Time and a ship encountering
rough weather.

Outside the two doors were black sheepskin rugs and one also laid at the main staircase, for no reason at all. Immediately inside the front door was a mat, sunk into the floor, on which boots should be wiped. What the Boy liked and coveted most in that hall were two trophies of arms which hung above each door—Drawing and Dining Room. They contained curved cavalry sabres of the Crimean and Waterloo period, bayonets of the same time, and light, curved and businesslike-looking Indian scimitars. The Boy would stand halfway up the staircase and gaze at this deadly array. He yearned for them. And, one day, he got them. A sabre fell off its hook and nearly dashed out the brains of a lady entering the Drawing Room one Third Thursday. The arms were taken down—and the Boy put in his claim successfully. It never dawned on his people that they would be dangerous to him or to those with whom he played. And there was never the slightest accident.

Lighting of the hall was achieved by a fair sized octagonal lantern, with stained-glass windows, which hung from the ceiling and had to be lighted by standing on a chair and using a taper holder—a long, hollow brass affair, into which the lighted wax taper was stuck. The illumination was pretty but did not give much light, so it was reinforced by two ordinary gas brackets with opal globes with stars on them. There were four chairs, of solid mahogany, but the seats were hinged and lifted up, disclosing receptacles which could hold all sorts of things—and did.

There was no form of heating in the hall, which could and did get very cold in winter and would have served as a good fridge. Guests had to be content with the warmth of the welcome before going into the rooms, which were warm and cosy enough after a fire had burnt for about eight hours.

That hatstand held something not seen today. In the Victorian House it was a sizable silver tray—or basket—it was a bit of both. Callers, finding the family not at home, would 'leave cards'. There was an etiquette about this—a card was left for the caller, of course, and if it was a formal call, one was left for the husband of the lady making it and for each of her adult family as well. This was always the case when people moved into a new house. After a decent interval, neighbours would 'leave cards' but not come in on that occasion. It was just a manner of breaking the ice. It was a good idea, too, for it showed the newcomers who their neighbours were, what their names were and how many there were in the family. The cards were of the very best 'cardboard' and always engraved—a printed card was a social solecism and in those days even printed business cards did not inspire confidence. These cards were most useful as reference for names and addresses. They were a definite record of who had called—for there were hardly any telephones at all in private houses and, even so, calls of that kind are seldom noted and soon forgotten. But these cards remained for a long time in those card baskets, and could always be referred to. When friendship grew, addresses got into the address book. Ladies attending their first At Home Days and new friends of the family would also leave a card—but the old friends did not. Men did not come to 'At Homes'—although an occasional clergyman or curate might drop in—they were Ladie's Day.

There was another card which was left persistently and sometimes was not at all welcomed. Every afternoon, round about three, the ladies of the house would go upstairs to their rooms to 'dress'. Nobody wore the same dress all day. It was a recognized thing and nobody 'called' about that time; it would have been difficult for them to do so, for nearly every lady was 'dressing'. Often the servants went upstairs to dress at the same time—it was the most convenient. If there was a gap in the domestic ranks, it was almost certain that nobody would be downstairs. Then, on such an occasion, would come a knock on the front door and also a ring, too (if the bell worked). This would cause consternation. Who could it be, coming at such an inauspicious hour? The caller was out of sight because of the front porch. So a maid would have to make herself as presentable as possible in the shortest space of time and rush down four flights of stairs to answer the door. Outside stood a man, who regarded her. "Any answer to Mrs. Mitchell's card?" he would demand. Now, Mrs. Mitchell's card had been pushed through the letterbox earlier in the day with a note to the effect that a call would follow it. Nobody paid any attention to it. But here was the caller. He would be well 'told off', informed that in future he must go to the side door. 'Come knocking on the front door at this time of day, like one of the gentry,' the incensed maid would say, 'whoever 'eard. . . .' She would slam the door and remount the stairs, calling to the ladies of the house what had happened, to reassure them. Mrs. Mitchell's card was a very regular caller, for she was—and the firm still exists—a 'wardrobe dealer'—in other words she dealt in old clothes. The card said 'Best Prices given'. Once made to understand that the side door was her social status and only one knock —and not in the afternoons—Mrs. Mitchell, in the person of her representative, did a good business with Victorian and Edwardian households, to mutual satisfaction. Nobody, to general knowledge, ever saw Mrs. Mitchell, but her card was very familiar. It was printed and did not go into the card basket. It still comes round—and callers still follow it up . . . an old-established firm indeed.

The banisters of the flight which led from the state apartments to the next storey were the very best in the whole house for sliding down, because the longest and, if anything, the most highly polished. The fact that you usually slipped on the mat at the bottom only gave an added zest. This long flight led to an enormous landing, which was cut in half by doors, partly of frosted glass. Behind them was the hot-water cupboard as it was called in that household, where was the hot-water tank and in which things were aired. It was as large as an ordinary living room today; a small bedroom (again small by contemporary comparison), the bathroom and the lavatory. The bedroom was that in which the Boy slept. It had a big double bed—for if visitors came his Mother would move in too; she being an interloper, as it were, her room was sacrificed in time of stress and crowding.

This room was rather crowded. It had a washstand with curved mahogany legs and a marble top with a washbasin, jug, soapdish, water carafe and glass, toothbrush stand (earthenware) and one or two oddments. Towels hung from a rail on either side and there was a little bowl to hold a face flannel. The dressing table was of white wood, and enamelled in white. It had an American cloth covering, and a mirror which was a fixture and could tilt backwards and forwards, being secured by wooden screws at each side. There was a pin tray, brushes and combs —for which a bag was also supplied (in case of travelling) embroidered with designs by one of the ladies, silk being sewn over a transfer pattern thereon. A small wardrobe, with mirror in the door, held the boy's clothes. There was a fireplace, in which a fire was lit if he was very ill—and he was never very ill. As a rule it held a paper fan, specked with soot. He only remembers a fire there once.

The bed was a wooden frame and a feather mattress—you sank right into it. It was warm and comfortable—even in the rigorous winters of those times when the water froze in the bedroom waterjugs and had to be melted in the mornings. There were a couple of bookshelves in a corner, filled with books and 'comics', and a few pictures—some school groups, some football club groups featuring the uncles, pictures from Christmas Annuals and his favourite boys' magazines, all framed. One from a Christmas Annual was there when he took over the room. It showed a very demure girl, in a white lacy dress and kind of mob cap, wearing black mittens. She had brown hair and eyes and a delightful complexion. By her side was a basket of cherries and the name of the work of art was 'Cherry Ripe'. The Boy thought that young lady very lovely indeed, even at an age when as a general rule he held all girls in loathing, contempt and detestation. But he decided that when he got married that was the sort of girl for him. And indeed, when that time came, the girl was very much like that picture, except for the rather smug demureness. . . .

There was one window which was large and shielded with a short

lace curtain heavily flounced, and the view was of the next door house
—or that part of it corresponding with the room under description.
This room and its neighbours, like the scullery and the Little Room,
was in the kind of annexe which stuck out from the back of the house and
above it were 'the Leads'. This was the top storey of the excrescence. The
blind was of blue shiny cloth and went up with a satisfying rush and
bang. . . . The bathroom was long if rather narrow. There was a window
at the far end, not curtained but with a pull-down blind of dark blue—
shiny on one side and dull on the other—similar to the blind in the
Boy's room. The bathroom could not be overlooked. It looked out upon
the very long garden, beyond which was a field called 'The Back Piece'
—then came the long gardens of the road behind this 'Best' Victorian
road. The nearest houses were a good hundred yards or so away. Opposite
the door was a small table bearing a looking-glass—also with movable
mirror, and against the wall opposite the bath was a towel horse, very
easy to upset. The bath itself was large. It was of iron and was enamelled,
in this case the enamel was of green. It was enclosed with wooden sides
and at the end nearest the door, where the washbasin and taps were, the
wooden partition continued to the end wall. This bath did not have the
usual taps which turned on, they operated by flat levers, fastened into
the wooden covers, and there was no plug—the water went out through
a series of upright slits. Those tap levers turned round by means of knobs
—almost touching the wooden surface and the flow could be adjusted.
It was quite fascinating to use them—the horse trams of those days had
brakes which acted in much the same way—a fact which did not escape
the notice of the Boy. Tube train drivers have a similar lever now. The
washbasin was of blue and white. It resembled Willow Pattern Plate
except that it was not Chinese. It depicted what appeared to be a *Fête
Champêtre* in the extensive grounds of a Château, with groups of people
who danced, sang, played instruments, sat about or stood around
gossiping. The Boy liked to fill that basin until these people were all
submerged. It gave him the feeling that he was causing another Flood.
The basin had brass taps, and as the bath levers were brass there was a
good deal of daily polishing in the bathroom. The Boy was made to clean
his teeth here—an occupation which seemed to him a waste of time. He
used either white camphorated chalk, Calvert's Carbolic, which was
pink, or another tooth powder called 'Robin', which was in little white
jars or boxes with a robin on the lid. Toothpastes in tubes were unknown,
and the powder got very wet, was easily spilled and the whole method
was wasteful. What the Boy liked most in the bathroom was being
allowed to sail his boats therein. He had quite a fleet of all sizes and
well remembers one afternoon in his summer holidays when he was so

employed. He had the window open. A fresh breeze caught the sails of a little lugger he possessed causing it to heel over and scud along like a real ship. It happened only the once but it was quite unforgettable. . . .

A short flight from the Bathroom landing led to the next one, also vast—where were the two Best Bedrooms. The back one belonged to Uncle James. It was very simple and austere in *décor* and the bed was of iron with brass knobs. It had a large cupboard and a large dressing table and on the walls were athletic groups and gatherings of gymnasts in all of which Uncle James figured. But in the fireplace stood some things which made the room very individual, a pair of Indian Clubs so vast that they made that of Hercules seem like a child's toy, and a pair of dumbbells which it took two ordinary people to lift. Uncle James could swing the clubs like thistledown and exercised with the dumbbells every morning. . . .

Between this room and the Best Bedroom was a cupboard, very long and very deep. It held quantities of clothes—which were suspended from pegs. Here the ladies kept their 'things'—their heavy cloaks and coats, their capes—capes were largely worn—and all sorts of dresses which although not in general use were by no means discarded and had not reached the 'Mrs. Mitchell' stage. It was an amazing place. When, at children's parties, Hide and Seek was the game, this was a wonderful place of concealment. For one could be quite hidden amongst the clothes in the uttermost depths of it, and strange children were afraid of entering its dark expanse. And children who had hidden there had been known to get scared too and by their wails betray their hideout.

Then came the Front Bedroom, the Best Bedroom. This was an amazing room, immediately over the Dining Room, in the front of the house and of vast dimensions. If the Back Bedroom was austere, the Front Bedroom made up for it. It was crammed with things of all sorts. It had a thick Turkey carpet on the floor and a light wallpaper—white with immense flowers on it, species quite unknown, but partaking of the nature of a dahlia, a chrysanthemum, a rose and a cabbage all at the same time, and of a bright blue tint. There was a wardrobe of mahogany, large enough to live in, with a long mirror in the panel of its door. There were six small chairs, painted white with floral garlands on the backrests, forget-me-nots and roses intertwined. They had cane seats —and there were two small armchairs, swathed in loose covers, which were white with a blue floral design, but of nothing like the same violence as the wallpaper. The embrasured window had Venetian blinds, long lace curtains, draught protectors—covered in blue and not the usual turkey-red, and heavy blue velvet curtains to pull across. There was a large cheval glass which tilted backwards and forwards so that the lady could see all of herself in her voluminous dress. The fireplace was plain white marble and bristled with ornaments. Prominent amongst these were objects of white china, the main feature of which was a little naked boy. He might have been a Cupid or just a boy who had mislaid his clothing. Sometimes he wore a very short vest, which only reached his hips, it seemed to have shrunk badly in the wash. This urchin was not idle. He pushed a wheelbarrow, he held a kind of large egg, with a circular hole in it. Sometimes he leant against a vase and supported it—and sometimes he even wrestled with a swan. Sometimes he was in coloured china, but mostly plain white and his 'lead finish' was usually so shiny that he looked sticky. The object with which he was occupied usually held a fern, as often as not maidenhair. There were a lot of these ornaments about, all over the house, except in the Dining Room, and also rather majestic-looking swans which also carried ferns. There were at least six in the Best Bedroom. A clock made of what appeared to be quartz and rather heavily decorative stood in the centre of the mantelpiece, but it did not go. There was no overmantel or mirror. The walls bore watercolours, in white frames. Some of these were landscapes, some were of flowers. In some families they were the work of members thereof, but more often than not they were purchased. There was a centre chandelier of white metal bearing four gas globes, highly chased and blue rimmed. Two further gas globes were stationed as sconces each side of the Dressing Table, which was the most important article, apart from the bed, the room possessed. It had, of course, a washstand, with a white marble top, which held two of everything—the china being blue and white—this was naturally a double room. On the rail below the washstand was a blue and white slop pail, the other utensils sometimes found there being in a white wooden pedestal and so out of sight, thus preserving the modesty of the period when lavatories were not things of fun, but quite unmentionable. No water was laid on, of course, it was all brought up by hand. All the articles on the washstand were blue and white, even the water carafe and the glasses.

The dressing table was something at which the present generation might wonder. It had a mirror running almost its entire length with a narrow flanking mirror at each end, so that the lady could study herself completely. What could be seen of the table was white, with again sprays of roses and forget-me-nots painted on it, but little enough was seen. All round the edge of the actual table top was fastened white muslin over a pale blue foundation. This formed a kind of skirt for the table, split at the front and caught up by a blue bow—so that the legs could go underneath. The muslin was usually spotted—the spots being thick and white. Then from the edge again and over this skirtlike swathing was a valance of what was known as torchon lace. Behind the mirror hung a muslin pall, fastened again by little bows of blue silk, which indeed were dotted all over the place. The whole effect was extremely charming but made an awful lot of washing. There were little nests of drawers beside the mirror—which were kept empty so that visitors could put their personal property therein. But the dressing table was heavily furnished. It bore the best silver set, silver-backed brushes and mirror and a silver tray. The rest of the furnishing was of china. There was a curious thing, rather like a stag's antler, sticking up into the air from its base, on the prongs of which the lady hung her rings. There were little boxes and pots, mostly of china but sometimes cut glass and silver-topped—these were for powder and the like. There was a scent spray, of blue glass and gilt decoration, which operated by a tube and bulb and was kept filled with the best eau-de-cologne. A watchstand was there, for the lady's watch, a sensible precaution as the clock never went. There were, as a rule, a couple of little oblong boxes for holding hairpins, most necessary then. These were of white china with little embossed and coloured flowers round every edge, quite attractive and charming and likely to be collector's pieces in the future. And over a knob of the mirror hung a little white bag into which the lady put her 'combings'—the pieces of hair which came out into the brush and which were taken to the hairdressers to be 'made up' into 'switches' and 'transformations', for the elaboration of the coiffure. There was also a little silver tray, for casual things—probably more hairpins—and a little plated stand for curling irons which had a small methylated stove under it. Millions of hairpins must have been used in those days—every time the carpet was swept—and that was every day—there was a harvest and they could be found all over the pavement in the streets as well. There were always a lot on every dressing table, although the visitor always brought her own. There were little boxes for pins and safety pins and other accessories. The Dressing Table was indeed an altar to femininity.

The Bed was remarkable. It was of tremendous proportions—and very high off the ground. One had practically to climb into it. And having done so the occupant sank almost out of sight in its feathery depths. The bedstead was of plain brass with knobs at the four corners. It had a flounce of white muslin and torchon right round it. The bedspread was of white net or lace, with a blue foundation which showed through—like the dressing table but of more delicate material. The sheets and blankets were of superfine quality, and so were the bolster and the pillow cases, all of which had lace edges. There was a blue eiderdown quilt. But the bed had something hardly ever seen today. It had a canopy which extended almost half way down it, supported on a brass frame

with arms, and curtains hung down on each side, which could be looped
back or pulled forward, to exclude draughts. They were all of muslin
with blue foundation and torchon edges. The whole thing was an
offering to Morpheus, if the user thereof was not too overcome by the
grandeur. This was the room occupied by important visitors and also,
by a contrast, into this room went any member of the family who was
very ill. It was thought to impress the doctors. If a married couple had a
large family—then they used the room. There was a dressing room
attached, rather more plainly but very comfortably furnished, and this
could be locked off from the bedroom and used independently, for it
had a door of its own on to the landing. It was here that Frederica slept
—and when she was ill the Boy gave up his room and used this. One
thing about the Best Bedroom—a fire was always lighted and kept
burning when visitors came in the winter.

From the landing outside these apartments a staircase led to yet
another, on either side of which were tiers of trunks belonging to the
family for which there was not room in the Box Room. Some were
flat topped, some had domed tops and all were leather and large. They
were covered by sheets of green serge. The Boy liked that landing,
because to him the trunks were mountains whereon he was Rob Roy
fighting the English—or vice versa, outlaws in the hills—or he would
conduct a campaign on the North-West Frontier—the trunks being the
Himalayas and the landing between the Khyber Pass. The window
from the landing opened on to the Leads, and it was only a question of
stepping over the edge to get out. On the Leads was the cistern, which
supplied the whole house with water for all purposes. This water was
pumped in at intervals though later came what was known as 'constant
supply'. The water flowing in caused all sorts of odd gurgling noises
over the whole house—but everyone knew what it was. That cistern
was supposed to be cleaned out at periods—it had a large wooden
cover—but there was usually a dead bird or two in it. But nobody else
died, except the bird. The Boy liked the Leads because to him it was
either a castle or a fortress. A wall ran round two sides of it, the house
forming the third, but the fourth side, for reasons best known to the
builder, was quite unguarded. A chimney stack rose at the garden end.
The Boy went up there and played his games. He defended it against
immense odds, sometimes with pike and sword or axe—he had them
all, the pike being an old alpenstock found in the Box Room. Sometimes
he attacked it from the landing, gaining admission through the window
and, of course, captured the stronghold. He had fixed up a pole from
which he flew the Union Jack. At times he would be more modern and
then was armed with his Daisy Air Gun. He had a constant succession of

these air rifles, which cost only three and sixpence. They threw a dart or a slug quite a considerable distance; they were loaded by 'breaking' them in the middle and clapping them to again—which drew in the air. They had an inner tube which could be removed but its loss lessened range and accuracy. It was the method of loading which broke them— usually the top joint of the barrel, where it tapered off to the foresight, would break off—it was only soldered on—and then a new rifle had to be wheedled out of the grown-ups. The Boy had another airgun with a solid straight barrel, which outlasted all the Daisies, but did not look as good and he never liked it as much.

The Leads gave an extensive view over gardens on both sides and across the beloved 'Back Piece' into the next road. The Boy could, and did, observe what went on amongst hostile tribes which inhabited such regions. Steel helmet on head, sword by side, pike in hand, he would pace the battlements, gazing under his hand from time to time to see who or what was coming. If foes were sighted he 'wound his horn', and he had one slung around him, for he did everything properly, even to a dagger to balance his sword. He had a bow and arrows too, which he discharged on the foe beneath, recovering the arrows from the garden. He had gone in for realism, or as near as he could get it, by carting up some pails of water which became to him hot lead to be poured on the besiegers. But one day he drenched the gardener and that part of the performance was cut out. He was always expected to fall over, but he never did. If the game was modern and he used his rifle, he fired real slugs—until the supply ran out. There was a family of hostile boys who lived at the last house higher up, who would sneak down the Back Piece and destroy fortifications set up by the Boy and his friends—if they could do such destruction unobserved. But the Boy frequently spotted them from his battlements and kicked up such a row and kept up such a fire from his Daisy that, although out of range, they mostly retired. He and his friends took punitive action later. He would sometimes see, in a garden a couple of doors up, a girl watering the flowers. She would get shot at, and sometimes she was hit but not hurt. Mostly he made the slug ping against the fence and she would take to her heels. That was one way in which Boy met Girl because that couple got married—and are married still. He made all his games very real and elaborate. He played up there quite alone, he was not allowed to take his little friends out there. But he had the gift which Shakespeare begged his auditors to assume—'into a thousand parts divide each man and make imaginary puissance'. And all the time he kept up a suitable narrative, aloud. He was in trouble once. He had been to the Alexandra Palace and witnessed a parachute descent. It thrilled him to the core. It fascinated him. He set about making a parachute for himself. He got an old sheet and some ropes and he made one which seemed to him just the article. It was his intention to have a parachute descent of his own—from the Leads. He did not mention this to anyone, fearing he would be refused permission. Fortunately his parachute was discovered by his Mother on the very day he had planned the descent—and the intrepid airman was foiled. He has never made a parachute descent—and nowadays he does not want to. They are no novelty today but they have lost their charm for him. He would often sit out there in fine weather and clean his equipment. He kept all his arms in first-class condition, especially the swords. There was one genuine and straight sword, not very long but thick and satisfying, which he esteemed above all others. It had come from one of those trophies of arms and had probably been used either by a gunner or a sapper. It had a double edge and a cross hilt. It was a sword of many names, according to what he was playing; it could be 'Excalibur', it could be the 'Whitefire' of 'Eric Brighteyes'—he was a great reader of Rider Haggard—and it could be the 'Hneiper' of Harald Hardraada—he was never sure about the name. He carried it as often as possible and never hurt anyone with it, which shows that children with imagination can be trusted. He even pressed the Virginia Creeper which covered the back of the house into his games, for when it flamed red in the autumn his castle was on fire. . . .

From the landing of the Leads and boxes, another flight of steps rose to the top storey. Here was another big landing with doors opening from it, and here in adjoining bedrooms, one back and one front, slept Miss Bessie and Miss Mary. Miss Bessie had the back room, which was the larger. It was an attic and the roof behaved accordingly. It descended almost to the forehead of the sleeper in the bed and one had to be careful not to get a nasty knock on the forehead if rising quickly. The bed was never turned round the other way, for reasons nobody could understand. It was a black iron bedstead with brass knobs and the room was comfortably though plainly furnished. Miss Mary's room was also an attic, but she had a larger and wooden bed and it was not so placed as to endanger the head. She had far more ornate bits and pieces and a small cupboard which looked like the door of a castle, clamped with steel, which fitted into a corner and held a little collection of dolls in the costumes of many nations. She could never explain why she got them or kept them. But she had many odd habits. She probably meant to present them to children of her acquaintance, but could not bring herself to part with them. The Boy despised them as being girls' toys but found a use for them at times, regarding them as maidens in distress kept in a castle by recreant knights whom he slew. . . . Aunt Mary, who adored children, was

sometimes out in her judgment as to what they liked. She would waste
much time making scrapbooks for little friends. Now, children then
liked scrapbooks, provided they were scrapbooks, filled with highly
coloured scraps (mostly printed in Germany). But Miss Mary's scrap:
books held a minimum of them. She cut out advertisements from magazines and filled the books with those. The children despised them,
knowing them for what they were. She would collect up all the odds and
ends of coloured paper out of crackers, the silver or gold coverings and
the old torn paper hats and give bundles of these to children—who did
not want them and had no possible use for them. Yet she could enter
into a game with the best of them and would never spare herself to
amuse them. They knew it and persecuted her, she had not the heart to
refuse them. They made a slave of her—and her great-niece would make
her sit on the stairs whilst she, as a child, danced in the hall of her home
—and Miss Mary was an old lady then—for hours on end. Miss Mary
never failed to make the right comment or to applaud. She was a follower
of every popular fad. There was a craze for 'Rubbish Plates', a most
absurd affair. Tin plates, costing a penny each, were purchased and
covered with putty. Into this was pushed pieces of broken china, and
then the putty between was painted with gold paint. Or the putty was
filled with old nails, broken pieces of metal, any rubbish which was
quite useless and unornamental and the whole thing covered with gold
paint. A third method was to cover the putty with discarded pieces of
torn lace—embroidery or worn-out crochet—there was always a lot
about—and again it was all painted gold. These things looked terrible
and exactly what they were. Miss Mary would present them to her friends
who had to pretend gratitude. She had another odd habit. Wherever she
was a guest she did a little petty larceny, some minor pilfering. She would
pocket sweets, crackers and almonds—anything she could get into her
pocket (women had pockets then at the back of their skirts, most
difficult of access) or into her handbag—which was of large size and
of leather. She would bring them home in triumph. She did not want
them but she had to take them. Thank goodness it never developed into
kleptomania.

Both these rooms were comfortable in summer but very cold in
winter. Fires were seldom lit. But if there was a case of infectious disease
in the house the sufferer was hurried up to one of these rooms and there
treated. One of the family did the nursing. A sheet smothered with
disinfectant screened off the stairs. But as the servants slept on the same
floor, they had to risk it—and so did either of the ladies—for Miss
Bessie—it was always her room which became the ward, stayed there,
and Miss Mary had to use her room next door. However, there was

An early Motor Car—the driver is Isabel Jay

Three Edwardians see something they think attractive—wolf whistles were not invented. The Girl takes no notice—but she knows they are there. This was called "clicking"

Lewis Waller as "Henry V"

Sir Herbert Tree

always the Best Room into which she could go—and she mostly did. She believed in creature comforts. The servants slept in two rooms, one was usually sacred to the Cook, and the two maids shared the other. There was plenty of room and they had a bed each, although they shared a wash basin. When the Cook was dispensed with, they had a room each. In that Victorian house both of these rooms had gas—although many servants were only allowed candles. It was considered likely they would read in bed, waste the light and cause expense. They were mostly too tired to read after their day's work and the early morning rising (they were up at six) and they had the evening in the kitchen to do so if they wanted. It never dawned on the Victorians that candles in servants' bedrooms might—and did—occasion fires. The servants' rooms in that house had carpets too and very plain bedsteads—camp beds they were called—but plenty of bed clothes with counterpanes made of some thick material pitted like honeycombs and an old eiderdown each. In this room the servants kept their private belongings and their boxes. These were mostly of tin and painted either yellow or brown. They were old and battered; they had had them when they first went 'into service' and they made them do for years. Hardly any of them would close—the locks were always broken—and when a maid 'left' she tied rope round her box to keep it safe. Maids were sometimes suspected of pilfering and then the mistress would search the box and the room. But mostly the girls' privacy was respected. They did not have any heating in the bedrooms—and the water for all that floor had to be carried up six flights of stairs—unless they got it from the bathroom— and it was not easy to fill jugs in that bath, in which case they had only three flights to negotiate. They kept as warm as they could under their bedclothes and their mistresses presented them with bed jackets and woollen coats which they themselves had no further use for and so passed on.

That landing had a long narrow cupboard down one side which was an overflow or safety valve for the other room up there. And that room was the Box Room. The landing overhung that beneath it and there was a kind of well in the staircase, protected by banisters. That too had its use for the Boy, and there he made his major fortress when winter or wet weather prevented him from using the Leads. The staircases were lighted by gas and there was gas on each landing, besides the big windows. There was no lack of light in those houses—not a dark room or corner anywhere, except by the coal cellar.

Miss Bessie had on the walls of her room—which seldom got repapered—photographs of friends and of places she had visited. There were a lot of the German town of Giessen, where the famous Uncle

P

Peter had his mine, and of Frankfurt-am-Main, nearby. Also views of
the Rhine. There were also views of that Scottish village of Newabbey
where her Uncle was Minister. Miss Mary had a lot of these too, and a
picture of Mr. Gladstone, who was her hero, hung on the line with George
Alexander, Lewis Waller and Hayden Coffin. Both rooms had extensive
views and the Boy could look from Miss Mary's window right across the
reservoirs behind the houses opposite—which were detached—and see
many wild duck thereon. He always wanted to get a closer view but
never did.

Miss Bessie, who was really pious in her way, had a framed text
on one of her walls too. It showed an immense eye of a very penetrating
blue and the legend was 'Thou, God, seest me'. What satisfaction she
derived from it was never known. It frightened the Boy, who had the
measles in that room. That eye seemed to watch his every movement.
For a long time he was made most self-conscious and afraid, as he thought
that awful eye was upon him. That may have been the idea, but he can
assure the originator of it that it did not make for religious feelings—it
made for concealment and deceit if anything at all. Miss Mary also had
a text which was more comforting. Hers was 'The Lord is my Shepherd,
I shall not want'.

Not a night passed but both those ladies knelt by their bedsides and
said their prayers. Those prayers may have proved beneficial to others
for whom they prayed but they did not have much luck, poor ladies,
for a great part of their later lives. But perhaps they had their compensations and happiness. An attempt was made to make it so. Another thing
those two rooms had in common at afternoon dressing time was a smell
of singed hair. Ladies then curled their own hair and used curling tongs
to do so, which they heated over little stoves of methylated spirit. They
poured the spirit on to a kind of container which looked like a pad
such as is used for rubber stamps, only it was metal, and covered as to
the top with metal gauze. Arms at each end supported the curling tongs
or they could be just held in the flame. When hot enough, the ladies
seized their hair in the tongs and twisted it. Somehow it curled. They
held it wrapped round the tongs for quite a while sometimes and if a bit
too hot the tongs singed the hair which, mingled with the smell of the
methylated spirit, was perhaps the all-pervading aroma of all Victorian
bedrooms which contained a lady. They curled their fringes when such
things were popular, their side hair into little corkscrew curls, sometimes
almost all their head. The curling tongs were sometimes straight—with
a bit scooped out of one prong, and sometimes they were wavy, as if to
induce and help curls by their very shape and by having a permanent
wave in the tongs to ensure one in the hair. The curls were not as per-

manent as those now acquired at hairdressers at considerable expense, maybe, but they were just as good and cost nothing to do daily—for those who had not naturally curly hair. But there was always a hint of that singed perfume in all Victorian bedrooms which were used by the Ladies. . . .

The maids had texts in their rooms, put there by their employers— and there was a Bible in each room too. But they covered the walls with photographs and coloured pictures from the annuals.

And the visitor to this Victorian House, which the author has tried to recall through the mists of over forty years, is now back at the hard core—the real hard core of Victorianism itself, the Box Room. That was the storehouse of possessions retained not because of their usefulness but merely because they were possessions and could not therefore be thrown away. That was how the English—or the British, whichever is preferred, only the English started it—got together and held together the British Empire until such time as the nature of the race changed.

The Box Room was the Valhalla of the useless, the discarded, the almshouse of rest for objects which had served their time and done their duty. The Box Room is far more the essence of Victorianism than all the hansom cabs, the antimacassars, the top hats and the aspidistras in the world. There the things of Yesterday gathered the dust of Today and mixed with them were objects still in use but too bulky or perhaps a shade too domestic to be kept downstairs, such things as that dress-maker's dummy for instance. But then nothing in that room was really considered out of date or useless. It was believed that anything there might come in handy at any odd time. In reality the Box Room was the Memory of the Victorian House filled with all sorts of things seemingly forgotten but ready when evoked. And today—when Box Rooms have gone—there still remains one's own Memory to take their place. . . .

CHAPTER SIXTEEN

Victorian Garden

VICTORIAN Days, like the days of the first Elizabeth, are now called spacious and the word is well used. Young people of today, if they have been able to struggle through this book, have realized by now that the Victorian houses were spacious and they may be assured that the same remark applied to the gardens. For Victorians liked privacy. They liked possession, they liked to be aloof from the crowd and to be 'on their own'. Their House was their Castle and if they had sufficient ground round it to form a barrier against the world, like a moat, they were well pleased. Those magnificent Victorian mansions which stood in their own grounds, of anything from four to six acres, still remain. Their glory has departed, nobody lives in them now as private personages—they are either boarding houses, clinics, schools, some sort of local government offices or taken over by one of the Boards which manage to interfere between the public and the supply of public services like coal, gas and electricity and make these things, once so cheap and simple, expensive and difficult to obtain. Although flats had appeared in Victorian times, they were not popular. Subconsciously, Victorians regarded them as being Continental—and that was very much against them. For Victorians were essentially insular and none the worse for that. Dickens drew 'Mr. Podsnap' as a comic character yet one true to life, with just the slightest exaggeration as a caricature.

Such an outlook obviously did not favour Flats—and also there was always a lurking idea in Victorian minds that living in flats was very little different to living in lodgings—and gentlefolk—unless reduced —did not do that. Single gentlemen might reside in 'chambers' but that was a very different thing to lodgings—though they would have been hard put to it to explain, if tackled on the subject. No, it was houses for the Victorians and as big gardens as possible. The Best House which is the heart of this book did not stand in grounds. Its owners—who actually rented it, anyway—were not people of sufficient wealth for the large mansion with the semi-circular drive of golden weedless gravel, the stabling, the footmen and butler and coachmen—and the gardener and assistants and a staff of maids. Their house was not even detached, but it was big, spacious and the Best of its Kind in the Road. It had a front garden which has been described and which was not over large but it had an eminently satisfactory back garden, which made up in length for what it lacked in width, yet it was wide enough.

There were two ways into it. One, as already described, through the door by the scullery and one through an archway, closed by a large massive door, from the passage by the side door. That was seldom used, because the long tunnel-like entrance which ran below the popular Little Room was a splendid storage place. There were no sheds in these gardens, nor place to put them. They were not regarded as proper accompaniments to such houses—the place for a shed was out of sight and concealed. But this archway supplied all the accommodation needed for all garden tools, hoses, rollers—and although in this Best House the grass was cut by a scythe, some go-ahead people already had a new-fangled thing called a mowing machine, which was very heavy and very cumbersome and often out of order. But there were more in those arches than mere garden tools. The household bicycles and tricycles were kept there, and the Boy's Mail Cart, all the clothes lines, the clothes props, the watercans, tin baths and galvanized baths for soaking clothes in. And in the Best House archway were a number of large washing tubs, of wood, immense affairs they seemed to the Boy, which stood on stands of their own and were carted into the scullery on washing day. These were kept half full of water because it was believed they would otherwise burst. The Boy once decided to employ them to a better purpose than merely standing there half full of water, waiting for the next washing day. He drew a lot of water from the waterbutt close by—which collected rainwater from the roof—and filled the tubs up. He then raided the house and got a lot of old newspapers. These he made into paper boats, a thing at which, allied to paper helmets of the Field Marshal persuasion, he was adept. He put the paper boats into the wash tubs. He had made some very big ones and some very small ones. The big ones represented the Spanish galleons of the Armada in Calais harbour. The small ones were Drake's fleet and more especially his fire boats. He set fire to a lot of the small paper boats and propelled them amongst the great paper galleons. It worked splendidly. Great pillars of fire ascended almost to the roof and the vessels burnt to the water's edge. But of course a certain amount of soggy slightly charred paper remained and had to be disposed of. The Boy had not reckoned on that. Nobody had discovered his splendid fire—but he was discovered bailing out the tubs, a very long job and a wet job, because it was tea time and he did not come when called. He never played that game again.

There were a lot of clothes props because there was always a big wash, and the washing, if fine, was dried in the garden. Along each side of the lawn were six or eight square holes, lined with wood, sunk in the path and right against the edge of the grass. Into these went square poles, painted green and with pieces of rounded wood pierced through the top, round which the clothes line was fixed and from which it extended right across the lawn to the corresponding pole on the other side. The washing was then hung on the lines which were raised from sagging to the earth by other clothes props, small trees and saplings with bark still upon them and natural prongs at the ends which supported the lines. Washing day was quite a business and putting out the clothes, lines, props and the pegs was a labour. The garden was out of action as a place or resort of recreation for the day. The washing was brought from the scullery in large oval washing baskets, and from there put on to the lines. Woe betide the maid who dropped any.

Clothes lines had other uses. Carpets and rugs were hung upon them to be beaten and have the dust taken out. Very few things of that nature went to the cleaners—muscle was used upon them at home. And the beating was done by special instruments, called carpet beaters. These were made of cane and had a longish plaited handle and then a head something like a tennis racket in shape, only made up of lots of whorls and curves with spaces in between for the dust to escape through. It is believed they can still be obtained but they are not in the same demand in these days of Hoovers and dry cleaning.

The way through the door by the scullery, about which the Aunts always apologized when taking friends into the garden, led first into the tiled court where the permanent dustbin was, and which had a wooden and trellised fence between it and the garden proper. The garden was a long parallelogram. The lawn was of the same shape and lay in the middle with gravel paths all round and the flower beds extended right down either side. At the house end there was no flower bed in this garden because a Virginia creeper ascended and covered the entire annexe, looking like a cascade of fire in the autumn. And here also was the water-butt, the reason for which was that Miss Mary's delicate skin required rain water and she got it this way. It was carted up to her room in buckets and had to be strained. But the softness helped her, and she used a kind of prickly oatmeal soap.

At the end of the garden too was that grave of Miss Bessie's matrimonial hopes, already described, and a couple of circular wooden tubs which held box trees—the box being the badge of the clan to which the Family belonged. On the left-hand side, by the end of the archway, was a clump of evergreens, which always held a lot of magpie moths and their black and yellow cocoons, assiduously collected by the Boy—both varieties were there, the large and the small. There also stood that plum tree which could be gazed right into from the window of the Little Room and which not only bore a lot of plums, and good ones, but oozed gum from its bark which the Boy collected and reduced to liquid by means of putting it into egg-cups and adding boiling water. He had ideas about bottling this and putting it on the market—of forcing the sale of plum gum amongst his school friends, but the gum mostly got hard and was dealt with by the servants, by means of remelting and throwing away—and the Boy was not popular over that—long before he ever remembered to find any bottles. He had an idea too of turning that archway into a great aviary and breeding pigeons there—his cousin Jack had recently acquired pigeons—but he got no support and this too fell through. Along that left side of the garden were, besides the plum tree, two pear trees, which became snowy domes in the spring, an apple tree which had masses of lovely blossom but never yielded an apple, and a cherry tree which in spring was a dream of silver chalices which set and turned to promising looking black cherries which were for no known reason so sour as to be quite uneatable. Not even the Boy could manage them. There was not much in the way of flowers for the Family were not horticulturally minded until Uncle James took up gardening in his old age—but that was in another garden. Some perennials bloomed. There were funkias, Solomon's Seal and masses of lemon thyme and green and white grass called Gardener's Garters. There was one rose bush on that side which did bear a lot of large old-fashioned cabbage roses—the gardener pruned it—and there were also big clumps of marigolds. Slight variations were made by the gardener—a very old man with a long white beard, who, when he scythed the grass, might well have been Father Time—and as a small lad the Boy believed he was. He was slow and timeless in his movements—he seemed to belong to Eternity and there was never a hurry. To watch him swing his scythe was to understand how near movement can come to intertia, and to see him hone it—his hone being kept in a little sling in the small of his back—was to believe that things could move and stand still at the same time. Yet he kept both back and front gardens very tidy indeed, and was most understanding of small boys and their liking for bonfires. He touched his hat to everybody every time he saw them. He had a brown face which was a mass of wrinkles, and blue eyes of a startling brightness which held a perpetual smile. When asked when he was going to do a certain job he invariably replied 'Now directly, mum'—that meaning, to him, any time that week. He wore a kind of square-cut thick cloth coat with a turn-down collar and short lapels, which it took him the best part of ten minutes to take off before he started work, a cotton shirt of various degrees of dilapidation, but although faded to a neutral tint always very clean, and had its sleeves permanently pulled up, corduroy trousers strapped at the knees, a waistcoat which was of a dark material but never buttoned up, and very heavy boots which had never been cleaned and were consequently earth coloured. His only chance of displaying his art with flowers in that garden was on a large deep bed which stretched the whole width of the top of the lawn and sloped upwards, the back being a rockery. In that bed he put bedding-out plants of various kinds. There would be borders of the kind of daisies known as bachelor's buttons and golden feather, there would be geraniums, stocks and marguerite daisies and lobelia, also some heuchera and asters. So the seasons went round. But in the side beds he planted little, save some antirrhinums to please the Boy who liked them and called them snapdragons. That left fence was covered with ivy which was a haunt for moths which the Boy would hunt and capture with a large net and kill in a proper poison bottle given him by his Uncle. It was a fenced garden, not a walled one. And right at the far end of the bed were some substantial lime trees. At the end of the garden was a broad path behind the sloping rockery, holding ferns, London Pride and golden feather, which all competed for a foothold and existence against the Boy's fixed impression that this was (*a*) a fort, (*b*) a stronghold of savages and/or pirates and (*c*) a trench to be held at all costs.

That garden end was a nice shady nook, for there was a row of well-grown limes, one of which had a convenient fork which could be reached by standing on a large green garden seat and a little scrambling. Seated astride this fork, with his Daisy Air Gun, the Boy awaited the coming of the tiger—and plenty of tigers in the form of cats on their travels passed that way. They usually left the garden rather more speedily than they entered it, for the Boy was a good shot. But he never touched the house cat—Old Dick, whom he loved—or any cat he happened to know. Trespassing cats had short shrift and had he not helped them on their way with a pellet, Old Dick would have fallen upon them in fury, for he was jealous of his own domain. At the top of the right-hand side of the garden, the fence of which bore no ivy, was a great cluster of lilies of the valley which scented the whole garden in their season, and much the same sort of flowers and plants as on the other side. But there were two pear trees here, too, which bore pears of such hardness that it was almost incredible and one cherry tree which produced a small crop of immense and fine quality whiteheart cherries. There was a lilac bush and a large clump of blue cornflowers, beside the lemon thyme and gardener's garters and some mullein and evening primroses grew there too. At the end nearest the house was an apple tree, which not only blossomed but bore splendid large Granny Smiths. It was a very pleasant, tree-filled garden. Miss Mary, who had wonderful ideas for children, would let the Boy, on a Summer Saturday night, invite his little friends to supper—in the Garden. She called these things Alfresco Fêtes. He would invite a couple of Bernards of his acquaintance, a Frank, a Maurice and a Michael and sometimes two boys with the odd names of Newham and Luther— whose parents were of a strictly religious turn of mind—as shown by their sons' nomenclature—the sons of course being really disreputable little desperadoes. They would come and play and then Miss Mary would hang Chinese lanterns of all shapes and sizes on all the trees. Some would be concertina shaped, striped red, white and blue, others, which also folded up in the same way, would be globular and of all colours from orange to green, from scarlet to white and blue—and some were shaped like dragons and odd Chinese architectural forms like temples. They all had candles in them and she lit them up. There under this coloured glow, with great clusters of the largest lanterns on the apple tree beneath which their supper table stood, those Boys would feast in the deep blue of the summer night, surrounded by pools of soft and tinted light. They thought it wonderful and so it was. They had sandwiches piled high— beef and ham and tongue—they had lovely little meat pies—which melted in the mouth, made by a baker who lived some mile or so away but whose name was Musson. They were always called Musson's pies, and a dear old lady in black silk dress and a white cap sold them over the counter. She was, one presumed, Mrs. Musson, though whether Grandma Musson or not did not matter much. There were sausage rolls, too, for those who liked them. There were tarts of all kinds, open jam tarts, some of which had dollops of four kinds of jam in them, cream cornets, jam puffs, flaky and three-cornered, Banbury cakes, a blancmange or two and some custards in glasses—much the best way of having custard—it tasted like ambrosia that way with its sprinkle of nutmeg and its floating ratafia— and some jelly. The blancmanges and jellies were made in shapes, the most popular being a lion, couchant regardant. There was great competition to get the head. There would probably be a *gâteau* and a particularly nice concoction of Miss Bessie's called 'Italian Honeycomb', which was a mixture of jelly and blancmange and of a delicate honey colour and of a flavour all its own. This feast, just what every boy adored, was washed down with great jugs of home-made lemonade, made with real lemons, glass bottles of fizzy lemonade for those who liked it, mostly corked by glass marbles (which had to be forced in by means of a special opener and was prevented from getting into the drink by a couple of ledges which held it—boys mostly broke those bottles and got the marbles)—or stone gingers, which had either screw tops, or corks held by string. If the latter, then you shook up the bottles, cut the string and the ginger beer went off with a pop like champagne and tasted much better—or so the boys thought. Those alfresco suppers are remembered yet by those who still survive, though their numbers are lessening. The boys laughed and talked without ceasing and Frederica would get her pleasure in serving them with food. They needed no pressing. Each boy went home with a packet of sweets. The only drawback was the boy named Frank who, because of excitement and lots of food, usually managed to be sick. Sometimes a girl named Annie was invited, a sister of one of the Bernards.

The Boy had a hammock at the end of the garden slung between those trees, and on fine Sunday afternoons in the summer he would lie in that hammock, look at his comic papers and eat his dessert and his sweets. And very often a girl with large dark eyes and dark hair would come peering over the end fence, to which she would have access on account of the curious field at the back, and try to engage him in conversation, mainly with an idea of getting offered some sweets and fruit. She never got it. The Boy thought little of girls then. He tolerated this one but not to the extent of giving her a share of his good things. Well, he has shared many things with her since—his life and his success and failure and his belongings for over forty years. . . .

This House was the Last of the Big Houses and it so happened that the smaller houses which adjoined it and carried on the road had longer gardens. But this was made up for in another way. At the back of that section of the road in which the Best House stood was a long narrow rough field known to the Boy and his friends as 'The Back Piece'. The Family made a gate through their fence so as to gain access to it, although they probably had no right to do so, and other neighbours did the same. It was ideal for the children though not all of those children were friends. How this piece of land came to be there, unoccupied and quite waste, between the Best Road and the slightly inferior one behind it—which was shut off from the Back Piece by a wall—has never been clear. There was only one way in from the outside—through an archway which gave on to a side road—that in which the Pillar Box stood, and that archway was used by a builder to store his ladders, trucks and impedimenta. There was a general impression that it belonged to the New River Company. It had never been a river bed, there were no manholes or hydrants and nobody had ever seen an official of the New River Company upon it. The New

River, it is true, wound its devious course not far away and the New River Company was a splendid gilt-edged investment in those days. It ended in Islington and it brought fresh water to London—had done so for centuries, and had been the idea of Sir Hugh Middleton. But the New River legend was generally believed, however, and nobody ever asked the residents in the road for any rent for using the place, nor did anyone ever object to the gates. So the residents came to regard it as their own property. There was another version of the story which said it was part of what had been a highway known as Cut-throat Lane, and that it was a right of way, which some old law prevented any buildings from being erected upon. If so, then that law had not stopped many houses from being built at the lower end, for presumably it had run much further than the Back Piece extended and it was only the houses from numbers 123 to 147 which had the open space. The rest was covered by gardens. This had never been challenged. Anyway, whatever the reason, there it was. The inhabitants of the lesser road which also backed on to it were prevented from getting in by their high walls which kept them at a distance and which was considered very right and proper by the residents of the Best Houses in the Best Road. Sometimes the children of that lesser road would climb the wall and drop into the Back Piece. At once the children of the Best Road, who used the Back Piece as their playground, would rally to the attack and repel boarders. They always won because the invaders were at a disadvantage by being cut off from their base, their reinforcements, if any, and had a difficult line of retreat, having to scale the wall, which made them singularly vulnerable whilst so doing. So they would hurry back over the wall when the occupying army arrived, and from behind their battlements would hurl words of disdain and winged insults. They would also throw stones and chuck their rubbish over the wall. This was instantly returned. The children in possession might be at a disadvantage from the point of view of lack of cover, but the Boy was in command and he had his Daisy airgun. The moment an enemy's head appeared, he fired—and he was a good shot. So the foe just threw things without aim from the safety of the garden. If the refuse they sent over was inflammable, the children of the Back Piece used it to make a bonfire, seeing to it that as much smoke was produced as possible. A constant feud raged, fierce encounters took place with no quarter asked or given. Only the youth of two families in that lesser road were allowed access, because it was finally agreed that they were 'decent chaps' and knew how to play games. But these favoured ones always understood that they were there on sufferance and that permission could be revoked at any time. It it feared they became traitors to their own side and helped the Back Piece Boys. The Victorian Boy was Lord of the Manor of the Back Piece for years and ruled with a rod of iron. Not all the Boys of the Best Houses were on the right side, however. There was one family which were sworn enemies. They did all they could to annoy and upset the small group of lads who considered the Back Piece their domain. There was a real vendetta which lasted for years and constant fights. The stalwarts kept that Back Piece clean. They piled up all rubbish which was shot in and burned it. They looked upon it as their own property. When the Boer War broke out, they built a quite elaborate fort, with entrenchments and walls made of half bricks, of which there was a good supply—and some whole bricks which they were lucky enough to discover in the builder's yard. It was a first-class piece of work. Their adversaries, who lived at the top end, would come sneaking out and endeavour to demolish it. They seldom did this if any of the boys were about, but waited their chance of finding the Back Piece empty. But they would be observed, sometimes, by the Boy from his eyrie on the Leads. He was too far away to stop them, but he would blow his horn or bugle, whichever he happened to have handy, to warn them they were spotted and fire his airgun at them, although they were out of range. Then reprisals would be planned—and carried out. A favourite form was to besiege the garden gate of this horrible family, throw over a barrage of stones, if the foemen happened to be safe behind their fence, whilst the Boy, who was a dead shot, smashed, with the pellets from his airgun, the flower-pots which stood on sticks above the dahlias in that garden, flowers which were the apple of their owner's eye. They would fix wires across the gate and trip up the unwary when entering surreptitiously. And they had their best revenge one Fifth of November. At that season of the year a great Firework Display was held in the Back Piece. All the boys would save up and often get as much as One Pound, which bought a tremendous amount of fireworks then. A great bonfire would be built, which the malcontents always tried to destroy—every such attempt meant that lighted Chinese crackers were put through the letterbox of the offending House, with most satisfactory results to all save the occupants. But the Fifth would come, and a party be given. Prayers had gone up for a fine night and it often happened not to be raining. The Firework Boys always meant to let off their fireworks one at a time, so as to make them last the longer, but that never worked out. Enthusiasm got the upper hand. The Bad Boys would hang about just outside their garden gate, ready for flight to shelter, and jeer. So, one Fifth, when the struggle to maintain and destroy the bonfire building had been more desperate than usual, the Back Piece Boys invested in four Line Rockets. They fixed four wires from a pole in their fort right up to the gate of their enemies, in such a position that they would not be noticed. The Bonfire was lit and the display commenced.

The Bad Boys came out and howled insults and derision. The Victorian Boy gave the signal. Four hissing, screaming fiery missiles swished through the air straight at those jeering boys, taking them quite by surprise, hitting the fence above their heads with a terrific thwack and exploding all over the place. The Bad Boys fled, yelling with fear, in complete rout. They never interfered again. Those Bonfire Nights were most exciting affairs, the only blot on them being the boy Frank before-mentioned, who was frightened of the fireworks but would not stay away and always ended up with a bad bout of sickness. Perhaps it was his form of enjoyment.

One of the neighbours, whose son was a Back Piece Boy—it was the boy Michael—kept chickens in the Back Piece, and the Boys were not sure if that was quite in order. It is doubtful if the chickens laid to any extent, they led a pretty active life. But the lady added two ducks. This, the Back Piece Boys felt, laid a responsibility on them. Ducks should swim and there was no pond. The kindhearted Boys thought this rather cruel. So they set to work and dug a pond. They laboured like navvies. If they had been told to do it, they would all have rebelled. But they achieved—over several weekends, a tidy foundation for a pond. But, of course, there was no water. It was found also that there was no hose-pipe in the posses-sion of any of them long enough to supply the deficiency. So those Boys got buckets and pails and with tremendous efforts—it took an entire Saturday—managed to get enough water into that pond—of course at first it sank into the ground the moment they put it in—but at least they got enough in it for the ducks to swim. The ducks ignored the pond. This was considered unnatural on their part—and also ungrateful. The Boys determined that if these wretched birds did not know what a pond was for, they must be instructed. So they chased those ducks, which resisted capture with squawks and flutterings, and having caught them, they threw them in the pond. The ducks were not grateful even then. They swam to the edge, got out and ran for their lives. But the Boys thought they had justified themselves. The pond dried up during the night but afterwards heavy rain often left some water in it—and the ducks actually swam therein. It just goes to show what children will do. Present a thing as a game and they will break their backs at it. Present it as a task and the methods of evasion are as marvellous as ingenious. The Boys built an enclosure of sticks and poles which was a zareba, a laager or a stockade according to the game in hand. It was so well made that it became a permanency.

Once the grown-ups of the road got the Boys to co-operate with them in a little exploit of revenge. Some new people had moved into one of the Best Houses which ran on to the Back Piece and had assumed an air of complete superiority to their neighbours. That was not well received. Next door to them lived that lady who was one of the most English of all Englishwomen. She was of immense size and had a temper to match. She spent her life behind her lace curtains keeping her neighbours under observation. She was the lady who was allowed to come to the Select School and watch the dancing. It was her daughter at whom the Boy fired his rifle and denied dessert. It was her son who went to school with him, one of the two Bernards who came to the alfresco suppers and was a Back Piece Boy. This good lady never seemed to go out yet heard all the news. She was a remarkable woman, and had remarkable manners. She used curious phrases and could never explain them. She would say that a thing was 'as queer as Dick's hatband'. She referred to people in their Sunday best as being 'all dressed up like a Ramsey Man'. There was a particular time of day known only to her, which was called 'Bull's noon'. When her progeny enquired after certain people in her family, with a view to improving their knowledge of their ancestry, they would be told that 'he was more of a gentleman than you will ever be a lady'—which advanced their knowledge hardly at all but put them severely in their place. Her chief philosophy was that 'we shall all live till we die, if we aren't killed by a cart'. That gave her great satisfaction. But she liked the Victorian Boy and he liked her. They were to become related by marriage, indeed she became his Mother-in-law. His was really a Back Piece wedding. Well, this good lady heard that the haughty newcomers were going to give a garden party. They were ill advised in that. Their own garden was devoid of trees or shelter and did not lend itself to such a festivity at all, although it blazed with geraniums, marguerites, lobelia and alyssum. She heard that the catering was to be by Gunters, that distinguished people were to be present and that eminent artists had been engaged to entertain. But not a single resident in the Best Road had been invited. She interviewed the Victorian Boy on the matter and he placed at her disposal, without hesitation, the organization known as 'The Ever Victorious Band of Revenge'. This seemed right up its street. Word got round of the slight which was offered to the entire neighbourhood. Many of the neighbours, in the courteous Victorian method, had already called and 'left their cards'. It now dawned on them that this ordinary courtesy had not been returned, as the convention demanded. This fresh impertinence rankled. The large lady let it be known to all and sundry that in her opinion the newcomers were "more R than F"—which was her way of indicating that she regarded them as more rogues than fools. Miss Bessie and Miss Mary, who had 'left cards', felt very affronted. They were both of an inquisitive disposition and they adored parties. So when their Nephew disclosed the fact that the Boys of the Back Piece were to take revenge, help was forthcoming. The method chosen was a large and very nasty bonfire, to begin with. It was considered that a bonfire, built near the fence of this garden and composed of the right materials, would be most effective, if the weather was propitious. The boys collected all sorts of rubbish, nothing was too bad or too nasty. The elders, who now understood, helped splendidly. Miss Bessie contributed an old rug mat, dug out from the Box Room, calculated to smoulder and stink. Miss Mary, from an old chest of drawers in the same apartment, found some ancient pillows full of feathers. . . . Old paint-pots, spare bits of oil-cloth, old sacks, anything calculated to provoke smuts, were all added. The foundation was of good burning material. And at the last minute there was a small sack of soot, destined for a garden, but now much better employed. The evening of the Garden Party came, and the guests rolled up. All the lights blazed in the house, although it was not dusk. The host and hostess in full evening dress paraded round the garden displaying their house and its purlieus to their admiring friends. They must have observed that they had an audience. For not only the children were in the Back Piece but their elders and betters as well. They were all watching that garden. Waiters appeared with trays of refreshments and hostilities began at that time. A wild rumour spread that Mrs. Patrick Campbell was reciting in the kitchen. It could not have been true but anything seemed possible that night. The Boys began—with band practice. All the toy drums were assembled, all the whistles and the horn and bugle belonging to the Victorian Boy, who performed on them himself. There was not much music out of them but a terrible amount of noise. One of the prized possessions of the Back Piece was a very large and rather old metal tank. This had all sorts of uses—it was pressed into service as an Altar when the games took an historical turn and Human Sacrifices were the order of the day—it could be an armoured train—anything desired. That night it was a Bush Drum, or a thunderstorm, for two boys beat upon it without ceasing, producing a prodigious din. The host and hostess were perturbed—their neighbours looked on stolidly, not disguising their curiosity at all. Then silence fell. The host and hostess breathed again—and it was about the last clear breath they drew for hours. The silence was the cue for lighting the bonfire. The Boys, in Indian File, yelling incantations to Manitou, danced round the fire—and then they lit it. It went off in a blaze as the foundation of straw, dried grass and twigs caught and crackled. But then—the bad stuff began to work and Boys were on hand with water-cans to damp it if necessary. Nothing had been forgotten. It was a hot, still evening. There was nothing to disperse the immense cloud of thick, acrid, evil-smelling smoke which rose lazily from the fire and descended like a fog on all around—

and which showered down a perfect rainstorm, as it were, of heavy, black, clinging smuts. By this time the grown-ups were right against the fence, anxious to see how the newcomers took it. The host and hostess beat a retreat. They had to go indoors, they had to shut the windows, despite the sultriness of the weather—but the smoke had got into the house and so well stocked and replenished was the fire that there was no keeping it out.

Victory was complete and only the Boys were disappointed. They had prepared stink bombs made out of old tins with rags, brown paper and some noxious mixture one of them had procured from school. They had wanted to throw them—but the fire had done the trick. It was an evening of heaven, when bad behaviour was good behaviour—a chance of a lifetime! This story goes to show that, when occasion served, Victorians could be just as bad mannered as any Moderns—but only in defence of Convention. It cured the newcomers, who from then on adopted a conciliatory attitude and were finally received into the fold. The large lady, whose victory it really was, got quite friendly with them, for it appeared that the master of the house had been to Australia and so had she. Both had made the trip in the days of sail and found much to talk about.

But the end of the Back Piece which adjoined the garden of the particular Best House which is of this story was put to a real use. Frederica seized it. She impressed the gardener into her scheme—and she and he were friends. She called him Old Parr. Together they built a fence of twigs and then she got the man to dig up that rough ground—it took him a long time—but the next spring she sowed vegetables and got some fine crops. Nobody interfered with this piratical bit of squatting at all. . . .

The Victorians loved their gardens and they arranged those gardens for posterity. They planted many trees of all kinds. They knew that most of them would never come to maturity in their day, but they thought of the Family. They were of true descent from their ancestors of the 17th and 18th Centuries who laid out their estates and planted their avenues, which would not come into their true glory for at least a century afterwards but which they regarded as a contribution to the beauty and greatness of their land and for the enjoyment of that Family which would come after them.

Alas, those Families are going—and have in most cases—gone. The tree-girt Victorian mansions—which if they were not entirely embowered, yet had their back gardens full of trees of all kinds, are now mostly in decay or vanished. Many were blitzed, some pulled down to make room for flats. But, in that ring of decaying culture which surrounds London, which was once on its outskirts and the resort of prosperous merchants, some still remain. Their fronts are crumbling, they have no paint, they are scabrous and leprous, time and weather have taken their toll. Those steps have never known the ministrations of the stepgirl for a couple of generations. But still, if you glance their way from the top of a bus, you see those trees behind them, bringing a flourish of blossom in the spring, a hint of glories which once delighted simple, prosperous people, and brought the annual miracle of the awakening world to them, and in summer there is still greenery to refresh tired eyes, although the green is not so bright and fresh as of yore, but the struggling, weakly verdure of the city. The trees stand, relics of the days when the world did not move so fast, when the district was a good one, when commercialism and the outward surge had not brought it down to mere industrial or tenement locations—the trees, which outlast so many human lives and which outlast the buildings with which they were planted—the trees in those Victorian gardens still hold and keep a memory of the days when Beauty was enjoyed—when people had the time and leisure to look at it and appreciate it—standing there as monuments to a time when Progress did not demand their removal so as to leave the way clear for mere speed and noise—when people could enjoy a quiet evening in the air amidst the perfume of living natural things—long since surrendered to the noise and smell of a mechanical age which appreciates only the roar of an engine, the explosions of that internal combustion engine which has caused more trouble than any benefit it ever conveyed.

CHAPTER SEVENTEEN

Unwillingly to School

IT was a pleasant Victorian fiction—and one which still survives—that schooldays were the happiest time of one's life. No decent self-respecting Boy believed that—unless he was that detestable thing which the boys of the period called a 'swot'. Boys who liked school were not well regarded —there was something wrong in their mental make-up. It is doubtful if even they found their school days very happy, for their life was a martyrdom from the actions of more normal lads. Most boys regarded school as a natural evil and something to be endured until the years which advanced so slowly freed them from its toils. It is, of course, never safe to generalize about such things, but personal feelings of one who was quite a normal boy of his period can be set down and the Victorian Boy of this chronicle hated school life like poison. It was not so much the school to which he went—he admitted that was not so bad—nor the lessons which for some portion of his youth he found quite easy. It was the fact of having to go to school which revolted him—the repression, the restriction, the grim inevitability of passing through those gates to be herded with other small boys into a room and there made to sit still and be quiet—metaphorically speaking—for what seemed an eternity. Life, to him, was in two sharply divided portions—In School and Out of School. The former was purgatory, the latter bliss. He was the fortunate possessor of an extremely good memory. He could memorize anything. He could read through a lesson once and know it. But figures, mathematics of any kind, however simple, were to him a mystery to which there was no clue. Normally intelligent, he might easily have mastered them but he closed his mind against the subject. Euclid held no terrors—memory conquered that. He had been told all about the difficulty of the *Pons Asinorum*. He found it nothing at all. He was sometimes a bit nonplussed when wily masters altered the letters around the triangles and symbols from A.B.C.

etc. to S.X.Y.Z., but a little thought and memory overcame that snag, nine times out of ten. But what Euclid meant, what it proved and of what use it could possibly be never entered into his calculations at all. He knew quite well it had nothing to do with him. Mental arithmetic to him was agony and frustration, he never got an answer right. He struggled through ordinary arithmetic, rather sketchily, as far as Practice and then he gave up. They tried to get him to learn Algebra. It was part of the ordinary curriculum. Everyone had to learn it. Had they indeed? He was quite certain he would not. He went on strike, he put down his pen and he refused. He was kept in, he was derided, he was put on parade in front of his form and made an Awful Example. He stuck it out. He sat there, in detention, his book open, but he did not attempt it. He just gazed into space.

So he was sent to the Head. This was about the worst thing which could befall a boy at that school. There were two Heads, partners, one a youngish man of ebullient nature whom the boys liked and found amusing but who did not unduly impress them, and the other, a man of mature years, who was bearded and who could be as kind and understanding as a woman or as austere and frightening as an enraged God. This was the Head before whom the Boy stood in the forbidding atmosphere of 'The Study'. The Head knew, of course, all about him and his character, knew his background, his talents and his failings. He knew far more about that Boy than the Boy knew himself. He was indeed a wonderful man. He did not bully. He just asked why the Boy would not learn his Algebra. And it was he who got the shock, not the Boy. For the Boy told him, quite simply and frankly, that he did not believe in Algebra. After a few seconds of stunned surprise, the Head enquired the reason for this disbelief.

'Well, sir,' said the Boy, 'it seems to be based on hypothesis and that can't be right. You say, let X equal so-and-so. You don't know that it does. You just suppose it. And then of course you work it out by supposition and it must come right because you make it so. That's how it seems to me, and I'm sorry, but I don't believe in it.'

The Head took off his spectacles, polished them, resumed them and gazed at the Boy with interest. It was quite a new point of view to him and one which he apparently did not see his way—short of a lot of trouble—to cope with. He took a new line. 'What are you going to be when you leave school?' he enquired. The Boy mentioned that his people wanted him to go into the Navy. The Head beamed. 'Well, my boy,' he said, 'you will want Algebra there and mathematics of all kinds, you know. You cannot navigate ships without them. How about that?' The Boy made up his mind instantly.

'Then I shan't go into the Navy, sir, although I'd like to. I cannot do sums, I never could, I never shall. I shall go into the Theatre and perhaps write books. You don't want mathematics for that, do you, sir?' The Head coughed. He knew the Boy's family history. 'But you are an intelligent boy,' he said, 'you have a good record, you have won a lot of prizes, you have passed public examinations. Why won't you learn to do mathematics?' 'I do my best, sir,' replied the Boy. 'It is not so much that I won't but that I can't. And I can't do Algebra for the reason I have said. I think it will be a waste of my time to try. I'm sorry, sir, but there it is.'

The Head pondered. He was a wise man. 'Well, you know,' he told the Boy, 'you just can't sit about or play whilst the others are learning Algebra. If I make a concession on your account, you will have to take a special subject and work hard at it.' The Boy brightened. 'Oh, yes, sir, please, sir,' he said. 'I would like to take special History if it could be done. I like that.' The Head was not going to give in so easily. 'It is not what you like but what is good for you,' he said severely. But his mind was made up. Only two days before he had been escorting a Very Distinguished Visitor round the school and had entered the class room where this Boy worked during a History Lesson. It so happened the Boy was on his feet answering questions. He answered them all without a slip. The Head, to show off, asked him some extra questions. The Boy knew the answers. The Head asked some more questions, throwing them open to the whole form. The embarrassed boys, awed by the Head and the Visitor, fumbled and hesitated. The Boy shot up his hand. The question had been the ancient name of York. The Boy gave the answer, 'Eboricum.' And he embroidered on it. He informed the Head and the Visitor that the Archbishop of York, to this day, signed himself 'Ebor' and the Archbishop of Canterbury—the senior—signed himself 'Cantuar'. The Head was very pleased. So after much severe lecturing and deliberation, he told the Boy he might take special History and that he would himself set him the papers. And he did. The Boy thanked him and continues to thank him today. He has never had the slightest use for mathematics or Algebra since, but his History has stood him in good stead. He is still grateful to that understanding Head, although he thought of him then, as he does still, by the nickname which the boys imposed upon him—which was 'Pigeon'. He got the name because he moved very fast and his scholastic gown fluttered around him like wings.

School days were black days for that Boy. He lived for coming home from school, he hated the going. He had a long walk, but everybody walked then. No public transport went anywhere near his school and it was the best part of two miles away from where he lived. He came home

The Victorian Boy—grown into the Edwardian Young
Man—aged twenty-one

Edwardian Young Ladies on
Holiday go for a charabanc ride
—drawn by horses

The Victorian Girl and Boy—now a newly married Edwardian Couple,
go for a boat trip on their honeymoon. They are the couple seated in
the centre

to lunch, so he walked about eight miles a day. Sometimes he went with his friends who lived nearby. Sometimes he walked alone like Kipling's cat. He usually went to school alone because of his most unfortunate habit of punctuality. He had a horror of being late. He never was late once in his whole school career and the habit persists today. His punctuality has wasted more time in his life than anything else. So usually his outward journeys were undertaken on his own. He would come home with a mob of friends. He did not mind being alone at all. Satchel slung around him, he left the world about him and entered the world which existed in his own imagination. He played serial games. And sometimes he played several, dividing the walk into chapters as it were, each portion of which had its own place in his imagination. For the early part of the journey, when the Boer War was on, he was a trooper in a regiment of his own creation called Grey's Scouts. On his speedy horse, with his unerring rifle, he accounted for hordes of Boers. Then, when the big main road had to be crossed, the game changed. He became a Greek Warrior—and he spun his own Odyssey, based roughly upon Homer and culled from his books. He was not Ulysses, he was a hero named Gualtierus—and the land to which he journeyed was Brotonia. His galley had the most amazing escapes, he battled with Titans, with Cyclops, with human enemies—and always he won. He had bronze armour, a red cloak, and crest to his helmet, a circular shield and spear and he also carried a bow. His sword had a great ruby in its hilt which held magical qualities. Some of his adventures would have startled the Blind Poet himself. That game lasted until about half a mile from school and then he became a knight. Sometimes he varied this last chapter by being a Jacobite pursued by English dragoons. He had little sympathy really for the Jacobites but he always inclined to the losing side. This habit of mental games has stood him in good stead.

The way back from school was different. Here he was with friends. It was necessary to gaze into most of the shop windows passed *en route*. Or at least into special shops, mostly sweet shops. There was a pet shop which often held those boys for some time. They would long for the puppies, the tortoises, the birds, fish and even monkeys therein displayed. There was a newsagent's shop which always had a tempting array of comics, 'dreadfuls', and which the boy sometimes patronized if there was a 'dreadful' there which was new to him. Mostly he went to another shop which had a better selection and which he visited on Saturday mornings as it was off the main route. And that shop still enjoys his custom at times for it still sells comics and has now added toys—and there are grandchildren to consider. . . .

There was a shop which sold foreign stamps, showing packets of them in the window. Once he bought a packet there and it held a prize coupon. He got an extra packet for that. He was never so lucky again and the stamps were mostly duplicates, anyway. The stamps jostled cheap stationery and bits of paper in the window which bore advertisements of wonderful bargains for sale or exchange, situations vacant or people 'seeking sits', as was the phrase. Somehow the owner seemed to get a living although the value of the stock could not have been more than a pound or two. The chief objects of interest were the sweet shops. These were gazed into and what to purchase was hotly debated amongst the boys. It was primarily a financial question—what they wanted was as much for their money as possible. A penny went a long way. It would buy four ounces of good sweets or eight ounces of a rather inferior quality. It was also quite agreeable to the shopkeepers to make up half-pennyworths, to please their young clients—which meant that for a penny you could have quite a quantity of two different lots of sweets. Nor were farthingworths despised. There were several sweet shops on that school route but only two got the boys' custom. The one which got the most was a large shop with a big window display—trays of all sorts of sweets, large bottles of them, all clearly marked with the price. The Victorian Boy was regarded as almost a millionaire by his friends. He had sixpence a week pocket money and could mostly cadge another sixpence as well. So sometimes he patronized a better-class shop, which had not so lavish a window display but much better quality. The sweets were displayed in little glass stands, like cakestands, and they were of the best. He would buy an ounce of super chocolate creams there, which cost two-pence—but were worth it. The shop was kept by a very charming lady, who seemed terribly old to him but who was probably under fifty, who always had a nice smile and made much of her little customers. You got speed but not much personal attention at the cheaper shop. His favourite sweets were those expensive chocolate creams and a special brand of Cadbury's chocolate called 'Mexican', which was wrapped in silver paper bound with a light blue band. He would, at the superior shop, also buy acid tablets which were very strong indeed. They took the skin off the mouth, but were worth it! At the cheaper emporium he and his friends invested in gold and silver fishes (there were red ones as well) and boiled sugars—sugar babies—all sorts of toffee, but Everton toffee in great lumps was most esteemed and did indeed have a rich creamy flavour—cocoa nibs—lime juice tablets—cocoanut slices, which were thin slips of cocoanut, some white but some coloured pink, plentifully sprinkled with a very shiny kind of sugar—Cupid's Whispers, a flat sugar sweet about the size of a halfpenny (not a boiled sugar and quite opaque) which had messages of an amorous nature printed on them. Not that the boys troubled about the messages but the sweets, which were of all colours, were very nice. There was another kind of cocoanut sweet, which looked like a piece of cocoanut scooped from the shell, a perfect segment properly curved, the shell being represented by a thin layer of chocolate which might have been applied by a camel-hair brush, it was so thin. But this was a very popular form of confectionery and completely sickly, therefore esteemed. Many brands still obtainable today were on sale, like toasted cocoanut caramels. The Boy was very partial to what were called 'Pic Nics'. They were small sweets made of some kind of paste flavoured with cocoanut, sometimes round, sometimes heartshaped. They were chocolate-coloured underneath, the top being either pink or white. You got a lot for a penny and they tasted delicious. The size was a shade smaller than the old silver threepenny piece. There were bars of chocolate cream in all shapes and makes. The kind made by Fry had its champions— it was either vanilla or strawberry, whichever you favoured—and so had that made by Cadbury, which was of a different shape. Rowntree's had its champions too. Plain chocolate was bought in penny slabs, large, thick and satisfying. Fry's had a good line here, a flat slab which could be broken into pieces by means of grooves, whilst Cadbury's (if memory serves) had long and curved pieces. The Boy used these bars of chocolate not only to eat as such, but he would grind a portion of them into a fine powder with a penknife and ruler, mix it plentifully with sherbet and then drink it. Strange to say, it never made him sick!

It is not worth while to enumerate the sort of sweets still on sale, but there were some things not met with today. Tiger nuts, for instance, a small sweet nut with a brown crinkled skin and very white inside. You got a tremendous lot for a penny and could eat every bit of them. Large flat slabs of fig toffee had many devotees but was rather full of little pips. It was long-lasting and very glutinous, but not so long-lasting as what were called Everlasting Sticks, long, thin strips of some rather soft form of toffee wrapped in transparent paper. This lasted long enough, required as much chewing and made hands and mouth of such stickiness as to ensure its complete popularity with boys. For those who liked liquorice, there were many forms, quite broad-ribbed pieces like ribbon, long thin strips like bootlaces, little ladders of liquorice, Pontefract Cakes (more expensive) and thick solid pieces of liquorice which looked like coshes. Also there was liquorice root, capable of making the face of a consuming boy browner than the sun of the Sahara could have done. The Victorian Boy's own favourites were small chocolate creams, Cadbury's Mexican Chocolate, raspberry (or it may have been strawberry) bars of chocolate cream, acid drops or tablets (those of special strength preferred), chocolate drops with tiny white hundreds and thousands on the tops of them, fruit drops, wine gums (which bore the name of a wine on them and were coloured accordingly) and everlasting sticks. He would also buy 'Hundreds and Thousands' and dissolve them in water, drinking the sweet sticky result with gusto. And he liked Gelatine Lozenges—which were rather expensive. He was nearly choked to death by one of these which stuck across his windpipe—they were more adhesive than glue—and caused a real fright in the family and a very purple face. That rather put him off them. He did not like 'locusts', which were some form of fruit like dates, heavily sugared. He presumed this was what had formed part of the diet of John the Baptist, along with wild honey. That he had no objection to at all, especially in honeycomb form—there was always some in the house. You could also buy Surprise Packets, but there was never much of a surprise. Quite a few boys bought paregoric lozenges and liked them and some would buy Skuse's Herbal Tablets, in little tin boxes with yellow corners. There was a medicinal flavour which—as it was taken from choice and not from necessity—had much to recommend it. You could eat a lot because, strangely, they were doing you good.

Coming home from school was so much better than going. You kicked a ball from one to the other, you played a kind of gutter golf with a couple of stones, hacked out of the road with your heel, and at the right season of the year it was possible to come home—and even go to school—on your roller skates. Tops had their season, so had marbles, so had conkers, and no self-respecting boy ever played them at any other time. Hoops, too, were seasonable but were not taken to school. It was quite safe to bowl them in the road. And coming back from school was best of all on Friday nights, for there was no school on Saturday.

The Boy and his friends adored Friday evenings. They would go round to each other's houses in the winter, or into the Back Piece in summer. If that or the garden was too wet, there was always the road. Despite the fact that it was the Best Road, the children used it as a playground and it was quite safe. So little traffic went up and down after early afternoon that there was no fear. They played many games. For the younger boys, there were variants on games which included horses. Every boy had a pair of reins amongst his toys, with proper bits which those who were the horses held in their mouths, the driver directing them as if they were indeed steeds. They could be Roman chariots racing—and teams of boys often competed in this—a lamp-post would be the winning-post and loud arguments ensued over close finishes; or they could be a stage coach, with another boy, pretending to ride a horse, as a highwayman. They were buses, trams, fire-engines, any form of transport, and sometimes the galloping horses bringing up the guns—a game introduced by the Victorian Boy after a visit to the Royal Military Tournament then held at the Agricultural Hall in Islington. He did, indeed, in the Back Piece, stage quite a fair representation of this grand naval and military spectacle. It took a lot of preparation and the whole of Saturday to perform. Hardly a detail was missed. For the Royal Tournament then was an affair of horses—the cavalry were in being, and there was no mechanization. So the boys had tilting at the ring, tent-pegging, Turk's Head—a dummy head smitten off at full gallop by means of cutting a stick which held it; riding and jumping—the jumps were specially prepared—a musical ride, the naval men with the guns—which entailed the use of the Boy's mailcart (which was in nearly all games); a display by the Gunners and, finally, the battle which in those days brought the proceedings to a close. There was also an attempt at the Balaclava Mêlée, a most popular event at the Tournament, in which two mounted teams competed. They wore leather jackets, they were armed with single-sticks to represent sabres and on their heads were pretty solid masks, each topped with the paper plume—a colour to each team. The object of each team was to knock the plumes to pieces and a very spirited contest ensued with plenty of hard thwacking and quite a realistic exhibition of warfare. It was not so successful amongst the boys. They had no leather coats, and the few fencing-masks available from the Box Room were small protection against the singlesticks, of which there was a good supply. The item was cut very short, by mutual consent.

Conkers, marbles, tops, hoops, all these things could be and were played in the street. So was football and ball touch, whereby a ball was hurled at the other players by the one who was 'He' until he hit one, who in turn became 'He'. There was not room for 'egg cap' nor rounders—but 'Widdy' was possible. It exists apparently under another name, 'Chain He'. As the cricket season approached, lamp-posts became stumps and good practice was had on a hard wicket with a soft ball. Jumping was practised too with a rope tied round the lamp-post and, when the Sports Day grew near, races of all kinds were run as part of the training. Venturesome boys would hang on behind vans, and the others would yell at the driver, 'Whip behind!' And when he did lam round with the whip, the boy leapt off. It would be suicide today—but was safe then.

There were other games, less innocent. There were slapbangs, little harmless-looking paper bags with some mild explosive inside, to be dropped behind unwary passers-by—elderly preferred—or thrown at the back wheels of cyclists. If the rider dismounted, fearing a puncture, that was full marks. This throwing was done with the most innocent air. There was the game of 'Dares', which speaks for itself, and the little matter of tying black twine to a door-knocker and then to the gate, so that rat-tats could be made and escape effected without much danger. There were crazes, such as asking everybody 'Please could you tell me the correct time?'—or 'the right time'—as if any time could be of any use if it was not right. This game demanded an innocent exterior and a good memory for faces, for the danger was that you asked the same person after too short an interval. Also you must never ask anyone who had the slightest chance of noticing you making the previous request. The trouble with the Time game was that people got wary and, even when children really wanted to know the time, would not answer. The Boy had a watch which his mates envied him. It was a Waterbury, an enormous thing in white metal with a loud and satisfying tick. It was wound from the top. It cost five shillings, kept excellent time and lasted for years, despite hard usage. It was only discarded when he was given a silver watch, much smaller, with an elaborately chased case and flowers painted on the dial. He was not too sure about that watch, he thought it might be a bit girlish. Also, it required a key to wind it and, of course, he always lost the key. He liked the Waterbury better, but one of his Aunts gave him the other and he had to make a show of using it.

A very popular game was 'Mind the cotton, please'. This entailed the involuntary assistance of passers-by, as did the Time game. It required two active players and one innocent victim. The rules were simple and the victims picked. One boy stood inside a gate and had a cotton-reel in his hands. The other boy stood on the kerb and also had a cotton-reel. They would wait until a likely-looking person hove in sight—usually an old lady or gentleman—never a young man, though a young lady might fall for it. Then the boy in the gate would begin winding invisible cotton on to his reel whilst the boy on the kerb apparently paid out. To give verisimilitude to the game, a kite of some kind lay beside the boy in the gate and there was actually a little black cotton round each reel, firmly fastened thereto. As the pedestrian approached, the boys wound assiduously and then became aware of the would-be passer-by. Dropping their hands a little they would say, with great politeness, 'Mind the cotton please, marm', or 'sir' as the case might be. And the poor deluded lady or gentleman would be good-natured and go to the utmost trouble to step over the non-existent cotton, whilst the boys made the appropriate motions of trying to get it clear with their hands and little noises of apprehension with their mouths, in case the cotton got broken or tangled. It was quite amazing to see the trouble people would take, by means of contortion and high steps, to try to prevent themselves stepping on the cotton. Sometimes, if they were shortsighted or judged so by the boys, one would say: 'Oh, please, it's just got caught over your foot. Don't move, oh, please.' And the good-natured victim would stand on one foot until the boy disentangled him with great artistry. The boys always thanked their victims most politely and these good people passed on their way with a warm glow at having helped two such very well-behaved small boys. The only danger was the necessity of keeping serious over it all. A laugh or a grin meant instant flight.

If boys played in the street on a Saturday morning, or during holidays, there was a fresh danger. That was Errand Boys. Now between Errand Boys and Boys who were socially above that sort of thing there was perpetual war. It was inherent enmity, it required no starting, it was there—perhaps part of what is now known as Class Warfare. Boys who went to private schools and to whose homes errand boys delivered goods had to be careful because of this desperate, bitter vendetta. It was a matter of general hostility with personal feuds thrown in. Sometimes these latter had a cause. An errand boy would declare that he was 'after' a certain young gentleman—although that was not what he called him— and the young gentleman knew what to expect if the errand boy caught him alone or far from his base. Boys would tell each other that the butcher, or the baker, or whoever it was, was 'after him'. It gave them a sense of outlawry—of having a price on their heads. If by any chance the boy who was after the other came upon him at some distance from his house, there would be a chase. This the non-errand boy usually won, unless he was a very bad runner, because the errand boy was encumbered by his basket which he dared not abandon, it being full of goods—in case allies of the hunted arrived and scattered the contents. But errand boys were expert stone-throwers and did not hesitate to prove their power and accuracy of aim. Once a boy reached his garden he was safe. From there he could hurl derision and insults and if he managed to stand in front of a window, he could also deride stones, for the errand boy did not dare assault him on his own land, nor run the risk of breaking a window. It would have meant dismissal and to lose one's job then was a bitter disgrace. Also a bad 'character' might be his lot, and with a bad 'character' his chances of a job were small. So he would curse the boy under his breath, shake his fist and mutter 'You wait'. Like the villain in melodrama he was foiled again—but a time would come. Some Best Road boys of a daring nature and possessed of physical strength would even be 'after' errand boys and pitched battles ensued. It was fairly even as regards fighting. Butcher boys were avoided—they were a class apart, they were reputed to have the strength of three—and they certainly looked as though they had, being for the most part very sturdy, loud-voiced and red-cheeked. If a butcher boy was 'after you' you told your big brother, and if you had no big brother, then some sympathetic big brother of a friend—or, as a last resource, an adult member of your family. And you went about in threes and fours, so as to outnumber the enemy. Sometimes these small gangs would fall upon errand boys and really give them a hiding, to say nothing of upsetting the baskets or trays and strewing the contents all over the road. The errand boy was always handicapped by that basket. . . . Hardly ever was there peace between boys of the Middle Class and those whose living belonged to errands.

Boys had a slang of their own. Things were 'topping', 'whizzing', 'spiffing', 'fizzing', 'ripping', 'jolly decent', 'corking', 'scrumptious'—but never 'smashing', the universal term today. You did a thing 'like Billy-ho'. It could be 'frightful', 'absolutely rotten', 'putrid', 'stinking'—but never 'lousy'. An unpopular person could be a 'lout', 'cad', 'outsider', 'rotter', 'dirty rotter', a 'bounder' or a 'blag'—but never a 'louse'. There were no American terms in use at all. English was the language and even the slang was native. 'I guess' was the only American term used—and that was a joke.

'Catch-words' were popular and lasted for about a year—although some like 'What Ho She Bumps' got into the language and can still be heard used by elderly gentlemen. Most of the catch-words came from the Music Halls and swept the country until panto came round again. 'Get Your Hair Cut', 'Ginger, You're Barmy', 'Where Did You Get That Hat?', 'Whoa, Emma', 'There's Hair' (usually with the aspirate missing), 'Now We Shan't Be Long', 'Ever Been Had?'

These boys of the Best Road went to a Good Day School and wore school caps. The fees were as high as £4 4s. per term. That can be compared with a girls' school of the period which advertised:

The Course of Instruction embraces English, Reading, Writing, Arithmetic, Geography, History and French. Fees for each term are payable in advance and the hours are from 9.30 to 12.30 and from 2.30 to 4, with Saturday as a whole holiday.

And references were permitted to the parents of present and former pupils. A considerable reduction was made for children under seven. The fees worked out in this way: English, Writing, Arithmetic and Latin, all in for £1 10s. per term. French came to 10s. 6d. per term and Music was 15s. The young lady on the bill which still exists, found in a Box Room, had extra instruction in English, which came to 17s. per term. This may surprise parents today who face ever-growing school bills—bills which seem to grow as fast as the children.

The Victorian Boy liked the weekends. But he would melt into depression as Sunday evening approached. When holidays arrived—that was the time! Breaking-up day was a joy; one ran home with whoops and yells, and eternity stretched between you and the next term. No matter which season of holidays it might be, each had its own special joys.

The Court of Honour at the White City

Skindles at Maidenhead

Four Regulars at the "West End". *Upper left:* Horace Mills. *Upper right:* Bertram Wallis. *Lower left:* Maurice Farkoa. *Lower right:* George Graves

Christmas held the Feast itself, the Pantomimes, the Minstrels at the St. James's Hall, or at the hall adjoining the Agricultural Hall in Islington, where one saw The Mohawks—it was the Moore and Burgess at the St. James's Hall. There was the World's Fair—at the Agricultural Hall in Islington; there was the circus at Hengler's (where the Palladium now stands) or Wulff's Circus at the Crystal Palace. There was the Egyptian Hall with its thrilling, frightening mysteries—and all the presents to play with and new books and annuals in which to wallow. Easter holidays, although much shorter than nowadays, brought open-air joys. And the summer holidays were of course quite limitless. One was free, that was the great thing. Free to do as one wished, and one made plans beforehand as to what must be done. Needless to say these things were never accomplished—or only a small part of them. But there was cricket, to play one's self and to watch at the Oval or Lord's. The boys then studied cricket seriously. They knew all the averages, both bowling and batting, they knew the exact position of the County Championship, and if there were Test Matches the tension and anxiety were acute. No radio gave them the scores, they had to wait for the papers. But the papers ran many editions —and the contents bills were exciting. 'Lunch Scores', 'England Collapse', 'Surrey Centuries', 'Yorkshire Fighting Hard', 'Leicester All Out'—'Close of Play'. The Boys always found the halfpenny to read about cricket and to see how their own particular heroes had fared. There was not nearly the same interest in football—there were no pools—and football, when professional, was not approved in many families. But when the Spurs brought the Cup south for the first time, the Boys of the south were proud indeed.

Those Boys made their own amusement and were never bored. They never went to their parents and said 'What shall we play now?' They had no radio, no television—the gramophone was a new thing and scarce; films were another rarity seen at music halls as a last item or at the Egyptian Hall, as part of the show. Yet the Victorian and Edwardian children had no difficulty in amusing themselves at all. They were inventive and creative. They never found the day long enough for half they wanted to do.

That Victorian Boy remembers the joy with which he came out of the school gates with his Summer Holidays before him. School broke up at the end of July and did not begin until mid-September—an infinity of time which seemed on that day to be endless. August alone was an era, a complete month and still a bit of September at the end of it. He never found it a second too long. The only thing he feared was being taken out on visits by his grown-ups. That, to him, was horror unspeakable. His Aunts were greatly addicted to calling on their friends, especially on

Sunday nights. Sometimes they would go quite a long distance on ordinary week-days to see old friends. And sometimes, to his deep regret, they took the Boy as well. He liked the travelling part—either by horse bus, horse tram or train, but his spirits sank as the house to be visited drew near. There he had to sit and be quiet, whilst his elders and betters talked and talked and talked about things which to him seemed the essence of boredom. He would get asked the usual foolish questions and force himself to reply brightly. But he would call those mental games of his to his rescue. He would sit there and let himself go into another world —he was on his travels, a hero facing perils and overcoming them, covering all periods of time—his eyes dreamy and far away. He was often complimented on his good behaviour. It was nothing of the kind—it was merely escapism which he practised so well.

At times there were other children. He was not so keen on this at first because he was really a very shy boy but never dared admit it. But he often found that these other children were just as shy,—and after a bit they understood each other and had a good time. Somebody made a good suggestion for a game which broke the ice and often the Boy would introduce his own games, which always proved popular. He did not like Christmas Parties and dreaded going but usually thawed out all right, especially if there were charades, of which he took immediate charge. That was up his street. He was acutely embarrassed by Kiss in the Ring, Poor Jenny, Postman's Knock and the game where the girls sat in a row and the boys went outside. Then a name was called and the boy had to come in and kneel down before the girl who he thought might have chosen him. The complete and devastating humiliation of being wrong . . . that was terrifying. He liked giving parties himself but disliked going to others.

The great joy of the holidays, too, was the awakening in the morning with the knowledge that there was no school and the day was your own. He would get his Mother to call him and tell him it was time for school, as she did in the ordinary way. That was a magnificent sensation. . . . And Sunday evenings in holiday time, these were almost best of all. For the fear of school was not present. He would spend the late evenings in the Dining Room with his books. He would look at the bound annuals. *The Boy's Own Paper*, called *The B.O.P.*, was quite a large periodical, and it changed its cover, though not its size, during the time the Boy took it in. It had little vignettes all round the cover to start with, sailors in crow's-nests and things like that. Then it got a bit more subdued and had an illustration across the top which included sporting paraphernalia and, if memory serves, a pheasant. It had good tales but was a bit informative. This probably suited a lot of lads but was not much use to the Boy, who was no good with his hands at all. He liked the serials and the short stories, and he read the articles about cricket, but those which told him how to make things he ignored. He had a large red book called *Every Boy's Book* which he did not like at all. It was a complete mine of information. It dealt with wrestling, boxing, fencing, gymnastics, rowing, riding, shooting, fishing, football, cricket, tennis, Badminton, rackets, every form of sport. It told, with multiplicity of diagrams, how to make model ships, steam engines, whole villages, rabbit hutches—almost everything which could be made. He felt he must be an inferior kind of boy not to be able to do these things—for apparently the editor of the book was convinced that every boy should be able to do so. He consulted his Uncle James, who looked at the gymnastic diagrams and letterpress and snorted loudly. He advised the Boy, in a usual phrase of his, 'not to pay any attention'. The Boy was relieved and followed the advice. He had a copy of *Sandford and Merton* which he despised, and another called *Eyes and No Eyes* which was saved from neglect by its information on Natural History.

He liked *Young England*, which had first appeared in about 1880 and was well established when he became a subscriber.

But best of all was *Chums*. That the Boy read over and over again. His favourite story in all the annuals of it which he had was 'Rogues of the Fiery Cross'. When, a few years ago, he wrote a book and mentioned that tale, with a pretty full description, he did not imagine that anyone but himself would recall it. How wrong he was! Letters poured in from men of his own age all over the country. They remembered it too and some of them remembered the author's name, which he admitted he had forgotten, and merely guessed at. So many were there that he considered forming a 'Rogues of the Fiery Cross Club'. And finally, to his immense joy and pride, the actual author wrote to him personally. The author told him he had just been reading the book and had enjoyed it immensely

. . . as I have been privileged to live all through those wonderful years, so splendidly described by you. I am getting quite an old fellow now and it is a long time since I wrote that yarn for Chums, *'Rogues of the Fiery Cross', which you appear to remember so vividly and which ran as a serial in* Chums. *You were under the impression that the author's name was Anstey (see page 85 in your book) but my name is Walkey (S. Walkey) and for about 30 years I wrote adventure stories for* Chums *and* The Boy's Own Paper. . . .

With best and kindest wishes,

Yours sincerely,
S. Walkey.

The Boy takes delight in mentioning that author's name now. They had quite a correspondence, for Mr. Walkey was pleased at being remembered for his 'yarn'. He lived, and it is to be hoped still lives, in Devon, and his handwriting had the virility of his stories although he was, when he wrote that letter in 1950, in his eighties. The Boy pays him a grateful and humble tribute and still considers 'Rogues of the Fiery Cross' the best story he ever read. He wishes he could get a copy for his grandson.

Those Sunday evenings, with no school next day, were joy. Each day was a joy. Even when September came, there still seemed a lot of time. The evenings drew in, in those days before Daylight Saving, but the nights seemed scented, warm and happy and the Boy would stay out as late as he could, treasuring every moment of that glorious freedom. But the time came when one thought 'It's only another week' and games got feverish— and then 'This is the last Sunday before school again'—and the last couple of days were times of complete and deep depression. That was the most awful period of all, those last few precious days, when one realized how little one had done, when ideas for games which might have been so glorious crowded upon one—too late—when one remembered what one had anticipated doing—and had not done at all. And then, the last dread evening—and bedtime, with the clothes and books ready for the morning and blackness in the soul. How horribly cheerful the grown-ups seemed to be and how sad was life in reality. Too late to shut out the future, too late to close one's mind against it—it was Tomorrow Morning, which would bring slavery, and nothing could put it off. Sleep at last and the hopeless dawn.

A tasteless breakfast and the walk to school. And the Boy, who hated school, always left far too early on the first morning—he would sometimes be so early that he had to wait for the school gates to open—the whole walk had been full of poignant memories of passing that way during the free time . . . now over for months to come. Still, he was always early. It was his way of facing up to trouble—and he does it still. He cannot bear waiting.

CHAPTER EIGHTEEN

Fin de Siècle

THE Victorians were very much stirred by the fact that a new Century was upon them. The closing years of the 19th century were very eventful and the idea of the date being 1900 instead of 1800 was confusing to the mind. A phrase borrowed from France was upon everybody's lips—*Fin de Siècle*. It was smart to use it. Hats dresses, muffs, bonnets—everything was advertised as *Fin de Siècle*. All sorts of prophecies were made as regards what would happen in the new century, yet in the hearts of the people nobody expected much change. But the New Woman had arisen—who was demanding her rights. She was a most amusing idea to all Men and to the great majority of her own sex. Comic papers had pictures of women as jockeys, of ladies as Barristers, and even soldiers— which were regarded as 'highly comical'. Yet so many lived to see it all come about. There were pictures of women in a sort of fantastic male dress, smoking in public, going into public houses, playing billiards and even coming home intoxicated. Well, it all came to pass without the world being much better. Women had already made a small invasion of that very Male Territory, the City, on account of the typewriter. They were, how- ever, not very welcome and they retained their femininity. No lady smoked in public. No lady appeared in male attire—actresses who did so on the stage were, of course, not ladies. The sight of girls in tight vests and abbreviated shorts riding bicycles, rowing or hiking, was unknown. They would have been arrested as masquerading in male attire. The sight of women in trousers as a matter of course was beyond credence. Yet by the time the new century had run half its course all those things were the most natural in the world. Yet somehow they don't seem acceptable to the few remaining Victorians.

But *Fin de Siècle* gave excitement. It gave the ladies much to gossip about at the At Home Days. It gave the men matter for conversation in the train, over lunch and at their clubs. Every After Dinner speaker dragged in the phrase and got a laugh. *Fin de Siècle* was News.

What were the last years of the dying century bringing to Great Britain and the British Empire? Well, there was some degree of change and even Progress, although that word seemed to have a slightly different meaning then. Death duties had arrived in 1894. That was revolutionary and was introduced by the Liberals. The Grand Old Man, William Ewart Gladstone, resigned the Premiership in that year, at the age of eighty-six. He was succeeded as Prime Minister by Lord Rosebery, much to the disappointment of Sir William Harcourt, who just became Leader of the House, but who got through that Death Duties Bill. This was the Government which was eventually defeated because Campbell Bannerman had not got sufficient cordite for the nation's need. The Marquess of Salisbury came back to power, that statesman who really looked the part—bearded and leonine. Joseph Chamberlain was in this administration and during the Election he had broached the question of Old Age Pensions, which did not become a fact until very many years later. But it was on the *tapis* as long ago as that. It was an idea planted by Victorians.

Other important Victorian innovations were the establishment of public baths, washhouses and conveniences; foundations of museums and public libraries, and many parks and open spaces, allotments and lodging-houses for the poor, all to be supported out of the rates. County Councils arose, including the London County Council. Tramways, gas and electricity were municipalized—and private enterprise produced such remarkable things as the Salvation Army and Toynbee Hall. General Booth of the Salvation Army was one of the very great Victorians. The Victorian Boy saw him once only, on Broad Street Station. He thought the General looked like his idea of an Apostle.

Chamberlain went to the Colonial Office and it was by a stroke of real statesmanship that he invited the Colonial Premiers to the Diamond Jubilee and held the first Empire Conference ever known. Another thing which had great bearing on the whole life of the country was the establishment, in 1899, of Borough Councils, which did away with the old, effete and inefficient system of the Vestries. There was a bit of bother with America over the question of the frontiers of Venezuela, which might have been nasty. The Sultan of Turkey, known popularly as 'The Sick Man of Europe', carried on wholesale massacres of the Armenians, who were his subjects. Great Britain did nothing about this, although Dr. Parker, the great preacher at the City Temple, cried 'To Hell with the Sultan' from the pulpit! But she did assist Greece to turn the Turks out of Crete. There was one of those little wars which were always happening somewhere in the Empire and this one blew up on the North Western Frontier of India, the perpetual trouble spot. This frontier had to be securely held because the general idea was that the Russian Bear was lurking on the other side of the Himalayas, ready to pounce on India, given the opportunity. This uprising of the fierce tribes involved this country in a difficult and costly minor war in Diamond Jubilee Year, 1897. But a good show was put up in Egypt in 1896 where the Anglo-Egyptian Army—the accent being the Anglo—occupied Dongola. And in the following year Lord Kitchener broke the power of the Dervish might—whose Mahdi had brought about the murder of General Gordon —by completely smashing the desert forces, under the leadership of the Khalifa, at Omdurman, and later expelling the French, under General Marchand, from the Sudan, over which territory Britain became supreme until today.

The storm-clouds loomed over South Africa, and might have crystallized into a great outbreak in 1896, when Dr. Jameson, who was Administrator of Rhodesia, made his now historic raid, with a very small force, into the Transvaal. He was outnumbered by the Boers and captured. There was a whole lot of trouble. It could never be proved that Cecil Rhodes knew about this, though there is not the slightest doubt that that very great Empire Builder was behind the whole thing.

But all that bother faded into insignificance in the sparkle and glitter of the Diamond Jubilee of Queen Victoria—an event of such magnitude and glory that it dazzled the world.

For sixty years this small lady, mighty in mind, power and sovereignty, had reigned over a vast and ever-growing Empire and had, by her own sheer force of character, given her name to an epoch for ever. Nothing like it had ever happened before and can never happen again. The glory of that day of Jubilee has been described elsewhere. Here it is simply registered as an event of the *Fin de Siècle* period, for it so happened that it was the very zenith of the Victorian Age, which although nobody knew it or realized it, was drawing near to its end in actuality if not in its richness and power.

The end of the century drew nigh. The last day of 1899 dawned—and it did not dawn on a day of Peace so far as this country and its Empire was concerned. For the Boer War had broken out in October 1899. The old Queen was not to end her days in serenity. Her people were to be at war. And that war began very badly for the British. It was the first time they had fought a white foe since the Crimean campaign. And in many respects it resembled that unfortunate affair. For there was bungling, mismanagement and incompetence. The good old British custom of under-estimating the job was apparent almost at once. The small Army, gallant and brave in personnel, was entirely and utterly ill-equipped for the task before it. The Commander-in-Chief, a very gallant soldier, Sir Redvers Buller, V.C., was as ill chosen for the job as the equipment of the men he led. There were setbacks, and defeats—which were called 'reverses'. That tradition of invincibility which had become inherent in this land was badly shaken. Three times in a week were British forces defeated by the wily, mobile and sharpshooting Boers, each complete in himself as regards arms, ammunition and supply, and moving with great speed in companies called commandoes. These men, whose marksmanship and bravery were both remarkable, made rings round the slow-moving, heavily armed and burdened British infantry. For the Boers made it a mounted war, knew the country backwards, fought it in direct opposition to the Drill Book and took advantage of every scrap of cover. They struck—and they were away before the British could retaliate. They ensconced themselves on their rough boulder-strewn hills called Kopjes, and the British had to try to dislodge them. The troops paraded as trained and charged with the utmost gallantry—to be mown down by a shower of perfectly-aimed bullets fired by a foe they could not see. When they did get to close quarters there was only one side in it, but the Boers knew better than to risk coming to grips with those gleaming bayonets. Three times in a single week did they inflict defeats on the British troops in the closing days of the 19th century. A pretty *fin de siècle* indeed. But Queen Victoria set an example. She issued the statement that there was no depression in her house—and that truly British phrase came up again to stiffen the resistance of her people long after she had passed away, for it was displayed in many homes and largely quoted in the dark days of the Second World War. It was the basis of the battle-cry of World War One: 'Are we downhearted? NO!'

But the century was not ending auspiciously. Maybe it was a portent of things to come. There was a great discussion as to whether 1900 or 1901 was the actual beginning of the Twentieth Century—but most people did not care. 1900 was good enough for them; it was a new date, was it not? Very well then. And the last day of December 1899, despite the trouble in South Africa and the heavy casuality lists, was nevertheless a New Year's Eve to be remembered. Those who were then alive no doubt remember it as they spent it.

The Victorian Family which figures in this chronicle saw it in at home. That was their custom. There were fewer gay parties in restaurants and hotels in those now distant days. Earlier in the evening, the Family, with the exception of Uncle James (always a law unto himself), went and visited other members of the Family living nearby, to wish them not only a Happy New Year but a happy New Century. They had refreshments wherever they went and for the moment all old feuds were buried. They even called on the unpopular branches of the Family. A time like this demanded it. At Uncle John's, hospitality overflowed. At Aunt Maggie's the usual austerity of the household was thawed and even Arthur seemed a little excited at the great change ahead. The Victorian Boy of course accompanied his Mother and his Aunts. He was himself in a state of great excitement. His Mother and his Aunt Bessie had made him a complete khaki uniform, a replica of that worn by the British Tommies. Instead of the helmet he wore a smasher hat, for one had actually been found in the Box Room. He had a belt, a bandolier, a revolver holster—with pistol—a haversack, and even puttees, which he found great difficulty in rolling—a thing he never conquered in the days of the First World War. His Aunt Mary had contributed a new Daisy Air Gun, but he did not take that with him on the visits. He was prepared, however, to recite 'The Absent-minded Beggar' at any moment—and saw to it that no household escaped his rendering of this poem, to which Sir Arthur Sullivan had contributed music. The Boy did not sing it, he recited it. He was much applauded. He is now of the opinion that probably he did not do it too badly, either. Blood will tell.

They got back home at about eleven o'clock. There was a table full of refreshments, and the Boy, who could do his share of eating and drinking, had a lot of sandwiches, blancmange, *gateau* and home-made lemonade— made with real lemons. The clocks approached the hour of midnight. The new century was on the edge of birth. Everybody went out of doors—and it happened to be a fine night. That Victorian Family stood on the top step of that big flight which led to their main entrance. All down the road, neighbours were doing the same, or were at their gates. There was an air of tremendous excitement and voices and laughter resounded on all sides —more remarkable because as a rule there would have been a dead hush. . . .

The clock in the dining room began to strike twelve with its silvery chime. This was the moment for which the Boy had been waiting. He sprang his surprise. He let off a large cannon cracker which he had saved from Guy Fawkes Night. The New Century came in with a bang. There were shouts, cheers, messages of goodwill called across the dark road and then someone started 'Auld Lang Syne'—and the Road—the Best Road— joined in together. The time wasn't very good, the singing was question-able and some had finished before the others had reached half-way. But the Spirit was there. The Victorians were greeting a new century. So much of the last one which had just died had been in truth Victorian. But the Victorian Age proper had only one more New Year's Eve to live. . . .

Despite the setbacks, the country went war mad—or perhaps this was because of the reverses. Volunteers flocked to the colours—patriotism ran riot. The boys of the land were not behindhand in this and the Victorian Boy and his friends were well to the fore. Some of them cajoled or bothered their Mothers into making them khaki uniforms too, and presently the Boy had a small troop of juvenile warriors—all about twelve years old—under his command. The Back Piece became the Veldt, they fought the Boers, they always won. Boys from adjoining roads found themselves cast for the rôle of Boers whether they liked it or not, and had a pretty thin time against the well-armed and—up to a point— disciplined forces from the Back Piece.

All those Boys thought war and talked war. Khaki was the only wear. The war was the first khaki war, for the scarlet coats were far too conspicuous a mark in South Africa. This had been proved when Briton and Boer had clashed before at Majuba Hill—a battle had provided a lesson which the British had not learnt. This previous defeat and the patched-up unsatisfactory peace which followed it was regarded as a slur on British arms. It was the meaning of the line in 'The Absent-minded Beggar' which said 'He's out on active service, wiping something off a slate'. But that something seemed very deeply ingrained and not easy to erase. But Boys—like their elders and the Queen herself—never considered anything but ultimate victory. They were avid in collecting cigarette cards— stamps went by the board temporarily—and those were all of war interest. They were pictures of British Generals, and scenes from the front—and also the wicked Boers—commanders like Cronje, De Wet, Botha, Joubert and even old President Kruger himself—'Oom Paul'—popularly pronounced as 'Kroojer'. Boys compared cards and swopping was a tremendous trade. Frederica made it her business to find a friendly tobacconist and persuade him to get some of his customers to give him their cards and bought them off him for a few pence. So the Boy did well. Those which were given with Ogden's Guinea Gold Cigarettes were the most popular, for they were real photographic prints—shiny and handsome. But greatly esteemed also were the cards which accompanied the Gold Flake and other brands of Wills' cigarettes. These were matt prints. Boys not only swopped the cards, they played games with them. They stood in a line, cigarette cards held lightly between finger and thumb of the left hand. They flicked them with the nail of the forefinger of the right hand. The boy whose card went the farthest scooped the pool. They all collected the little round buttons, as they were called, which bore photographs of the British Generals—they were printed on some form of metal and fastened in the lapel of the coat. The Boy had a perfectly complete collection of these and still has the majority, all lined up on a piece of cardboard covered with green velvet, with a little tartan ribbon to hang it up by—this being the work of Frederica. He had also a wonderful collection of Diamond Jubilee medals and tokens of which, alas, only one remains.

That poem 'The Absent-minded Beggar' was to help raise funds for the dependents of the soldiers—and did so nobly. Carnivals were held for this purpose, too. Long processions of people in fancy dress paraded the streets, like the processions of guys which had been usual on 5th November on Hampstead Heath—with carts specially decorated and bearing either large emblems or living tableaux of a warlike nature. Britannia was much to the fore. Soldiers—sometimes real Volunteers— but more often civilians dressed in uniforms—posed in warlike attitudes. Officers pointed swords and exhorted their men to attack—pointing presumably to show their men where the foe were, a fact of which they would have been uncomfortably aware.

One such procession had a very realistic tableau of that favourite pastime of the British Army, The Last Stand. This much impressed the Boy, and he and his pals had many such Last Stands—the Boy mostly bandaged and wounded but prepared to sell his life dearly. Another procession included a real machine-gun drawn by real horses, on its mobile carriage. At once the Boy's mail-cart became a machine-gun carriage—an old discarded Daisy Gun being thrust through the rails of the back rest and, all things considered, looking very well. And if anyone today does not know what a mail-cart looked like, an illustration is provided. And the mail-cart in the illustration is quite a famous one, for it belonged to the family named Agate, of which James Agate, the famous dramatic critic, was one—he played with and rode in the mail-cart—whilst the girl pictured in it is no less a person than that excellent actress, his sister May. The Boy's mail-cart was all sorts of things on the veldt of the Back Piece, from the battery of the Royal Horse Artillery and a veldt wagon to the land carriage of a naval 4.7 gun. . . .

No need to trace the war's rather sad history. Lord Roberts, the beloved 'Bobs', was sent out and with him went Lord Kitchener, the conqueror of the Sudan. The cavalry got active under General French. The Boers were met on equal terms. Proper organization was set up by Kitchener. Three towns in which small British forces had been beleaguered were relieved—Ladysmith, Kimberley and Mafeking. Victory shone ahead—for the Boers were in disorder and full retreat. The 20th century was starting much better than the 19th had finished.

And then, right on its threshold, just as she had entered the door, the old Queen died. She left her people in the early part of 1901. When the new century was opening its eyes to begin its hundred years of sovereignty, Queen Victoria, who had lived for eighty-two years, ended her reign of sixty-four years. She passed away at 6.30 p.m. on Tuesday, 22nd January, 1901. The true Victorian Age had closed as the new century opened. Her people mourned her as they would have mourned a beloved mother, the depths of the feeling for her is almost unbelievable today. It had seemed that she and her times were permanent and would never pass away. When she died she had forty grandchildren. When she came to the throne as a young girl she reigned over 168,000,000 people. When she died her subjects numbered 400,000,000. An old newspaper from the Box Room gives some astounding facts about her. The *Evening News* of 23rd January, 1901, second extra edition (its number was 6021), had a front page full of them, in short paragraphs. They are of the greatest interest today. Territory thirty times the size of the United Kingdom had been added to her empire during her reign—over 3,000,000 square miles. The first to be annexed in her name was Aden, in 1839, and the last was The Transvaal, in 1900. In the first year of her reign, the s.s. *Sirius* and s.s. *Great Western* crossed the Atlantic, the first steamships to do so. The population of the United Kingdom had risen in her reign from 25,000,000 to 45,000,000. The tonnage of the mercantile marine rose from 2,335,000 tons to 12,293,539 tons. On the night of her Coronation the Theatres of London were thrown open to the public free—at her own request. There were only about twelve that mattered. She had a staff of no less than 1000 at Windsor to uphold her proper state. She disliked smoking intensely and never approved of it—men were put to all sorts of shrifts and it was only at Prince Albert's earnest request that the officers of the Royal Yacht were allowed a whiff or two . . . in the special cowhouse aboard the vessel in which two small Alderney cows supplied the fresh milk for the Queen's own table; fresh butter was also made aboard. She was autocratic, yet she could be gracious. The *Evening News* recounts a story told by Mrs. Keeley, the famous actress. She suffered acutely from rheumatism in her knees and when she had the honour of being presented to the Queen she apologized humbly for this disability and explained with embarrassment and humility the reason why she had just to bow to her sovereign. 'I can't curtsey, Your Majesty,' said the actress. 'I can't either,' said the Queen.

Victoria had seen eleven Lord Chancellors, ten Prime Ministers, six Speakers of the House of Commons, at least three Bishops of every see and five or six of some, five Archbishops of Canterbury, six Archbishops of York and six Commanders-in-Chief. There had been eighteen Presidents of the United States, eleven Viceroys of Canada, sixteen Viceroys of India (according to the *Evening News*, when she became Empress of India in 1877, 'she set herself assiduously to learn Hindustani'), and France had been ruled by one King, one Emperor and seven Presidents of the

Republic. She outlived every member of her first Privy Council and all the Peers who were alive on her accession save one, The Earl Nelson, who was then fourteen, all the members of the House of Commons in her first Parliament and every Duke, Duchess, Marquis and Marchioness who held that rank when she came to the throne. During her lifetime no less than five Dukes of Norfolk had been Earl Marshal.

The tributes in the foreign press were amazing and also accurate. *Voce della Verita* of Rome said, 'With the passing away of Queen Victoria there disappears the principal guarantee of the peace of Europe.' 'No sovereign had ever ruled with so great a success with a life which was simple and immaculate. She raised the prestige of the Kingdom and encouraged the sentiments of morality' (*Popolo Romano*). 'Victoria was a perfect ruler for the 19th century.' 'Posterity will forget that her last hours were clouded, and will remember the Victorian era as the Golden Age of English history' (*Journal*, New York). 'No living sovereign in like degree embodies the idea of sovereignty which for Americans, with quadrennial changes, is embodied in the flag. To her subjects she stood for all they had achieved under her unexampled reign, which made her even in life a mythical embodiment in her person of the glories of her race, and her nation a kind of Avatar' (*New York Times*).

'The subjects of the Queen thank her for having in her family life and as a Queen set them an example of purity and truth which will endure for all times' (*Vossische Zeitung*). 'The manifold threads of relationship which stretch between Great Britain and Germany and which cause Germans to look upon the Queen as above all the grandmother of our Emperor, have proved to be one of the most enduring bonds between the two countries' (*Berliner Tageblatt*). 'The principles which guided Queen Victoria were impartiality and moderation at home, prudence and humanity abroad. It will be to the honour of Queen Victoria that she took them as her guide and left them as an example and a lesson to her successor and her peoples' (*La Journal*). 'The English people will keep in profound recollection the grandeur which marked the reign of Queen Victoria, who was an object of veneration for the whole world and particularly for Russia' (*St. Petersburg Journal*).

Those are a few of the foreign comments which the *Evening News* printed on its front page on 23rd January, 1901. They are of special interest as showing the impact which the Queen made abroad. For France had been on the verge of war with this country in 1896, over Fashoda. Germany, of course, looked upon her with different eyes, for she was the maternal grandmother of its Kaiser—who was himself probably not too pleased about it—and as regards Russia, there again were family ties between Victoria and the Czar Nicholas, who met that tragic end not many years later, and who bore such a remarkable family resemblance to George V. She was not only the Mother of the English but she was almost Grandmother of all the Courts of Europe. And America recognized her worth, despite the rupture over Venezuela not so long before her death. Thirteen years later Germany was at war with Great Britain and Queen Victoria's grandson fought against her people—and lost. Russia was on Great Britain's side but she lost and the Bolshevik regime came to power as a result. Nothing makes these personal tributes more striking than the fact that, owing to the Boer War, practically every nation in Europe was anti-British, save only Austria-Hungary. But Queen Victoria's greatness impressed itself upon them all. The fear expressed by the *Voce della Verita* concerning the peace of Europe being endangered by her death was too true.

Nowadays it has become customary to laugh at Victorians and the Victorian age. The British themselves would do well to remember that phrase used by the *St. Petersburg Journal* and also by the *Vossische Zeitung*— to say nothing of the *New York Journal*. Those indeed were true words and should be borne in remembrance. They were not just lip service to a dead Queen. They were facts. Those who lived under Victoria and live on now can testify to it. . . .

That *Evening News* from the Box Room shows other things of interest. It shows by its advertisement columns how all the Theatres closed at once (the usual procedure in a Royal Demise) but they made no announcement of their reopening. They remained closed until the evening of the day of the funeral, 4th February, 1901. So many of those theatres have now gone altogether or have become cinemas. Arthur Collins was in command at Drury Lane. Tree at Her Majesty's (which was not then four years old), Comyns Carr was running the Lyceum, with Lewis Waller and William Mollison in *Henry V*. Theatres now vanished or derelict include the Gaiety; Daly's; Kennington; Grand, Islington; Borough Theatre, Stratford; Britannia Theatre, Hoxton; Alexandra, Stoke Newington; Shakespeare, Clapham; Duchess, Balham; Holloway Empire; Crown, Peckham; Pavilion, Mile End Road. D'Oyly Carte was at the Savoy and William Greet at the Lyric, Shaftesbury Avenue and H. E. (afterwards Sir Edward) Moss was in command at the London Hippodrome. The World's Fair at the Agricultural Hall closed down and a Mr. H. R. Johnson announced the postponement of his Ball until 15th February, but he did not say where this was to be held.

Old advertisements are always intriguing. Samuel Brothers Limited of 65–67 Ludgate Hill (half a column on the front page) announced their great sale—first for eight years—with everything at below cost price. Taddy's Myrtle Grove Tobacco and Cigarettes took space, so did

Gallaher's 'Two Flakes' tobacco. Bovril had a double half-column stating that it was liquid life. Scotts Emulsion had a similar space given up to a testimonial from Mr. Wm. Maher, who declared it had given him a fresh lease of life. He got his picture in, too—a good-looking, clear-featured man with a lot of well-brushed hair, a very high collar and a Lord Kitchener moustache. Maconochies Marmalades, Jams and Soups, Powell's Balsam of Aniseed (with the familiar trademark of the netted lion being freed by the mouse), Dr. Ridge's Food 'For Infants and Invalids', Epp's Cocoa (Grateful—Comforting), Nixelene Stove Paste and California Syrup of Figs were other advertisers. You could obtain a New Century Phonograph (Marvel of the Age: Loudest, Simplest and Cheapest, for 24s. 6d. Waterfield, Clifford and Co., who marketed it, stated they had a stock of 10,000 records. The Hackney Furnishing Co. announced their hire-purchase system. They manufactured their own goods, they said so; there was no middleman's profit, no interest was charged, a deposit was optional and they gave free Life Insurance. The terms are illuminating:

£10 worth of goods ..	6s.	per month
£20 ,, ,, ,, ..	12s. ,, ,,	
£30 ,, ,, ,, ..	18s. ,, ,,	
£40 ,, ,, ,, ..	£1 6s. ,, ,,	
£50 ,, ,, ,, ..	£1 9s. ,, ,,	
£100 ,, ,, ,, ..	£2 15s. ,, ,,	
£200 ,, ,, ,, ..	£5 10s. ,, ,,	
£500 ,, ,, ,, ..	By Special Arrangement	

Carriage was free up to 300 miles. Carpets and linoleums were laid free. Their hours of business were 9 a.m. to 9 p.m. and on Thursdays they closed at four. The Midland Furnishing Co.'s terms were practically the same, except that they announced that £500 worth cost £13 15s. per month. It was possible to furnish a house adequately for £100. There was what was stated to be an admirable flat to let in Westminster (Vincent Square, just off), fine modern block, let only to superior classes, four rooms and bath, first floor; £4 18s. monthly. One on the ground floor with three rooms for £3 10s. monthly and another on the first floor (accommodation not mentioned) for £2 16s. monthly—all inclusive. A cottage was offered at Ponders End, five rooms (redecorated), good garden, open situation, close to station; rent, 6s. 6d. per week. There were flats in Tooting, four or five rooms and scullery and separate front doors, close to bus, train and tram, for 8s. 6d. weekly. The neighbourhood was stated to be healthy! Four-roomed flats at Earlsfield, within ten minutes of station, where workmen's tickets could be obtained, the advertisement said, cost 7s. per week. And good light offices in the centre of the City were going for £15, £25 and £40 per annum.

There was only one 'Personal' advertisement: 'Sunbeam. Will wait at home for interview every afternoon this week.' It gives no clue as to who was waiting for whom or what.

With the Queen dead, there was little room for other news, except that about the new King, who came to London for a special Privy Council. He had sent the death message from Osborne the night before. King Edward VII arrived in London at five minutes to one. He had crossed from the Isle of Wight on the Royal Yacht, with the Dukes of York and Connaught and with Mr. A. J. Balfour, the Home Secretary, in attendance. That London crowd which gathers automatically was at Victoria Station to see its new Monarch. And that crowd was in deep mourning—already it had assumed it. The King, looking very strained, stepped speedily into his waiting carriage, a closed one, and drove off, whilst the crowd stood with bared heads, to be followed by the Duke of York (afterwards George V) and the Duke of Connaught (Queen Victoria's son). They went straight to St. James's Palace. That Privy Council was fully attended. Among those present were The Marquis of Salisbury, A. J. Balfour, Lord Rosebery, The Duke of Portland, Sir Henry Campbell-Bannerman (who had been short of cordite), Lord Ripon, The Speaker, Sir Michael Hicks Beach, The Lord Chancellor, The Duke of Devonshire, Lord Strathcona, The Lord Chief Justice, Mr. Walter Long and the Duke of Devonshire. The Lord Mayor called on the new King, who had gone across to Marlborough House and who now came to his first Privy Council attended by an escort of Horse Guards. And he was loudly cheered by the mourning crowds. It was announced that he would be proclaimed next day and that his title would be Edward the Seventh.

Thus passed the Victorian Age and thus entered the Edwardian Era.

But London was full of signs of mourning, which the *Evening News* described. It mentions that many buildings flew flags at half-mast, including the Union Jack and—the Royal Standard, which nobody but Royalty has the right to fly. . . .

The Victorian Boy saw the proclamation of King Edward VII from outside St. James's Palace. But the Victorian Age had one more day of grandeur. The old Queen did not lie in state but passed through millions of her subjects on her last passage across her capital—being driven on a gun-carriage. Behind her rode her sons and grandsons, including the Kaiser, who came straight across to England immediately his Grandmother died. That funeral and that very small coffin remain clearly in the Boy's memory, and a picture of the Kaiser, looking grimly across the vast crowds, and wondering maybe if one day they would be his subjects. He stared at them in silence and the crowd stared back at him, equally dumb. There was a spatter of cheers, speedily suppressed, for Lord Roberts. Grey skies, bitter cold and the sound of the Funeral March by Chopin with an undercurrent of horses' hooves and marching feet—that was the keynote to which the Victorian Age made its exit. The funeral did not pass off as expertly as it should have done, although the crowds knew nothing of that. The tiny coffin had nearly been dropped in the sea at Cowes, by its soldier bearers, and for the last stage of its journey the horses of the Artillery proved intractable, so the Navy came to the rescue, and at the King's direct orders pulled its Queen to her last home . . . as it has done ever since. She might not have liked that—the Army always came before the Navy in her affection. . . .

There are a few other items in that *Evening News* from the Box Room.

Tucked away at the bottom of a column was: 'Signor Verdi. Slowly Sinking. The condition of Signor Verdi is today worse and his end is believed to be approaching. The news has caused profound sympathy throughout Italy.' . . . So a King of Opera was following a great Queen into the realms of death.

The telephone number of the *Evening News* was 124 Holborn. That must have been a busy number, but the *Evening News* gave splendid coverage to the epoch-making event.

The Victorian Boy remembers that when he saw King Edward VII's proclamation he wore a black tie, his darkest suit and a crêpe band round his arm. His Aunts and his Mother wore black, with heavy dark veils. Every woman had her 'black' handy in those days. The Boy had wanted to wear his school cap—green and yellow—but this was disallowed and he had a dark blue cap instead. His womenfolk wore their furs—which were of bear—and had muffs of the same skin. The Boy had black knitted gloves bought for him as they went along and was upset about this. He despised all gloves and especially woollen ones. The only comfort derived from wearing kid gloves was that one could nibble the finger-tips and he rather liked the flavour. But black woollen gloves were a horror. He disliked the sensation when the fingers rubbed each other, it made him shiver. It does so still, but now he need not wear them. It rather spoiled his day but eventually he slipped them off and kept his hands in his pockets, the pockets of his dark grey overcoat which had a cape attached with little slings inside to rest the arms. He escaped detection, too. The ladies were too busy staring about them. They had tea at Fuller's in Regent Street. And they took a yellow bus to King's Cross and the train home. The Boy enjoyed the day—he had missed school but what he saw was of more value to him afterwards. He had hoped the schools would close down like the theatres—the board schools had closed for the day. It did not seem at all fair to him. But he got the day off anyhow. And was excused homework.

The Victorian Age was over—and a loosening of convention was soon to follow, to keep pace with the vigorous, keen-witted man on the Throne. The change, when it came, started from the exalted circles and was some time before it reached the Middle Classes. They had to get used to singing 'God Save the King' instead of 'the Queen'—to realize there would be a new face on the stamps and coins—that it would now be K.C. instead of Q.C., and *King's Regulations* instead of *Queen's Regulations*. The habits of sixty-three years had to be shed. The new Royal Cipher would soon make its appearance and naturally did so. But still, dotted about the land are letter boxes and pillar boxes which bear the cipher V.R. There is one outside the Royal Theatre—Theatre Royal, Drury Lane —to this very day.

CHAPTER NINETEEN

Edwardian England

UNDER the new King, things moved fast. Life changed its tempo and took on a gayer, more colourful tint. A man at the head of affairs made a difference, it seemed, a man who mixed more freely with his people, who was a sportsman who, indeed, won the Derby twice. That was the sort of King who was, in the slang of the day, 'Just the ticket.' The stiffer and more austere methods of Victorian life changed and were changing. Peace came to the Empire with the end of the Boer War. The treaty was signed, Cronje was sent to St. Helena, a very much lesser prisoner than his predecessor Napoleon. But the public thought it right he should be sent there. The nation was annoyed with these Boers for having given them so much trouble. Kruger had fled and was safe from arrest. With him had gone much of the Transvaal Treasury, too. And when the war was over, the British, in that easy-going way, forgot any enmity it might have felt for the Boers. A large section of the public had, it is true, disapproved of the war but had not been able to do much about it owing to the intense Jingoistic patriotism of the great majority. The Unionists, as the Tories then called themselves, were convinced it was a just war, but Campbell-Bannerman, now the leader of the Liberals in place of Harcourt, said he thought that a better turn of statesmanship could have avoided hostilities altogether. There is little doubt he was right, but Salisbury, with his keen political foresight, had suddenly sprung an election on the country at the height of war fever and the Unionists came back with a huge majority. It was called The Khaki Election. But at any rate the war was over. Very shortly the Boers were given self-government, which made men like Botha and Smuts, statesmen both, friends and helpers of this country.

Salisbury resigned and Balfour succeeded him. And it was becoming apparent that a very good statesman indeed was sitting on the Throne of this country.

The man who had stood so much in the shadow—the enormous shadow cast by the small figure of his Mother—was now emerging as somebody who knew and had studied affairs of State. Thanks to Victoria, the Throne was more secure than it had ever been before. It was the very core of the living rock of the British Empire. And he who now occupied it was very much beloved. It was a different affection to that veneration which his Mother had aroused. It was tempered by a real friendliness which mixed in the alloy of respect with which the Monarch was regarded and made Kingship something intensely real and not aloof. The people called him 'Teddie' amongst themselves, but he kept the atmosphere of Royalty just the same.

The country, despite the bill for the war, was prosperous. That war bill was a thing of almost nothing compared with the cost of the succeeding World Wars, but the British felt it was heavy at the time. Still, in the main they were very rich. Many had made large profits during the hostilities; some, however, had been ruined. And the Victorian Family which is the centre of this book was one of the latter class. Disaster had befallen them, reducing them to great straits. The Best House must go, it could no longer be their home, they could not afford it. They must all be separated—they must earn their own livings if they could—how they did it has been described. For a time at least, and nobody knew how long that time must be, they would have no home, but must stay with relations until things got straightened out. The Boy sensed something wrong and then he was told that the house he loved so much would soon cease to be his home. He was stunned at first and is not ashamed to state that he shed many tears. For he loved that house, that garden, that Back Piece, that road. It had always been his haven in the nomadic days when his Father was alive, but now, for some years, it had sheltered him and all his cherished toys and possessions. He knew every cranny of it; every stair was a friend of his. He knew every article he owned, every book he possessed. His friends envied him his seemingly vast possessions. For some days he was inconsolable. He asked where he was to live. He was told that it was not quite certain yet. He demanded that wherever it was his Mother should be with him and on that point he was reassured. He did not realize the day of parting was so close. Then they told him that he and his Aunt Mary, as soon as his school broke up for the summer holidays—only about a fortnight away—were to go up to Scotland, to that little village in Galloway which he had already enjoyed, and there they were to spend a glorious holiday. The resilience of boyhood came to his rescue. A holiday on the hills and moors, in the pinewoods, clambering over the crags, playing in the old abbey, tickling for trout in the burns and bathing in the nearby Solway Firth—that was scrumptious. He loved his Scottish cousins and his great-uncle the Scottish divine, a kindly, learned and very good man—a real Christian. Already his mind was busy with the games he would play, and the adventures he would have. He discussed them eagerly with his Mother, not noticing how ill she was, how she would stop and go pale and hold her side—indeed, she hid it all from him. Then the question of his toys arose, of which he had such numbers. His swords, his guns, his uniforms, his helmets, his rocking-horse, his books and, above all, his own army—his leaden soldiers, which now numbered nearly two thousand! Realization came that he could not keep them.

But no child thinks much about the future. The present, with that glorious six or seven weeks in Scotland, was enough. It was eternity to him. He did not look beyond it. So with a certain amount of heroism and inward sorrow he began to bestow those toys on his friends and some of his cousins. Great was the joy amongst them. His swords he would not part with. One of his aunts, Maggie, promised to keep them for him and she kept her word. At last everything, save his Daisy airgun, a prized dagger, a couple of model revolvers and about a dozen books—the bound volume of *Chums* which contained 'Rogues of the Fiery Cross'; *Harald the Norseman* and a few more he could not part with—were dispersed. Maggie took care of his school prizes and his rapidly selected pick of a few more volumes as well—he has them still. And when the day came to go to St. Pancras Station—he went all over the house, as yet untouched and as it always had been—and bade it good-bye. He could hardly believe it would not be there for him to return to. He went out on those leads, he went into the Box Room, he went all round the garden and all round the Back Piece and he made his final farewell in the Little Room, which he had always loved.

Then they called him to come and get into the cab. His Mother and his Aunt Bessie were coming to see them off. He stood for one moment on the top of the front steps, he patted the front door and he went down those steps for the last time. And as he did so, something seemed to fall from him—he seemed like something emerging from a shell. It was his childhood he was leaving behind, to stay in ghostly form in the place where its happiest hours had been spent. . . . He took his first step to maturity that day; he really started to grow up. And, indeed, things were never the same again. . . .

But life in England went on. The next thirteen years were fraught with great events. It was remarkable how soon the Edwardian veneer spread over the solid foundation of Victorianism. Broadmindedness was the order of the day, and although amongst the Middle Classes the

s

conventions held, life on a higher level was much less strict than in the days of the old Queen. That barrier round the Court which had been so hard to pass was easier to penetrate. Money, as well as birth, now had the entrée. People whose claim to fame was riches could now rub shoulders with those whose blood was blue and whose descent was impeccable. The country was still tremendously rich, the richest in the world. It had emerged from the shadow of a bad war and had been victorious. The victory had cost it dear in blood and treasure.

Now the sun shone, and a new Sovereign had set a faster pace. The country followed it. And that thing which was to alter the whole world began to get more into general use—the Internal Combustion Engine. That was in keeping with the tempo of the times. The Dining Out habit spread, hotels were commonly used for entertainment and so were restaurants. But the Middle Classes still made Home the headquarters. Money was spent and everyone benefited. Income tax was infinitesimal, rates were hardly noticeable, costs were so amazingly low as to be unbelievable today. British prestige stood high and the Royal Navy ruled the world. When the battleship *Dreadnought* appeared, it was the last word in naval might. Now indeed the British Empire seemed firm and secure and the Homeland, as it was still called, was impregnable and invincible. But across the North Sea a challenger was rising. That grandson of Queen Victoria, the Kaiser Wilhelm, had made up his mind that his country and not England should lead the world. There was no love lost between him and the King of England, his cousin Bertie—for Edward VII was Bertie to his family. The two had never liked each other. Queen Victoria had kept the peace between them. But Edward VII had laid down his dictum. The Kaiser was no gentleman, he said, and that, so far as he, and his subjects, were concerned, was sufficient to place the German, Emperor though he might be, without the pale.

For Germany, now a complete Power instead of a conglomeration of small states, kingdoms and grand duchies, was going steadily ahead. She was making tremendous progress in commerce and was, when King Edward ascended the throne, a serious challenger to British commercial supremacy. Her people had great concentration and the will to work— and obey. The British derided their rivals, in the good old British way. 'Made in Germany' was a term of contempt. It meant things were cheap and nasty. But Germany was selling her goods abroad and taking British markets. Wilhelm the Kaiser wanted world domination and he meant to have it. King Edward knew all about that.

There was a thing in Europe called The Balance of Power. This was represented by groupings of the Powers in alliance and had been the result of the Napoleonic Wars. When King Edward ascended the throne, the main groupings were the Triple Alliance, which included Germany, Austria-Hungary and Italy, and the Dual Alliance of France and Russia. It seems strange to find two Latin countries like France and Italy in opposite camps, but politics and the Vatican were largely responsible for that. Great Britain sat outside it all, alone and powerful, determined not to enter into Continental Alliances but to play the part of intervener if need arose. She held the seas and her position was wellnigh unassailable. She had not been involved in a Continental war since the Crimea.

The average Briton cared little about what went on in Europe. That Continent, to him, was a playground. Paris was a naughty city to be spoken of with a wink. Rich people went to the South of France to dodge the English winter—they had villas on the Riviera. Some went to the Italian Lakes as well. Quite a few followed the example of King Edward by visiting Baden-Baden, Homburg and the German and Austrian spas. And those who liked what was called 'scenery', or who happened to be mountaineers, took holidays in Switzerland or the Tyrol. Some few patronized the seaside resorts on the French side of the Channel, where one could gamble—the reason why so many went down south to Monte Carlo—a few whose purses were not long went to the Belgian resorts, Ostende or Knocke—but by and large they did not travel to anything like the extent which was general between the World Wars. Few people indeed had been to America, little was known of that amazing country. Yet the British dominated all parts of the world. They did this in order to trade and to administer the Dominions and the Colonies and Dependencies. Few families but had some of their number scattered about the Empire in a more or less outlandish spot.

For this country it was an era of peace and prosperity as it had been for many years. There seemed to be no reason for a change. Except that there was more outward gaiety and show, life went on much as it had done under Queen Victoria. But King Edward went about the Continent. He went to nearly every country and he did much good. He took the grandeur of his realm with him. Besides that, he saw for himself what was going on. His astute mind and his dislike of his cousin Willie made him a careful observer of that Balance of Power which interested nobody in the ordinary way, save politicians and those in the actual Government or Opposition. But it was obvious to the knowledgeable eye that the alliance of France and Russia was not too stable and would not be very efficient in the case of war. England and France were hereditary enemies with a thousand years of battle between them. It is doubtful if they could have been brought together by ordinary political or diplomatic means. It needed the hand of someone above such things. King Edward accomplished it. He entered into no Alliance, such things were alien to the race over which he ruled, but in 1904 he arranged an Entente between France and this country, which although not an alliance was one in everything but name. This brought Russia, France and Britain into step in the event of war and it set up quite a new Balance of Power in Europe. It was immensely popular on both sides of the Channel. Old feuds were forgotten and Frenchmen and Englishmen grasped hands. At the Gaiety Theatre Gertie Millar sang:

> "So come to France
> When you've got a chance
> You'll feel so gay when you are landing
> Each maid you meet
> You'll find so sweet
> There is a Cordial Understanding."

Many Englishmen took that advice and found it true enough, though maybe if the crossing was rough the gaiety on landing might be missing.

King Edward became known as 'Edward the Peacemaker'. And at the time it was true enough. Although the Triple Entente went to war in 1914, during the King's reign there were no wars worthy of mention so far as his subjects in all parts of the world were concerned.

He was much beloved. He gave his subjects a nasty shock when he was taken ill in 1902 just before his Coronation. He had a new trouble which was called appendicitis. He was operated upon and soon got well. Appendicitis became fashionable, not to say popular. He was crowned later the same year—in August. It was a month which did not exist fashionably in those days, but that year naturally the London Season was prolonged. The Nation rejoiced and celebrated gaily over that Coronation. In comparison with the Coronation which took place whilst this book was being written it was a gigantic affair with far more troops and a great deal more splendour. But whereas all the nation watched that recent Coronation by means of an everyday affair called Television, which would have been a miracle in 1902—fifty-one years before, the Coronation of King Edward was seen by a comparative handful and what went on inside the Abbey was only made known by the work of artists who drew the scene, very often from their own imagination. But the rejoicings were general.

> On Coronation Day
> On Coronation Day
> We'll all be merry
> Drinking whisky, wine and sherry
> We'll all be merry
> On Coronation Day.

And they were. Beer was consumed in quantities although not mentioned in the song, but all forms of liquor were plentiful and cheap. The public houses were open all day. And there was another song about King Edward which was typical of its kind:

> There'll be no war-er
> So long as we've a king like Good King Hedward
> There'll be no war-er
> 'E 'ates that sorter thing
> Mothers, don't worry
> So long as we've a king like good King Hedward
> Peace wiv onner is 'is motter
> So—Gawd save the King.

Sung on the Music Halls by the nigger minstrels (who were in process of being displaced by the Pierrots), sung outside and inside pubs and by buskers to theatre queues—the only queues there were—it was just a plain, palatable truth. War did not come in his days although the storm was gathering. The world went very well then. Progress was showing its hand. That internal combustion engine, as applied to transport, had come to stay. King Edward championed the motor-car. It was to push the horse off the roads in a remarkably short space of time. It is possible that the King's love of the car may have been fostered by the fact that he was a rather indifferent horseman. The first official body of motorists—The Automobile Club—had been officially recognized in 1900. In that same year there had been a run from London to Edinburgh and back—it had gone on for a long time, from 23rd April to the second week in May. In Diamond Jubilee Year, 1897, a car had actually gone at twelve miles an hour—downhill. It was a Daimler. It was a Daimler, too, which first had pneumatic tyres and that car was built in Coventry in 1901. And in the same year King Edward said that by the end of the summer he would have made motoring so popular that every English gentleman would own a car. It did not go quite as fast as that, but motoring certainly became fashionable and what was called 'all the rage'. It received a great impetus when King Edward ordered a car especially for Queen Alexandra. It was electrically driven and made by The City and Suburban Electric Carriage Co. The King's new car was a Gardner-Sepollet, driven by steam. One of their cars reached the astounding speed of seventy-five miles per hour. The only trouble was that they soon became overheated. In 1902, a corps of automobile volunteers was formed and cars were offered to the Army as part of its equipment. Tests were watched by Field-Marshal Lord Roberts, with General Kelly-Kenny (one of the few generals to come through the South African War with enhanced reputation) and General Sir Leslie Rundle, of whom the same may be said. The tests were satisfactory and the seeds of a mechanized army were sown. By 1905 the first A.A. Patrol was on the road. He operated on the Brighton road and did not wear the smart uniform of today. He had a cap, a tweed coat, cycling knickerbockers, stockings and boots to match. He had a brassard bearing the letters A.A. and a badge like that worn by a bus conductor, marked A.A. and with a number. He rode a push-bike! But speed was getting on. In 1905 the Post Office began the use of motor-mail coaches instead of the old horse-driven mail-carts. And motor buses were making their appearance. The first was exactly the same to look at as the horse bus it was to displace. The driver still sat aloft and the engine was down where the horses used to be. But these were actual horse buses converted to motors and still relied on the old form of brakes applied to the outside of the wheel. Later came the buses which were the true forerunners of the giants of today. The 'Germain' of the London Road Car Company which plied from Hammersmith to Oxford Circus had the engine underneath the driver's seat. That too was in 1905. When 1906 arrived the battle between horse bus and motor bus was really joined—and the motors were little, if any, faster than the horses. King Edward used a car wherever possible, but never, of course, on state or semistate occasions. The horse trams did not surrender to the internal combustion engine but to electricity, which began to be applied to them in 1902—the same year as in which the London Road Car Company tried out a steam bus. Electricity replaced steam on the Metropolitan Railway in 1903, not only underground, but out as far as Harrow. By the opening up of this then rural district, great suburbs arose. Yet newspapers were still distributed by means of the horse.

In 1903 the Brothers Wright got their flying machine off the ground and the aeroplane was accomplished—to advance with rapidity which astounded everyone. In the same year the Prince of Wales (afterwards George V) drove an electric tram at Tooting, and his wife (later to be Queen Mary) was a passenger. The motor cab arrived in 1904. It was a sort of converted hansom, for the body of that kind of cab was fixed on to a primitive chassis. It had no taximeter. The driver followed the old custom, "I leave it to you, sir."

Under Edward the Peacemaker the world moved faster than it had ever moved before. Styles of buildings changed, houses were less heavy and solid looking, those front steps disappeared. Red tiles replaced slate roofs. The houses were spacious, airy and gracious. They were typical of their time. And modern conveniences kept on arriving and being installed. But life moved in much the same way. There was the London Season, a thing which those who never saw it cannot understand today. All the rank and fashion were in town. The houses of the West End were all repainted and shone with colour, also they were decked with window boxes which set them off like jewels. Great parties were held in the great houses—now almost all vanished away. Footmen in livery, coachmen as well, smart 'tigers' in their cockaded tall hats and shining high boots with the brown turned-down tops. Butlers in their pride and pomp marshalled the guests arriving at the evening receptions, as the shining broughams with perfectly matched pairs or, occasionally, the little gleaming electric broughams, set them down under the awning and they walked up the red carpet into the huge house, which blazed with light. Crowds of curious onlookers surveyed the scenes, craning their necks for a glimpse of interiors as the doors opened, and they heard the strains of a string orchestra—dressed like hussars in pink or blue and all owning the title of Viennese. Bond Street at the fashionable hour was a parade of English gentry, male and female, in their best clothes, as was Church Parade in Hyde Park on Sundays. It was a sight to see the fashionable people driving in the Park, too, and to watch the riders in the Row. None of the ladies rode astride. They wore 'habits' and used the side saddle.

The West End of London was a place which wore a smile. Commerce had got into Piccadilly, Oxford Street, Regent Street and Bond Street but residential districts were intact. Mayfair and Belgravia had a knowledge of, and perhaps a bowing acquaintance with, Bayswater. Berkeley Square, Belgrave Square, Grosvenor Square—those were places where people lived, as was Mayfair. For in those days people had a town and country house. They spent a 'Season' in London and would appear again in fewer numbers for what was known as The Little Season, round about Christmas time. They gathered soon after Easter and by May the Season was in full swing. The Courts were held and Presentations were made. It mattered a lot then. Debutantes really were debutantes, spending their first Season in a ceaseless round of parties, receptions and balls. Hostesses stood at the top of marble staircases and welcomed their guests. Mothers watched the impact the debutante daughters made on the eligible young males. The Derby, the Opera, Oxford and Cambridge and Eton and Harrow, Lord's, Newmarket for the Guineas, Ascot in its supreme glory, Henley and then Goodwood—and the Season was over. The rich and smart went to Cowes Regattas. But by 12th August they were in Scotland and the north shooting the grouse. September found them potting the partridge amongst the stubble.

> The month is now September
> And shooting has begun
> Across the wheaten stubble
> Is heard the frequent gun.

October meant pheasant shooting and the hunting season. House-parties for shooting and hunting and fishing. House-parties in the summer with cricket under ideal circumstances. And, of course, the river—the Thames at Maidenhead. Tea on the lawn at Skindles—many had their own river-side villas, too. Company was a little mixed but very jolly and Bohemian. If you saw the Guardee of your acquaintance with a very pretty and slightly overdressed young person who was surely a chorus-girl, you looked the other way. The zenith of the river season was Ascot Sunday at Boulters Lock, where fashion displayed itself to wondering eyes—fashion which was the latest word in everything but suitability for boating. But who cared about that? This was what convention and habit decreed. So they did it. Morals seemed to be getting looser. There arose what was known as 'The Smart Set' whose reputed goings-on shocked the respect·able Middle Classes (who might have been rather envious) but whose 'fast' behaviour would have passed quite unnoticed in any stratum of society today except that it might have seemed rather staid and respect-able. But great divines thundered against it. Father Vaughan filled his Mayfair Church every Sunday with the very people whose behaviour he indicted. They loved it, it made them feel so delightfully wicked. A house in Mayfair was not a luxury to these folk but a necessity. It did not cost much, from the modern point of view. People now live in the mews where once the coachmen and servants had their free quarters and pay rents therefor which the Edwardians would have considered scandalous for their mansion. So does the world improve.

When the Middle Class went 'Up West' it wore its best clothes. For London was a well-dressed city—the best-dressed city—certainly so far as men were concerned—in the world. English tailors were supreme. Englishmen led the world's male sartorial fashions. They dressed quietly but they dressed well. They all looked very much alike, it is true, but was that a drawback? They all looked English—or perhaps one must say British—and that was a great deal. You might see them in the mornings having a stroll on the way to their clubs, well built, perfectly-tailored young men, pink and clear of complexion or sun-tanned according to their calling, walking quietly and sedately, never in a hurry. They might wear a lounge suit—and in Edwardian times the trousers turned up and the last button of the vest was left undone. The shirts were white or coloured but never loud. The collar was double fold, starched and white. The tie was quiet and discreet. Along Piccadilly and the adjoining streets between it, Pall Mall and St. James's, the tie was almost always that of an old school, a regiment, a well-known club or the Navy. They wore boots, of glacé kid, or patent leather, according to their attire. If they had a function to attend they would wear a morning coat and shiny topper. In this case the collar would be straitup or butterfly and the tie either black and white or grey—it could be in a knot or it could be an 'Ascot.' There might be a fancy waistcoat, in which case it would be grey, or white with black stripes. The shirt would be white, the trousers striped, beautifully cut and creased and the boots would be patent, with perhaps brown or even white uppers. In that case they were laced. If just plain patent, they were mostly buttoned. Men of middle age wore frock-coats but otherwise the dress system was similar. But when these young men were in lounge suits, they wore bowler hats or—in summer—straw hats. They never called them Boaters. In the latter instance the band was usually that of a club. But King Edward set a fashion. He popularized the Homburg hat, the universal wear of today—but of green velour. They soon became popular and ousted the straw hats. But in Town men clung to bowlers in winter. It was the English hat and they were Englishmen, which was the generic title covering people of Scots, Welsh and Irish birth as well. One sees plays produced on television today which show young Army Officers walking about in uniform, attending private parties therein and even wearing it at theatres. That never happened. The officer's one idea was, when off duty, to get out of his uniform and into mufti. He was proud of his uniform in its right place but he was extremely self-conscious of it when not on parade. He got into mufti as soon as he could. There was not nearly so much smoking. Pipes were never smoked in the street and cigars seldom—it was ostentatious to do so. All young men had their pipes and smoked them in clubs and at home and in the country. They selected their pipes with as much care as they chose their suits, their ties, their cricket bats and their guns. They had them with amber mouthpieces, with vulcanite mouthpieces and they kept them in cases supplied with them, lined with velvet. Pipes were for the most part silver mounted and the best came from Loewe and Co. in the Haymarket. Some men smoked a meerschaum and took pains to 'colour' it. They handled it with gloves on and treated it with reverence. Some of these pipes had modelled bowls of extraordinary ingenuity and even artistic merit. There was a short vogue for calabash pipes, but they were heavy and cumbersome. Cigarettes were usually Turkish or Egyptian. Only the very best Virginia was smoked—the 'gasper' arrived at universal popularity during the first war when Turkish and Egyptian cigarettes fell from favour never to regain it. There were no automatic lighters. Matches for lighting up were usually wax vestas, and carried in a gold or silver match-box, with a place to strike the match at the foot.

Brown boots could be worn without a solecism being committed, but only with suitable suits. Never, of course, with a frock- or morning-coat. That was barbarian and the wearer was a self-confessed outsider.

The ruling convention amongst men was 'Good Form'. There were certain things one did and certain things one did not. To do the latter was to be a cad, a bounder, an outsider, hairy at the heel. Bad form got one blackballed at clubs or expelled, if a member. Good form was essential.

Women were treated with respect. Hats were raised and if the lady stopped to speak, not resumed until she gave permission. One walked on the outside, one opened doors and the lady went through first. No man who was good form remained seated when a lady entered or left a room. He would never have sat down whilst she spoke to him, without permission. He carried her parcels, he fetched and carried for her on all occasions. Always, she came first. Women were supposed to be the weaker vessel. Men did not smoke in their presence without permission. And no man, whether of Mayfair or Mornington Crescent, Belgravia or Brixton, Bayswater or Balham, would have retained his seat in any public vehicle when a woman entered, if there was no seat for her. 'Allow me' he would say, jumping up. This was done maybe with more alacrity when the lady was young and pretty than when she was old and plain, but it was always done without hesitation. But, of course, in those days women had not attained equality with men, so they were treated as superiors.

London glittered, London glowed, London wore a smile. It was rich, happy and free. Its money went a long way. It always had plenty to spend. It had good manners and a good time. But although the tempo of life was faster under Edward VII, it never swept away Family Life. That endured and parents had the respect of their young. And the young wanted to marry and set up a family of their own. Edwardian women knew their way about and how to attract men. They were essentially feminine. There was no swooning—that Victorian Boy has attested to the fact that he only saw a woman swoon once.

There were other alleged conventions firmly believed in by the people who were never Victorians or Edwardians. It is not to be believed that any man, making his proposal of marriage, ever heard the young woman he was thus honouring say 'This is so sudden!' Bless you, the Victorian and Edwardian Miss was never taken unawares. She used her wiles—she knew how to glance under the brim of her hat, over her fan at a dance or across the top of her attractive muff. The young man knew pretty well what were his chances. There were what were called 'flirts', who lured men on to turn them down, but the average Edwardian young man knew about them. If he had his share of brains he never fell for the 'flirt'. He knew about them. He heard the other men talking about them. For although in the Mess 'a lady's name was never mentioned', young Edwardians would discuss the young ladies they met at dance, tennis clubs and the like. How they met and the manner of approach has been described. And the young men who might indulge in a little gossip about the ladies would take care that they never mentioned one to whom anyone in company might be 'paying attention'. They had their share of tact. Sometimes, of course, there might be a slip-up and a row. And there was often quite a bit of trouble, conducted in a gentlemanly way, off the premises, if a young lady honoured by a young man's attentions had been, in his view, a little bit too friendly in the manner of too many dances with a rival. That was settled outside—and sometimes there was a bit of a fight, but not very often. By and large they played fair and so did the girls. The girls wanted to get married even more than the men. It was their calling, their profession, as it were. And there was still a code of morals. A man expected chastity in a girl to whom he got engaged. He expected modesty, too. A young lady dressed in taper trousers and a tight jumper, with a cigarette in her mouth, which did not impede her extreme freedom of speech, and with make-up on her face, would indeed have attracted quite a few young Edwardians. But—their attention would have been of a different kind to that which they offered to the Edwardian Miss. And their intentions would not have been at all honourable. Other times—other manners.

CHAPTER TWENTY

Edwardian Youth

THE early years of the reign of King Edward VII were not too fortunate for that Victorian Boy who had now become an Edwardian Youth. He had entered his teens, an orphan with no home of his own.

He lived with his Uncle John and was far from happy. He felt he was an intruder—something of a figure of charity, although the money on which Uncle John lived was earned by Uncle James.

He retired into himself; he made no complaints. He had said good-bye to toys—he had none left, anyway—but he clung to his few books and read avidly those of his Uncle John. He became very silent and self-centred, and he dreamed his dreams. He still played his mental games on his way to and from school—now four miles each way—and those dreams sustained him, for pocket-money was a thing of the past—or almost. His Aunts did their best to keep up the sixpence a week. But his Uncle James, who was living with his own sister Maggie, never forgot his promise to Frederica. He did his best to look after that boy. He knew his tastes and, even when they did not coincide with his own, he pleased the Boy. He took him to see as many of the sights as could be managed. Amongst these outings was a visit to the Royal Albert Hall, in the cheapest seats—for now every penny mattered—to hear Sousa and his Band when they first played there in 1902.

That was an 'occasion'.

This man, of Spanish extraction and born in Washington, was a sensation. His real name was 'So'—but that did not look well on the bills, so Mr. 'So' added the initials of his country—U.S.A.—and became John Philip Sousa. It fitted with his own genius.

Sousa gave America what was perhaps its first national music—loud, dashing, crashing and wide-awake. There was nothing sleepy or old-fashioned about Sousa or his Band—or his Marches.

He wrote those himself and, for his first success in that line—'The Washington Post'—he received £7. The publishers sold millions of copies, for this was the heyday of sheet-music, because most people played the piano.

Sousa learnt his lesson. 'The Stars and Stripes for Ever' brought him in over £10,000, and 20,000 copies of 'The Invincible Eagle' were sold on the day of its publication. Sousa knew his business.

He glorified America, and the titles of his compositions tickled the young, enthusiastic patriotism of that land, which had so recently thrashed the Spaniards—from which race Sousa had sprung.

His Band was magnificent. Strangely enough, although billed as 'Military' its composition was mainly wood-wind, which made it more flexible. Sousa had it under perfect control. His concerts at the Albert Hall and all over the country were packed. He played in the massive Olympia and thousands were turned away.

He was great on 'Request' items. He said it was his duty not to play only what he liked himself, but what his public really wanted to hear. This was first-class showmanship and he was a first-class showman and a musician as well. He would swing from the classics to Plantation Melodies, from a light, sentimental waltz to one of his own stirring marches—and that delighted his audiences.

He was not tall, but he had a tremendous personality. He and his Band wore dark blue military-looking uniforms. Very dark, with *pince-nez* perched on the bridge of his nose, his hair parted in the middle, a sweeping moustache and a spade-like beard, Sousa made that Band into something alive. He performed all sorts of tricks; he did amazing things with his baton.

Sometimes he leaned against his music-stand, twirling his moustache with one hand, twiddling the baton between finger and thumb of the other, whilst he gazed around. Sometimes he seemed galvanic, and conducted by upward jerks and downward thrusts, as if he were digging it out of his musicians. At other times he became a veritable whirlwind and seemed to be flailing the players. But always his beat—and the *tempo* —was perfect.

Of course he had hosts of imitators at once. That was what he wanted. Not only did cartoonists adore him, but comedians burlesqued him and in every pantomime that year somebody gave an imitation of Sousa. It was grand publicity.

Sousa and his marches vied in popularity with the year's most popular song—which happened to be 'The Honeysuckle and the Bee', originated here by that lovely lady Ellaline Terriss, who still graces this world and is as beautiful as ever. Nay, more so, for the silver hair gives a character which enhances the sweetness of the days when that hair was golden.

She was Everybody's Sweetheart. Sousa was everybody's hero. He and his Band seemed tireless. They would give several concerts a day. Once when he was engaged at the Alexandra Palace, in North London, he and his Band arrived very late. Something had gone wrong. The Great Hall was packed with many thousands.

Sousa apologized and gave a magnificent show, but had to cut it short owing to the lateness of the hour.

The Trustee in charge objected to paying him his full fee—which was gigantic. The money had been taken, but he claimed that the full show had not been given.

It was a very moot point. But Sousa waved away the difficulty. Let the Trustee pay him for the portion of the concert he had been able to give and all would be well. That was done—and Sousa got a good Press story out of his magnanimity. But he was never late again.

There was only one other slip during his visit here. He was given, soon after his arrival, a Complimentary Luncheon at the Trocadero Restaurant, London, to which all the celebrities of the time—and the Press—were invited. That famous journalist, George R. Sims ('Dagonet' of the *Referee*), was, of course, a guest. He could make or break a reputation with a paragraph.

Mr. Sims duly arrived but could not find the place said to be reserved for him. At last it was discovered—under the name of Mr. Sims Reeves, the famous tenor, who had died a couple of years before. And that gave George R. Sims—and Sousa—a nice little paragraph for Sunday.

Uncle James took the Boy to see the Coronation of King Edward. They stood in the crowd in Whitehall, but saw it well.

For the Diamond Jubilee there had been seats in St. Paul's Churchyard—magnificent seats—but things had been different then.

He went to see 'Buffalo Bill' at Earl's Court—he had seen him on his previous visit. It was a wonderful show, and a Royal Lady who was to become Queen Mary visited it three times.

In the 'bill' was a lady who galloped about on a horse and performed great deeds of marksmanship with a rifle. She shot down, with unerring aim, plates, saucers and small glass balls as they were flung into the air. Her name was Annie Oakley. Uncle James was of the opinion that the lady's rifle was in reality a scatter-gun. Well—you never know.

The Boy remembers being taken by his Uncle for a ride on an electric tram as soon as they came into commission. He thought it wonderful— but you could not jump on whilst it was going or drop off on one foot with the indolent ease which had been possible on the old horse-trams. No young man, or boy, would have dreamed of getting on or off a horse-tram unless it was in motion. It was almost a point of honour. That applied to horse-buses, too.

He caught a glimpse of the King of Italy when that sovereign came to town.

But there were two red-letter days. By means best known to herself and her sister—the ankle-kicking came into use here—Aunt Mary with Aunt Bessie and the Boy got themselves into the old Gaiety Theatre to see that memorable 'Last Night'.

And Aunt Mary kept a place for the Boy until he could join the queue for the opening night of the new Gaiety. Aloft in the gallery, lost in delight, he saw *The Orchid*—Gabrielle Ray's triumph—and King Edward VII and his lovely wife, Queen Alexandra, made history by attending the opening night of the show and the Theatre. Later—and at not such a distant date—the Boy was to work in that theatre, become friends with all that Cast and even to act as Receptionist to that King and Queen. . . .

Those were indeed red-letter days.

But back to more intimate matters. That Victorian Family—now Edwardians—were together again. Uncle James' good name and his expert knowledge of his business had begun to pull things round. They lived in lodgings now very near that old Victorian home of theirs. Indeed, they lodged in the next road, that lesser road which had been a frontier of the 'Back Piece', although the portion in which they lodged did not abut thereon. It was higher up the road.

The Boy was growing up. He was still much alone, and his school-days were nearing their end. That gave him great joy.

For when the Family broke up and he became a nomad again, he began to lose what little interest he had ever had in his work. He dreamed the longer, he played games with avidity, but he did not work in school. He took no more prizes.

He would neglect his work to ride around on his bicycle. He had one of the very early American bicycles—very light, with dropped handle-bars, wooden rims to the wheels and no brakes at all. It was a marvel he never had an accident—save once when, unable to stop, he fell under the spray of a watering-cart and was soaked completely but not hurt. In modern traffic he would have had no chance at all. But the roads were safe then if you could ride at all and keep your head. He would go for evening spins with his Uncle, as far as Cockfosters, in Hertfordshire, and have ginger-beer—his Uncle had something much stronger—at the old Cock Inn, then a most picturesque old hostelry of very ancient foundation

—once it had been *Le Coq Forestieri* in the old Enfield Chase, hunting-ground of Tudor and Stuart monarchs, and hence the name 'Cock-fosters'. Now it is a very well-run modern hotel—and that Victorian Boy and his wife frequently lunch there on Sundays on the fringe of the Hertfordshire Woods, near where they live.

But when the Boy rode there on his American bicycle, it was in the heart of the country. Southgate, now a large borough, was a village clustered round a Green—which is still there—and then straggling along a high-road. By that Green was a mansion with an old horsepond and water-splash outside, in which mansion lived the famous Walker family—who could put an entire Cricket Eleven in the field—and did so.

And nearby also was Osidge, where Sir Thomas Lipton lived, the errand-boy who became a millionaire and who made such a gallant attempt to recover the American Cup—the Blue Riband of the Yacht-racing world. He challenged with a succession of yachts all named *Shamrock*—for he was Irish—and these had to be built so that they could sail across the Atlantic to race. It was odds against them and the gallant Sir Thomas, who had made his millions out of groceries—and, above all, out of tea. 'Lipton's Tea' was on every hoarding—on every tea-table.

His repeated attempts to bring back the Cup, although they did not succeed, had success in another way—they sent up the demand for Lipton's Tea. He never lost a chance of advertising or of making money.

When *Shamrock* was engaged in a tussle for the Cup, rockets would be sent up from Osidge to give the public some idea of the situation—a green one if *Shamrock* led and a white one if the American yacht was ahead. The white always predominated, but sometimes a succession of green raised hopes—never, alas, fulfilled.

Lipton did deserve to win that Cup. But there is a road on what was once his private estate, which is called 'Shamrock Way'—so the gallant effort is not quite forgotten.

The Boy still read as much as he could. He had not many books of his own now they were in lodgings, but he clung to his old favourites. He went to the local Lending Library—which was some distance away. It was not like the Public Libraries of today, where borrowers go in amongst the books and sample them. You had to make a list of the books you desired to take out from a catalogue. Each had a number. There was a tremendous Indicator in the Library which shut you off from the books. It was divided into hundreds of little squares and each had a number—corresponding with a book. If that label in the square was red, your book was 'out'. If it was blue, it was 'in' and you could get it.

Trouble arose if the librarians forgot to make the change, which only happened very infrequently and mostly when a young inexperienced

Souvenir Programme
OF
"THE FOLLIES"

Under the Direction of H. G. PELISSIER.

NEW ROYALTY THEATRE,

Dean Street, Shaftesbury Avenue.

Lessee and Manager - - Mr. TOM B. DAVIS.

Every Evening at 8.30.

Matinees : Wednesdays and Saturdays at 3.0.

GENERAL MANAGER (for "The Follies") ... Mr. WILLIAM ALBERT.
ACTING MANAGER (for Mr. Davis) ... Mr. A. C. BELSEY.

Programme of *The Follies*, H. G. Pelissier is third
from the right

Philip Raphael—the Boardmen King

Lady bicyclists.

Women in breeches riding bicycles were regarded as just a joke made by a humorous artist. Times have changed—and so have the bicycles

The Derby of the future.

Regarded then as a ridiculous impossibility—women may yet ride in the Derby, but they will not ride side saddle as depicted here

Two pictures from Back Numbers—the paper was *Fun*, a serious rival to *Punch* in Victorian Days

librarian was working himself in. For in those days people really took an interest in their job. They wanted to keep it and get on. It was a disgrace to lose it. They never said: 'I Could Not Care Less'—they said the reverse—or thought it—because the need for saying it never arose.

The Boy still read Henty, until the books ceased, with the death of that great writer in 1902. G. A. Henty—the 'G' stood for 'George' and the 'A' for 'Alfred'—was born in Trumpington in Cambridgeshire, on 8th December, 1832. He went to Canterbury to live when he was five and remained there for five years. The house in which he resided was on the River Stour, and he used to watch the trout therein.

He went to a Dame's School in the cathedral city, but he was a weakly lad—so delicate that his parents did not expect to rear him. His health was very, very bad until he was fourteen, so his schooling both at Canterbury and later at a private school in London—where the Brompton Oratory now stands—was irregular and intermittent. But he had a taste for reading, history and general science, which was fostered by his grandfather—whom he adored.

He read everything which came his way, and laid up that store of knowledge which went to the making of his books.

At the age of fourteen he went to Westminster School, where he was a day-boy, and was rather scorned by his fellow students because he liked writing poetry. He got a poem printed—and the whole school felt ashamed. But it was his first taste of literary success. He was bullied and that gave him the idea of learning boxing—at which he became proficient.

From Westminster he went to Cambridge. His improved health made him, whilst still at Westminster, fully acquainted with the athletic side which was so important there. He did not play cricket. He went in for rowing. When he first went to Cambridge he was still very thin, gaunt and delicate, although much better than in his youth. He had a chest measurement of forty-two inches which was right out of proportion to his figure. But he filled out, and Cambridge did him good.

He went into journalism and became a War Correspondent. He was working in that capacity during the Garibaldi Campaign of Freedom in Italy.

His early boating training gave him a love of the water, and eventually he owned his own yacht—*The Egret*. He got his material—which afterwards stood him in good stead—at first hand.

He had been in the Commissariat of the Army in the Crimea, but was invalided home; but he remained in the Service for five years, travelling around. He had been War Correspondent for the *Advertiser*, but he got on the staff of the *Standard*—the old 'Thunderer'—and writing became his trade.

T

He wrote a novel in 1867 and his first boys' book—*Out on the Pampas*—in 1868.

Then came *The Young Franc-Tireurs*—a story of the Franco-Prussian War—and the immense flood of wonderful books for boys followed. He wrote three a year—and by the time the end of the century came he had turned out over ninety of them—all first class, all exciting, and all very correctly informative without appearing to be so.

He was every boy's hero, and he looked the part. For he had grown into a giant of a man, weighing over seventeen stone, with grey hair, a grey moustache, bushy beard, bushy eyebrows and loose comfortable clothes.

There was always a briar pipe in his mouth and a dog not far away—he had what amounted to a pack of them, of all sorts of breeds.

He wrote his books in a big study, filled with books and the walls covered with trophies of arms he had collected from all over the world. He looked what he was—the ideal writer of books for boys; the sort of man every boy would trust, respect and hold in adoration.

And the boys did that in no small measure.

It is good to see that now his stories are being reissued for another generation of boys and, as boys do not change a great deal, there will be another spurt of popularity for G. A. Henty, the Victorian giant of juvenile literature.

His books did much good, and gave the youngsters a proper view of the greatness of their history, their country and their race.

Another thing seems to have changed, too, since Victorian and Edwardian times. Then, every dog, the moment he saw a cat, would immediately chase it. There was deadly enmity between the canines and the felines. One spoke of 'A Cat and Dog Life'. Dogs killed cats if they could catch them. Nowadays that seems entirely altered. Dogs pass by cats as if they did not exist. Some even seem to be friendlily disposed.

Have the animals changed over? Were they the warlike things in a peaceful world that have now decided to set the humans a good example of peace in a world given over to war and thoughts of war? True, those owning dogs no longer tell them to chase cats, as they used to do. But the dogs needed little telling. They enjoyed it. Now it is another change in a changing world.

The Victorian Boy had decided that his education was over. He was, at this particular time—1902—still at school, but the span of the days of servitude was wearing out and by 1903 it had worn to snapping point. He could hardly endure the last two terms. He did not work at all.

As soon as the Spring arrived he spent his evenings on his bicycle.

This machine had not a new-fangled gadget which was just coming in—a 'free-wheel'—which was just as well, for his only method of 'braking' was to back-pedal. The cycle had an enormous gear-wheel, and was capable of considerable speed.

Near where he lived was a 'Best Road', which had been paved with wood—which was quite a novelty then. It was a long road, quite a mile-and-a-half in length, and to it resorted all the cyclists of the neighbour-hood, and there they rode up and down on this remarkably smooth surface—such a different sensation to that provided by the macadamized roads or those roads made of granite setts—smooth, easy and with the risk of a puncture reduced to a minimum.

You met your friends there—and you made new ones. It was almost a great Club. Young men and women, previously unacquainted, went through the Edwardian process known as 'clicking'. They got to know each other without the formality of an introduction. The day of what was known as 'The Glad Eye' was not yet—although soon to be—but the Edwardian girls on the cycles knew just how to catch the eyes of the young men. They did not wear shorts, of course. They wore skirts which just cleared the ankles. They rode ladies' bicycles, without the cross-bar, and the back wheels of which were protected by a sort of netting made of strands which resembled boot-laces, to stop their skirts from getting entangled with the rear wheel. They wore all sorts of hats, from round straw ones like men's straw hats to quite large and feminine ones. They had bracelets and bangles on their wrists; blouses—and sometimes even a feather-boa draped their shoulders. They were not serious cyclists, but very feminine. They did not lean over their handlebars and travel at speed; the handlebars curved up to them and they rode along sitting upright with as much grace as their proficiency permitted. A few wore flat shoes, but there was a preponderance of high heels.

Up and down that delightful road they went, and glances would be exchanged which often ended in a young man raising his hat—or cap—and perhaps, if he looked all right, he would get a bow and a smile in exchange. The rest was easy.

Or maybe a young lady would dismount and appear to be in some trouble with her machine. A gallant young man always came to the rescue, and it was quite surprising how it seemed to be just the one the girl wanted to know.

The Victorian Boy did not worry about 'clicking'. He went in for speed—and as there was no traffic except for an occasional horse-bus, which was the only means of communication between two prosperous suburbs, he could whizz along. All he had to watch for was that ubiquitous 'Man-in-Blue'—for 'scorching' was a serious matter. But there were only three places in that long, straight road where a 'copper'—or 'rozzer'—could lay in wait, and somehow one always knew—and slowed down. . . .

Sometimes, as real dusk was falling—and it seemed to fall much more gently in those days before 'Daylight Saving'—he would turn off along other nearby 'Best Roads', and there pedal slowly between great gardens which enclosed detached mansions, the walls of which were overhung by lilac, laburnums, May and other blossoming trees, which made the gathering dusk a mass of colour.

Hardly a soul would be about—except for young couples immersed in each other and oblivious to the world, or a servant standing at a gate, watching the world go by—that leisurely, happy world which never thought of war, danger or insecurity.

The Boy should have been studying for the last and biggest examination which was the climax of his educational career. It was a very stiff Public Exam. He did not do one hour of study. That was wrong of him because failure meant a minor disaster, and would upset his Uncle James and his Aunts. But he had already put school out of his thoughts. He had grown up—his lack of a home and his forced self-reliance had done that.

At school he had announced that he would fail, and this was generally believed.

He sat for the Exam. His memory stood his friend, in all save Mathematics—against which he had closed his mind. He handed in that paper—and knew he had failed. It was necessary to pass in every subject; one failure and—however brilliant the rest—the axe fell. . . .

The whole School was assembled to hear the results. The Sixth Form sat in embarrassed prominence—that was the Form which took the Exam. The Boy now began to be worried. He thought of what would face him at home after he had endured the scorn of the Head Master. He did not worry about his school-friends. They understood. He felt pretty bad, did that Boy, but he put on a smile and a slightly defiant swaggering air.

The Head Master, after a glance at the Sixth, announced that on the whole the result was satisfactory. There was only one failure out of all the entrants.

Everyone looked at the Boy and he did his best to meet their gaze. The Head Master proceeded to read out the names of those who had passed—the failures were omitted from mention. The Boy, to salve his conscience, wrenched his mind on to other things. Suddenly he was electrified—he could not believe his ears. His name was read out—not only read out, but he received the astonishing intelligence that he had passed—with Honours—and was Top of the Kingdom in two subjects.

He heard no more. His friends around him thumped him on the back until he was nearly sick. Even the Head Master beamed upon him. The incredible had happened.

It transpired he had managed to get just enough marks to scrape through the Mathematics. To this day he is sure there was a mistake. He is certain somebody else's paper was taken for his. He did not believe he had got a single answer right—but there it was.

The day passed in a whirl of excitement and when his Uncle came home at night, he announced the result at supper in a suitably offhand tone. He asked to leave school that term. His Uncle agreed to that. It did indeed seem to be flying in the face of Providence to attempt anything more.

And so the day came when, at the end of July, the Boy left school for good. Now that he was going, the old place did not seem so bad.

According to his custom, he went all over it—into every classroom, recalling his time spent in each—its triumphs and disasters. It was all vividly clear.

He said 'Good-bye' to the Masters and, finally, to the Head, who asked him about his future. The Boy was evasive about that. But they all wished him luck and then—he passed out of the big iron gates—no longer a schoolboy but, in his own estimation, a young man.

And he left the last vestige of his boyhood at those gates as he walked through. A feeling of exultation surged over him. Holidays ahead and then—well, that could wait. He knew what he wanted to do. Whatever it turned out to be like, it could not be as bad as school. . . .

And during those holidays the Family moved. They had begun their climb back to their old estate.

But the Boy spent those holidays, and, indeed, all the time he could spare, in the 'Best Road' where this story started.

Most of his friends there had moved away—one family had gone to South Africa—but another family stayed on; that which had the little Frenchman for the Father and the large Englishwoman for the Mother. Not only had they been neighbours in the 'Best Road' days, but the boy of that family had gone to the same school, largely because the Victorian Boy went there.

The family also consisted of some girls, amongst whom was a very lively, very slim, brown-haired girl, with very big brown eyes—the girl at whom the Boy had shot with his air-gun from the leads—the girl who had tried so often, and always in vain, to coax some of his Sunday dessert out of him.

The Boy was always in and out of her house in those days—he was like one of the family. He had paid little or no attention to the girl then; but he had, of course, seen her in all sorts of informal attire—in comfortable old dressing-gowns and shoes, with her hair not done; indeed all lank and sagging, from a shampoo.

He still spent a lot of time there—a great deal of time. Now he had ceased to be a schoolboy he was beginning to take a different view of girls. He was beginning to realize their place in the scheme of things. He began to perceive that they were not all rotters, sneaks and stinkers, as once he had classed them. It seemed to him that this gay, sparkling big-eyed girl, with the strong and melodious mezzo-soprano voice, who could play the piano so well and who shared his enthusiasm for the Theatre, was a bit better than most of them. A bit better? A whole lot better! This was something very different to the rest.

This piece of dainty femininity, who dressed so well, and who shone like a jewel, was 'a bit of all right'. And then he realized that he was in love. He had no job, no prospects, no money, and he was just a lad—but that did not matter to him.

He was far more mature than most youths of his age—his rather hard life had seen to that. He made up his mind. This was the girl for him—this was the girl he was going to marry. Quite a number of young men, all much his senior, had the same idea. But he had an advantage over them. He had the friendship of the family, and the *entrée* to the house at any time. And his time was his own. So he saw a lot of the girl.

It is doubtful if she thought much about him. She never troubled to look her best while he was about; she treated him just as a boy and her young brother's friend. There was no ceremony at all. They knew all about each other. But it made no difference to the Boy—he had made up his mind. He was always about, he was always in the way of the other young men when they called round. He saw to that.

And, being free of the house, he often did the honours, and put them at a disadvantage.

There was one whom he had to take seriously. They had been at school together, but this rival had been above him in class, because he was older. They disliked each other, these two. They had fought several times, and the Boy had always won. He took little credit for that—the other was a foreigner. As he had beaten him in War, he reckoned he could beat him in Love.

The chance came. The girl wanted the first copy of a recently-issued magazine about the Theatre. She had the others but she wanted Number One.

Those two rivals promised it to her and both began to search. The elder boasted that it would be easy. The Boy just went about the job. He won.

His rival had to attend to his job of learning engineering. The Boy had all day. He found the magazine; he presented it to the girl, who was genuinely pleased—and a little touched. Thereafter, every time he came, he brought a little offering—a bunch of violets, a magazine, a few sweets. The girl began to look out for him. She found him round the corner by the pillar box when she took the dog out. Nobody saw their meetings as a rule except the crossing-sweeper who swept a clean crossing at the top of the road. Crossing-sweepers have gone, but then it was quite a calling— and they did well, especially on muddy days. All they needed was a broom and a hat to touch. Charitable people did the rest and the pennies mounted up. A good crossing was a valuable possession.

This particular crossing-sweeper had a technique. It was his habit when anyone not a 'regular' used his crossing, to touch his hat and say, with a vacant, simple smile, "My birf'day ter-day." It nearly always worked.

He knew the young couple and all about them. It was no business of his. They disregarded him. They would stroll along the roads, and maybe through one of the adjoining parks. And every evening the Boy came round to the house.

It had a double appeal—it was exactly the same as his old home, the rooms being built the same way. And it held this Girl. And when he left —using the side door, as an old friend and almost one of the family, the Girl usually saw him off.

And then one night, when she was wearing a red blouse and a fawn skirt, and her hair was in two long curls over her shoulder, she stood looking up at him under the flickering light of the gas-jet. He just took her in his arms and kissed her. They gazed at each other for a moment, breathless—and then he left.

But something had happened to both of them. He knew for a certainty this girl was to be his wife. He must make a start to earn money. He did so, without delay.

This was Romance for these two young Edwardians, who were both born Victorians—a thing of sidelong, fleeting glances, touching hands, furtive but precious meetings. Not a soul would have minded them meeting—but that would not have been romantic. So they kept up just a friendly appearance in the house—and outside they were young lovers— he waiting at the rendezvous always early, she hastening towards it. Both hugged their secret to their breasts. Both thought it was simply wonderful and were starry-eyed. They had an 'Understanding'.

But that girl was very popular at dances—little subscription affairs of great respectability at a local hall, over a furniture shop.

The Boy did not dance. He decided that there must be a properly-forged link between them. He must, like Lovelace, put his fate to the test. He must Propose. . . .

CHAPTER TWENTY-ONE

Happy Days

THERE is still a legend to the effect that Victorian and Edwardian men, when proposing to the lady of their choice, went down upon their knees—or at least on one knee—and held one hand over their hearts whilst they stretched forth the other in supplication. Nobody has ever yet been able to produce proof of this, and no Edwardian or Victorian alive ever remembers it being done—much less doing so himself.

The Victorian Boy, when he proposed, certainly did nothing of the kind. He and his girl were in what, in his old home, had been the Little Room—his favourite room—and it was in that equivalent room in his Girl's house that he took that momentous step. It seemed to him the right place. But there was no kneeling, no romantic protestation, no oaths of deep and eternal devotion.

There was a piano in that Little Room, and the Girl was playing it. It was during the Pantomime season and she had been playing and singing a song which had been popular in all of them. It was a sentimental ditty, beloved of the time. It was called 'Good-bye, Little Yellow Bird'—and it told the story of a lady sparrow who was cold and perhaps hungry and who perched on the windowsill of a mansion. Inside the window was a canary in a golden cage—a cock bird—who looked at her in admiration and told her that he had been pierced by Cupid's arrow, and asked her to share his cage with him. The sparrow refused. She surveyed the golden cell of captivity in the warm room, with its little glass receptacle for water and seed—and she replied in mournful tones, according to the song:

> Good-bye, Little Yellow Bird—
> I cannot mate with you.
> I love you, Little Yellow Bird—
> But I love my freedom too.

> So good-bye, Little Yellow Bird—
> I'd rather face the cold
>   On a leafless tree
>   Than a prisoner be—
> In a cage of gold! . . .

Impeccable sentiments, of course, for the dwellers in a country which was really free.

They both liked that song.

Then the Girl sang another love-song—of a more cheerful kind. It was called 'The Little Irish Girl'—about a colleen who was wooed by an Irish youth and he finally won her heart when he told her that he had a cabin—and pigs that numbered seven:

> Her eyes looked up in mine—
> And my heart was in a whirl—
> The little pigs had done it—
> Och, the dear little girl!

The Girl stopped and looked up at the Boy, who was standing by her. He looked down at her. It seemed the right minute.

"Look here," he said, "don't you think it is about time that you gave me the right to look after you—now and always? You know how I feel. Will you let me?"

That was all. She looked up at him, swayed against him—and they kissed.

That was a long engagement, but they enjoyed every moment of it. They went everywhere and saw everything, doing it as economically as possible—but money went far then.

They saw every show in town from the pit. They always managed to get the end seats in the front row. He always bought the Girl a packet of Velma Chocolate—long cardboard packets coloured crimson and gold, with Napolitains inside, each in its own little crimson envelope.

They watched the rich people come into the stalls, and he told her they would be there one day. They graduated there via the Upper Circle and the Dress Circle. But somehow the old pit days seemed the happiest. They had no cares then—and were both very much in love. That has not altered.

They became ardent First Nighters and when, in the early days, there was a First Night at either the Haymarket or His Majesty's—as it then was—they got seats in that wonderful Upper Circle at the Haymarket at two and sixpence and the equally wonderful Upper Circle at His Majesty's for two shillings. He believed that he would eventually work at both those lovely theatres—and he did.

They went for country walks, going out by train, and having tea at little village inns. Wonderful teas, with watercress—lots of everything and new-laid boiled eggs. And they went several times a season to Earl's Court and the White City. They loved both resorts—perhaps the Girl liked the White City best, but the Boy had a sentimental regard for the older place—which the White City eventually killed—because he had been there so often as a child.

Sometimes he would tell the Girl it was to be a Golden Day. That meant he had a golden half sovereign to spend on the outing.

They would go in the afternoon—have a grand tea at the best place; go to the most attractive Side Shows—on the Scenic Railway and the Flip Flap—and the Great Wheel if it was at Earl's Court. And when darkness fell and the lights blazed out and sent golden shafts across the rippling waters of the Court of Honour at the White City and the canal which wound through the grounds—they would sail in the little boats which plied thereon, past the illuminated waterfall, over the sound of the falling waters thereof, came the strains of a string-band playing melody— a waltz or a musical-comedy selection. They had a little dinner; they sat at a table in the open air listening to the band and had a little drink—the Girl had lemon squash—and the Boy would smoke his cigarettes—he liked a special brand called 'Du Perfex' which a firm named Sandorides marketed—and, quite late, they would go home—and would always arrange to do part of the journey either by hansom or taxi. And there was still change left out of that golden half sovereign.

On days when they did not see each other, the Boy always wrote to the Girl, and would send her every new picture postcard of the stage idols as they came out. He believes he sent her every picture postcard of Gabrielle Ray that was ever issued. They have come in very handy since.

They would go to the early Cinemas—often in what had been a shop— where the operator was in full view and the film rolled into a basket whilst the pianist pounded out suitable music to the flickering silent picture—or, in more style, to the now vanished Parkhurst Theatre in Holloway Road, which had surrendered to films when overshadowed as a playhouse by the handsome Marlborough Theatre next door. There they saw, for ninepence each, all the beginnings of the Film Saga—the rise of men like Max Linder, John Bunny—and a funny little fellow who afterwards got his name into the captions—and the bills—and who was Charles Chaplin.

Or they would go up to Frascati's—which has just breathed its last. There, next door to the old Oxford Music Hall, they would sit at a table just outside the inner circle of the restaurant proper, and either have some food or a drink—wonderful Turkish coffee was made there, served by a man who might—or might not—have been a Turk, but who was most suitably attired.

You could stop as long as you liked without being pestered, and watch the people. It was the only place in London where this could be done. It was, on the whole, very respectable and mainly Middle Class—the couple were Middle Class themselves, and aspired to nothing better. But now and again a gentleman would bring in a smartly-dressed 'Lady of the Town' and all the respectable ladies around would bridle slightly, and take in all that the outcast was wearing, without ever seeming to look at her.

In the middle there was an excellent orchestra. The surroundings were of their period and luxurious. The prevailing note of *décor* was not garish at all, it was gold and blue. There were plenty of mirrors and marvellous chandeliers, but the lights did not blaze and bewilder—they were soft and kindly.

Up in the Balcony a dinner was served at seven and sixpence. You got so many courses, with a *Sorbet* halfway to cleanse the palate, that even the appetites of those days were satisfied. More was eaten at a meal than in a week now.

Frascati's was the Winter Garden of London, and supplied a real want. There was nowhere to go for a rest, a drink and some music, but Frascati's. It had a Continental air and yet it was British.

It had been founded by one Krasnopolski, in the late 19th century, and he named it after the Italian village. Most of the *habitués* imagined that Frascati was the owner's name. Foreigners went there and often a man might be seen sitting silently at a table with a glass before him, which was surmounted by a little white metal cup with holes pierced in the bottom. Some colourless liquid was in the glass and the waiter would place a piece of sugar in the metal receptacle and then put in some water. As it seeped through and fell into the glass the liquid therein became milky and slightly opalescent.

That drink was *absinthe*, sold freely then.

Frascati's was a great place for Family Celebrations—Silver Weddings, Engagement Parties, Club, Firm, and Masonic Dinners. It was a real piece of London before the days of the Milk Bars—and if you wanted a drink you got it at no higher cost, but well served, in much comfort, in charming surroundings—and with music. Any brand of whisky was threepence, and a 'splash' was free.

That young couple always dined there on Christmas Eve, when a vast Christmas Tree stood in the middle ablaze with lights. They carried out that custom for many years.

There was no dancing in Restaurants then—although Frascati's surrendered later, and never seemed the same again. In its last phase it was, to its old frequenters, a place of sadness and the ghost of their youth . . . but to that Boy and Girl it was Heaven.

When they first got engaged, being so young they kept it a dark and romantic secret—or so they thought. He gave the Girl a little posy-ring of his Mother's—a little gold affair with a cluster of pearls surrounding a little ruby, and she wore it round her neck on a ribbon.

There was really no need for concealment. And it was not long before the engagement was fully accepted.

The Large Lady told her daughter, 'He'll be all right, my girl, so long as you play second-fiddle!'

The Boy's Aunts even approved the Girl, and Uncle James was very fond of her. Her gaiety pleased him. She could cheer him up.

The Family had moved into quite a large house of their own now, with a threequarter-size billiard table, in a room so big that the short cue was only needed at one corner on account of the enormous sideboard— which was like a young cathedral.

The Aunts, of course, did not think any girl good enough for their nephew; but if it had to be one, then this was the best.

Aunt Bessie had only one criticism. "She's not very well-set-up," she said. That was her yardstick of femininity. She herself was stout and by 'set-up' she meant plump. She divided women into two categories: 'Skin-and-bone'—those were the tall and lean; and 'Little Dutch Skippers' —which were the short and fat.

They had known the Girl for many years and approved of her. They never said so to her face; but they did so at the Church and at the Croquet Club—an offshoot of a big Bowling Club where they belonged, with all their friends, which they adored. There they sang her praises along with those of their Nephew.

The small French Father of the Girl was quite a rich man, but that had never entered into the Boy's calculations. He was always independent and would make his way himself.

And then he had a bit of luck. He got a job which was a regular one and in the West End. He was, of course, in the Theatrical Profession. He also wrote little plays and music-hall sketches, and had quite a success. But this job meant Marriage at last. He was to earn four pounds a week —more than enough to marry on in the days when families were reared, clothed and educated on a weekly wage of two pounds ten shillings.

There was to be no more waiting. The marriage was to take place. Then the Aunts did a little bit of rebelling. It meant them losing their Nephew.

Their expressed idea was that both the prospective Bride and Bridegroom were far too young—mere children, in fact.

But the Boy—and Uncle James—soon settled that, and both families paid ceremonious visits to each other. Elaborate meals were served—and the Girl's Family even went to the length of serving supper in the Dining Room—one of the few occasions it had ever been used for that purpose.

The wedding-day was fixed for the 1st July—when the Boy got his holiday. He was working very hard.

To please his Father-in-Law-to-be, the couple agreed to be married at a Register Office. They knew nothing about Special Licences, so the names were put up in the usual way of that time, and as—although they lived near each other—they were resident in different districts, the ceremony had to take place at a neutral Office some way off. The Girl was instructed to find out where it was, and give the Boy directions. She did so, but they were a bit vague. He was too busy to be able to find out himself.

The Girl was busy, too. She was busy with her trousseau. And if there is any curiosity as to an Edwardian Bride's trousseau, this was it:

Half-dozen vests; half-dozen chemises; half-dozen pairs of knickers—bedecked with lace and embroidery; half-dozen camisoles; half-dozen night-dresses; half-dozen petticoats; two Princess petticoats. Dressing-gown and dressing-jacket.

All the underclothing was of nainsook, fine linen (the Princess petticoats were of Japanese silk) with a lot of lace and embroidery and yards and yards of *bébé* ribbon threaded through everything. The dressing-gown and jacket were quilted blue satin.

As regards dresses, that Bride had a white pearl-embroidered satin dress—which was her wedding-dress and made an evening-dress after, minus the train; a blue chiffon evening-dress, and a black velvet evening-coat. She had four afternoon-dresses: one of powder-blue satin (what would now be called Slipper Satin); one black dull satin embroidered with braid, short sleeves and a tiny basque; a cream lace dress, pink-edged, in flounces, complete with pink parasol and large lace hat to match, and muslin gloves; a plain and beautifully-cut navy-blue satin dress; two tailored suits, one in beige (the Going-away dress); hat, shoes and bag to match, and thick pure-silk stockings; four summer cotton and print dresses; travelling-coat of camel-hair, and an afternoon coat of stiff taffeta, in blue shot with gold.

There were innumerable pairs of shoes, stockings and gloves—and all, save the plain blue dress, went on the honeymoon in an enormous trunk.

And the Bridegroom of Edwardian days? Well, men's clothes don't matter—but he had a very smart morning-coat, vest and grey striped trousers, patent boots with kid tops; a blue lounge-suit (plain navy-blue), a brown tweed suit—with patch-pockets and with a cap to match—and a grey flannel suit. He wore the blue suit to go away in, with a grey shirt and collar and a light-blue-and-white spotted tie, and grey velour hat.

The wedding-morning came. The Bridegroom felt very well—for he had not, according to tradition, spent the night out with his friends. His Best Man had done that, and looked ghastly at the wedding. The Bridegroom, flouting traditional custom, had gone to see his Bride.

His only fear on his wedding-morning was that he would cut himself whilst shaving—for there were no safety-razors then. He did not do so, however.

He had a good breakfast with his Aunts and his Uncle, who were rather more nervous than he was. They were to go to the Register Office in two cars—he and the Best Man and his Uncle in one, and the two Aunts in another.

The cars came, and received general directions. The chauffeur of the Bridegroom's car said he knew where the place was.

They went on and on—and found themselves out in the country. Now the Bridegroom was really upset. He began to fear he would be late and that the Bride would arrive first—an unforgivable calamity! They asked the way—and got worse confused. A policeman then directed them, and they arrived at a big red-brick building with great iron gates— which were closed.

The Bridegroom, in a panic, leapt out and pealed the bell. After a pause—which seemed endless—a very old and toothless man shuffled out and opened the gate.

"Is this where you get married?" demanded the Bridegroom. The old man roared with shrill, senile laughter.

"No, 't'aint!" he said. "This is where you come to after you're married. This is the Work House."

Everybody talked at once, and Uncle James could be heard saying they would have to make other arrangements!

But the old man knew, and gave them clear directions. They went off at top-speed—and they got there three minutes ahead of the Bride. . . .

She wore full bridal array—she was not going to be cheated of that— white satin, veil, wreath and train complete! For the Reception was to be at the Waldorf Hotel—then quite new and smart.

The ceremony did not take long. It was a lengthy drive back to the West End—partly through the City—and everybody spotted them.

For some time, in the thickest of the traffic, they were tagged on behind a Carter Paterson's van, and an object of interest to the van-boy, who swung on the rope in the rear and regarded them.

Suddenly a seraphic smile overspread his face. He retired into the van and reappeared with a bassinette—which was a species of baby-carriage. To this he directed the young couple's attention with huge delight—and then they managed to get ahead. . . .

The Wedding-breakfast was a big success.

This was what a Middle Class Wedding-breakfast was like in Edwardian Days, for, although George V sat on the throne then, the Edwardian Period persisted.

Melon Canteloupe
Canape Moscovite.

Truite Saumonnée à la Royale.
Homard à la Parisienne.

Mignonette d'Agneau au Beurre Noisette.
Crème Favourite.
Pommes Macaire.

Mousse de Langue au Paprika Rose.
Poularde en Casserole
Cœur de Laitue aux Pommes d'Amour.

Asperges Verte Froides.

Macedoine de Fruits Glacée Waldorf.
Charlotte à la Russe.
Gelée aux Marsale.
Coupe de Patisserie Française.

Corbeille de Fruits.

Café.

Wines: St. Julien 1900; Rudesheimer 1900.
George Goulet, Extra Quality
1906.

Liqueur Brandy.
Benedictine.
Crème de Menthe.

Apollinaris.
Iced Syphon.

There was an orchestra, which played the Wedding March as the Bride and Bridegroom entered, and everyone enjoyed themselves.

And amongst the music the Band played was: Léhar's 'Count of Luxemburg'; Finden's 'Indian Love Lyrics'; Dvořák's 'Humoreske'; 'The Pink Lady' Waltz; 'Barcarolle' from *The Tales of Hoffman*; Archibald Joyce's Waltz, 'Dreaming'; Sousa's March, 'El Capitan' and—as a portent of the future, 'Alexander Rag'. . . .

What the Large Lady, the Bride's mother, said to her daughter when leaving for her honeymoon, is worthy of note: 'Good-bye, my girl. You might as well be dead as married!'

Bless her, she did not mean it. She was very fond of the Bridegroom and was a good friend to him always. But she liked to make remarks like that. . . .

And so that Victorian Boy and Girl—now an Edwardian married couple—went on their honeymoon—spent at the best hotel at a favourite Devon honeymoon centre—returned to their nine-roomed house with its large garden and general servant—and started their married life on £4 a week.

The married life still goes on—forty-two years have passed since that day and these words being written—and still they go on—he earns many times that amount now, but they are not nearly so well-off as they were in Edwardian times . . . and concern with them finishes here. . . .

But there is much to say of the life which had gone on during that engagement and during the first two years of the married life—they were married in 1912 and the First World War brought their own world crashing about them only two years later. . . .

The Edwardian Era was the richest and most colourful through which this realm has ever passed in its long history. Those were peaceful times and, although there were many domestic excitements, nobody considered War. And nobody considered being killed by bombs in their own homes. That was never dreamed of. Not even the first Zeppelin (Zeppelin II) scared them. They called it a German Sausage. Sausages and Germans were synonymous—and nobody took sausages seriously.

Life went easily if more speedily. The weekend habit grew and grew. The motor made that easier. Crazes came and went; bicycling and roller-skating were two such fashionable habits. Cycling, of course, remained but roller-skating was left only to its devotees when the fashion ebbed.

Aeroplanes of curious type sometimes crossed the sky and brought everything to a standstill whilst crowds stopped, stared into the air—and maybe wondered.

Paulhan the Frenchman and Graham White the Englishman had an aerial race from London to Manchester for a prize given by the *Daily*

Mail. They followed the railway-line, and Paulhan won. Bleriot flew across the Channel and the *Daily Mail* blazed headlines, 'England no longer an Island!' The aeroplane had come to stay!

But still people lived the same happy lives.

Politics had been exciting. In 1906 an attempt had been made to alter the old tradition of British trading. It was generally regarded that the basis of Britain's commercial supremacy was Free Trade.

Joseph Chamberlain did not think so. He told the country about the inroads Germany was making; how she dumped surplus goods here at a ridiculous price, and cut out our own working-men. He demanded the erection of a Fiscal barrier against foreign goods, and the Unionist Party adopted Tariff Reform as its policy.

The Liberals at once raised the cry that 'Your Food Will Cost You More.' The Tariff question split the country.

Never before, even over Home Rule, had Party feeling risen so high. Families quarrelled amongst themselves, old friendships were broken. Men who had voted Conservative all their lives could not follow Joe Chamberlain, they now discovered. But the Conservatives believed they would win.

With Balfour as their Leader, they went to the polls. There was a good deal of unemployment, and they thought this would be their strength. Indeed, in the summer of 1905 there had been quite a battle in Manchester between the Unemployed and the Police. Yet the majority of people considered that the Unemployed were really the 'Unemployable'— and said so.

The election in February 1906 was one of the most exciting the country had ever seen. The Conservatives—Unionists, as they were called—had been in power for years. The Khaki Election had given them a huge majority. They believed in the driving-force of Chamberlain, the business man.

Free Trade or Tariff Reform was the issue—with sidelines about Chinese Labour in South Africa.

Polling Night was one of seething excitement. Shops showed the results, either by writing them on transparent paper held before a lamp, or by verbal announcement.

And the results were surprising.

Manchester polled first—and heads fell. Free Trade swept the poll. Balfour was defeated, and other great Conservatives followed.

The Industrial North was solid for Free Trade. Only Birmingham stood firm for its own Statesmen—the Chamberlains.

The Liberals were returned with a majority of 104 over all other Parties combined. They held that power for many years.

That election swept Labour into the House, too, for twenty-nine members of the Independent Labour Party were returned. And the Irish Members—who so often wrecked the plans of all Parties—were there, too.

The result was more than a mere change of power in the House of Commons. It was the dawn of a new era—the ending of the great surge of Imperial Expansion of which Chamberlain was the spearhead and Kipling the Poet Laureate, for the more moderate age of Liberalism and Dominion status. This was really the beginning of the end of the Old Regime, although nobody realized it. The British, by refusing Tariff Reform, were starting another Reform—a Social Revolution.

Things moved very fast, to the beat of the Internal Combustion Engine and to the beginning of the age of Flight and Speed.

Campbell-Bannerman had resigned in 1908 and the man who had been his Chancellor of the Exchequer took his place at the head of things—his name being Asquith. And a little Welshman named Lloyd George became Chancellor in his place.

Old Age Pensions arrived in 1908—there is an idea that they are quite modern, but they were Edwardian.

And in 1909 the Veto of the House of Lords was assailed bitterly. It was a desperate struggle and—whilst it was being waged—the heart and centre of the Edwardian Era passed away. King Edward the Peacemaker died.

His greatness will be assessed—is being assessed—by History. His reign was short, but more eventful than that of many a sovereign who had reigned for a much longer period. He saw the rising power of science and machinery; he saw the Old Order begin to pass; the beginning of the Suffragettes; the decline of power in the House of Lords; the rise in power of the Commons; and the immense and growing menace of Germany. But he had kept the Peace, and as these lines are being written, that Entente, which he brought about, is celebrating its Jubilee.

Under him, his country had been prosperous and happy. It had been carefree. It had a golden sovereign, who was a man of the world, and a sportsman, on the throne. It had a golden sovereign in its pocket to spend. It did not worry much about what went on abroad. It lived its life as it wanted to live it—nobody interfered with it. Taxation was light and there was real freedom. The Englishman's Home was still his Castle.

The more elderly of the Middle Classes were perhaps aware of a restlessness—a slight lessening of parental authority—a demand for more independence on the part of their young people. More and more women went out to work—until they got married—marriage was still woman's ultimate aim.

But there was a distinct restlessness.

Still Family Life held on and was the bedrock of Society. People lived in much the same way as they had under Queen Victoria, even if many things were done in a less formal manner. But still the Middle Classes gave their little dinner-parties in their own homes, with all their possessions on view; with the silver and the *epergne* on a damask table-cloth decorated with smilax, and still the At Home Day was of supreme importance. And so were Morals.

Scandal was to be avoided at all costs—Divorce was social death for a woman and not much less for a man—and for the men Bankruptcy meant social banishment.

Women were still essentially feminine, despite the growing uproar of the Suffragettes. They still wore purely feminine attire. Some of them smoked now—mostly in private. But most girls did not care two hoots about the Vote; they cared more about the Tennis Club, the Amateur Dramatic Society, the Social Life of their suburb and the Theatre.

They cared most about the places where they could meet young men who might 'pay attention'.

It was still possible to ring a bell and have it answered immediately. And the Middle classes deemed it necessary to have a servant—two if possible—but certainly a 'General!'

Domestic Servants were an Industry—and newspapers catered for their advertisements.

The *People* charged them a special cheap pre-paid rate of one shilling for eighteen words.

The rate for 'Situations Vacant', 'Articles Lost or Found', 'Apartments', etc., was three lines or under, two and sixpence; ninepence a line after—two lines of words of average length came to about twelve words, so the 'Servants' did very well.

Here are some advertisements of those who took advantage of the cheap rates:

General seeks situation, 19, strong country servant, cook and wash, excellent references.

Girl, 16, as General. 9 months character; 5/– weekly; also General, 3 years character, £12.

General Servant, age 20, strong, willing girl, can do plain cooking, tall, neat appearance, 11 months character, £14.

General Servant, age 20; neat and willing; good personal character, wages £14–£16.

It will be noted that the girls insisted on their 'willingness' and their characters. And that they did not object to being called 'Servants'. They described themselves as such.

And the 'Situations Vacant' column in that old newspaper dug out of the 'Box Room'—that 'Back Number' which holds such a comparison with today and whose mirror reflects such a different life, is also illuminating. Here are some extracts:

Wanted. Lad (sharp) in the Physiological Department of the Charing Cross Hospital Medical School, 52, Chandos Street, Strand, W.C. Must have passed sixth standard at school; hours 8 till 5-30. Wages 10/- a week. Apply personally, Monday 11th May at 10 a.m.

It is safe to conjecture that a small army of boys, all neatly dressed, with hair brushed and clean faces, all very scared and self-conscious, sent on their way with their Father's blessing and their Mother's care, were lined up for that job. Ten shillings a week to start—why, most office-boys got 7s. 6d.!

And the advertisements for servants show the growth of the Flat habit.

General (superior) wanted age 25, small flat, 2 in family, plain cooking, easy and comfortable home, £18–£20.
Superior General, 18–28, small flat, 2 in family, no washing, good outings, £18.
General Servant wanted, 3 in family. Abstainers. £16.
Superior General Servant wanted for small flat, 3 in family, plain cooking; wages £14–16.
Cook-General Wanted; plain cooking, early dinner; house-parlourmaid and nurse kept.

The address to that was 100 Gleneldon Road, Streatham.

General Servant, age over 20; small family, no cooking, no washing, good home, good outings, wages £16.
General Servant Wanted, age 16–30; 4 in family, mistress superintends cooking, no washing, early dinners, wages £16–£18.

Those were the degrading servile jobs which nowadays a housewife has to do herself. And if the idea may linger that those wages were disgracefully small, that old 'Back Number' can supply some idea of what it cost to rent or buy a house which would have had a 'Box Room' for 'Back Numbers.'

Overlooking Epping Forest, Forest Lodge Estate, Whipps Cross. Freehold 24 ft. frontage. 4-bed. bath (h. & c.), 2 sitting rooms, good garden, electric light and gas, close station, excellent market, price £500, easy payments.

Bush Hill Park, Enfield. 5-roomed houses, close to station, cheap fares to City; rent 6/9 per week.

Croydon (healthiest town in England). New houses, six rooms (extra large kitchen), garden, close Mitcham Common, 8/6. No rates.

Chingford. House to let, containing five bedrooms, bathroom, 2 parlours, kitchen and scullery; rent £26 p.a. 20 mins. from Liverpool Street.

Villa Residences, Poynter Road, near Enfield 3 min. walk Bush Hill Park Stn. G.E.R.; with penny workmen's trains to Liverpool Street, containing 2 sitting, 3 bed, bathroom (h. & c.), good garden. Rent 10/– or lease (ground rent £5) £170; or freehold £290.

One finds illuminating matter indeed in the Back Numbers. The Allan Line of Steamers would take you to Canada and the U.S. for £10 Saloon; Second Cabin, £7 10*s*.; Third Class, £5 10*s*. The Birkbeck Bank offered 2½ per cent on deposit accounts, payable on demand. But the Birkbeck Bank went broke before the First World War.

The firm of J. W. Benson Ltd. offered 'The Best English Lever Watch made' for £5 5*s*. in silver cases or in 18-carat gold cases £12 12*s*. John Noble Ltd., of Brook Street Mills, Manchester, offered knock-about frocks for girls from 1*s*. 6*d*. The price—for hopsack or cheviot—varied according to size and ran from the 1*s*. 6*d*. advertised line through 6*d*. rises up to 5*s*. 6*d*. Postage was 4*d*. extra. Costume skirts for ladies—in black or navy serge—were 4*s*. 11*d*. each; a full dress-length of Zibeline (48 inches wide) or Cheviot Serge (52 inches wide) cost 7*s*. 6*d*. for six yards. And Ladies' ready-made costumes in Zibeline or Cheviot, coat-and-skirt, or bodice-and-skirt, could be obtained for 10*s*. 6*d*. The colours available were Heliotrope, Turquoise, Electric, Old Rose, Green, Brown, Grey, Navy or Black.

Ward's VI-Clothing Co., of Gateshead-on-Tyne, announced that 30,000 Tailors were panic-stricken at their prices. And well they might have been, for Messrs. Ward offered a gentleman's suit for 13*s*. 3*d*. They exhorted you to see the London Papers. Thousands measure themselves, they proclaimed. Readers of this paper thunderstruck! 'See our printed letters of Delight and Surprise! We supply you with Gentlemen's Business Suit, specially made for the coming season, guaranteed to stand sun, rain or sea. Our "Wholesale Price" to readers is only 13*s*. 3*d*., carriage free. Before you buy please send us a post-card for patterns and tape-measure which you can keep. Size of gentlemen no object. "The bigger the better." Gentleman's suit to measure only 20*s*. Gentlemen's Waterproof Over-coats with vertical pockets, only 13*s*. 3*d*. See our 13*s*. 3*d*. Gent's Over-coats. Thousands of Testimonials. Exact Copy: Beulah House, Audlem, Cheshire. Dear Sir—Suit to hand and delighted; splendid fit, better than ever, another order soon. A man that works for his wage and doesn't support your firm must be mad. Yours truly—Rev. W. H. Bishop.'

Messrs. Ward's final offer was £1000 if their testimonials were not genuine.

An older 'Back Number' than that copy of the *People*—the *Morning Leader* of 23rd June, 1894—contains some astounding advertisement bargains.

The Association for the Promotion of Home and Foreign Travel offered a Return-ticket to the Antwerp Exhibition, with substantial breakfast and table-d'hôte dinner—and six days' hotel accommodation, for £3 3*s*.

Messrs. Hetherington's, of 334 Strand, would transport you to New York for as little as £2. Canada for the same price. New Orleans £7 17*s*.; River Plate £7 10*s*.; Cape Town £9 9*s*.; Australia £13 13*s*.; New Zealand £15 15*s*.

No wonder so many people 'Made up their minds to sail away'—it seemed a shame to stay at home.

The 'Wanted to Sell' column had bargains, too; a nearly new mail-cart for two children was going for 15*s*. A Nearly New American Organ, with full gadgets, was offered at 5 guineas cash; a nickel-plated banjo complete with case could be had for 15*s*. A landau-shaped bassinette which cost 5 guineas was offered at 37*s*. 6*d*.; another with high wheels and good condition was only 15*s*.; and a third which was 'nearly new' and complete with rug was a bargain at £2. There was a Piano—a Chappell—with check-action, trichord, handsome walnut case and nearly new, for which the owner wanted only £13.

But perhaps the biggest bargain was a Wagonette to carry six, in good condition and complete with lamps and cushions for the knock-out price of £9.

You could get bargains in the best makes of bicycles which varied from £2 15*s*. for a Humber up to what appeared to be a perfect miracle by Barratt of Wolverhampton and which cost £10 with complete equipment down to the oil-can.

The *Morning Leader* itself was a bargain at the price of one halfpenny. Its advertising rates were 14 words for 6*d.,* three insertions for 1*s.*; 'Situations Wanted' and 'Apartments to Let' got three extra insertions if unsuited, and Classified Trade Advertisements were 6*d*. a line. . . .

And out of the pile of magazines in the Box Room comes another 'Back Number'. It is the *Coloured Pictorial*, Vol. I, No. 1, and the date is 24th May, 1902.

On the cover was an excellently-coloured picture of Miss Maidie Hope, the actress. The frontispiece was a picture of the Countess of

Westmorland, a beautiful lady in a wonderful hat, who was to have a stall at the Imperial Coronation Bazaar. The price of this magazine was 2*d.*, and it ran to thirty-two pages of illustrations (many full page) and much editorial.

A feature called 'Random Reflections' gave interesting information.

Mr. Cadbury, the great manufacturer of chocolate, was advocating Old Age Pensions of 6*s.* a week for everybody over sixty-five years of age, 'from the King downwards'. The paper had some caustic remarks about this—and was satiric about Andrew Carnegie trudging to the Post Office to draw his little bit, and Alfred Beit, the great financier, overwhelmed with monetary problems, drawing comfort from the fact that at least he could count on his 6*s.*

It appeared also from this column that the Boer Delegates in Pretoria, discussing the final Peace, purchased two ping-pong sets. Ping Pong was the original name of Table Tennis. It was first played with rackets covered with vellum, like small banjos. When they hit the ball it went 'Pong' and when it hit the table it went 'Ping'. Hence the name.

There were illustrations of H.R.H. the Duke of Connaught; Mr. Beerbohm Tree (as he then was) as Ulysses—and Mrs. Brown Potter as Calypso in the same play, at His Majesty's, both drawn by Buchel; a double-page centre in colour by Tom Browne, in his inimitable style, which showed a tramp of the period facing a housewife (also of the period). The joke was: "Tramp, 'I lived without food for a month, Mum.' Housekeeper, 'How did you exist?' Tramp, 'Why, Mum, whenever I thought of me 'ome and fr'ens a lump used to rise in me throat, and I used ter swaller it. By that means, Mum, I was able to——' Then the dog was let loose. . . ."

There was a full page in colour of the Imperial Court at Earl's Court Exhibition ('Paris in London'). A full page in colour also of Marie Studholme, and another of the volcano in eruption at St. Pierre in the West Indies.

Other illustrations covered a sketch of the new Gaiety Theatre and many photographs of Colonial troops in London for the Coronation of Edward VII; the trial of a man who had forged £5 notes, with Mr. Charles Mathews, K.C., cross-examining; a feature about the Theatres and the Military Tournament.

It was wonderful value for 2*d.* It carried good advertising including: Pear's Soap; Wright's Coal Tar Soap; Edwards's Harlene for the Hair, with illustrated testimonial from Mrs. Langtry herself; Mellin's Food (for Infants and Invalids), which showed a baby—presumably before birth—imbibing food from a bottle of the period; one with a long rubber tube, seated in a stork's nest, whilst the stork waited for the child to finish before taking it to the expectant and anxious parents.

Dr. Mackenzie's Complexion Wafers were offered at 2s. 6d. or 4s. 6d. per box, to cure freckles, blackheads, pimples, vulgar redness, rough, yellow or muddy skins.

Allen Foster & Co. offered Ladies' costumes, as per their coloured illustration, at 30s. each; coats at 10s. 6d. and skirts at the same price. They all appeared to use a lot of material.

There was also a picture of Lord Roberts' new house, Moor Park, near Farnham, Surrey, which he had taken, it stated, so as to be near Aldershot. Moor Park was where Dean Smith first met his Stella.

The *Coloured Pictorial* was a wonderful twopennyworth—and typical of its day.

CHAPTER TWENTY-TWO

'Out of the Box Room'

IT is time now to go back into that Box Room—and to make it a composite box-room, partly of the Victorian House and partly of the Edwardian House into which the Victorian Boy and Girl started their married life.

Many things were common to both—in each there was that pile of unbound magazines, in each those old newspapers. There comes to hand a pile of copies of that magazine *The Captain*—one of the best periodicals for boys ever issued. In it are the Victorian and Edwardian 'Giants' who were heroes to the young—and in the case of Sport, to the grown-ups as well.

And in a very early issue there looms the immense figure of Dr. W. G. Grace. The Editor himself had gone down to interview this wonderful man, and found him in his home at St. Andrew's, Lawrie Park Road, Sydenham.

It was a real Victorian 'Best' House, with a high pointed roof, a bay-window and a porch over the front door.

That Editor—whose name was R. S. S. Warren Bell—wanted to see W. G. Grace, because that amazing man was going to embark on a new venture. He was going to start a new County Cricket Club—the London County Cricket Club—to play on the ground at the Crystal Palace.

'W.G.', as everybody called him, was then fifty-one. That rather disposes of the idea that Victorians were often on the shelf at forty, attired in velvet jackets, circular smoking-caps and carpet-slippers. Grace was wearing grey tweeds and a woollen waistcoat. He weighed eighteen stone, but his weight only seemed to increase his agility. He had given up his medical practice at Bristol—Heaven alone knows how he ever found time to attend to it at all, especially in the summer, and was now immersed in his new scheme with the utmost enthusiasm. He

313

gave much detail, and when asked if Ladies would be admitted, stroked that long, world-famous black beard of his and said: 'I think all Members will have the privilege of taking ladies and friends, without payment, into the Members' Enclosure, except on certain big Match Days—when they will be charged admission. It is not customary, on any grounds, to admit ladies to the Pavilion.' Evidently in the Doctor's eyes, Ladies were Not Cricket. He would not listen to the idea of moving trolleys to sell refreshments, either. Refreshments, also, were NOT Cricket.

But he got his Club started with some very good fixtures.

'W.G.' was fifteen when he played his first really important game —being included in twenty-two of Gloucester against All England. He made an excellent 32 and hit one ball right over the boundary, into the scoring tent.

Three years later he scored 224 not out for England against Surrey at the Oval. His record that year was 2168 runs in forty innings, not out seven times. Not bad at eighteen.

He made two 'centuries' in the same match in 1868 and again in 1888; between 1866 and 1890 he made ninety-three 'centuries'.

He was now the greatest figure in the world of cricket, as famous in Australia as at home. His name in the team filled the ground. He was Captain of England.

Perhaps his bitterest moment was in 1882, when he led England against Australia at the Oval and, despite a handsome lead in the first innings, suffered defeat by seven runs.

It was the amazing performance of Spofforth, the Demon Bowler, that beat England. This match was destined to go down in history, for the *Sporting Times* printed that immortal 'In Memoriam':

In Affectionate Remembrance
of
English Cricket
which died at the Oval
on
29th August 1882
Deeply Lamented by a large circle
of sorrowing friends and acquaintances
R.I.P.
N.B. The Body will be cremated and the Ashes
taken to Australia.

Hence the 'Ashes'—still competed for.

Grace lost them first, but played a fine game himself. There was another notable thing about that match. An Englishman, moved to horror at the way in which the game was going, said to the lady with him in the Stand:

'If only they would play with straight bats, they would be sure to get some runs!' To which the lady replied:

'Would they really?—Why don't you get them some? . . .'

Victorian ladies knew little about cricket—and cared less.

No need to go through 'W.G.'s' wonderful career. It is in the reference books for all to read.

There he was, at fifty-one, having just played in what was to be his last Test Match, starting a new Club.

On the cricket-field Grace was the perfect 'all-rounder'. He could bowl tirelessly, he was a wonderful fielder and a master-bat. He never appreciated being given 'Out'—and as this dislike was shared by the crowd which had come to see him play, it is suspected that umpires were often stricken with sudden blindness when 'W.G.' was in trouble. He would make remarks in his curious voice, which contained a squeak and a deep rumble, just when an opponent was going to make a stroke or deliver a ball. He believed that was Cricket.

His beard was everyone's delight, and once he was caught off a ball which went right through it. He was the cartoonists' joy, especially to 'Rip', a sporting artist who did wonderful sketches of the mighty man—and others.

Every year people said, 'This will surely be "W.G.'s" last season'— but it never was. At the end of it he would have made several centuries and piled up well over a thousand runs.

He was idolized. He never became a 'Back Number'.

After a hard day's work he would go home and drag a heavy horse-roller all over the lawn, with his crowd of dogs and cats walking at his heels.

He made his big scores mostly on wickets which would have scared the modern player out of his life. When he played his last Test, in 1899, there was a young player in the team making his first appearance for England as a slow bowler, who afterwards became England's opening-bat and who, in 1926, at the Oval, too, came back to bowl again and skittled out the Australians, winning the Ashes again.

He made his entrance as 'W.G.' made his exit, and his name was —and is—Wilfred Rhodes.

W. G. Grace was a fighter who never tired and whom it was difficult to beat. He was the 'Grand Old Man' of Cricket and there has never been such a dominant figure since. He exercised more influence over the game than anyone before or after. He died in 1915, at the age of sixty-seven, during the First World War. He had not played for some time, but his spirit pervaded the game as he and his laugh—as immense as himself—pervaded the Pavilions up to the end of his life. His body died in 1915, but his spirit goes on, for he is not only an Immortal—he himself was really Cricket.

There was another idol of those days who was the direct opposite of 'W.G.'. He figures in the Box Room, too. This was no bearded English Giant, but a slim dark-skinned young man with a moustache—who was indeed an Indian Prince—and whose name was K. S. Ranjitsinhji. No Englishman could say that—or wanted to. One and all they called him 'Ranji'. Ranji was educated here at school and University, and he loved England and Cricket—the only thing he did not like here was the cold weather. He was one of the best—and certainly one of the most graceful—players of all time. He played for Sussex and there he partnered another giant—Charles Burgess Fry. *The Captain* sent Keble Howard—journalist, novelist, and playwright—to interview 'Ranji', and little enough he got out of the modest, elusive Prince save the admission that his name meant 'King of the Field'—not the Cricket—but the battlefield, he explained modestly.

For Ranji was always modest about his amazing exploits. Under pressure, he admitted to having had a good season in 1896, saying that he 'fluked' 2780 runs—he first played for England in a Test that year and managed to 'fluke' 154 not out at Manchester. Not a bad start.

He did some good 'fluking' in 1900, collecting 3065 runs, with the staggering average of 87.57. To watch Ranji play cricket was to watch poetry in motion. No ballet-dancer ever moved with more grace or precision, and nobody ever had such amazing wrists.

In the days of hard hitting and driving, he went in for cuts and miraculous glides. He would get in front of his wicket and, when the ball arrived, there would be a lightning-turn of the wrists, scarcely perceptible to the eye, and away would go the little red sphere to the boundary. 'L.B.W.' was about the only way to get him out. When he ran between the wickets it was with panther-like grace. He was worth his place in any team for his fielding alone. Woe-betide the batsman who gave him an eighth of a chance.

When he and Fry went to the wickets together to open an innings, then indeed it was Paradise. That indeed was Cricket.

Boys were torn in loyalty between the two idols. Yet perhaps Fry carried the day.

What indeed can be said of C. B. Fry, the complete all-rounder, the 'Admirable Crichton' of Athletics—champion and amateur International in almost every known form of Sport? And a fine journalist into the bargain.

He, too, was on the staff of *The Captain* as Sports Writer. He was every boy's hero in the early 1900s—they took him as their model, they spoke of him with bated breath, they knew all his averages, his records and his scores. To them he was god-like. There seemed nothing he could not do. He was either first, second or third in the averages—often turn-and-turn about with Ranji—from 1898 until 1911.

He was in the select band who scored over 3000 runs in a season. He was at his best when things were most difficult. He topped the averages in 1903 with a total of 2683 and an average of 81.30—the runner-up being 56.

That was a year of terrible rain and bad wickets, but he made nothing of it. Invincible in a tight corner, he would snatch victory for his side from seeming certain defeat.

He had not the beautiful style of, nor was he so attractive to watch as, 'Ranji' or the magnificent Victor Trumper of Australia, but he played cricket as it should be played—he was absolutely correct, a text-book of orthodoxy.

He was most modest about his prowess—he said he thought he might be as good as Tom Hayward. But Tom Hayward was very good indeed.

Charles Burgess Fry still lights the world—that face and figure of distinction, that monocle worn so naturally, that characteristic voice is still seen and heard everywhere cricket is played. Nobody worshipped him more than the Victorian Boy of this chronicle. And when that Boy was a man turned fifty, he got C. B. Fry to do some broadcasts for him, during the Second World War. And although he had half-a-century behind him he felt, in that presence, as humble as a schoolboy again. It was, for him, one of the thrills of his life—and he has had a few.

C. B. Fry has turned eighty—but then he always stood high in the averages. Once he scored six centuries in consecutive innings. He is still—Not Out.

Tom Hayward, with whom Fry compared himself, was Surrey and England—an amazingly sound bat. A large man, going a bit bald towards the end of his career, he turned his face, with its heavy moustache, to the bowling—and he trounced it.

He opened the Surrey innings with his partner Robert (Bobbie) Abel, who was his opposite in almost every respect, for Abel was a very small and slightly bandy man.

Both of them were persistent century-makers. Hayward knocked up 3518 runs during the 1906 Season, which was a record for many years. He never actually topped the averages but was often second, third—or well-placed. His middle name was Reliability—and that is exactly how he looked—a grand reliable Englishman. He and his partner Abel knocked the edge off the bowling attack and one partnership between them at the Oval against Yorkshire produced 448 runs.

Abel was not so orthodox as Hayward—he had a knack of scoring runs between his legs so the bow thereof was useful. He did not top the averages but was, like Hayward, always well-placed.

His bat seemed as big as he was himself, and he was a Surrey Idol—and his idolatry was not confined to that County. Those in the field against Surrey breathed a sigh of relief when Abel was out. But he had a knack of staying—he scored 357 not out against Somerset in 1899, and the Oval-ites went mad with delight.

Both he and Tom Hayward played in many Tests and in the season in 1901 Abel made 3309 runs. He was an enchanting little man to watch.

There are so many names in the Box Room annals which clamour for notice. Great Cricket-Captains like A. C. MacLaren, of Lancashire—who was also a fine bat and who made 424 in one innings against Somerset; Lord Hawke, of Yorkshire, calm, skilled in judgment, sound in all he did, who led Yorkshire and England to many victories—and Pelham F. Warner, who was known as 'Plum' and whose Harlequin Cap made him as noticeable on the field as his superb cricket—under whose Captaincy in Australia R. E. ('Tip') Foster of Worcester (known as 'Fostershire' because so many of that family played for it) collected 287 runs at Sydney in an innings which materially helped Warner to bring home the Ashes once again. P. F. Warner, honoured by a knighthood, bears one of the great names in English Cricket—and that game still has the advantage of his presence and his advice.

There was George Hirst, the burly Yorkshire all-rounder, who invested his savings and benefit-money in a Toffee-factory, and every boy deemed it his duty to buy that excellent 'Hirst Toffee'. He it was who said to his colleague, Wilfred Rhodes—last man in and fourteen runs to get at the Oval Test in 1902:

'Wilfred, we'll get 'em by singles.'—And they did.

Nobody who saw it will ever forget that Match. When the scores stood level, a clergyman in the crowd, who had miscounted, careered over the field towards the wickets, cheering wildly. He had to be 'fielded' himself and sent back.—What an ordeal for those two batsmen at that tense moment! But Hirst and Rhodes were from Yorkshire—and they did it all right.

There were other heroes in that match who helped turn what seemed certain defeat into a victory by one wicket—the Hon. F. S. Jackson, also of Yorkshire, who made a score of 49, worth several centuries! and G. L. Jessop—who, with Jackson, stopped the rot.

That sturdy man of Gloucester, of whom the Australians thought little, came striding to the wicket with his rather rolling, sailor-like gait, and his bat held projecting and sword-like before him, almost at the 'engage', the very embodiment of attack.

It meant nothing to him that the cream of English cricket had succumbed. He was going to show them. He was going to hit. He did—to the tune of 104 runs in 65 minutes.

It was terrifying. They called him 'The Croucher' because of his stance—and indeed he crouched to spring at the foe. He was, indeed, Olympian. He hit everything they sent up, sometimes running out to make a well-pitched ball into a full toss. He hit fours, he hit sixes—he ran between the wickets like something inspired—he and Jackson ran a six and it took Jackson quite a while to get his breath back. Jessop seemed the fresher for it.

He made the Australian bowling look like that of a 'Prep' School. The Victorian Boy saw every ball bowled in that game, and can remember it as if it were yesterday.

He adored the name of Jessop—and that wonderful man still lives, it is pleasant to record.

Nor must the Australians be forgotten: Victor Trumper, fair and handsome and one of the best bats of all time; Noble, Gregory, Bardsley, Darling, Duff, and Hugh Trumble, that tall figure who ran round the corner before delivering his deadly bowling—and many more.

Cricket was indeed the National Game, and interested far more people than did football.

Professional football was looked down upon by the Middle Classes to a very large extent. But Cricket—that was the stuff! You did not really worry who won the match, save in the Tests or in a last battle of the giants for the County Championship—or, of course, the annual Oxford and Cambridge Match. You went to watch the game, to observe the fine points, the variety of strokes, the skill of the manipulation of the ball, smart fielding, stumping, catching and returning the ball.

It was a game of detail in which every movement matters. It was—Cricket.

And to an Englishman the greatest joy in life was either to play himself or to watch a good game. Those away from London were best, and those in a tree-embowered field, or on a village green, the best of all.

The sun, the smell of the grass, the leisureliness, the appraisement, the 'Well-played, sir!'—the spatter of applause, the 'How'z'at?' and the real good sound of a bat meeting the ball in the right place—that was England—and that was Cricket.

Wrestling had never been a sport to draw the crowds until there was a boom in professionalism. Britain liked 'Catch-as-Catch-Can', but it was again a North Country preference. There were the native styles, such as Cumberland and Westmorland. In 1891 Antonio Pieri, the 'Terrible Greek', came here and appeared on the Music Halls in demonstration and challenges in the 'Catch-as-Catch-Can' style.

A rival arose in Jack Carkeek, who issued challenges from the Music Hall stages, notably the Tivoli, and made wrestling a top-of-the-bill attraction. And one night the challenge was taken up by a young man called Georges Hackenschmidt, the Russian Lion.

Carkeek, who knew all about Hackenschmidt, kept dodging the challenger, so Hackenschmidt determined to show Carkeek and the world what he could do.

Hackenschmidt had a great match at Olympia with a tremendous man from Turkey—Madrali, the 'Terrible Turk'.

Madrali was immensely strong, and much bigger than his Russian rival, but Hackenschmidt made nothing of him and smashed him—and his arm—in no time.

Hackenschmidt, a wonderful figure of a man, became a big star of the Music Halls, packing them to suffocation when he appeared.

He lives today, as strong and fit as ever, in a nice house in a 'Best Suburb'. He is just the opposite of what a professional wrestler might be expected to be. He is quiet, thoughtful, well-read and studious—he studies philosophy and has a philosophy of his own—a very good one— and is quite sure that if it were only known and adopted, there would be no more war in the world. He is very likely right, for philosophers are no prophets in their own country, and Hackenschmidt is British now.

The Victorian Boy who saw him beat Madrali is proud that Hackenschmidt is a friend of his—and is delighted to see him and to listen to that quiet, charming voice which always calls one 'My Dear' . . . and long may he live in the pride of his strength—he looks little different now from when he smashed Madrali.

At the same time a small, smiling Jap came here and introduced the science of Ju-Jitsu. He, too, went on the Halls—and once appeared at the Gaiety Theatre as partner to Gaby Deslys, the fabulous Frenchwoman. They demonstrated Ju-Jitsu—and Tani—to show the great George Edwardes how easy it all was—threw that immense man right over his head—but was careful to bring him down safely on his feet. 'The Guv'nor' never went near him again, however.

Tani still lives and looks just the same.

There was during the late Victorian and Edwardian period a great craze for physical development, and one of the leading exponents was Bankier, who called himself—with good reason—'Apollo'.

But the most famous of all was Eugene Sandow, who—like Hackenschmidt—had taken up a Music Hall challenge at the old Royal Aquarium, issued by a strong man called Samson.

Sandow beat Samson easily. He was a man of great physical beauty, with a handsome face—a Swiss. He made physical culture into big business.

He had premises in St. James's and there he trained men and women alike to give them physical strength and the body-beautiful. He did so, too.

He sold all sorts of exercisers, he went into the Cocoa business and he did a roaring trade in corsets. Sandow was a popular idol and a really strong man, who knew his business. He was a great believer in publicity —and took advantage of every opportunity. There was a very popular number in a most successful Musical Comedy produced by Robert Courtneidge at the Apollo Theatre in 1906 called *The Dairymaids,* in which the Sandow Girls figured. The song was sung by Carrie Moore—a very clever Australian who still graces the world, and one of the 'Girls' was a young, tall, striking and very pretty red-haired young lady who is now a great star—and one of the best Principal Boys pantomime ever knew—Dorothy Ward.

It was in *The Dairymaids* that Dan Rolyat, a magnificent comedian, made his first London success—a man destined to be stricken down by an accident which crippled him at the very zenith of his career.

That Victorian Boy and Edwardian Young Man was not an athlete like the men of his maternal side. He adored cricket and played quite well.

Behind the sticks was his place. He was a moderate slow leg-break bowler, and as a bat he would have a go.

He was a more than useful boxer and fencer. His eye was good—and that was his reason for being a good wicket-keeper.

When, after the sensational story by Robert Blatchford in the early 1900s, forecasting a German invasion, he joined a rifle-club, he won many competitions and prizes.

At football, he played centre-half and was reliable. He was no good on the track, or at gymnastics—at the latter a complete wash-out.

But he, like all boys, had a hobby—he had two—one for the summer and one for the winter.

His summer occupation, apart from cricket, was Bird-Watching. His winter passion was stamp-collecting. Up in that Box Room were many old stamp-catalogues. He liked decorative stamps and did not specialize. He would gloat over his Labuans bearing the heads of a sambhur deer—he believes now that they were actually printed for collectors like himself—a Canadian Christmas Stamp which showed a

x

map of the British Empire, those of Newfoundland bearing the head of a small boy—now the Duke of Windsor, and then Prince Edward of York; Malta stamps showing a felucca; three-cornered Cape of Good Hopes; an American stamp showing a Special Messenger actually in the act of hurrying, which was sur-charged Cuba—a relic of the American victory over Spain, and also U.S.A. stamps bearing a picture of the battleship *Maine*—the blowing-up of which caused that war.

He liked the picture of the old Queen Victoria as printed on the stamps of Canada, and those of New Zealand bearing tropical birds. The Nigerian stamps bore a good picture of the Old Queen, too, and he got a full set.

A Sudan stamp showing a man on a camel, a much more picturesque postman than the home variety, was also a favourite, and the Russian stamps with the double-headed eagle in relief, also appealed to him, especially one printed in orange, and one in blue and rose.

Many Japanese stamps were most artistic, and those of Korea were amazingly complicated in design.

There were very attractive Egyptian stamps, too, showing the Sphinx and the Pyramids; and he liked those of India.

The stamps of his own country seemed to him very dull and uninspired, and much of a muchness. He still has the same opinion. Yet this country had invented Postage Stamps.

He never troubled about perforations, surcharges or faults. The Borneo stamps with the Orang-utangs thereon—and those of Nicaragua with some sort of volcano—were much more to his taste. And he prized highly another from Newfoundland which, delicate grey in colour, bore, very fittingly, the head of a Newfoundland dog.

Poring over those stamps, examining the advertisements of dealers in *Chums*—who sent stamps on approval—whiled away the evening hours of the winter delightfully.

He mostly studied them with the album on that table in the Little Room whilst he knelt on a chair—and on Wednesdays a piano-organ always played—and the tune he liked was, 'A Little Bit Off The Top'.

CHAPTER TWENTY-THREE

Give Me Yesterday

IN one of the great melodramas of Victorian Days, *The Silver King,* the author, Henry Arthur Jones, made his hero, in his distress, cry out, 'Oh, God, put back Thy Universe and give me Yesterday.' There is a general belief that Yesterday cannot be recalled. But it can, and that is one of the consolations of Age. Old scenes, old faces, old characters, old places can be re-created—they can be called back by those fortunate enough still to possess a Box Room, although that Box Room is only their own memory. But into that Box Room has gone the lumber of the years and that lumber remains, to be taken out and examined at leisure.

Things hitherto seemingly forgotten are vividly recalled—and the present scene fades into the Past, which lives again. It is not possible to travel far in memory here but still some of the articles, the places and the faces that remain in the Box Room can be taken out, dusted and re-examined, even if that examination covers only a tiny section of such a minefield of Memories as the West End of London. For in Victorian and Edwardian days people went 'Up West' for a complete change from their own surroundings—and got it. They get it still but in nothing like the same way. To go 'Up West' was something of an event, for which one dressed in one's best, put on a smile of anticipation—which was always realized—and entered a region which was totally unlike that of today, in spirit, in life and in personnel. Those who worked in the West End naturally have the most vivid impressions for their daily life engraved deeply on their memory—but even for the visitor, much remained.

People went 'Up West' to shop, to see Life, to go to the Theatre, to dine, and to sup. They went, in ninety-nine cases out of a hundred, for pleasure—and they got it. They got it for a mere fraction of what they pay today and in far more generous measure. They also, if going 'Up West' at night, felt a thrill of adventure—for part of the West End—the

323

Pleasureland thereof—was naughty and people living by Convention found that exciting. And so it was. It was a far quieter and less garish West End. It was more real and less artificial. The places which competed for custom did not find it necessary to indulge in Neon signs (there were none, anyway), blinding, flashing lights, lurid colours and huge pictures or cut-outs of semi-nudity. That was considered vulgar. They relied on what was on their bill, on the names set forth upon the posters, and those names then had more drawing-power than a million Neon signs. The Theatres were still like Theatres and not like booths at a Fair. There was no need for flagrant display—the names were good enough. They were, those Theatres, the places in which Illusion was for sale, where that other life—nearer heart's desire—could be glimpsed; portrayed by mysterious people of the Land of Illusion who did not hobnob but kept behind the frontier of their land—and that frontier was the footlights. The Actor Managers ran the Theatres with dignity—and people appreciated dignity and good taste. The great Managers who were not actors offered their wares with a guarantee of that Quality and Tradition which had made their success, and neither dared nor desired to fall below it. The Theatre was a full-time job—there were no sidelines like radio, films, television or recording. The players either acted well—or they got out. That gave a high standard of performance. So many of those men and women have been dealt with elsewhere that here they must waive their right of entrance. But one of the best beloved of them must have a little space—just to show how different things were in her days—and she is still as gracious as were those days.

Publicity as understood today was then not considered in good taste. The best publicity a player could have was a good performance and the applause of a well-satisfied audience. The word 'Star', if used at all, was used sparingly and the title had to be earned—it was bestowed not by Gossip-writers, journalists and young men who are said to produce radio and television programmes, but by a grateful Public. It was their accolade to one who had given them pleasure. Not much space in the papers was given to individual artists except in respect of their plans, productions and performances. Only a few periodicals peered into their private lives. And the players knew that, as Dr. Johnson had said, 'We who live to please, must please to live.' Although Vincent Crummles was in the habit of writing paragraphs about himself, though never admitting it, and although players were pleased if a newspaper noticed them, not all of them rushed for the limelight of print and the blazoning of their photographs. They knew, bless them, that too much publicity, given too soon, aroused hopes which might not be fulfilled in the minds of that critical Victorian and Edwardian public. They adored applause for Achievement but they did not want unintelligent anticipation. And here is a letter written by a young actress, in the year 1888, to a prominent lady journalist who desired to put that actress's picture in the magazine for which she worked:

Dear Madame—wrote the young actress from her address in Russell Square—*Miss Frost has kindly forwarded me your letter and allow me to thank you for the great compliment but I must decline it for the present on the grounds that I have as yet done nothing to deserve it; but should my forthcoming appearance on the stage at the Lyceum on 14th March be successful, I shall be only too happy to afford you every facility for the publication of my portrait.*

Truly yours,
Julia Neilson.

That's how young actresses behaved sixty-six years ago.

And did she—Julia Neilson—lose by it? She made that appearance at the Lyceum—only it was on 21st March instead of 14th—playing 'Cynisca' in *Pygmalion and Galatea* and she made a resounding success—for she had not been heralded by a deafening fanfare of publicity. She never looked back—she became the idol of the playgoing public, that lovely gracious woman who sits today in her Best House, that mansion by Primrose Hill —enthroned like a Queen and looking far more Queenly than most regal ladies—still ruling that kingdom of hers in the hearts of thousands of playgoers who cherish her memory.

But there she sits, in her favourite chair, which is one of those used in *Sweet Nell of Old Drury*, in which she and her splendid husband made such a vast and lasting success. And there in the room is his portrait—Fred Terry—painted by an eminent artist and given him as a present by the Managers of Theatres to which he and his wife had brought such crowds and such custom. . . .

The Theatre, in Victorian and Edwardian Days, was the aristocrat of the Entertainment World. That is still its title, but like other members of the aristocracy it finds it rather hard to live and maintain its position in a Welfare State which sends, as competitors, machine-made rivals which are either shadows on a screen or which take entertainment right into the homes of the Public, giving them no trouble save the turning of a knob, satiating them without calling for the slightest effort, destroying the great incentive of anticipation and piling one programme on another so fast that no memory remains.

One wonders how much will be left in those Box Rooms of the Memory twenty-five or fifty years hence. . . . Maybe the older, slower Victorians and Edwardians had the best of it there. . . .

Naturally the Theatre in those days presented every form of entertainment, too, but you took it in limited doses, and it registered. Old playgoers are rich in such things—and hold their memories dear—the nights at the Gaiety, Daly's, His Majesty's with Tree, the Haymarket with Cyril Maude, Charles Wyndham and Mary Moore at the Criterion or the New, Alexander at St. James's; Marie Tempest, Charles Hawtrey, Lewis Waller and many, many more wherever they might be. Those people all dealt in laughter, romance and tears, as did Martin Harvey, Forbes Robertson, Seymour Hicks and Ellaline Terriss; Weedon Grossmith, Henry Ainley, Zena and Phyllis Dare, Willie Edouin—and all their noble company.

By and large the Theatres had each their own policy and sold branded goods. You knew where to go to satisfy your taste or your immediate mood. When it came to laughter there was a little company in those days who dealt in that commodity and who always had the good sense never to outstay their welcome. They came to Town, they did their season, often a long one—they vanished into the Provinces—and they came back again with a load of laughs, burlesques and melody, all purveyed with the perfect simplicity of true art, and they were called 'The Follies'. At first glance they might seem just a troupe of Pierrots and Pierettes, for when the curtain rose—there they were in black-and-white Pierrot clothes, against a simple setting—just as you might see such things at the end of a pier. But in the corner, seated at a piano, was a huge, colossal figure—a Pierrot in Black. This was the heart of the show, the brains of the show, the inspiration of the whole thing—this was H. G. Pelissier. Fat, not at all good-looking and on first sight ungainly, this man was a Genius in the real meaning of the word. He had a gift for melody, he was a superb actor, he was a grand comedian and—above all—he was a Wit. His wit flashed, coruscated like a diamond. It had a rapier point. He used satire and irony with such a delicate art that the British Public, always afraid of such things, were powerless in his hands and gave themselves up to helpless laughter. He knew exactly how to handle them. He was one of the first *Compères* the British Stage ever knew. There are hundreds today— but there remains only one genuine *Compère*—H. G. Pelissier. Nothing escaped him; his whispered comments to himself were gems, his announcements volumes of comedy and his audience control something at which to marvel. He had attempted to be a music-hall comic and failed. But Harry Gabriel Pelissier was not to be beaten. He formed his own little Pierrot show—and many of the Company stayed with him up to the end—and they fought their way upwards. They practically 'busked' in the open air at Earl's Court Exhibition, they played in the small theatre which was then part of the famous and mammoth Midland Hotel, Manchester. They

were brought to the Palace Theatre—as a wild experiment—in 1904.
They opened on a night of fog which was the 'Father' of all the 'London
Particular' Pea-soupers. But they shone through that fog like a beacon
light. And they came back year after year. They burlesqued everything—
even themselves. And then they took their own seasons at West End
Theatres, mostly at the Apollo, in Shaftesbury Avenue, and became one of
the 'musts' for theatre-goers. It is not possible to set down in cold print
what those amazing people did under the leadership of their many-stoned
genius. They opened in approved Pierrot style, singing songs of all kinds
—one of them just had the plain announcement on the Programme—
'Morris Harvey Cannot Sing.' Well, Morris Harvey did imitations, which
were the supreme zenith (if there is such a thing) of cartoon and yet
perfectly lifelike. He even looked like the people he imitated. Then, the
pace quickened. In the second half they 'potted' plays—they took the
successes of the moment and held them up to ridicule—and they gave
what would be called now 'productions' but which were the highest
order of Burlesque. They were like a kaleidoscope, the pattern always
changed in the twinkling of an eye and every man and woman played
many parts—each distinct and clear-cut. Nobody who saw them will ever
forget their 'Music Hall', their 'Voice Trial'—even the property-man went
on in that, and 'Everybody's Benefit', which got right to the heart of every
benefit performance ever held and had a tear behind its laughter. It was
Comedy in its best and most difficult form. And there was never a
suspicion of vulgarity or suggestiveness from start to finish. Being really
clever funny people they did not need that.

Pelissier believed in making his audience laugh before the Curtain
went up. His printed programmes alone were worth the money paid for a
seat.

An Apollo Programme—when Morris Harvey, Muriel George and
Ethel Allandale were also in the cast—shows the amazing 'Everybody's
Benefit', the aged beneficiary, Sarah Judkins, getting a postal order for
6d. On the back of the programme was a map: 'How to get to the Apollo
Theatre', which marked innumerable 'pubs'; the War Office with an inn
next door called 'Ye Old Sleeping Sickness', Colney Hatch and Hanwell,
Mr. Pelissier's Garage, Romano's, Fitz's Bar, Public Wash Houses, Bow
Street and Bedlam—everything except the Apollo—with finger-posts
contradicting direction arrows and No Thoroughfares everywhere. But
the advertisements which they codded were, from the amusement point
of view alone, worth the ten-and-sixpence charged for the stall.

The Follies were Laughter. A modern comedian recently issued
posters reading, 'If It's Laughter You're After . . ." and gave his name.
He was right. But the Follies did not only supply it on the stage but all the

time you were in the Theatre—and by memory all the way home—and even today!

There was, of course, Publicity, and advertisements were issued. One of the most popular forms of this was by use of Boardmen, Sandwich-boardmen, poor creatures who made human sandwiches of themselves between two boards and carried another in an iron frame, supported by their shoulders, above their heads. They stood at picked points, they paraded either singly or in long lines in the gutter. They were the failures of the world earning their living, and they were sad to look at. But few people looked at them—they looked at the advertisements on the boards. Sometimes these men wore costume—sometimes their own clothes, more fantastic than any costume a Costumier could provide. They were adepts at 'miking', at vanishing up alleys to have a smoke from the fag-ends they collected in the road—and who shall blame them?

But if you wanted Boardmen—and everybody did—you went to a small, dark man who was a genius in advertising and whose name was Philip Raphael. He could supply them and their impedimenta in any quantities, at any time. He paraded them all before they went out and would pop up to see they were on their jobs. He knew them all and they all knew him. They liked him as their Boss, for he was just and fair. He would listen to their troubles and help them. Boardmen sent out by Phil Raphael seldom dodged their work.

Philip Raphael was dark and he was handsome—something maybe of Spanish ancestry was in that olive skin and distinguished calm face—something of the eternal East in the dark eyes. But he did his job as a job should be done. He had always loved the Theatre; he had gone to all the plays when he was a child. He was no actor, and had the sense not to try, but he made up his mind he must work in the Theatre. He got on the original advertising staff of the London Hippodrome when it opened and was Publicity Manager for the Lyceum in the Smith and Carpenter days of romantic melodrama and pantomime. Then A. E. Felton, the Boardman King, offered him a job as manager. He took it, and he made an offer of partnership which was refused. He opened on his own and he swept the pool. He saw to the placing of all the Posters, the Bills for the Libraries, the contracts for space on the Tubes and Buses. He publicized the International Horse Show every year as well as all the best Theatres. And every year, King George V and Queen Mary received a telegram from Phil Raphael's sandwich-boardmen on their birthdays and the men always received a reply. Raphael supplied men to sell newspapers and periodicals. He built up a very big firm; he never spared himself. At no time strong or robust, he nevertheless served his country in the R.N.A.S. in the First World War. He was a regular First

Nighter and everybody knew this dark little man with the quiet voice, unobtrusive manner and charming friendly smile.

Ernest Trimingham—a coloured man who was an actor and haunted the Theatres—had such a respect for him that he insisted on calling him 'Sir Philip'. He said it was even less than his due.

Times began to change—the thunderous traffic drove the board-men off the road. But he kept on, and his staff was never reduced.

The Second World War was a tragedy for him, but he weathered it somehow. He had no thought for himself; he worked from 7 a.m. until 11 p.m. He never let anyone down in his life. The world of the Theatre is the poorer for his going; for he now takes his rest. But his firm goes on, controlled by his beloved wife and by two other Directors, one of whom started there as office-boy and the other as typist. Philip Raphael, good friend and Gallant Gentleman, was a Back Number in quality who never became a Back Number in reality. His friends remember him. . . .

But it is not possible to embrace all the West End or even Theatre-land—let the last survey be circumscribed.

Much of this book has been written at a window which looks out upon Coventry Street, London, W.1. From it one sees right across Piccadilly Circus down as far as Burlington House, with Eros in the middle distance. Opposite is the Prince of Wales's Theatre. And but a stone's-throw away, and just in sight, is Leicester Square. Coventry Street is one of the main arteries of the West End connecting two of the great nerve centres—Piccadilly Circus and Leicester Square.

The man who sometimes glances out of that window sees a very different street to the one he knew when he was Edwardian and Victorian, too. Just across the road by his side—which is Rupert Street—is that vast Corner House which covers a haunt of his youth which was Challis's Hotel and Buffet—almost a Club to him. All trace of it has gone now, and that enormous *caravanserai* has covered another old landmark, too. Arundel Place—a little *cul-de-sac*—ran into an odd little square of Georgian houses and three hotels. On the corner of Coventry Street stood a silversmith's, with a beautiful old Georgian shop-front, and a window full of Sheffield Plate. The name was Lambert, and the very fine sign which hung outside was taken in every night. There was a night-watchman on the premises, but for further security, because of the valuables in the shop, the firm arranged with Vine Street Police Station to have a policeman on night-duty there, for fifty shillings a week. The policemen liked the job, for some very distinguished people had rooms in the little Square—and quite a lot used the 'West End Hotel' up to a very late hour—the 'West End' was one of the three hotels, the others being the Previtali and the Mathis, and the tips were lavish. Also the policeman and the night-watchman would have conversations through the grille in the heavily-barred shop door. They would laugh and joke, and smoke, to the annoyance of a man who lived at No. 18, who would throw things, including his sponge, soap and even tooth-brush, the missiles inducing a short silence, broken as soon as the conversationalists hoped the man had gone to sleep.

The 'West End Hotel' was a queer little place. It was at the time under notice owned by a man named Da Costa. He was an Italian, who came to this country when he was fourteen years old with about fourpence in his pocket. He got work at a Boys' School, doing odd jobs and cleaning the boots. He cleaned twenty-five pairs of boots every day before breakfast. He slept in the boot-cupboard; his pay was 2s. 6d. a week and his food was what he could get. The proprietress of the school was a German woman. The first time young Da Costa got a day off, he had a month's wages in his pocket—ten whole shillings—and he felt rich. Somehow he lost it all, and had to borrow a few pence from an old Chef who was his only friend in London. But he worked on and on—he did not know the meaning of 'hours'. He rose and he rose—he was for a time at the Pall Mall, in the Haymarket, where that remarkable lady 'Mac' presided over the little bar—and eventually he borrowed some money and got the 'West End Hotel'. He made it a real success and repaid all the backing he had been advanced. He acquired the Burlington Lounge as well.

He married an Englishwoman and had two daughters, to whom he gave a good education. One married a waiter at the Carlton and the other an official in the Italian Embassy; and both husbands rose in the world.

The 'West End' did a very discreet business. It had a restaurant where the food was first-class and the service perfect. It had private sitting-rooms upstairs in which food was served and privacy maintained for the customers. Bedrooms could be hired—and sometimes the object was not slumber. But its *clientele* was of the *élite*—names well known in every walk of life went to the 'West End' and no scandal ever resulted. Da Costa kept secrets as tightly as the grave. His prices were high but value was given.

There was security and tact. Earls, Barons, Lords and ladies—with a small 'l'—rich business-men, knights and baronets, admirals, generals—all sorts of people turned up that little street and went into the 'West End'. Men who directed the government of the country, writers, actors, artists—and Horatio Bottomley. Some had suites there which housed fair guests. It was all very quiet—and outwardly respectable. The place was within a yard of Piccadilly Circus—yet off the map—a strange little backwater left over from a former age. The freehold of the square in which it stood had been lost over a game of cards in the days of High Play—in Georgian days. In Victorian days it belonged to two old ladies and once a year a barricade was out across the entrance of Arundel Place to preserve the right-of-way. The Georgian houses dreamed of the more romantic days—and secret romances went on still under their tiled roofs, and card-parties, too. Cabmen knew it, and were particular about the pronunciation—they always put the accent on the last syllable. There was a tennis-court at the top of it, which was still in use up to the First World War.

There was more in the 'West End Hotel' than its lounge, its restaurant and its bedrooms. There was a Bar. This was all in white enamel and had large mirrors round the walls with some perfectly frightening paintings on them; nobody knew who had done them, but it may have been artists in debt paying off old scores. Still, despite that, the bar had an atmosphere. It was by way of being the most exclusive Bar in the whole of the West End—it was more secluded and therefore more exclusive than that of the Pall Mall. That entrance was right on the Haymarket, and anyone could drop in. But at the 'West End', one had to know where it was. It had tables and chairs, seats by the walls, and over it presided Bunny. She was about as unlike the popular idea of an Edwardian or Victorian barmaid as chalk is from cheese—as Apollo Belvedere from a Zulu. Those who did not know the ladies who served refreshment in those days draw pictures of monstrous women with immense bosoms and thighs to match, towering piles of dyed golden hair and powdered, simpering faces. Well, they were to be found—and still are—but not in the best places, and, indeed, they needed hunting for.

Bunny was the direct opposite. She was a small woman, with very dark and glossy hair, drawn back from her forehead and done at the back. She had a red-cheeked face, a dominant but well-shaped nose, and very dark, penetrating eyes. They missed nothing, those eyes—and she read men's and women's characters as one reads a newspaper or a book. A quiet woman, she kept perfect order with unforced authority. She tolerated no nonsense, and indeed none of her regulars would ever have broken a rule. For she had rules and enforced them. Outsiders who got 'fresh' found themselves 'outsiders' in a brace of shakes—outside the 'West End Hotel'. She could hold a conversation with anybody on most topics, for she was well-read and well-bred. Her father had been at Christ Church, Oxford. She liked the life—she was a rebel at heart. She found it interesting. She had had bad times and remembers still meals at coffee-stalls—and good meals, too—for a few pence. But she established herself, and she was a personality in London, known by all who were really inside West End life. She treated everyone with courtesy and she expected courtesy and respect herself. She got it, too, and she got friendship and affection. She could and did give both herself. If you were a friend of Bunny—if she approved of you—she never forgot you. Into her bar came all sorts of people. Amongst the very regular regulars were Maurice Farkoa, the musical-comedy star, the Turk who was more French than the French and who was regarded by ladies as a real Parisian. His manners were as faultless as his singing—and he sang love-songs with great charm. Sometimes they were considered a little *risqué*—they would not raise an eyebrow now—but he never gave offence. He played the banjo well and sometimes he would, with Bunny's permission, play it in the bar and serenade her.

Bertram Wallis, that fine handsome musical matinée idol, was another 'regular'. What a figure of a man; a real Victorian Edwardian, tall, strong, upright, resonant-voiced and with just the suspicion of a British Bulldog on his handsome face.

George Barrett, the comedian so often at the Prince of Wales's Theatre almost opposite—the West End was almost a Club for the actors there—would be in at lunchtime and before—and after—the show. He was a splendid actor; he made a great success as 'Tom Lambert' the trainer in the record-breaking *The Whip* at Drury Lane. He had the kindest heart, and every Friday night he would go down to the Embankment with fifty shillings in his pocket, and give money to the broken, hopeless men, sheltering under Hungerford Bridge, bringing a gleam of light into their darkness. Bunny collected for separate shillings for him. His mind was unhinged by the First War—he served gallantly on a minesweeper, and eventually he committed suicide.

There was a tall, very thin but distinguished-looking man who was an *habitué* of Bunny's Bar. He was always accompanied by a greyhound which looked very much like him. He was Frederick George Fenn—son of George Manville Fenn, the famous writer of books for boys. But this son was a dramatic critic, and a playwright with successes to his name. He wandered round town all day with his greyhound, calling at the various Bars, and the West End was on his regular list. Sometimes these visits would make him, well, forgetful, and he would lose his dog. But the dog never got really lost. It knew its master's last place of call, and when he got there, however late, there on the steps of Queen's Hotel, in Leicester Square, was the greyhound. Both dog and man were delighted at the reunion.

E. H. Kelly and George Graves—the original Baron Popoff of *The Merry Widow* and, with Arthur Roberts, one of the greatest gagsters of all time—were in and out each day. And a very frequent caller was that Edwardian young man who now, much older, sits in his Coventry Street window delving into his mental Box Room.

It was an odd but atmospheric place, that little hotel, with all the charm of the unusual. Da Costa's manager was his nephew, who was blind, but a splendid man of business.

Frank Otter, a strange character who drank only champagne, whose face was the colour of a Victoria Plum and whose voice matched it, except that it had a slow somnolent note, was a great West End-er too, and Bunny knew him well. And outside the West End was a small area covered by a barred grating. Nobody working at the West End ever need be in want of a hand-bag; there were always half a dozen or more, many of them in excellent condition, in that area. For when the pick-pockets and bag-snatchers got away with their capture and were lost in the crowd, they made their way to Arundel Place, removed the money and things of value—and slung the bag down the grating.

Bunny had also been at the Queen's Hotel, Leicester Square. It is still there, still a first-class place, but very much altered since Victorian and Edwardian times.

This was the place of meeting for the sporting fraternity. Its Grill Room was unique. It was a painted room, divided into four pictures, each representing one of the Seasons of the year with every flower, fruit and animal—game animal for eating—depicted with great artistry. There was an excellent orchestra presided over by Mr. Barbirolli, father of Sir John, the great conductor. In that orchestra was De Groot, the violinist, who wore such a beautiful diamond-ring and was a law unto himself. He was told he must not use the lovely marble staircase, which was reserved for guests and customers, he must come in the Staff door. So he walked down that staircase and out of the front door, over to the new Piccadilly Hotel, where he became famous.

Great characters used the Queen's. A gentleman rider from Ireland, named Adam Black, who always wore a blue and white vertically-striped collar, once rode his horse into the front entrance, up that same marble staircase forbidden to De Groot, round the landing on the drawing-room floor, down the stairs and out of the front entrance again. That was the sort of thing which happened at the Queen's in those days.

Another regular customer, a professional Backer, who used it as his headquarters when in Town, always brought his own solid silver dinner-service and gave marvellous dinners and suppers there. That Front Hall had a mosaic floor, and a clock which carried the Signs of the Zodiac; and flights of very well-painted swallows decorated the walls of the staircase down to the dining-room and Restaurant. The Wootton family, famous trainers and jockeys, were always in and out. So were Peggy Bettinson and the Boxing fraternity. Indeed, all the jockeys were to be found there; it was like an enclosure at Newmarket. They used to cheek Bunny but she could hold her own.

Many of the frail but fair ladies of the Empire Promenade dined and supped at the Queen's. But real celebrities like Adeline Genee, the dancer, herself often lunched there and so did many smart Society people. The bar downstairs was quiet in the afternoons, but there was a bit of a surprise one day when Bunny was sitting there at rest. Down the stairs fell a very flash-looking woman indeed, ending up in a sitting position on the floor. Bill Adams, the waiter, was equal to the occasion.

"No ladies served down here, Madam!" he said sternly.

The semi-recumbent lady looked at him.

"Bless you," she said, "I ain't no lady. I'm 'One of Those' and I want a brandy-and-soda." She got it. Bunny saw to that.

But Bunny herself caused a stir down there once. It was Derby Day and all the staff had backed King Edward's horse, Minoru. It won—by a very short head. There were celebrations at the Queen's, and a German *commis* waiter declared that the second horse had been 'pulled' by arrangement to let the King win. Bunny set about him, verbally and physically, and he came off second—by many lengths.

Bill Budgeon in the Queen's Bar, when cocktails came into fashion, was the best mixer of them in Town.

A last glimpse of the old West End discovers other customers, too, such as John Goulden, manager of Mudie's, in Coventry Street, the smartest stationers in London. He used to go down to Buckingham Palace and take Queen Mary a selection of their goods for her to choose Christmas presents from. He looked like a prosperous country gentleman, and he lived at an hotel in Hounslow. When off duty, he would come to Town and to either Challis's or the West End—or both—in rough tweeds and a tweed hat decorated with flies, for he was a mighty fisherman.

And once the Crown of England itself entered Bunny's Bar at the West End. In came a 'regular' of hers, dressed as usual. He was a short man and a bit stout, wearing striped trousers and a black coat and vest. His tie was of black with red spots—the colours of his native county of Durham. He popped in every day for a glass of sherry. This time he had a small black bag with him, and he called in the early evening. In that bag was actually the Crown. He was the man from the Court Jewellers, who always accompanied the Crown Jewels, or any portion of them, when they left the Tower. He had collected the Crown from Windsor Castle, for it had been on Queen Victoria's coffin that day. He should have had an armed guard, but they had lost each other in the crowds. So he was taking the Crown back by himself, and he came into the West End for a drink, in the ordinary way.

The Crown got back all right. He and his daughter had seats in the

Abbey for the Coronation of King George V and Queen Mary, so he was near the jewels even then.

Mervyn Dene was another West End regular; so was that excellent comedian Horace Mills—but the list could go on interminably.

Bunny ran the place perfectly. She knew all the secrets and never breathed one—she keeps them even today. She was one of the best-natured and most generous women living, and she remains so today. When she went out, she used to give poor, hungry-looking children some money, until a cabman told her she was wasting her time and her cash.

"They'll only 'ave it took orf 'em, my dear," he said. "If they look 'ungry, better ter give 'em a meal." She saw the point and she would collect hungry boys and girls, take them to Lockhart's and fill them to bursting-point. They thought the Age of Miracles had come to pass!

Bunny and Mac, opposites in appearance but of the same heart and spirit, are very old friends. They worked together at times. They are friends today.

'Mac'—who is Helen Macdonald—so calm and serene, with such a twinkle in her eyes and a sense of humour, which she shares with Bunny, was as dominant at the Pall Mall as Bunny at the West End. She knew everyone and all about them. She stood no nonsense and, like Bunny, she knew secrets and kept them. She was as kind and helpful to young beginners as a woman could be. She had—and has—a big heart and is a wonderful woman. Indeed they both are, these two ladies whom the unknowing might class as 'Barmaids'. Mac was at the Westminster Theatre during the Second World War. She ran the refreshment side, and saw that it ran like clockwork. She braved the bombs, she slept in the Theatre so as to be on her job. It did not do her much good. But she is still the same generous soul and good friend.

Bunny clings to the old friends who remain. Letters go to her from that window in Coventry Street—the street she knew so well—and she replies gladly. She made that Edwardian young man's grandson a delighted boy when he received two walking-sticks from her; one a memento of Victoria's first Jubilee, and the other from the timber of a famous old Wooden Wall of England. And the grandfather got a beautiful Malacca cane, the property of a celebrated Victorian, and found his own name, in the shortened form used by his friends, engraved on the silver knob. It goes everywhere with him now—passing its old and much-changed haunts. And on his walls hangs a picture which every frequenter of the Pall Mall knew well—that is from Mac. The two ladies still brighten this world, and Mac goes down to the little Lincolnshire village where Bunny now lives—and they talk about old times. Bunny's name is Emily Hartley. . . . They are Victorians of the real vintage, genuine, big-hearted, understanding women who know the world. They are not titled, of course, but they are more than that; they are ladies in their own right, these two delightful women who once stood behind the Bar in Victorian and Edwardian days . . . bless them both!

And up and down Coventry Street go the crowds daily. It is a different crowd and they pass many different buildings. Some of those buildings went because of bombs, some by rebuilding. What was once the Globe Restaurant, next door to that window where this book took shape, became the Café de Paris, and held tragedy one night of blitz. It is open and working again now. It is much grander and more resplendent than in the days when it was the Globe—but then it saw life, too. It was a quiet-looking place, much frequented by the Ladies of the Town with their escorts. Little lamps stood on discreetly-shaded tables. And often, by some strange mischance, the lights would go out, and then there were high old times. What was its ground floor is now a first-class Cinema with a policy of its own, run as a place of entertainment should be run by an expert manager, whose name is Ernest Luke and who comes from Cornwall. He does things as they were done in the days of the Back Numbers. The crowds go by and the Edwardian Young Man—now a Back Number himself—watches them. They are, to him, strangely attired, they speak a slang which is not of this country. They do not seem to smile as much as they did. But probably they enjoy life and would think the way of life to which *he* was accustomed 'a perfect scream'.

There are Milk Bars and Pin-Table joints instead of places he used to visit and shops at which he dealt.

But that is Modernity, too. It is sometimes quite a surprise to see English people amongst the crowd of young men with no hats and odd-looking shirts and odder-still-looking ties, who speak with a Trans-Atlantic accent, but then that accent seems general nowadays.

But the 'Back Number' can close his eyes and wrench his mind back; and it seems to him that the past comes through and he almost believes it time to drop into the Pall Mall or the West End, to see who is in Challis's, or to go down to Stone's in Panton Street, or over to the Queen's for lunch . . . and then he opens his eyes and remembers.

But nevertheless he has his 'Box Room' into which to retire, and from there he can bring the lumber of the past and spread it out for others of his age and period to see, with an almost certainty that they will have a stirring in their memory and delve into their 'Box Rooms', too.

He watches life closely now, and he watches the shy oncoming of an English spring very closely indeed. He notes each tiny change, each step forward in season, the coming of the almond blossom, the dusting of the chestnuts with buds of gold, the daffodils, the crocuses—and he hears the birds tune-up. He knows each note. That has always gone on and will always go on. He may see a few more, he may have seen his last. Who knows—and in these days who cares? But he has a great affection for the spring. He and his wife both came into the world then, and he knows that, whatever happens to them, to the rest of the people, spring at least will never become a Back Number . . . for no Back Number really does.

CHAPTER TWENTY-FOUR

Old-Fashioned, Obstinate and Unashamed

AT no time was it intended to make the book which finishes here a chronological chronicle of its period. It does not pretend in any shape or form to be a history. But it does attempt to be a picture of the period with which it deals, and as the characters that appear herein are drawn at first hand from close relations—and in one case the very closest possible —it does claim that they are correct. Also, the description of the house and its furnishing is actuality—for that house existed until a bomb destroyed it completely in 1941—and was known intimately. The prices mentioned, the service described—all is factual. For the writer has got so tired of seeing Victorian interiors and exteriors designed by young gentlemen who were probably not alive even when George V reigned, and of hearing equally juvenile gentlemen on the British Broadcasting Corporation—with its acquired American accent—dismiss the Victorian Era as being entirely composed of aspidistras, antimacassars and hansom-cabs, whilst its people were all sanctimonious, pompous idiots, hysterical and impossible females or sneering villains, that he thought it as well to put on record what things were really like. And this book tells the truth about them.

As regards Edwardian Days, they are here, too, and when good King George V succeeded his great father, there was very little change. It was still the Edwardian Era, hastening to its doom. This land was still the heart of a Great Empire; it was still the richest place in the world and London was still the nerve centre of finance. A Briton—or Englishman if preferred—was safe in any part of the world. The Royal Navy 'Kept the Seas'. And, except for a small minority, a good time was had by all.

There were, it is true, signs of change even then. There was a greater restlessness, and parental authority was not so strict. The 'Child' began to come into its own, to be glorified—no longer to speak only when

338

spoken to—to be both seen and heard. There was an almost imperceptible slackening of discipline and a little more looseness of speech. But not much. Women began to go about more freely and even to smoke, sometimes in public—but never in the street. But Family Life held on. By-and-large, people lived and did much the same things as they had done under Queen Victoria—and because there still remained so many Victorians, that was natural. You could not forget the old Queen. A handful of small change is a constant reminder of her—and she can be met with still. The writer has just tried it—not that he had much money in his pocket to take out. There were only nineteen coins in all—and twelve of them were pennies. But there she was—solitary but still present—on a penny dated 1898 and remarkably well preserved. Another penny bore the head of King Edward, dated 1903, six other coins were of George V, and the rest of George VI. Thus the Victorian and Edwardian days hold on—the numbers of their units lessening constantly as they go back to the Universal Mint—but still in circulation.

The couple who figure in this book, married when young Edwardians, although Victorians by birth, can act as a standard of how Middle-Class people then managed to exist. They took a house in a nice Northern suburb, not too far away from their respective families, but far enough to prevent too much 'dropping in'. Both were agreed about that. They paid £42 a year rent. They would not buy outright for £350, because it was not a freehold and they were quite sure they would move to something even better in a very few years' time.

Their dining-room was furnished with an oak suite which they still use today—and there is not a creak in it. All that has gone is the table, which they sold back to the manufacturers, who admitted they had nothing like it (between the Wars)—and got several pounds—and a refectory table thrown in.

The dining-room was green and brown: a green Axminster carpet; plain brown paper on the walls; an oak book-case and Welsh dresser, which displayed their silver—both still in use—blue-and-white ornaments; sepia prints on the walls; casement curtains of fawn with lace insertion—all made to measure—and a bronze club-fender.

The drawing-room—or lounge—was grey and mauve. The furniture was of Sheraton type and there is still some in their home—with a rather charming upholstery, six chairs, two arm-chairs and a settee. Again, casement curtains and also long curtains of heavy corded grey silk, with key-pattern in mauve and pelmet to match, across the french windows.

Their large kitchen and scullery contained everything they could possibly want. The hall and the stairs had green Axminster carpet—that in the drawing-room was grey Axminster with clusters of pale pink roses at the corner. Their 'Little Room' was blue and comfortably furnished with bits and pieces of their own. It had blue linoleum of the best quality.

Their own bedroom, in the front, was a pale lime green, with a mahogany suite—a double-bed, four chairs, wardrobe, washstand with marble top, and dressing-table—light in design but solid in quality, and again the room was linoed and covered with a thick green drugget and rugs. And again casement curtains to match the room.

The back-bedroom was furnished in oak and the scheme was blue and pink, with blue lino.

The servant's bedroom—for they had a 'General'—was a comfortable room with a lovely view; and then, across the entire width of the house, ran the Box Room—which they had linoed as well in case they should want to use it as a room at any time. There was a separate W.C. and bathroom.

The whole job—blinds and all—was done by Maple's and cost well under £300. The house was lit by electricity.

His fare to and from the West End cost the young man a shilling a day. It costs him much more than that for a single journey now. The rates were £5 a year. They lived well and entertained their friends to little dinner-parties. Their outlook was quite rural, for their long garden ran down to the grounds of a large mansion which were full of fine old trees and flowering shrubs. Masses of laburnum and lilac bordered their fence, and the birds sang. Tradesmen almost fought for their custom— especially when it became known that they paid cash—and up the road every morning came a man crying 'Hot Rolls' which they bought and had for breakfast.

It was all very wonderful—but two years later the world crashed in the First War. Luckily for them, they managed to preserve their home. . . .

But up to then the world had gone very well indeed. If strict formality was lessening, morals were still of the utmost importance. Women were still essentially feminine, despite the activities and din of the militant Suffragettes.

One of the great arguments advanced by the Suffragettes was that if women had a say in things there would be no more War.—Well, they got the Vote—but there was a little bother known as World War the Second. . . .

But so far the world had changed very little—to the outward eye. Actually it was changing very fast. From what did that change start; where was the beginning? Most people would say the First World War, but that was not so—it changed the whole world, but this country had begun to alter before it.

Such a soundly built, old-established affair could not crumble at short notice, of course—but the alteration into what is now known as 'The British Way of Life' had begun in 1906.

That was the beginning of the change in the structure of this land and its Society—its social economy and condition. And the inherently conservative British brought it about by refusing reform and sticking to their old customs. This conservative stand was not the work of the Conservative Party—but of the Liberals. By voting for a conservative idea in 1906 the nation defeated the Conservative Party. They clung to an old belief, sponsored by the Party of Progress—according to Liberal ideas—and rejected a radical reform sponsored by the Party of Reaction —again according to Liberal ideas. That conservative principle was Free Trade. The overwhelming victory of the Liberals on that issue put the Conservative Party out of office for many years. And being firmly in the saddle, on account of conservatism, the Liberals proceeded to work Reforms.

Many of those reforms were needed and all of them were good. Nothing was dashed at and done without counting the cost—social reform was carefully thought out and due attention was paid to the burden it would lay upon the nation. And taxation remained low. Wages also were low, judged by present views. According to the annals of a great store, which still carries on—in 1899 and for years afterwards a top-grade clerk got £2 a week and senior counter-assistants were paid 35s. But look at what living cost them! There is a list of Christmas presents which could be given—these were all packed for transport— which would cost about 1s. or 1s. 6d. by Carter Paterson.

There is a case which contained three bottles of Full-Bodied Port, one bottle medium sherry, three bottles of Old Scotch Whisky, one bottle of unsweetened Gin, one bottle of Brandy and three bottles of Good Claret—and the whole cost one guinea.

And if you wanted to send a real Christmas Hamper, this Store had just the article. Here are the contents: One turkey or York Ham (13 lbs. in weight), 3 lbs. Plum Pudding, 1 lb. finest Muscatels, half-pound Jordan almonds, 2-lb. box Mixed Fruits, 1 lb. Crystallized Ginger, 1 box Carlsbad Plums, 1 'Verona' cake, 2 boxes 'Cosaques', 1 bottle Fine Old Scotch Whisky, 1 bottle Old Port.—And the cost?—£1 10s.

That is a microcosm of the cost of living when cigarettes were sixpence for twenty; a good suit made to measure was £2 2s. and a pair of boots good enough for anyone cost 8s. 6d.—real leather, too. And the cost of living did not vary until the First World War.

The new Liberal Government had its eye on the House of Lords— referred to in the Commons as 'Another place'.

Hereditary Government was going to be scrapped—if not at once then by degrees. This reached a climax when the Lords rejected the Lloyd George Budget of 1908. He had to find an extra fourteen million pounds to meet increased expenditure on the Navy, brought about by the German expansion of their fleet, and to meet the Old Age Pension scheme.

There was a General Election. The Liberals won but by a reduced majority and the state of the two great parties was almost equal. But the issue had been the Veto and on this point the Irish Members and those representing Labour were on the side of the Liberals. So there was a majority against the Veto of one hundred and twenty-two. In face of this the Lords passed that disputed Budget without any change in it—although some of the money required was to come from Land Taxation.

Then the Government proposed to abolish the Lords' Veto on matters of finance and to limit it anyway to a period of two years, and to reduce the life of any Parliament from seven to five years. Lord Rosebery saw the red light—he was a Liberal Peer. He produced a 'Reform the Lords' idea of his own, the most striking feature of which was the abolition of the hereditary right to sit there at all. The warring parties faced each other for a death grapple—but King Edward caused a cessation of hostilities by dying himself.

The combatants were hushed and had a Conference. But as soon as the mourning period had passed, war broke out again. The Conservatives now produced a scheme for the House of Lords' Reform. There was another election and the Liberals came back again in power. They put forward their scheme and Asquith announced that he had received the consent of the new Sovereign to create as many Peers as he needed to put this Bill through the House of Lords. Lord Lansdowne—a Conservative Peer—and A. J. Balfour, head of the Conservative Party, counselled surrender; but Lord Halsbury led the 'Die Hards' in a last stand.

The Bill which destroyed the Lords' Veto on Finance and limited it anyway to two years, became Law.

That was the beginning of the change in the social structure of this country.

Bills for Home Rule for Ireland, Disestablishment of the Church in Wales, Abolition of Plural Voting—very near the hearts of the Lords—and Insurance of the Workers for Health and Employment now became Law. Japan joined France and Great Britain in a Triple *Entente*; unconditional arbitration was agreed with the United States of America, and the maintenance of a Supreme Navy was agreed to by all. And the following—quoted from a book written in 1913—is illuminating, in view of the World situation today:

Few men on either side any longer wish to increase or diminish the size of the Empire. The problem to-day is to defend, develop and consolidate the vast territories which owe allegiance to the British Crown. Canada, Australia and South Africa are now less daughter-nations than Allies. The Colonial Conference has become the Imperial Conference, the Colonies have become Dominions and their Governments negotiate commercial Treaties with foreign Powers. Canada and Australia are creating their own Fleets. More frequent and systematic consultation between the Governments is desirable, and an important step was taken at the Conference of 1911, when the Foreign Policy of the Mother Country was explained to the Dominion Premiers. But every project of Fiscal, Military and Political Unification must be tested by its bearing on the sovereign principle of local autonomy. . . .

That is an interesting piece of statesmanship which comes out of the Box Room. Some of that vast Empire still exists—huge tracts and myriads of people have broken away—although some still remain in what is called 'The Commonwealth of Nations'—and people in power still make exactly those same remarks.

But the change inside this realm began at the top. Certainly Old Age Pensions, National Insurance—'Ninepence for fourpence' was its nickname; the employer paid ninepence and the employed fourpence (and Lloyd George said the outcome would be 'rare and refreshing fruit')—workmen's compensation and child welfare helped the working classes immensely. It was the other end that felt the beginning of the pinch. Their land was taxed and their veto gone—the hereditary right to govern which had ruled this kingdom for so long, was no more. The Aristocracy stood aghast. It was the beginning of a Revolution! But no heads fell. Revolutions happen in this country by legal instruments instead of guillotines.

Comic papers began to publish drawings of Peers in full regalia doing menial jobs, with their coronets on their heads. Few of them, nowadays, can rustle up their own coronets or robes for a Coronation. They showed, too, impoverished peers conducting parties round their proud mansions and taking tips for so doing. Well, that is the saving of what is left of the Stately Homes in these days—only there is no need to tip and half-a-crown is charged for entrance.

True, the Nobility, even with their Veto freshly shorn away, were still rich and still had the means to support their town- and country-mansions. It was from these mansions that the country had been really governed for so long—rather than just within the Gilded Chamber. Those houses were greater than the House of Lords itself—they were, indeed, part of England. They stood serene and aloof in the parks, girt about with woods and tall trees, led up to by avenues perhaps centuries old.

The village-folk still looked upon the Great House and its People with the utmost respect, and the People—who were called, locally, 'the

Family'—took the greatest interest in the village and its inhabitants. The villagers knew all about 'the Family' and, whilst a bit in awe of the heads thereof, they were firm friends with the younger members who had grown up amongst them. But they never felt a feeling of equality with the Family. They did not want to do so. Tradition was far too strong for that. The ghostly fetters of feudal times still bound them even if they did not realize it.

But there was the House, for all to see, and they were as proud of it as if they lived there themselves. It was a symbol of the British Way of Life (as known for centuries) and of the Kingdom itself—sound, solid, solvent; peaceful, strong and gentle at one and the same time—quite complete in itself and looking as though it had always been there—not made by Man at all but natural growth.

The tenants dealt with the Agent who knew all about them—and they knew that he knew. They asked for repairs, for new gates, new roofs, maybe for time to pay the rent when in trouble; and they considered that, by-and-large, he treated them fairly. There was a school of thought rising, which came from the big cities, which said that these estates should not be, that it was not right or social that so few people, by the accident of birth, should own and hold so much land. There was so little land—and so many people who had none.

Money, goods, trade, commerce, shipping, wealth—all that could be increased. But try as you might, you could not increase the land.

Of course, these suffering serfs were the virtual owners of vast tracts of land across the seas and emigrated to them—but that was not England, their own England. So it was whispered that the Land should be free and that these people who owned it, and lived like little sovereigns themselves, should be dispossessed. "The Earth is the Lord's and the fullness thereof!" thundered a demagogue. 'Yes, but that does not mean the lord—with a small "l"—who owns the land.'

That sort of talk did not particularly interest any but a very few of those who came under the jurisdiction of the Great House. They did not particularly want change. They had never known any other system and it seemed to work all right.

Besides, they had pride in those Great Houses and Estates. They liked to see the carriage—and, later, the car—sweep through the opened gates between the great brick pillars, whilst the lodge-keeper touched his hat and his wife curtseyed. They touched their own hats and curtseyed, too, according to their sex, and did not feel degraded.

It appears now that they were shocking examples of 'Back Numbers' who should long ago have been swept away, and not even put in the Box Room.

The down-trodden servants of the House—the butler, the footmen (who actually wore livery!), the parlour-maids, house-maids, cooks, housekeepers, 'tweenies', kitchen- and scullery-maids; gardeners, odd-job boys of all kinds—even the lodge-keepers—had no idea that they were slaves. Not even the personal maids and the valets thought so—the latter believed that they were 'gentlemen's gentlemen'. There was great competition to join those ranks of slavery. Around those Houses were the outlying woods and brush, and great belts of bracken amongst which deer still sheltered and wild-life ranged free and undisturbed. There were the paddocks where the children of the House learned to ride, almost as soon as they could walk—for the Horse was still a power. And those who served the House by serving the Horses—the coachmen, the grooms, the ostlers, the stable-boys—they did not think of themselves as slaves, either. They took a delight in being trustworthy. For behind those protecting Park-walls, there were stables, and although the Horse might be in process of being driven off the roads and streets, under the wing of the Great House it still reigned. Saddlers still had plenty of work. The Horse came into its own when Hunting started—for there were many Hunts then. Men in 'pink' and women in habits with veils on their tall hats—riding straight, both men and women, astride or side-saddle according to sex, but taking their fences.

To shoot a fox was an unforgivable sin. There were huntsmen and kennel-men—slaves, as well, of course—and game-keepers in velveteens who protected the pheasants and other birds from poachers—who got their living off these Houses indirectly, although their poaching was on such a small scale to that which came later—and those keepers in their velveteens, with their dogs, their guns and their comfortable cottages, were, of course, serfs as well.

Presumably the very deer were slaves, although they never knew it. Cars began to creep into portions of stables—and the men who drove them—called chauffeurs—wore a livery like other slaves and touched their caps as well. Around the house were smooth-shaven lawns, great borders ablaze with flowers, rose-gardens, Dutch-gardens, pools of water-lilies in which slave-goldfish swam; fountains and terraces. On those lawns, under spreading cedar trees, the slaves served tea to the Tyrants. The Tyrants were themselves slaves to convention. They all dressed for dinner—not to do so was unthinkable. Everyone wore the right sort of clothes at the right time. The ladies left the dinner-table when their hostess gave her signal, leaving the men to their port and cigars—and the port still circulated according to the proper custom.

There were the great rooms of state, the smaller rooms of comfort, the majestic staircases; the picture-gallery where former Tyrants—who had also been the slaves to their Land and Conventions—gazed from golden frames. There was the library, and the special sitting-rooms, the billiard-room, the gun-room.

The seasons came and went and the same things were done.

There was the 'London Season' when the Great Houses were empty. The Twelfth of August was sacred to St. Grouse and the Northern moors; the First of September to the partridge and the stubble; the First of October to the woods and rocketing pheasants who had their protection withdrawn and fulfilled their destiny. . . .

It had always gone on and it always would. So they still thought—with the shadow of approaching dissolution already on them.

Cricket was played on its own field under ideal conditions—cricket as cricket should be played—country-house cricket, the finest of all.

Those Estates and Houses had been built up with loving care—for centuries. Men had planned for posterity. And in the Edwardian Era they were still in their prime. At the House-parties given by these idle rich people, affairs of State were planned and decided more quickly than in the regular place where Laws were made. Wires were pulled, it is true, and family connections were of more value than money—although there was enough of that. Politics were the topics, parliamentary campaigns were planned—garden-parties were given to which the lesser-breeds were invited—and how eagerly they came, and how proud they were to be there!

Those Houses did as much towards ruling the Empire as did the Houses of Parliament! And with considerably less trouble.

And in those days Members of Parliament were not paid for their services. These idle, rich people found a lot to do. The eldest son had his career around him—the estate. His 'coming-of-age' was a tremendous affair in which the whole of the neighbourhood—the whole County—joined. But as a rule he spent some time in one of the Services, too. The younger sons actually worked—yes, worked. They went into the Navy, the Army, the Church and the Law. They went into the Indian Civil Service, the Colonial Administrations, and many became Pro-Consuls and attained Peerages of their own. They went to the uttermost ends of the earth, serving their country, risking their lives, their health and much else, for very small financial reward. It was seldom they could live on their pay. And wherever they went they took England and some portion of that Great House with them, and ordered their lives thereby. It was all very absurd, all stupidly feudal, old-fashioned and, according to modern ideas, effete and wicked. But it was almost as much a Closed Shop as a Trade Union. It was not easy to be accepted in those Great Houses unless you belonged to that Union which in Victorian days admitted only Birth and Breeding, but in Edwardian days opened its doors to Wealth as well. But money was not the master-key. Artists, writers, poets, dramatists, actors and suchlike had little chance. Only the most eminent got invited occasionally. Yet Queen Victoria had given the Stage its first accolade when she knighted Sir Henry Irving; and under her, too, Tennyson had become a Peer. Actresses had no place therein. The Stage was still not 'respectable'.

The girls of those Houses got married after they had made their debut and their curtsey to their Sovereign—and made suitable marriages, too. If their luck was out, they lived at home and devoted themselves to good works. They had their allowance. And yet titles were already going into business. A titled lady ran a most successful exclusive and expensive dress-making establishment under the name of Lucille. She started a new idea—she gave the dresses she created special names. It was most thrilling.

Centuries before Victoria, and still in her early days, these idle rich had been the patrons of Art—they had by that patronage made it possible for geniuses to get recognition, and rise to fame. But that was dying out ... there are artists and writers today who would be glad of such patronage indeed.

The Great Ladies themselves did not attempt to retain a youthful appearance as their years increased. They grew old and mellow like the houses in which they lived. When they became Dowagers they wore easy, shapeless garments, making no pretence at fashion; shady and comfortable hats, and never worried about hair-dye or cosmetics. Cosmetics had seldom worried them. It would not have been easy to preserve a permanent wave or a complete make-up whilst riding to hounds in a gale of wind or driving rain. They took their ease and they were the Ladies Bountiful. They instructed the head gardener—or thought they did. They consulted with their Housekeeper; they drove about in little pony-carts and visited their tenants. They brought help and comfort to the sick and what was required for ailing or delicate children. They did not do this as an act of charity but as something which was natural and right—and so it was regarded by both parties.

These ladies pulled strings, worked their cunning wits and long experience for the good of their Party and their Family. They were indeed a part of England—and no unimportant part, either.

The First World War sounded the final knell of that peaceful England, lapped in security by the peace and progress of centuries. Those Great Houses wore mourning for their sons whenever there were any of the little Wars in which the country engaged. Few of them but lost sons or close relatives in the Boer War; and they were all up to their necks in the First World War—and never recovered from it. Those families and those Houses and Estates, all of them founded on some form of Private Enterprise, got their death-blow after their sacrifices in blood and wealth in two World-conflicts. Their money was gone, their land was going . . . has gone, in many cases!

Nationalization is the panacea for all ills. Well, Nationalism has done one good thing. It has saved many of those Great Houses from complete destruction by turning them into offices where hundreds of well-paid officials can work at innumerable forms. The others, which have not been Nationalized, rely upon the half-crowns of the trippers . . . those Great Houses which are so much a part of England and where so much of its history has been made.

And what has happened to those useless old Back Numbers—those doddering Victorians and ageing Edwardians who once lived in them and went all over the world from them? They have their day of pride still. If you go along the Mall, in London, on a summer's afternoon, in July, you will see unusual sights and think that the Master has indeed put back His Universe.

For your astonished eyes will notice scores of men in uniforms and many more in tall-hats and morning-coats.

A great many of them are aged, and of advanced middle-age. With them are their ladies, wearing their best silk dresses, obviously not new clothes but carefully preserved, and of old style. Quite a few are a little bewildered by the rush of the traffic, and hesitate on the kerb as the maelstrom sweeps by—they had, when accustomed to that part of the town, been used to horses.

Observant policemen help these old folk and even stop the traffic for them, receiving a courteous bow and word of thanks.

For this is their day, these old people, these hopeless 'Back Numbers' —their one day of the year when they can, for a few hours, get back into a world remotely resembling their own, and mix with people of their own type—mostly of their own type—in conditions similar to what they had once known. These old people are the remnants of the Victorians and the elderly Edwardians who were, in their prime, members of what was known as 'The Privileged Classes'. Those days seem so far off to them.

Whatever privileges they had then have long since vanished. It was their privilege once to serve their country in various ways in all parts of the earth—to write its books, its poetry, to paint its pictures, to advance its science, to fight its battles, to make its laws—in their own time and largely at their own expense—to plan its buildings, and to receive a very small remuneration for all these things. But they esteemed it a privilege to do it. And those who had spent their best years in such service—

especially those who served in the Forces or abroad in its Administrative Offices—retired on a pension which brought them with a bump from a Palace in the East to a lodging-house in Leamington. They did not complain about that—it was their job. They had known the privilege of stinting themselves to see that their children had first-class educations so as to follow in their own footsteps, to get a good start in life, to pay their debts and their doctors' bills, and contribute to the best of their ability to Charities and Hospitals. They had known the privileges of being able to live within their means in some degree of comfort and to have the privilege of domestic help, and of a little annual holiday. They had painted pictures which other privileged people bought and hung upon their walls—not knowing the greater artistic value of bare distemper —of writing books which people not only read, but bought because they had the money to spare, and room in which to keep the books.

They had paid to hear good music played as its composer intended, not 'hotted' and 're-arranged' out of all recognition. All sorts of absurd, old-fashioned and ridiculous privileges.

Now it was another form of Privilege: To live in a Welfare State, to watch their little pensions break under the strain of rising prices— because of increasing wages which went into other privileged pockets, not because it was earned by extra work, but because the last rise in wages had made things so much dearer. Nobody thought it worth while to increase the wages of those Privileged Back Numbers. Why should they? Most of them had a Decoration given them by a grateful—if economic—country. Was not that enough?

There was no such thing as their stratum of Society today, let them remember that. They were Back Numbers. But they had the privilege of existing on the border of penury, of going without comforts, of making their old bodies do work for which they had once paid handsomely to be done; to wear old clothes, to be pushed about on buses, to 'queue' and carry heavy parcels. To sit by fireless grates, to stand in trains in which there was once room—and pay three times as heavily for that privilege. Of seeing their houses—if they had them—grow shabbier and shabbier and rot, because they could not pay for repairs. The privilege of being told to 'Hurry along', and of hearing how men who drove a motor-van to deliver newspapers collected £28 a week in wages, which would have been wealth to them—oh, all sorts of other privileges. It was their own fault for ever being of the Privileged Classes and the Idle Rich.

But on this day it was different. They wore their rather pitiful 'Best Clothes' and their faces were alight with a smile—their eyes almost young and eager.

For they were going back in Time; they were going to the greatest of all the Great Houses as Privileged People once again—to meet old friends, to find themselves and their work not entirely forgotten because, just for this day, this afternoon, they were the men and women whom The Sovereign delighted to honour. They were guests at a Buckingham Palace Garden Party. They would, for a short space, walk again on a shaven lawn, meet people like themselves; greet old acquaintances—and note with sorrow the absence of those who were there last year—who would never be there again.

To step backwards down the years; to talk of old times in an English Garden under an English sky—to take light refreshment and strawberries-and-cream—and to stand erect, to bow and to curtsey with a little tremble of pride as their Monarch and the Royal Family passed by with a bow and a smile.

Once again they were privileged people—once again themselves— once again wearing their right attire, the tall-hat and the morning-coat; the silk dress and the parasol. . . .

For a little while—but what a precious little while. Just enough to sustain them in the hope that perhaps, next year as well . . .

Well, there it is. It is all old-fashioned and absurd, of course; anti-social and class-conscious. But those people have not had the good-fortune, as 'Back Numbers', to have the security and comfort of an actual Box Room, as had the furniture, the fittings; they hang on in the old magazines and papers, in the faded photographs of seaside resorts in ramshackle local railway carriages.

The writer knows he is likely to give offence, but he takes refuge in the fact that he is a 'Back Number' too. He lives, and he works on, still harder and longer than he ever worked before and for far less result. He pays in taxation annually five times the amount of his entire income when he first got married. There are very few things he can afford now that he could afford then, although a life-time of effort lies between.

He is awake to all that goes on around him and observes life keenly. He sees and notes the alterations. He knows that there are great improvements—free meals and milk for school-children; fine, airy schools—but he wishes the education doled out there was a bit more personal and a little less mass-produced. He is told that this is the Day of the Young—but he does not believe that. It was always the Day of the Young—or so the young people thought.

He observes great miracles of Science; immense advances in medical achievement—but he knows of dreadful cases of neglect and of deaths because of over-crowded hospitals.

He does not understand Modern Art—and, frankly, he does not

want to. He does not like Modern Music—but he is a Back Number, remember. He sees discomfort where once there was comfort. He sees Craftsmanship dying out; work indifferently done and a desire to do less—and get more for it. He sees discourtesy and rudeness publicly applauded. None of those things he quite understands. He hears politicians making the same speeches and saying the same things that were said when he was a boy. Also he fears that his race is losing its individuality and borrowing from another nation. He hears his language being infiltrated by foreign words and accents; the male fashions in which his people once led the world surrendering to another and—to his mind—not nearly so excellent a style.

He hears his country being derided and he sees it being kicked around. He is told that today there are no workhouses or paupers—and that nobody starves. He knows hundreds who face penury in their old age because their money is taken from them and they cannot save.

But he still believes that his land is the best in the world, even though it is not nearly so free as when he was not a 'Back Number'. He still believes that the glory it has won will survive and he does not believe that its spirit will ever be quenched.

It is a curious spirit which flares up at the most unexpected moments —for the race is inherently mad; it goes plunging towards precipices and pulls up at the last moment. He believes it will pull up soon and be British again. He remembers that it was the only Democratic nation to fight right through the Second World War.

But being a Back Number he is obstinate and unrepentant. He is quite sure that he has seen better days. He is quite sure that it was better far to live in a land which did not stand always in the shadow of war and spend its money on armaments to preserve a peace of fear.

He knows his history, and he knows that possession of what seems power sooner or later means the power being tested. He knows that preparations for war have always led to war. He knows that a 'straight left' in English Boxing led to victory; that a straight bat in cricket led to preservation of a wicket and to scores. He believes that a bit of straight talking today would do the same.

He also believes that in World Politics, experience and tradition carry more weight than wealth and numbers. He sees his country which once, small in size as it was, kept peace for a century, dropping far back in power and influence, losing its freedom after winning two Wars fought for Freedom, poor because it gave its treasures for its ideal and not for conquest.

But who is he?—Just a 'Back Number'.

He sees the literature of his land in which it led the world becoming

—because of taxation—a part-time occupation. He knows all about the Welfare State; he lives in it and helps support it; but he worries about the future of his grandchildren. What will that be?

His own youth was spent in safety and secure conditions. They have a Welfare State. But will the march—nay, the headlong rush—of what is called Progress allow them to live in their Welfare State and reap its benefits—if any? Or will they just be wiped out by a horrible death?

Well, he does not know—nobody knows. The Present is around us; we know the Past—but the Future is a closed door which at any time may become a scarifying Present. So this Back Number takes refuge in the Past—in a Past which he believes was far better than the Present. He knows that young people will sneer, but he does not mind that. He did his own share of sneering once. He just tries to show people by means of his discursive, rambling books, which so often annoy the reviewers but which bring him such piles and piles of happy letters, what that Past was really like.

He is told he is Superlative—well, the Past was superlative. He—and those who really knew it—know that quite well. So he goes on, quite impenitent. He thrusts himself back into the Bad Old Days and tries to draw accurate pictures of them. He goes back fifty and sixty years in his own memory and further still by means of his hardly acquired knowledge.

This time he has gone back to the Victorian Age, so much maligned; and to the Edwardian Age—now a classification for juvenile delinquents who in the real Edwardian Age would have been given the 'Cat'—and cured out of hand.

He has gone back to the Box Room which was such a feature. He has ventured into that distant misty time when people 'Rang Bells'—and got them answered. Nobody answers a bell today! When those bells were no longer answered, an Era passed away. So if he has 'rung a bell' which will be answered by a general opening of the Box Room of Memories—the Box Room which all people possess—then he will think these months of the Present, spent in writing this book, well spent indeed and will remain, in the language of his own Profession—the humble and obedient servant of all who rang the bell for him to answer. . . .

Easter Day, 1954.
*London, W.*1

THE END